UNDERSTANDING

a guide to the WHO, WHAT, WHEN, WHERE,
and WHY for each book of the Bible

THE
EVERYDAY SERIES

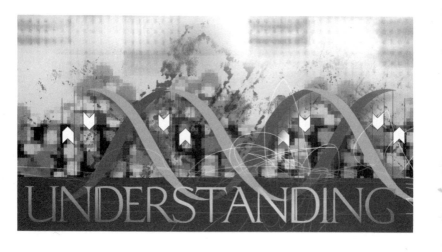

Everyday Understanding: Your Bible Handbook

Copyright © 2006 by Thomas Nelson, Inc.

Published in Nashville, Tennessee, by Thomas Nelson, Inc., Publishers.

Reprinted from *How to Get into the Bible* by Stephen M. Miller.

Interior design and typesetting by Kristy Morell, Smyrna, Tennessee.

ISBN 1-4185-0565-x

Library of Congress Cataloguing-in-Publication data available on request.

1 2 3 4 5 6 7 — 10 09 08 07

CONTENTS

HOW TO USE THIS BOOK

As you turn the pages of this book, here's what you'll find, and why.

• **How We Got Our Bible.** This is a fast-paced article that traces the story of the Bible from the days before it was written—when eyewitnesses told astonished listeners what they saw—to the computer age, when we can again see video recreations of the Bible events. It's astonishing to discover how God has preserved His message throughout the ages.

• **Top Stories.** Here you'll catch a glimpse at the 30 biggest scenes in the Bible, and a concise biography of a dozen main characters.

• **Genesis through Revelation.** From the first Bible book to the last, you'll get a thorough preview preparing you to read each book for all it's worth.

—**Famous Lines** from each book—quotes you've probably heard, but never knew where they came from.

—**Influential People,** briefly identifying each of the main characters in the book.

—**Points of Interest,** pointing out insights you might otherwise zoom right past.

—**Timeline,** helping you picture where the book fits into other events going on in the Bible lands and beyond.

—**Did You Know?** Intriguing nuggets of information about each book.

—**Author and Date,** evidence about who wrote the book and when. (Most Bible books were written anonymously, but clues in the text and in other ancient writings often suggest possible writers.)

—**On Location,** maps of key sites.

—**Outline**—the heart of *Everyday Understanding*—quickly acquaints you with the main events and teachings in each book.

—**Points to Consider,** a section that lets you listen in on what the experts are saying about the book. You encounter both affirmations and challenging perspectives.

—**For Further Study** pointing you to related books in the Bible. If you like the book of Ruth, for example, you'll also enjoy the dramatic story of another heroine: Esther.

GETTING STARTED

You don't have to read this book from cover to cover before opening your Bible. Our hope is that you'll read the two together.

Here's one approach you might consider.

First, read "How We Got Our Bible," then "Top Stories." These will pique your curiosity, which you should follow as sure as you follow your nose. If you find yourself drawn to the story of Jesus, for example, you can turn to the Gospel of Mark—the shortest and most action-packed of the four Gospels. Read the overview of Mark that we offer in *Everyday Understanding,* then grab your Bible and read the complete story with enriched insight.

There are dozens of Bible translations you can choose from. Or you might select one of the paraphrases of the Bible, which seek to convey the key ideas in the Scripture without sticking to the Hebrew or Greek words used in the passage. A few version deliberately choose to use only a limited vocabulary to tell the Bible's story. We especially like the *New Century Version* because of its readability and accurate translation. In fact, unless we indicate otherwise, it's the version we use throughout *Everyday Understanding.*

One tip about looking up Bible references. If you see "John 3:16," for example, John is the name of the book, and 3:16 means chapter 3, verse 16.

One warning, but a happy one. Reading and learning about what God wants to say to you through the Bible can change your life forever, but you will never regret the changes. After living with them daily for many years, the words of God continue to change my life and fill it with joy. I believe they can do the same for you.

INTRODUCTION

HOW WE GOT OUR BIBLE

There's a short version of how we got the Bible—and why.

It's summed up in a letter from the apostle Paul just before his execution: "All Scripture is inspired by God and is useful to teach us what is true and to make us realize what is wrong in our lives" (2 Timothy 3:16 NLT).

Paul was talking about Jewish Scripture, which Christians call the Old Testament; the New Testament was not finished at that time. But Christians believe that Paul's words apply equally to the twenty-seven books of the New Testament, which revolve around the life and teachings of God's Son.

Exactly how God "inspired" the many biblical writers is an intriguing mystery, and a source of sometimes hot debate. But all Christians who believe that the Bible is God's revelation to the human race agree on one rock-solid point: God guided the more than a millennium-long process, from beginning to end. He personally saw to it that humans got the message he wanted to deliver.

In the beginning, stories about God were probably passed on by word of mouth long before they were written onto clay slabs or tanned sheepskin. In ancient times, villagers and herders alike admired gifted storytellers who, with entertaining flair and evocative cadence, preserved and passed along the community's tradition and history. Listeners became familiar with the stories and typically refused to allow storytellers to skip or add material—much like children today monitor and supervise the familiar stories that their parents read to them.

THE WRITING BEGINS

No one knows when the first Hebrew put pen to parchment, or stylus to clay. Moses is the first person the Bible identifies as a writer. Perhaps as early as the 1400s BC. Moses wrote down the many laws God gave him—probably those preserved in the books of Exodus, Leviticus, Numbers, and Deuteronomy (Deuteronomy 31:9). But hundreds of years before Moses, Abraham, the father of the Jewish nation, may have written the dramatic stories about his life that are preserved in Genesis. He came from the Persian Gulf region where writing was already at least 1,000 years old.

Most of the rest of the Old Testament—stories, poems, songs, genealogies, nuggets of wisdom, prophecies, and all the other genres of Hebrew tradition—was likely passed along orally, then eventually collected and recorded by scribes. The writing probably began in earnest after Israel established itself as a powerful nation, during the reigns of David and Solomon in about 1000 BC. As scrolls began to wear out, scribes carefully duplicated the text onto fresh scrolls.

Exactly who wrote the Old Testament remains a mystery; most books don't say. The first five books of the Bible, for example, are anonymous. But ancient Jewish tradition says Moses wrote them. Some Bible authors, on the other hand, are clearly identified; many prophets wrote the books named after them.

All but a few sections of the Old Testament are written in Hebrew, the language of the Jews. A few passages are written in Aramaic, a similar language that the Jews picked up when they were exiled to Babylon. After twenty-some-year-old Alexander the Great swept through the Middle East in the early 300s BC, Greek became the prevailing language.

Within about a century, an Egyptian king decided to create a new holding for his renowned library in Alexandria. As legend has it, he asked

OLD TESTAMENT		Major Prophets	Letters by Paul to Churches
Law		Isaiah	Romans
	Genesis	Jeremiah	1 Corinthians
	Exodus	Lamentations	2 Corinthians
	Leviticus	Ezekiel	Galatians
	Numbers	Daniel	Ephesians
	Deuteronomy	**Minor Prophets**	Philippians
History		Hosea	Colossians
	Joshua	Joel	1 Thessalonians
	Judges	Amos	2 Thessalonians
	Ruth	Obadiah	**Letters by Paul to Individuals**
	1 Samuel	Jonah	1 Timothy
	2 Samuel	Micah	2 Timothy
	1 Kings	Nahum	Titus
	2 Kings	Habakkuk	Philemon
	1 Chronicles	Zephaniah	**General Letters**
	2 Chronicles	Haggai	Hebrews
	Ezra	Zechariah	James
	Nehemiah	Malachi	1 Peter
	Esther		2 Peter
Poetry		**NEW TESTAMENT**	1 John
	Job	**Gospels**	2 John
	Psalms	Matthew	3 John
	Proverbs	Mark	Jude
	Ecclesiastes	Luke	**Prophecy**
	Song of Songs	John	Revelation
		History	
		Acts	

the high priest in Jerusalem to loan him about seventy top scholars who would translate the five revered books of Moses into Greek. The result—the first Bible translation—became known as the Septuagint, meaning seventy. Over the next hundred years or so, the rest of the Hebrew Bible was added. When New Testament writers later quoted the Old Testament, they quoted it from this Greek translation.

Rome destroyed Jerusalem in AD 70, leaving the Jews with no temple for offering animal sacrifices. So the Jews began to offer sacrifices of praise and prayer by reading from the sacred writings. The problem was that the Jews had a wide array of revered books, and many versions of some books. No one knows exactly how or when the Jews settled on the books that make up their Bible, which Christians call the Old Testament. The five books of Moses, known as the books of Law, were probably among the first ones widely accepted. The books of the prophets likely came next, followed last by books known as the Writings: Psalms, Proverbs, and others. Eventually eliminated—partly because they were not originally written in Hebrew—were many books published in the popular Greek translation. They were called the Apocrypha, meaning "secondary" or "hidden" works, and would later reappear in Roman Catholic and Eastern Orthodox Bibles.

The Bible isn't one book, but a library of many books. Most Protestant Bibles have sixty-six books—thirty-nine in the Old Testament and twenty-seven in the New—arranged in the order and categories shown here. Old Testament books by prophets, for example, appear together—starting with the Major Prophets (meaning the larger books), followed by the Minor Prophets.

This arrangement is different for some other Bible-believing faiths.

Roman Catholic and Eastern Orthodox Bibles include the Apocrypha, a collection of books that appeared in the Septuagint, a Greek translation made from the Hebrew Bible about 200 years before Christ. (See "The Apocrypha, page 513.) Jews, however, later decided against keeping these books in their Bible.

THE LATE-BREAKING GOOD NEWS

The story of how we got the New Testament is quite similar, though the time frame is compressed. Instead of taking a thousand years or more for spoken stories to give way to writing and then to widely revered status, the process takes about a century for Christians. The earliest followers of Jesus didn't immediately write their stories, apparently because they expected Jesus to return soon. They urgently spread his teachings in person, by speaking.

TIMELINE								
BIBLE EVENTS	Moses writes God's laws 1440 BC	David writes songs 1000 BC	Solomon writes wise sayings 950 BC	Jeremiah wishes prophecy 600 BC	Old Testament translated into Greek 200 BC	New Testament written AD 100	New Testament accepted as Scripture 367	
	1500 BC		**1000 BC**		**500 BC**		**AD 100**	
WORLD EVENTS	Canaanites create first alphabet 1500 BC	Trojan War ends in sack of Troy 1190 BC	David becomes king of Israel 1010 BC	Solomon dedicates first Jewish temple 960 BC	Confucius born 551 BC	Jews win independence 164 BC	Paper invented in China AD 103	Pagan temples closed in Roman Empire 354

The first New Testament books were probably not written by Jesus' disciples, but by missionary-minded, circuit-preaching Paul. Scholars estimate that Paul's earliest letters of encouragement to young churches he had founded were written about twenty years after the death of Jesus. The rest of the New Testament was written throughout the remainder of the first century, roughly AD 50 to 100.

Christians had long respected the Jewish Scriptures as God's Word. But they also recognized that the message of Jesus, contained in the Gospels and other writings, was an essential part of God's revelation to human beings. Christians, however, didn't formally agree on which books to include in the New Testament until after Marcion, a Christian leader in the early AD 100s, proposed a short list: the letters of Paul and the Gospel of Luke—all of which he had edited to reflect his belief that Jesus was not human and could not really suffer.

ENGLISH BIBLES
A SAMPLER FROM PSALM 23

Readers today can choose from many Bible translations in modern English. To give you an idea of how they compare—and how they have changed over the centuries—here are excerpts from the most famous psalm in Scripture, a psalm often quoted in times of difficulty or read at funerals.

Wycliffe Bible, 1380s (first English Bible)	The Lord gouerneth [governs] me, and no thing shal faile to me; In the place of pasture there he hath set me.
King James Version, 1611	The Lord is my shepherd, I shall not want. He maketh me to lie down in greene pastures.

Jerome translates Bible into Latin 405	Caedmon, a monk puts parts of Bible to music 670	Wycliff produces first English Bible 1384	Tyndale executed for translating Bible into English 1536	King James Version of Bible 1611	English Revised Version 1885	Dead Sea Scrolls discovered 1947	Revised Standard Version 1952	Contemporary English Version 1995
	500		**1000**		**1500**		**1900**	
Muhammad has vision, recorded in Karan 610	Crusades begin 1095	Eyeglasses invented 1300	Bubonic plague kills one-third of Europe 1348	Columbus sails for new world 1492	Shakespeare becomes a London playwright 1592	Puritans land at Plymouth Rock 1620	Mark Twain writes Huckleberry Finn 1884	Israel becomes a nation again 1948

Over the next two centuries, Christians debated which books should be included. Many had been written, including about sixty of questionable content and authorship. By 367, most church leaders agreed to accept as authoritative only the twenty-seven books they believed were written by apostles—ministers who had actually seen Jesus, including the original disciples and Paul. The first known list of these books appears that year in the Easter letter that an Egyptian bishop, Athanasius, sent to his churches. He was the first on record to use the word *canon*—which originally meant "measure"—to describe the officially recognized books of the Bible. Church leaders decided that no other books should be added to the canon.

THE DANGEROUS ART OF TRANSLATION

Latin, the preferred language of Romans, eventually spread throughout

New International Version, 1973	The Lord is my shepherd, I shall not be in want. He makes me lie down in green pastures.
New King James Version, 1982	The Lord is my shepherd; I shall not want. He makes me to lie down in green pastures.
Contemporary English Version, 1995	You, Lord, are my shepherd. I will never be in need. You let me rest in fields of green grass.
New Living Translation, 1996	The Lord is my shepherd; I have everything I need. He lets me rest in green meadows.

the empire. Christian scholars began producing several Latin translations of the Jewish and Christian Scriptures. By 382, however, Pope Damascus decided the church needed a single, authoritative Latin translation. He assigned this arduous task to Jerome, leading Bible scholar of the time.

Jerome knew Latin and Greek, but not very much Hebrew. He was determined to translate the Old Testament from the original Hebrew language, not from the Greek Septuagint. So he moved to a monastery in Bethlehem and learned Hebrew from Jewish scholars. More than twenty years after he began, his monumental translation was complete. It became known as the Vulgate, meaning "common," since he wrote it in the common language of the day.

At first, his translation met stiff resistance. After one congregation heard his version of Jonah read to them, instead of worshiping, they rioted. They preferred the earlier version they were used to hearing and memorizing.

Because language changes, updated versions can sometimes sound dramatically different from previous version. To further complicate the process, it's not always clear how to interpret the ancient text. For example, ancient Hebrew had no vowels and no lowercase letters. If we wrote English that way, "once upon a time" would look like this: NC PN TM. But those same letters could also read "Nice pun, Tom." Ancient readers familiar with the story seemed to have little trouble reading it. Others had to look for context clues, which were plentiful. Solving the puzzle of one word gives you a clue about what the next word should be. When you put a lot of words together it's easier to figure out what the story is about.

At about the time Jerome was translating the Bible into Latin, a missionary named Ulfilas was inventing an alphabet for German tribes so he could translate the Bible into their Gothic language. This scene has been repeated throughout the world, throughout the ages.

As Christianity grew, so did the number of Bible translations. Most Bibles were too expensive for common people, because it took months of work to copy them. In the 1300s a Bible could easily cost a priest a year's salary. This changed dramatically in about 1456, when the Bible was first printed with movable type. By the end of that century, printers were busy in more than 250 European towns, publishing a wide variety of Bible editions.

Surprisingly, Christian church leaders resisted the notion of translating God's Word into everyday language. The prevailing opinion was the people should get their teaching from ministers, not the Bible—because it was thought most people were not capable of traveling through God's Word without a spiritual guide. Oxford scholar John Wycliffe became viewed as a heretic for creating the first English Bible—which was banned in England. He died before anyone killed him, but forty-three years later church leaders dug up his remains, burned them, and threw the ashes into a river. William Tyndale produced an improved English translation in the early 1500s. For this, he was publicly strangled with a rope and his body burned. His dying words, "Lord, open the King of England's eyes." Within two years the king ordered English Bibles placed in every church.

The most famous English Bible of all time is the King James Version, known in England as the Authorized Version. It remained the principal Bible of English-speaking Protestants for some 300 years, beginning with the time of Shakespeare. In 1611 the translation was presented to King James of England, who had commissioned about fifty of England's foremost scholars to produce it. Working at Oxford, Cambridge, and Westminster, they completed the task in about seven years.

Then, as now, people resisted change. It took forty years for the public to warm up to this new version and accept it as a replacement for the Geneva Bible, which was translated fifty years earlier and was used by the American Puritans.

BIBLES TODAY

Since King James commissioned his masterpiece translation, archaeologists have unearthed Bible manuscripts much older than the ones that his translators used—up to a thousand years older. For example, some Old Testament texts from the renowned Dead Sea Scrolls, a library cache preserved in a dry cave near Israel's Dead Sea, date as far back as about 200 years before Christ. Variation in the Scripture is surprisingly minor—a tribute to the care taken by copyists.

So far, none of the original Bible manuscripts have surfaced. But translators today make good use of the ever-emerging ancient texts, linking them with cutting-edge technology. To piece together brittle and broken fragments of leather scrolls, for example, some scientists are using DNA testing to determine what sections belong together.

Today there are countless millions, perhaps a billion or more, Bibles in homes throughout the world. At the moment, at least parts of the Bible have been translated. Surveys report that in the United States nine out of ten homes have at least

SAYINGS FROM THE BIBLE

Many frequently used sayings come directly from the Bible—especially from the King James Version. Here are just a few.

He'll go the second mile (Matthew 5:41).

I saw the handwriting on the wall (Daniel 5:5).

The leopard can't change its spots (Jeremiah 13:23).

She thinks she's holier-than-thou (Isaiah 65:5).

I escaped by the skin of my teeth (Job 19:20).

She's the apple of my eye (Deuteronomy 32:10).

He's a man after my own heart (1 Samuel 13:14).

It's a case of the blind leading the blind (Matthew 15:14).

This place is a den of thieves (Matthew 21:13).

That man is a thorn in my side (2 Corinthians 12:7).

one Bible—and the average home has about six. These are just the printed Bibles. People can now choose from a staggering array of ancient and new Bible translations on computer, via electronic disks, online services, and the Internet. People can also listen to narrated tapes of Scripture.

SOME FAMILIAR VERSIONS

King James Version • 1611

American Standard Version • 1901

Revised Standard Version • 1952

Phillips: The New Testament
In Modern English • 1958

The Amplified Bible • 1965

New American Standard Version • 1971

Today's English Version
(The Good News Bible) • 1976

New International Version • 1978

New King James Version • 1982

New Revised Standard Version • 1989

Contemporary English Version • 1995

For children, there are Bible stories in comic book style and other age-tailored editions. And for kids who would never consider curling up with the Good Book, there are Bible story cartoons and dramas, and even interactive Bible video games.

Adults, too, can choose Bibles targeting their interests. There are storybook Bibles for parents to read to their children, and devotional Bibles with inspiring articles for singles. Readers interested in studying the cultural background of each Bible passage can buy thick volumes such as the *Nelson Study Bible,* with 15,000 expository study notes based on the latest scholarship. The less scholarly, yet equally inquiring, can turn to the *Word in Life Study Bible,* designed for today's media-smart reader. In addition to in-text maps and charts, this edition contains hundreds of articles and features, including information on occupations in the Bible, geography and culture, and personality profiles.

The Bible has been the world's best-selling book since Johannes Gutenberg invented the printing press 550 years ago. With modern publishers producing niche editions that meet the spiritual needs of even the narrowest segments of the market, the Bible is likely one of the best-read as well.

DID YOU KNOW?

• Using the Bible at swearing-in ceremonies grows out of the ancient Jewish practice of making a promise and reminding each other that "God is watching" (Genesis 31:50). In the Middle Ages, Christians swore by kissing or touching a cross, a Bible, or a sacred object they believed once belonged to a holy person.

• The oldest Bible text is a Dead Sea Scroll fragment written in about 225 BC. It's from one of the Old Testament books of Samuel.

• The oldest surviving New Testament text is a fragment of John 18:31–33, which includes Pilate's question to Jesus: "Are you the king of the Jews?" The fragment dates to about AD 125, roughly one generation after the original was written.

• Bible typos produced dubious nicknames for some editions. "The Adulterer's Bible," also called "the Wicked Bible," dropped an all-important "not" and commands "Thou shalt commit adultery." The printer was fined a hefty sum.

• Bizarre translations of key words spawned Bible nicknames. "The Bug Bible" (more respectfully known as Coverdale's Bible, 1535) encouraged its readers not to be afraid of "bugs by night." The King James Version later replaced "bugs" with "terror."

• The word *Bible* comes from a Greek word for papyrus *(biblios),* a plant used to make paper.

• *Gospel* comes from the old English word *godspell.* English scholars used it to translate the Greek word *evangelion,* which means "good news" and from which we get the word *evangelist.*

• The most widely translated Bible book is the Gospel of Mark—the shortest of the four Gospels about Jesus. It's available in about 900 languages.

• Christians were among the first people to discard the 3,000-year-old tradition of using scrolls. They adopted the codex, or book format. Every surviving fragment of Christian writing from the second century AD comes from books. But only fourteen of 870 non-Christian works of that time are from books. Books, printed on front and back, were cheaper and easier to use.

• After Johannes Gutenberg of Germany invented the printing press in the mid-1400s, the first book printed was the Bible. The first press run, of about 180 copies, sold out before the presses started. Forty-eight copies of this masterpiece survive.

• The Bible didn't originally have chapters and verses. Scholars added chapters in AD 1231 and verses in 1551.

TOP STORIES

GOD THE FATHER

Before the first star began to sparkle, there was God. That fact opens the Bible: "In the beginning God created the sky and the earth" (Genesis 1:1 NCV).

When the last star fades and creation gives way to a celestial realm, God will be there—with his people. That fact closes the Bible in John's vision of the future: "Nothing that God judges guilty will be in that city. The throne of God and of the Lamb will be there, and God's servants will worship him. They will see his face, and his name will be written on their foreheads. There will never be night again. They will not need the light of a lamp or the light of the sun, because the Lord God will give them light. And they will rule as kings forever and ever" (Revelation 22:3–5 NCV).

Between Genesis and Revelation is a sacred library written over more than a millennium. It is the story of God revealed in history, biography, law, prayer, song, proverb, prophecy, parable, letter, and vision. Through this story we begin to understand God, though only in part. For as Job asks, who can understand "Can you understand the secrets of God? Can you search the limits of the Almighty? His limits are higher than the heavens; you cannot reach them! They are deeper than the grave; you cannot understand them!" (Job 11:7–8 NCV).

Why God reveals himself to humanity quickly becomes clear in Genesis. God created a good and idyllic world and placed it with humans with whom he could fellowship. These humans chose to disobey him. Because of this, and in ways we can't fully grasp, sin contaminated God's creation and severed his intimate relationship with humanity. Since that moment, God has been working to restore his creation and his relationship with humans.

God begins by teaching humanity about himself through promises made and fulfilled in obedient people, like Noah, and through punishing evil people. Then through Abraham, God produces a race of people chosen to receive his special insights and laws, and to guide others in the ways of the Lord. He also sends prophets to remind these chosen people, the Jews, to obey him.

Finally, God sends Jesus onto the planet and the Holy Spirit into the human heart to further reveal what he is like. The Bible doesn't explain how three distinct entities can be united as one. It simply states this as fact, then reports a wide array of astonishing miracles and testimonies to prove it. Who but God, for example, could silence a storm (Mark 4:39)?

From beginning to end, the Bible paints a detailed and complex portrait of God. But all the descriptions are best expressed by John, a disciple of Jesus: "Whoever does not love does not know God, because God is love." (1 John 4:8 NCV). Good news for humanity is that this love is offered to us, and when we accept it, it's ours forever.

God creates Adam (Genesis 1:27–31; 2:7).

After God creates the heavens and the earth, he finishes his creation with a finale: human beings. "Then the Lord God took dust from the ground and formed a man from it. He breathed the breath of life into the man's nose, and the man became a living person." Unlike all other creatures, humans are made in the image of God, "to be like himself."

Eve eats forbidden fruit (Genesis 3:1–24).

In the paradise garden of Eden, Adam and Eve are limited by only one rule: they are not to eat fruit from one particular tree because it will kill them. Eve eats it anyway, then convinces Adam to eat some too. Sin enters God's creation and changes it for the worse.

The flood destroys life on earth (Genesis 6–9).

"Because people have made the earth full of violence," God tells Noah, the only righteous man left. "I will destroy all of them from the earth." God says he will flood the land, and that Noah should build a massive houseboat to preserve his family, along with pairs of "every kind of bird, animal, and crawling thing will come to you to be kept alive."

God makes a contract with Abraham (Genesis 15:1–21).

As a key part of God's plan to save sinful humans, he makes a contract, or covenant, with Abraham. It establishes Abraham as the father of the Jewish people. God's promise: "Look at the sky. There are so many stars you cannot count them. Your descendants also will be too many to count." To seal the contract, Abraham offers animal sacrifices. He stands as the model for all who trust God.

ABRAHAM

When Abraham was seventy-five years old, childless, and married to an infertile woman, God asked him to leave his homeland and move to Canaan, now Israel. In return, God said he would make Abraham into "a great nation" (Genesis 12:2 NCV).

Abraham, a descendant of Noah's son Shem, was born and raised near the Persian Gulf in the culturally advanced city of Ur. This was a town where most people worshiped idols, yet Abraham worshiped only the Lord and trusted him explicitly. Once, God tested Abraham's loyalty by asking him to sacrifice his son, Isaac, who had been born when Abraham was 100 years old. Deeply saddened but steadfastly loyal, Abraham built an altar, then raised his knife to kill Isaac. An angel stopped Abraham, saying, "Don't kill your son or hurt him in any way. Now I can see that you trust God and that you have not kept your son, your only son, from me" (Genesis 22:12 NCV). Early Christians saw this episode as a foreshadowing of God's sacrifice of Jesus.

Abraham's flocks and family grew large in Canaan. His great-grandsons, the children of Jacob, produced the extended families that became known as the twelve tribes of Israel.

Jacob wrestles a heavenly being (Genesis 32:22–32).

One sleepless night, Jacob, Abraham's grandson, meets a mysterious man. Possibly recognizing him as a divine being, Jacob grabs him and says, "I will let you go if you will bless me." They wrestle until dawn, when the man blesses Jacob by giving him the new name of Israel. Jacob's twelve sons (the children of Israel) become the basis of a nation which later calls itself Israel.

Moses sees a burning bush that doesn't burn up (Exodus 3:1–10).

While grazing his flock near Mount Sinai, Moses sees a bush on fire—yet it is not burned. Out of the bush comes the voice of God, giving Moses a terrifying chore: Go to Egypt and order the king to free the Israelite slaves. Moses doesn't want to go, and says so. But God promises, "I will be with you."

MOSES

No one in the Old Testament is more heroic and influential than the shy and humble Moses. He freed the Israelites from Egyptian slavery, organized them into a nation, gave them the Ten Commandments and other laws that still guide Jews and Christians, and is credited with writing the first five books of the Bible.

Moses was born in Egypt to an Israelite slave, some 400 years after Jacob's family emigrated to Egypt to escape a famine. As an infant, he was set adrift on the Nile in a waterproof basket to escape the king's order to kill all newborn Hebrew boys. The king's daughter found and raised him. But at age forty, Moses fled the country after killing an Egyptian he saw beating an Israelite. He settled east of Egypt, married, and became a shepherd. While he was grazing his flock one day, God spoke to him from a burning bush and asked him to go back to Egypt and demand the release of the Israelites. Reluctantly, Moses did as God asked.

Israel's deliverance, characterized by many spectacular miracles—ten plagues in Egypt, parting the waters of the Red Sea, manna from heaven, water from rocks—is the Exodus, the most celebrated event in Jewish history, still commemorated in religious holidays each year.

Israelites cross the Red Sea (Exodus 14:1–31).

"Get your people out of my country and leave us alone!" the king tells Moses after a celestial being has killed the oldest child in each Egyptian family. But once the Israelites leave, the king changes his mind. His army traps the fugitives by the Red Sea. But God parts the water for the Israelites to escape and begin the journey to the land God promised to Abraham.

Moses destroys the Ten Commandments (Exodus 20:1–7).

Moses leads the Israelites to Mount Sinai, where God gives him the Ten Commandments inscribed on two stone tablets. These laws are the constitution for the nation and its faith. Moses returns from the mountain and sees the people betraying God by worshipping a golden calf. Furious, he throws the tablets, shattering them.

The wilderness trek to the Promised Land (Numbers 10:11–36).

A pillar of cloud representing God's presence among the Israelites rises from the tent sanctuary and moves. This signals that it's time for Israel to break camp and follow. Priests lead, carrying the ark of the covenant, the chest containing the duplicated Ten Commandments. (Moses broke the first set.)

Jericho walls come tumbling down (Joshua 6:1–27).

Crossing the Jordan River into the Promised Land, the Israelites meet their first Canaanites, who are protected behind the walls of Jericho. Six days Israelite soldiers march once around the city. On the seventh day, they march around the city seven times. Then the priests blow trumpets, the soldiers shout, and the walls of Jericho collapse.

SAMUEL

Once settled in their new land, the Israelites lived in a loose federation led by judges. Perhaps the most important of these judges was Samuel. Though Samuel had a family, from early childhood he lived with the priest in Israel's worship center to fulfill a vow his mother made. Infertile, Hannah had promised that if God gave her a son, she would return this child to the Lord's service.

Samuel grew into a wise and righteous man who served God in many capacities. While he was still a boy, he received messages from God and delivered them to the people, as a prophet. He offered sacrifices, as a priest. And he traveled the countryside settling disputes, as a judge. In fact, Samuel was the last of the judges in the era before Israel crowned.

When Samuel grew old, the Israelites asked him to select their first king. Samuel believed that the people should continue thinking of God as their king. But God granted Israel's request, though he considered it a rejection of his kingship. Samuel chose Saul. Later, when Saul sinned and became an unworthy leader, Samuel secretly anointed David as the future king. When Samuel died of old age, the nation gathered to mourn him.

David kills Goliath (1 Samuel 17:1–57).

Four centuries after the Israelites entered the Promised Land, they still have not captured the coastal area where the Philistines live. When Philistine champion Goliath challenges any Hebrew warrior to mortal combat, a shepherd boy steps forward and drops him with one stone from a slingshot. The shepherd, David, later becomes Israel's legendary king who forges a unified nation.

Solomon builds the temple (1 Kings 6:1–38).

On a hilltop overlooking Jerusalem, Solomon, David's son, builds the first of only three temples the Jews have ever had. In seven years, a work force of about 150,000 builds one of the most beautiful and expensive temples in the ancient world—a worship center with gold ceilings, walls, and floors. It lasts for 400 years.

DAVID

Israel's greatest king had a humble start in life. David was born into a Bethlehem shepherd's family, as the youngest of eight sons. But even as a lad he showed signs of greatness. He killed bears and lions that raided his flock. And with only a slingshot he defeated the Philistine champion, Goliath.

Invited to live in King Saul's palace, David calmed the moody ruler by playing a harp. When Saul erupted over David's growing popularity and tried to kill him, David fled and lived as a fugitive. David immediately began attracting an army of followers. After Saul died in a battle with the Philistines, Israel rallied around the still popular giant-slayer and crowned him king.

David chose Jerusalem as his capital, expanded the nation's borders, and launched Israel's Golden Age, which spanned his reign as well as Solomon's, his son. Yet David had failings: he committed adultery with Bathsheba and had her husband killed. And he raised an incredibly dysfunctional family—one son led a coup against him. Still, David never grew too proud to repent.

His dynasty began in 1000 BC and endured for nearly 500 years. Early Christians believed his dynasty was resurrected in Jesus, the Messiah promised from David's family and hometown.

Israel splits into two kingdoms (1 Kings 12:1–33).

By the time Solomon dies, the people of Israel are tired of paying heavy taxes to build cities, forts, and palaces. They ask Solomon's son and successor for relief, but he refuses. The northern tribes secede and start their own nation: Israel. Only the tribe of Judah, in the south, remains loyal to David's descendant.

Elijah challenges prophets of Baal on Mount Carmel (1 Kings 18:1–46).

Idolatry becomes the biggest threat to both Hebrew nations. Queen Jezebel, of Israel, sponsors an association of 850 prophets devoted to Canaanite gods. Prophet Elijah, however, challenges the association to a contest. The god who sends fire from heaven to light a sacrificial altar will be the god of Israel. The Lord wins, and the false prophets are executed.

ISAIAH

The prophet Isaiah lived 750 years before Christ, but his predictions about the Messiah—a deliverer who would save Israel—read as though he was an eyewitness to Jesus: "he was crushed for the evil we did. . . He was put to death; he was punished for the sins of my people" (Isaiah 53:5, 8 NCV).

Isaiah was an educated noble living in Jerusalem when, at age 20, he saw a phenomenal vision. In this vision God called him to become a prophet who would deliver messages of warning and hope to the Jewish people—a ministry Isaiah performed for 40 years. His style of delivery, preserved in the book of Isaiah, was dramatic and often symbolic. He even walked naked for three years to predict that the Egyptians would become slaves. This encouraged the Jews to trust in God rather than in an alliance with Egypt against Assyria.

During Isaiah's lifetime, Assyria crushed the northern Jewish nation of Israel. Isaiah warned his native Judah, in the south, that a similar fate awaited it. But he also offered hope, promising that God would one day send a messiah—promises the New Testament says were fulfilled in Jesus.

The sentence: seventy years in exile (Jeremiah 25:1–14).

Stubbornly the Jews break God's laws—for centuries. God sends prophets urging the people to repent, but few obey. So God invokes his rights under the covenant: "I will scatter you among the nations" (Leviticus 26:33 NCV). Speaking through the prophet Jeremiah, God vows, "these nations will be slaves of the king of Babylon for seventy years."

Jerusalem falls (2 Kings 25:1–21).

Assyria invades the northern nation of Israel, deporting the Jewish survivors as slaves, and repopulating the land with their own settlers. One hundred fifty years later, Babylon defeats the southern nation of Judah, destroys Solomon's 400-year-old temple, levels Jerusalem, and exiles most of the survivors. Suddenly, there is no longer a Jewish nation.

DANIEL

Hero of the prophetic book bearing his name, Daniel is most famous for surviving a night in a den of hungry lions. How he got there and what happened afterward enhance his fascinating story.

When Babylonians defeated the southern nation of Judah in 597 BC, and before they destroyed the cities a decade later, they peeled away the top layer of society—the most educated and influential—taking them to Babylon to serve the empire. Daniel, a wise young noble, was among this group. He became the elite of the elite, chosen to work in the palace, as were his friends Shadrach, Meshach, and Abednego. They are remembered for surviving a fiery furnace after refusing to worship an idol.

Daniel was a gifted sage, and a visionary, who interpreted dreams for King Nebuchadnezzar. The king became so impressed that he put Daniel in charge of all sages of the empire. Jealous rivals later tricked a subsequent king (of the conquering Persian Empire) into issuing a decree for all people to pray only to him for thirty days. When Daniel continued praying to God, he was punished by facing the lions. After surviving, Daniel was promoted to the number two position in the empire, second only to the king.

A time to cry (Psalm 137:1–9).

Exiled from their land and temple, the Jews endure bitter grief. Some of the most tender Hebrew songs are written during this time. In one such song, a Jewish exile paints a vivid and heartbreaking scene: "By the rivers in Babylon we sat and cried when we remembered Jerusalem. On the poplar trees nearby we hung our harps."

Rebuilding Jerusalem (Ezra 1–6; Nehemiah 2–4; 6:15–16).

After the Persians defeat Babylon, exiled groups return home—Jews included. The first wave of returning Jews begins work on the temple, followed by later Jews who help finish the job. Rebuilding the walls comes next—a project bitterly opposed by non-Jewish locals. But the work is finished in just fifty-two days.

God promises to send a Messiah (Isaiah 11:1–16).

Isaiah, like other prophets, says that God will fulfill his covenant through a ruler from David's family who will lead the people into everlasting peace: "Then wolves will live in peace with lambs, . . . and a little child will lead them" (NCV). Early Christians see these prophecies as describing Jesus and his kingdom.

Shepherds visit newborn Jesus (Luke 2:1–20).

Terrified shepherds watch the night sky burst into radiance, filling with angels, "Do not be afraid." one angel says, "I am bringing you good news. Today your Savior was born in the town of David. He is Christ, the Lord." The humble shepherds rush to nearby Bethlehem to see Baby Jesus, the promised ruler from David's family.

JESUS

Jesus, the Son of God, is a central figure of the Bible—from beginning to end.

He was with God when the world was created, says the Gospel of John. He was the hope that the prophets anticipated in the Messiah—a deliverer sent from God to save humanity from sin and to bring peace on earth. And he is the fulfillment of that hope, as reported in the New

Testament, especially the remarkable Gospels of Matthew, Mark, Luke, and John. His title, Christ, comes from the Hebrew word for messiah, translated into the Greek language of his day as *christos.*

Jesus' mother was the virgin Mary, engaged to Joseph, a carpenter from Nazareth. When Joseph learned his fiancée was pregnant, he planned to leave her. But an angel assured him that the child was from God.

On orders from the Roman emperor, the couple traveled to the hometown of their ancestors to be counted in a census; for Mary and Joseph this was Bethlehem, birthplace of King David. It was there, in a Bethlehem stable, that Jesus was born. Many Old Testament prophets predicted that the Messiah would come from David's family; Micah added that the birthplace would be Bethlehem (Micah 5:2).

As a growing boy, Jesus worked with Joseph. When Jesus was twelve years old, he traveled with His family to the Jerusalem temple to celebrate Passover. There he astonished the scholars with his spiritual insights.

The Bible says nothing more about Jesus until he began his ministry at roughly thirty years of age. This was a ministry that spanned perhaps only three years, in the heart of a tiny Middle Eastern country. But this ministry has changed the values and lives of people throughout the ages and around the globe. Whether Jesus was healing illnesses, calming storms with a word, or teaching compassion, he gave humanity an intimate portrait of a God full of power and mercy.

Executed by crucifixion, Jesus also gave the world its greatest proof of both his deity and of life after death, for three days later he rose from the tomb. Over the next forty days he met many times with his followers, urging them to take his message to everyone. Then he ascended to heaven, but not before promising to return. The Bible concludes with the greatest hope of early Christians: "Come, Lord Jesus!" (Revelation 22:20 NCV).

Sermon on the Mount (Matthew 5:1–7:29).

On a country hillside and surrounded by crowds, Jesus gives the Inaugural Address of his rule, the Sermon on the Mount. A concise summary of his main teachings, the Sermon is a call to life in his revolutionary kingdom: "love your enemies," Jesus says, "Pray for those who hurt you."

Jesus feeds 5,000 (Matthew 14:13–21).

Exhausted by their ministry, Jesus and his disciples sail away from the crowds for a rest. But the people follow along the shoreline. Though weary, Jesus is moved with compassion and heals all who are sick. Then, from one boy's lunch of bread and fish, Jesus feeds everyone. Dramatic miracles like these convince many that Jesus is the promised messiah.

The crucifixion of Jesus (Matthew 27:33–66).

Resisting Jesus' ministry, Jewish leaders condemn him of blasphemy for claiming to be God's Son, and Pilate bows to the pressure to execute him immediately. With this execution, Jewish leaders hope to prove that Jesus is no messiah, but is cursed of God. Yet the crucifixion fulfills the ancient prophecy: "But he was wounded for the wrong we did; he was crushed for the evil we did" (Isaiah 53:5 NCV).

Women at the tomb of Jesus (Mark 16:1–20).

Sunday morning, women who have followed Jesus walk to his tomb. Instead of finding a corpse, they find an angel announcing that Jesus is resurrected. In the following weeks Jesus appears to his disciples many times, then ascends to heaven. The apostle Paul later explains that Christians, too, will one day have resurrected bodies (1 Corinthians 15).

HOLY SPIRIT

The Holy Spirit is one of three persons in what early Christians called the Trinity: God the Father, Son, and Holy Spirit. The Bible doesn't use the word *trinity,* but it portrays all three divine persons as distinct yet equally God. For example, in Jesus' last words on earth he told his followers to make disciples all over the world and to baptize converts "in the name of the Father and the Son and the Holy Spirit" (Matthew 28:19 NCV).

The Spirit's role on earth has changed over history. When the universe was yet dark and lifeless, "God's Spirit was moving over the water" (Genesis 1:2 NCV), involved in the miracle of Creation. (Old Testament writers usually called him the Spirit of God, though occasionally the Holy Spirit.) Throughout Old Testament times the Spirit empowers the heroes and leaders of Israel. When, for instance, the prophet Samuel anointed David as Israel's future king, "From that day on, the Lord's Spirit worked in David" (1 Samuel 16:13 NCV).

In those days, the Spirit's work was apparently limited to unique leaders and special occasions. But the prophet Joel, speaking on God's behalf, promised that a time was coming when "I will pour out my Spirit on all kinds of people" (Joel 2:28 NCV). That moment arrived in a dramatic miracle on the day of Pentecost, a springtime Jewish celebration. Jesus had warned his disciples that he needed to leave, "I have told you all these things while I am with you. But the Helper will teach you everything and will cause you to remember all that I told you. This Helper is the Holy Spirit whom the Father will send in my name." (John 14:25 NCV). Jesus further instructed the disciples to stay in Jerusalem until the Spirit arrived. As the disciples waited, "Suddenly a noise like a strong, blowing wind came from heaven" (Acts 2:2 NCV). The Spirit had come, filling each disciple with spiritual vitality that gave them courage to preach about Jesus and to perform miracles proving that their message came from God.

Thousands began converting to Christianity and receiving the Holy Spirit. "You are God's temple," the apostle Paul later explained to believers "God's Spirit lives in you" (1 Corinthians 3:16 NCV). Christians guided by the Spirit, Paul added, will find themselves taking on the characteristics of godliness and rejecting sinful ways. "But the Spirit produces the fruit of love, joy, peace, patience, kindness, goodness, faithfulness, gentleness, self-control" (Galatians 5:22 NCV).

PETER

Lead disciple of Jesus, Peter is famous for trying to walk on water—and sinking. Ironically, his name was Simon until Jesus renamed him Peter, which means "rock." Jesus wasn't making a joke; the name change came later to emphasize Peter's rock-solid devotion to the Lord. Peter graphically demonstrated this allegiance when officials arrested Jesus: Peter cut off one's man's ear.

Peter and his brother Andrew were fishermen when Jesus invited them to become his disciples. Bold and strong-minded, Peter established himself as the leader, often speaking to Jesus on behalf of the others and vowing to defend Jesus to the death. Unfortunately, Peter is best known for his cowardice. While Jesus stood trial, Peter waited outside and three times denied knowing the Lord.

After the resurrected Jesus ascended to heaven, a reenergized Peter directed the emerging Christian church. He preached the first sermon, which produced 3,000 converts. And he defended Christians before the same Jewish leaders who tried Jesus.

Two New Testament letters bear Peter's name as author, and early Christian writers say that his sermons provided the source for Mark's Gospel. These writers add that Peter was crucified upside down on what is now Vatican Hill in Rome, when Nero persecuted Christians.

The Holy Spirit fills the disciples (Acts 2:1–3).

Before his ascension, Jesus tells the disciples to stay in Jerusalem until the Holy Spirit arrives to take his place. After about ten days the Spirit floods the room with the sound of a mighty wind and fills the disciples with courage. Boldly they preach about Jesus. On that day of Pentecost about 3,000 believe, and the Christian church is born.

Paul converts and becomes a missionary
(Acts 9:1–19; 13–14; 16:16–40).

On his way to arrest Jewish "heretics" who believe in Christ, Paul encounters a blinding light and the voice of Jesus. The experience makes him a believer. Instead of traveling to suppress Christianity, he begins traveling as a missionary to expand it. Convinced that through Jesus God's promises to Abraham now apply to non-Jews also, he starts churches throughout the Roman Empire.

Paul argues against making non-Jews follow Jewish laws
(Acts 15:1–21).

The church's first big controversy is over whether to make non-Jews observe the laws of Moses, especially laws about circumcision and diet. Paul and Peter convince assembled leaders that you don't have to be a Jew to be a Christian, because salvation comes through trusting Jesus, not through observing Jewish laws.

James leads the church to serve (James 1–5).

James, the brother of Jesus and leader of the church in Jerusalem, writes the letter bearing his name—a letter for Christian congregations, encouraging them toward holiness and compassion. "Religion that God accepts as pure and without fault is this: caring for orphans or widows who need help." Jewish authorities executed James, said a first-century historian.

PAUL

Next to Jesus, the person most responsible for Christianity was this fiery Jew who took the story of Jesus on the road for 10,000 miles and wrote over one-fourth of the New Testament.

More than any human being, it was Paul who turned a religion full of Jews into a religion made up mostly of non-Jews. In the earliest days of the church, if you wanted to be a Christian you had to be a Jew. If you hadn't been born Jewish, you had to convert and agree to keep all the Old Testament laws, including a painful one for grown men: circumcision.

Paul convinced church leaders that non-Jews should be granted full membership without having to obey Jewish laws. Old Testament laws, Paul argued, were part of God's old agreement with humanity. Jesus' death and resurrection marked the beginning of God's new covenant, prophesied by Jeremiah: "I will put my teachings in their minds and write them on their hearts" (Jeremiah 31:33 NCV).

Paul was often assaulted and arrested. His final arrest, in Rome, led to his execution. As a Roman citizen, Paul had the right to a swift death and was probably beheaded.

Paul preaches, under house arrest, at Rome (Acts 28:17–31).

After Paul's last known arrest, he is taken to Rome, where he waits two years for his trial. Constantly guarded, he freely teaches, preaches, and writes to his congregations. The Bible doesn't say what happened to Paul, but early Christian writers say he was beheaded in Rome.

John's vision of heaven (Revelation).

Exiled on an island, John, the last of Christ's original disciples, writes his vision of the future. He sees the promised return of Jesus, the gathering of God's people into a celestial city, and a new heaven and earth free from sin or evil. "The city does not need the sun or the moon to shine on it, because the glory of God is its light, and the Lamb is the city's lamp."

JOHN

When Jesus hung on the cross, dying, he looked down at his mother standing beside one of the first and dearest of his twelve disciples: an unidentified man that most scholars agree was John. "Here is your mother," Jesus said, entrusting Mary to John's care (John 19:27 NCV).

John and his brother James were fishermen whom Jesus nicknamed "Thunderbolts," perhaps because of their fiery personalities. Once they asked permission to punish some inhospitable Samaritans with fire from heaven—a request Jesus denied. Yet along with Peter, they were the closest friends of Jesus—the inner circle of disciples. They alone saw Jesus transfigured into his celestial form (Matthew 17:1–2) and witnessed agonizing prayer just before his arrest (Mark 14:33).

Early Christian writers say that John outlived the other disciples and settled in Ephesus (western Turkey), where he wrote five New Testament books: the Gospel of John, 1, 2, and 3 John, and Revelation.

GETTING INTO THE BIBLE

Genesis

WHEN THE WORLD BEGINS

Genesis answers some of the most basic questions we'll ever face:

- **Who am I?**

  "So God created human beings in his image" (1:27 NCV).

- **Where did I come from?**

  "Then the Lord God took dust from the ground and formed a man from it. He breathed the breath of life into the man's nose, and the man became a living person" (2:7 NCV).

- **Why am I here?**

  "Then God said, 'Let us make human beings in our image and likeness. And let them rule over the fish in the sea and the birds in the sky, over the tame animals, over all the earth, and over all the small crawling animals on the earth'" (1:26 NCV).

We are caretakers of God's creation.

Genesis is an ancient Greek word that means *beginning.* That's what the book is about: the beginning of the universe, human beings, sin, the Jewish nation.

Here we watch God breathe life into Adam and Eve, sail with Noah

> ### FAMOUS LINES
>
> - "In the beginning God created the heavens and the earth" (1:1).
>
> - "Am I my brother's keeper?" (4:9, KJV). *Cain's reply to God, when asked where Abel was, whom Cain had murdered.*
>
> - "Noah found grace in the eyes of the Lord" (6:8, KJV). *The reason Noah and his family weren't killed in the Flood.*
>
> - "I will surely bless you and give you many descendants. They will be as many as the stars in the sky and the sand on the seashore, and they will capture the cities of their enemies" (22:17 NCV). *God's promise to Abraham, father of the Jewish nation.*

during the Flood, marvel at the faith of Abraham, and travel with the families of Jacob as they escape a famine in Israel by migrating to Egypt where they will wind up as slaves making bricks for Pharaoh.

Without Genesis, the rest of the Bible makes no sense. The Bible talks about God's plan of salvation—his strategy for reaching out to human beings and saving them from sin and the destruction it causes. Genesis shows why salvation is necessary: God's good creation was invaded and contaminated by sin. And only the Creator can restore his creation.

BACKGROUND

INFLUENTIAL PEOPLE

Adam and Eve, the world's first human couple (3:20).

Noah, builder of the ark and survivor of the Flood (5:29).

Abraham, the man God chooses to become father of the Jews (17:4).

Isaac, the son God promises to Abraham; born when Abraham is 100 (17:19).

Jacob, father of the men whose descendents become the twelve tribes of Israel (25:26).

Joseph, Jacob's favorite son, who becomes a leader in Egypt (30:24).

THEME

God makes a beautiful, sinless world, and human beings to take care of it. These first humans, Adam and Eve, enjoy a unique relationship with God and with each other, and are entrusted to manage a wondrous world teeming with life. Adam and Eve, however, decide to eat fruit that God had warned would kill them. God expels the couple from the Garden of Eden, explaining that they will reap the promised consequences: they will die. But first, the woman will "have great pain" when

TIMELINE	BIBLE EVENTS	God creates the universe Before 2500 BC		Flood destroys the world Before 2500 BC	
		4500 BC	**4000 BC**	**3500 BC**	**3000 BC**
	WORLD EVENTS	First known Egyptian calendar 4230 BC -------		Floods devastate river basin of Iraq 3400 BC -------	Chinese develop acupuncture 2700 BC -------

giving birth. And the man will have to "sweat and work hard for your food" (3:19 NCV).

Humanity and God become estranged. Apart from God, the world grows so evil that God purges it in a vast flood, saving only Noah and his family. Afterward, God launches a plan to reclaim humanity from the grip of sin.

God begins his plan by creating through Abraham a nation of Jews. This nation is to learn how to obey him and "to live right and be fair" (18:19 NCV). Later, God promises, he will broaden the scope of his salvation, making the Jews "a great and powerful nation, and all nations on earth will be blessed through him" (18:18 NCV).

POINTS OF INTEREST

Truth in an ancient style. Don't read the creation story expecting it to be written like a modern laboratory report. What Genesis teaches about creation is true, and an increasing number of scientists think that the universe was born in a way startlingly similar to what Genesis has always said. But Genesis expresses this truth in the ways in which truth was expressed in ancient times, not in the technical, hyperprecise terms of modern science. It focuses on the *who* of creation much more than on the scientific *how.* Against all claims that creation happened on its own (through some unknown cause) or happened through the cavorting or

	God promises Abraham a nation 2100 BC		Joseph goes to Egypt, Hebrews follow 1800 BC	
2500 BC		**2000 BC**	**1500 BC**	**1000 BC**
	Most pyramids completed 2200 BC	Stonehenge built in England 2000 BC	Astronomy starts in Babylon 1800 BC	Dates are approximate

clashing of any number of gods (according to many other ancient creation stories), Genesis says simply, "In the beginning God created the heavens and the earth." Many of the details regarding *how* he did it remain a mystery. For example, Christians are divided over whether the days of creation were 24-hour periods or long stretches of time. (See "Six-day Creation" in Reviews.)

Reclaiming creation. Notice how the original sin of Adam and Eve grows to engulf the entire world, and how God sets out to correct the problem.

Adam and Eve disobey God. Cain becomes jealous of his younger brother and murders him. Lamech kills a younger man who wounded him and boasts that anyone seeking revenge will get punished ten times more than any trying to get even with Cain, whom God had given a special mark for protection. Meanness, violence, and murder cover the earth by the time of Noah, so God purges the world with a flood. A restored and sophisticated civilization repeats the spirit of the original sin, defying God, causing the Lord to scatter humanity to the four corners of the planet and to impose on them a variety of languages.

The very first sin corrupted God's "good" creation, with painful consequences not the least of which is a broken relationship between humanity and God. And from there sin spreads and infects the entire world.

God decides to reclaim his creation and make it good once again. He starts with one righteous man: Abraham. From Abraham he begins to grow a nation set apart to serve him and to become a model of godliness for the rest of the world.

Loving the underdog. Notice how God shows his love for people that society tends to look down on. Though ancient custom demands that the oldest son get the attention and glory, God shines the spotlight on younger sons like Isaac (instead of Ishmael), Jacob (instead of Esau) and Joseph (who had ten older brothers).

Then there's the matter of childless women, ladies often treated as though they have done something to deserve infertility. God saves them from their agony by turning barrenness into fruitfulness with Sarah, Rebekah, and Rachel, as he will do later for the mothers of Samuel, Samson, and John the Baptist.

AUTHOR AND DATE

The writer is never named. Many scholars say Genesis shows literary evidence of being a marvelously blended composite of several ancient sources. But Jewish tradition says Moses wrote the first five books of the Bible. Jesus agreed (John 7:19). If Moses wrote it, he may have received some of the information directly from God as he did the Ten Commandments. Other material may have come from stories passed on orally and in writing. Abraham, for example, came from the region where writing was invented; he may have recorded part of his story. Christians receive this book and the other books of the Bible as inspired by God, to reveal to human beings what he is like and what his will for us is.

It's uncertain when Genesis was written. It covers a time span from the birth of creation to the death of Joseph in Egypt, about 1800 BC. Some Bible scholars say the book was compiled from several sources, perhaps as late as the 500s BC, nearly a thousand years after Moses. But if Moses wrote the book, he probably did it during the forty years he and the Israelites wandered in the Sinai Peninsula after leaving Egypt. It is uncertain, however, when this long journey took place; some scholars say the Exodus, as it is called, happened in the 1400s BC. Others argue for the 1200s.

The book was written to show that God's creation was good, and that after it became spoiled by sin, God began His plan to reclaim it through the chosen people that come from Abraham.

On Location

Sites mentioned in the book cover a thousand-mile stretch from Abraham's hometown of Ur (in Iraq), to the land God promised him in Canaan (Israel), and to Egypt. It's uncertain where the Garden of Eden was located. Most persistent theories put it somewhere in the Middle East, especially in the fertile strip of land between the Tigris and Euphrates rivers in Iraq, or along the Nile river in Egypt.

GENESIS OUTLINE

God creates Adam (1:24–31; 2:7).

After God creates the heavens and the earth, he finishes his creation with a finale: human beings. "Then the LORD God took dust from the ground and formed a man from it. He breathed the breath of life into the man's nose, and the man became a living person." God makes Eve from one of Adam's ribs.

Unlike all other creatures, humans are made in the image of God, "in his image." Their job is to rule over the earth, taking care of it.

Eve eats forbidden fruit (3:1–24).

In a paradise garden in Eden, Adam and Eve are limited by only one rule: they are not to eat fruit from one particular tree because it will kill them. Eve eats it anyway, then convinces Adam to eat some too.

God expels both of them from the garden and promises that they will die after experiencing a harsh existence unlike anything they have known before. Eve will suffer in childbirth. Adam "will have to work very hard for your food." The presence of sin radically changes creation, for the worse.

Cain kills Abel (4:1–16).

Cain, a farmer, is the oldest son of Adam and Eve. Abel, a shepherd, is the younger son. Each man makes an offering to God; Cain gives crops and Abel gives livestock. God accepts Abel's offering but rejects Cain's, perhaps because Cain did not sacrifice the first and best of his crop (v. 7).

Enraged by jealousy, Cain commits the world's first recorded murder. He kills his brother.

As punishment, he can never again grow crops; if he tries, the ground will produce nothing. Also, Cain is doomed to become a fugitive, "I must wander around on the earth, and anyone who meets me can kill me." But God protects him with an undescribed mark that somehow alerts others not to kill him.

The Flood destroys life on earth (6–9).

Cruelty and violence have spread everywhere, God tells Noah, the only righteous man left, "I will destroy all human beings that I made on the earth."

God instructs Noah to build a massive, three-deck houseboat about 150 yards long, fifteen yards wide, and twenty-five yards high. In this boat, God will preserve Noah and his family, along with pairs of "every kind of bird, animal, and crawling thing will come to you to be kept alive." Torrents of rain fall for forty days, covering the mountains.

Only after five months do the waters recede enough that the boat comes to rest in the Ararat mountain range of Armenia, some 500 miles north of where many scholars believe civilization began.

People start building the Tower of Babel (11:1–9).

Noah's descendants speak one language, work together, and become arrogant because of their accomplishments. They decide to build a huge tower, perhaps as a staircase to heaven or in honor of pagan gods.

"This is only the beginning," God says.

God stops the tower project and puts human pride on pause by suddenly making the people speak different languages. As a result, they scatter all over the earth, apparently clustering by language groups.

Abraham goes to Canaan (12:1–9).

Through Abraham, God launches his plan to restore creation to its original goodness. He tells Abraham to leave his homeland and go into what is now Israel. God says he will give this land to Abraham, and "I will give this land to your descendants." Abraham is seventy-five years old and childless at the time. But he obeys and sets out for the Promised Land called Canaan.

God makes a contract with Abraham (15:1–21).

God makes a formal contract, or covenant, with Abraham. God's promise: "Look at the sky. There are so many stars you cannot count them. Your descendants also will be too many to count." To seal the contract, Abraham offers a sacrifice of a cow, a goat, a ram, a dove, and a pigeon.

Sarah laughs at the promise of a son (18:1–2).

Divine messengers, on their way to evaluate the situation in Sodom and
Gomorrah, visit Abraham. They promise that he and Sarah will have a
son. Sarah, listening from inside the tent, chuckles to herself. After all,
Abraham is ninety-nine and she ninety. But within a year a star is born:
Isaac. And the Jewish nation is begun.

Sodom and Gomorrah are destroyed (19:1–29).

After delivering this happy news, the divine messengers move on to
Sodom and Gomorrah, twin cities in a plain somewhere in Canaan.
Their investigation finds such a depth of depravity that God decides to
destroy them. In fact, the men of Sodom go so far as to try to gang rape
the angelic messengers that God sends to warn Lot and his family to
leave. The angels blind the would-be rapists.

    With Lot and his family out of the city, "The LORD sent a rain of
burning sulfur down from the sky on Sodom and Gomorrah" (19:24
NCV). When Lot's wife looked back, she became a block of salt.

Abraham prepares to sacrifice his son, Isaac (22:1–19).

To test Abraham's faith, God asks him to kill his son, Isaac, as a sacrifice.
This is the son through whom God promised to produce the Jewish
nation. Yet Abraham obeys.

    Isaac doesn't know what is going on. As Abraham builds the sacrifi-
cial altar, Isaac asks where the lamb is. "God will give us the lamb for the
sacrifice, my son," Abraham replies.

    As Abraham raises his knife to kill Isaac, an angel suddenly appears
and tells him to stop. "Don't kill your son or hurt him in any way," the
angel says, "Now I can see that you trust God and that you have not kept
your son, your only son, from me."

    The New Testament portrays this story as a foreshadowing of Jesus.
What Abraham was willing to do, God actually did, offering his only son
as a sacrifice (see John 3:16; Romans 3:21–25). John the Baptist introduced Jesus to the world, saying: "Look, the Lamb of God, who takes
away the sin of the world!" (John 1:29 NCV).

Jacob wrestles a heavenly messenger (32:22–32).

Isaac grows up, marries, and has two sons: Esau and Jacob. The two sons become estranged after Jacob, the younger son, tricks his father into giving him the deathbed blessing traditionally due the eldest son. The night before Jacob's tense reunion with his older brother, Esau, who has vowed to kill him, Jacob meets a mysterious man. Jacob possibly recognizes him as a divine messenger, for he grabs hold of him and says, "I will let you go if you will bless me."

They wrestle until dawn, when the mysterious man throws Jacob's hip out of joint. This man then blesses Jacob by giving him the new name of Israel. Jacob becomes the father of twelve sons, whose descendants will become the tribes of Israel. The most famous son is Joseph.

Joseph's brothers sell him into slavery (37:12–28).

Joseph is Jacob's favorite child, born of his favorite wife. Joseph knows this, and flaunts it by bragging and tattling. His ten older brothers are so fed up with him that they decide to get rid of him.

When Joseph goes to the pasture to check on his brothers, they grab him and throw him in a pit. As they argue over whether or not to kill him, a caravan of slave traders headed for Egypt happens by. Joseph's brothers sell him for twenty pieces of silver, in a scene that seems to foreshadow Judas betraying Jesus for thirty pieces of silver (Matthew 26:15).

In Egypt, Joseph lands in prison after he is falsely charged with trying to rape his master's wife. He remains in prison until summoned by the ruler of Egypt.

Joseph interprets Pharaoh's dream (41:1–40).

Pharaoh, the king of Egypt, has a dream that leaves him feeling troubled. He dreams of seven hungry, gaunt cows devouring seven fat cows, yet not becoming bigger. This dream is followed by one of seven blighted ears of corn consuming seven plump ears. Many people in ancient times believed that the gods communicated through dreams. Some kings consulted dream interpreters, as did Pharaoh. But when the king's wise men are unable to interpret the dream, he sends for Joseph, who has correctly interpreted the dreams of others.

Joseph tells Pharaoh that God is warning Egypt that the nation will enjoy seven years of good harvest, followed by seven years of drought. The grateful Pharaoh appoints Joseph as a top official, in charge of managing the grain reserves.

Joseph reveals his identity to his brothers (45:1–15).

Famine sweeps across Egypt, and Israel as well. Joseph's brothers make the several-hundred-mile trek down to Egypt in search of grain for sale. They don't recognize their younger brother, now a grown and married man. But he recognizes them.

At first, he keeps his identity secret. But eventually he can contain himself no longer. "I am Joseph," he says. Then he begins crying. When he is able to speak again, he asks if his father is still alive.

Indeed, Jacob is alive, but still depressed over losing Joseph.

To his frightened brothers, Joseph offers assurance that he has forgiven them. "Now don't be worried or angry with yourselves because you sold me here," he explains. "God sent me here ahead of you to save people's lives" (45:5 NCV).

At Joseph's request and with Pharaoh's approval, Jacob and his entire extended family move to Egypt to weather out the famine. But they are destined to suffer the fate of young Joseph; they will become an entire nation of slaves. And freeing them will take an act of God, working through a reluctant shepherd called Moses.

POINTS TO CONSIDER

Ancient lifestyles. Details in the story of Abraham and his descendants accurately reflect life in that era, according to records from Abraham's home region in what is now Iraq. For example, among the 282 laws inscribed on the seven-foot-high stone called the Code of Hammurabi is one stipulating that wives can use their slaves as surrogate mothers. In this case, the child legally belongs to the adopted mother. Sarah (wife of Abraham) and Rachel and Leah (wives of Jacob) all used surrogates to increase the size of their families. Prenuptial agreements inscribed on stone tablets at Nuzi, on the Tigris River, confirm this practice.

Sodom and Gomorrah. There's no trace of these cities that God destroyed in a firestorm of sulfur. But the region there is rich in underground gas, oil, and chemicals, sulfur included. The plain also sits on a major earthquake fault. One theory is that Sodom and Gomorrah were leveled when an earthquake opened a pocket of natural gas that rose, was later ignited by lightning or fire, and produced the effects described in Genesis.

Six-day Creation. The creation story reads like a myth, say many.

Specifically, the Bible account that the universe was created in six days does not jibe with current scientific theories that say creation took unimaginable eons. Christians are divided over whether days means 24-hour segments, or longer stretches of time; the original Hebrew word can mean either. Though Genesis doesn't answer our questions about the when and how of creation, it clearly delivers the main point it wants to make: God is the creator.

The Flood. Contrary to the story of Noah and his ark, there is no compelling archaeological evidence that a worldwide flood occurred on this planet. There is strong evidence, however, that at least one major flood swallowed up entire cities in the fertile region where human civilization possibly began: along the shores of the Tigris and Euphrates rivers in what is now Iraq. Traces of such a deluge date to about 3400 BC. Babylon epics also tell of a great flood there.

Some scholars wonder if the Flood covered just the known civilized world (the Hebrew term for *world* used in this story is not the most common term to describe the earth; it's a term that can also mean *land* or *country*.

Others wonder if the Flood covered the entire planet, and we simply haven't found the evidence yet. What we have turned up are flood stories from more than 100 cultures throughout the world: Egypt, Greece, North and South America, China, the South Pacific.

Repeatedly, Genesis shows that it was written in the ways and manners used to express truth in ancient times, not to satisfy modern scientific curiosity. It was written to reveal what God is like and how he began the long process of restoring his good creation and his relationship with the rebellious human race.

FOR FURTHER STUDY

- For more on the story of Abraham's ever-growing family, read Exodus. It starts where Genesis leaves off, with the Israelites in Egypt. Exodus tells of Moses leading the enslaved nation home to what is now Israel.

- For more about God's work in creation, read his reply to Job, who felt he had the intellectual savvy to argue with God (Job 38:4–40:2). Or try the prophet Isaiah's masterful poem about learning to trust in the God of creation (Isaiah 40:10–31).

- To learn more about why Abraham is so important to Jews and Christians, and how the New Testament presents him as a person who was saved through faith in God, read Romans 4:1–25 and James 2:14–26.

Sun
Mo
Tue
We
Thu
Frid
Satu
Sun
Mo
Tue
We
Thu
Frid
Satu
Sun
Mo
Tue
We

Exodus

MOSES LEADS THE GREAT ESCAPE

Ask a Jewish friend to tell you about the greatest event in the 4,000-year history of their people.

They'll point you to their Great Escape, an epic adventure reported in Exodus.

This wasn't just a hair-raising chase scene, wrapped around some of the most spectacular miracles in the Bible. If you freeze this frame of history, you capture the moment of Israel's birth. For though God promised hundreds of years earlier to make Abraham into a nation, this was the moment for that promise to become a living, breathing reality.

Into Egypt had come one Hebrew family, seeking relief from a famine and led by Jacob. Out of Egypt came one Hebrew nation seeking freedom from slavery and led by Moses.

During their trek home, to what is now Israel, they accepted their role as descendants of Abraham, and they vowed to obey God. So God, through Moses, set up the rules that would govern the people. At the heart of these rules are the Ten Commandments.

> ### FAMOUS LINES
>
> • "I AM WHO I AM" (3:14 NCV). *God's name, as revealed to Moses at the burning bush.*
>
> • "Let my people go" (5:1 NCV). *God's demand of Pharaoh, the Egyptian king.*
>
> • "You must not have any other gods except me" (20:3 NCV). *The first of the Ten Commandments.*
>
> • But if there is further injury, then the punishment that must be paid is . . . eye for eye, tooth for tooth (21:23–24 NCV).

The story is a classic—not so much because of what it reveals about the Jewish people, but because of what it reveals about God. He is the great deliverer, who can and will invade the physical world to save those who call on him for help.

BACKGROUND

INFLUENTIAL PEOPLE

Moses, who leads the Israelites out of Egypt (2:10).

Egyptian king, known as Pharaoh, who uses the Israelites for slave labor (1:11).

Aaron, older brother of Moses and builder of the golden calf (4:14).

THEME

To escape a famine in what is now Israel, Jacob moves his family to Egypt. They stay about 400 years. Sometime during this extended visit, Jacob's descendants grow so numerous that the Egyptians fear the Hebrews might take over. So an Egyptian king decides to turn them all into slaves. He forces them to make bricks for his massive building projects—including entire cities. The people ask God to free them. And God sends Moses to do just that.

DID YOU KNOW?

• The ten plagues probably aren't just attempts to twist Pharaoh's arm so he will let God's people go. Each plague seemed to target and overpower an Egyptian god, to show that the Lord is the only true God. For example, when God covers the land in darkness (plague nine he proves his power over Egypt's chief deity, Ra, the sun god.

• Israel capture the Sinai Peninsula from Egypt in the Six-Day War of 1967. But they returned it in 1979, under the terms of an Egyptian-Israeli peace treaty.

TIMELINE	BIBLE EVENTS		Moses born 1530 BC	The Exodus, Ten Commandments 1440 BC	Moses dies 1400 BC	*Many scholars say Moses lived about 200 years later, putting the Exodus at about 1275 BC
		Dates are approximate				
		3300 BC	2900 BC	2500 BC	2100 BC	1700 BC	1300 BC
	WORLD EVENTS	Cuneiform (picture-style) writing begins 3300 BC		Thutmose I rules Egypt 1530 BC	People in Canaan (Israel) and Sinai use first known alphabet 1500 BC	Rameses II uses slave labor to build monuments 1292 BC

POINTS OF INTEREST

God getting involved. Notice that God doesn't relax in the comfort of heaven, while expecting human beings to work out their own problems. He's a hands-on God. He produces a leader out of a man who wants to stay with the sheep. He generates breath-taking miracles to break the stubborn will of Pharaoh. And he blows a dry path through a standing body of water when the fleeing Israelites are trapped between a charging army and the deep blue sea.

Two sections. The first half of the book is the epic story about the Israelites escaping from Egypt. The last half, beginning with chapter 19, is made up of laws and worship instructions for the Israelites.

AUTHOR AND DATE

Probably Moses, though the book doesn't identify its writer. Other Bible books, however, speak of Moses as the author (Joshua 8:31; Mark 12:26). And Exodus 17:14 says Moses wrote at least part of the book. Critics once said Moses couldn't have written it, since the alphabet had not been invented. But archaeologists have uncovered many alphabetic writings from about 1500 BC in what is now Israel as well as the Sinai Peninsula, where the Israelites spent forty years.

Like the others of the first five books of the Bible, Moses probably wrote Exodus during the Exodus. That would have been sometime during their 40-year trek to Israel, perhaps in the 1400s BC.

On Location

The Hebrew captivity and the confrontation between Moses and Pharoah take place in the Nile Delta of northern Egypt. The Exodus and forty years of wandering in the wilderness take place in the Sinai Peninsula, a barren expanse between Egypt and Canaan, just north of the Red Sea. The map shows possible routes of the Exodus.

EXODUS OUTLINE

Israel becomes slaves (1:1–22).

The Israelites migrate to Egypt during the days of Joseph, to escape a famine in Israel. They produce a lot of children there—so many that when a pharaoh rises to power he complains that the Israelites pose a threat to national security. So he orders them enslaved to make mud bricks for massive projects such as the cities of Pithom and Rameses. They probably didn't build pyramids, since most of them were finished before 2200 BC, nearly 1,000 years earlier.

An early Egyptian record written on a tomb wall describes the slave brickmaker: "He is dirtier than vines or pigs from the treading under his mud . . . He is simply wretched through and through."

Pharaoh's daughter finds baby Moses floating in a basket (2:1–10).

To control the rapidly multiplying Israelite population, Pharaoh orders that all their newborn sons be killed at birth. But the mother of Moses puts her baby son in a watertight basket and sets him afloat near where the princess bathes. Big sister watches from among the reeds. When the princess finds the child and takes pity on him, Moses's sister walks over and asks if she needs someone to nurse him. When Pharaoh's daughter says yes, the child gets the mother of Moses, who serves as his nurse— and receives a salary as well.

Moses murders an Egyptian slavedriver and runs away (2:11–22).

Though Moses was raised in the king's palace, he knows he is an Israelite. And he feels a kinship to his people. When he witnesses an Egyptian foreman beating a Hebrew slave, Moses kills the Egyptian and quickly hides his body in the sand. When Pharaoh hears about this, he decides to execute Moses. So Moses runs away, east to Midian, which extends from the Sinai Peninsula to northern Arabia. There he marries into the family of a sheep herder.

Moses sees a blazing bush that doesn't burn up (3:1–10).

While grazing his flock near Mount Sinai, Moses sees a bush on fire, yet it is not burned. Out of the bush comes the voice of God, calling Moses to come close. "Take off your sandals," God says, "because you are standing on holy ground."

God then gives Moses a terrifying chore: return to Egypt and demand that the great pharaoh free the slaves. Moses doesn't want to go, and says so. But God promises, "I will be with you." So Moses goes to Egypt.

The angel of death visits Egypt (12:1–32).

"Let my people go" is the word that Moses delivers to Pharaoh. The king refuses.

Moses threatens—and delivers—plague upon plague to convince Pharaoh that the demand comes from none other than God. The Nile River turns to blood. Frogs invade the land, followed by gnats, flies, then locusts. The livestock get sick. Lightning and hail destroy the crops. Darkness shrouds Egypt for three days. The people suffer from boils.

But only the last plague breaks Pharaoh's stubborn spirit. God kills the oldest child in each family, Pharaoh's included. But he passes over the homes of Israelites who have obeyed his directions to splash their front door posts with the blood of a sacrificial lamb they have eaten.

Since that fateful day, Jews annually commemorate their deliverance from Egypt by eating a Passover meal.

Crossing the Red Sea (14:1–31).

"Get your people out of my country and leave us alone!" Pharaoh tells Moses that night. The Israelites leave the next morning, rushing east toward the Sinai Peninsula, nestled between the Gulf of Suez and the Gulf of Aqaba, which protrude up from the Red Sea like a couple of giant rabbit ears.

For Pharaoh, grief churns into seething anger. He assembles a massive chariot force that gives chase, trapping the Israelites on the banks of the Red Sea. God blocks the Egyptian advance with a pillar of smoke and fire. Then God sends a strong east wind to blow a path across the body of water. The Israelites walk across the sea floor.

When the Israelites safely reach the other side the Egyptians boldly—but foolishly—follow. The sea walls come splashing down, killing every Egyptian that enters the water.

The Israelites sing praise to God after the crossing (15:1–21).

In the moment it takes two massive, opposing waves to crash together, the Egyptian threat is gone and the Israelites are free. Exhilarated, the entire nation joins Moses in a song of praise to God. Miriam, the sister of Moses, takes out a tambourine and leads the women in dancing.

Moses destroys the Ten Commandments (20:1–17; 31:18–32:35; 34:1).

Moses returns to Mount Sinai, where he earlier met God in the burning bush. Here God gives him the Ten Commandments, inscribed onto two stone tablets. And here, God outlines other laws that will govern Israel and make it clear to other nations that Israel is devoted to God.

The meeting takes forty days—long enough for the Israelite to fear that Moses may not be coming back. So they talk his brother, Aaron, into building a golden calf, "these are your gods who brought you out of the land of Egypt!"

When Moses finally returns and sees many of the people dancing around the calf, he becomes so angry that he throws the stone tablets, shattering them. Already the people have broken the first and most important commandment: Do not worship any god except me.

Moses returns to Mount Sinai, where God replaces the inscribed Commandments.

The Israelites build a tent sanctuary (26:1–37).

On God's instruction, the Israelites build a portable worship center called the tabernacle. Wherever they go, they erect it in the center of their camp. The tabernacle courtyard—where people offer sacrifices to God to express gratitude or to atone for sins—measures fifty yards long by twenty-five yards wide. It is surrounded by a wall of curtains seven feet high. Inside the tent, fifteen yards long and five yards wide, the Israelites keep the Ten Commandments, secured in a chest called the ark of the covenant. Only priests are allowed inside the sacred tent.

The presence of God, in the form of a cloud, settles on the tabernacle. Whenever the cloud moved from the tent, the people would break camp and follow.

POINTS TO CONSIDER

Golden calf. The Israelites made a golden calf to worship, when they feared Moses would not return from his 40-day meeting with God on Mount Sinai. The story seems reliable since their choice of a young bull is not at all out of sync with the times.

Many countries in the ancient Middle East had bull cults. In fact, Egypt—where the Israelites had just spent the last 400 years—worshiped a bull god: Apis. People believed Apis provided fertile fields, flocks, and families. One Egyptian statue shows a king kneeling before a young bull.

When the Exodus took place. The Bible and archaeology seem to disagree about this.

First Kings 6:1 says the Exodus took place 480 years before Solomon's fourth year as king. His fourth year was 966 BC, which means Moses led the Israelites out of Egypt in 1446 BC. But many Bible scholars suggest the Exodus and conquest of Canaan (now Israel) took place in the 1200s. Their evidence? (1) Many Canaanite villages were destroyed during that century. (2) Exodus 1:11 says Israelite slaves build the city of Rameses, which Egyptian records say Rameses II built in his honor.

Some scholars in favor of the traditional date of 1446 BC say it is unknown who caused the destruction in Canaan two centuries later; it wasn't necessarily the army of Joshua. It could have been the Philistines. Regarding the mention of Rameses, scholars say that could have been a late editorial addition or a transcribing error (but the same argument could hold true for the 1 Kings verse that places the Exodus in 1446 BC).

Scholars remain divided on the issue. Many cling to the traditional date until stronger evidence compels them to do otherwise.

Parting of the Red Sea. Many find it unbelievable that God would miraculously create an escape path through the Red Sea—or that he would perform any miracle that would break the laws of nature.

The Hebrew term for "Red Sea" can mean "Sea of Reeds," suggesting the Israelites crossed a shallow marsh north of the Red Sea. For many people, it's easier to accept that a hot sirocco wind blowing in from the eastern desert quickly dried up the marsh. But whether the Israelites crossed a sea or a marsh, we seem confronted with a miracle. Either God parted a deep body of water, or he arranged for Pharaoh's chariot force to drown in a shallow marsh.

:00

:00

:00

:00

:00

oon

:00

:00

:00

:00

:00

:00

:00

:00

:00

:00

:00

======= **FOR FURTHER STUDY** =======

- For the rest of the story, read about the end of the Exodus, when the Israelites reach the Promised Land. It's found in Joshua, a book named for the man who led the nation after Moses died.

- To see how Israel later celebrates the Exodus in song, read lyrics from their song book: Psalm 78, 105–106, 136.

- To discover how the New Testament portrays Jesus as the Passover lamb whose blood saves us from spiritual death, read John 1:29 and 1 Corinthians 5:1–8.

Leviticus

ISRAEL'S SPIRITUAL HOW-TO MANUAL

It's not what you'd call easy reading, but essential reading.

It was essential in ancient times, for Jews serious about honoring their commitment to obey God. And it's essential today, for an unobstructed look at God's take on sin and how he made a way for people to get rid of it.

Jews long ago called this book the Priest's Manual. The name *Leviticus* came later; it means "about the Levites." The book earned this later tag because Levites were worship leaders in Israel, and the book is full of detailed instructions about worship. Both titles are misleading, however, because the instructions—about sacrifices, religious holidays, and ritual cleanness—aren't just for priests. They're for everyone.

In many ancient nations, only priests were uniquely set apart to serve the gods and to live by a special code. But the Lord set apart an entire country. He told Israel, "you will be my kingdom of priests and a holy nation" (Exodus 19:6 NCV).

FAMOUS LINES

- "You must be holy because I am holy" (11:45 NCV).

- "Love your neighbor as you love yourself" (19:18 NCV). *A command later popularized by Jesus.*

- "I will walk with you and be your God, and you will be my people" (26:12 NCV).

The book of Leviticus is their spiritual how-to manual. In a way, it's the volume preceding the new manual coming from Jesus, "the One who began our faith and who makes it perfect" (Hebrews 12:2 NCV).

To understand what Jesus did for us, we need to understand the Jewish faith on which he built.

BACKGROUND

INFLUENTIAL PEOPLE

Moses, who receives detailed worship instructions from God (1:1).

Aaron, older brother of Moses and the chief priest in charge of implementing the instructions (6:8).

THEME

There isn't really a story line to follow. After leaving Egypt, the Israelites camp at Mount Sinai for a year. This is where they receive the Ten Commandments, build a tent worship center, and receive some 600 laws that will govern them—many laws of which are preserved in Leviticus.

POINTS OF INTEREST

Plan of salvation. It's easy to get sidetracked by all the details of the law, and by trying to figure out exactly why God orders the Israelites to perform all these rituals and obey these

> ### DID YOU KNOW?
>
> • The Liberty Bell is engraved with words that describe the trumpet blast signaling the release of slaves at the start of Jubilee, a celebration every half-century: "Proclaim liberty throughout all the land unto all the inhabitants thereof" (25:10, KJV).
>
> • The idea of a scapegoat—a person who takes the blame for others—comes from Leviticus. On Israel's national day of repentance, known as Yom Kippur or the Day of Atonement, the high priest puts his hands on the head of a goat, symbolically transferring the nation's sins to the animal. Then he has the goat led into the desert to die. As the goat departs, so does Israel's sin.

rules—some of which may seem bizarre and even unfair. Instead, read the book as God's first step in his plan of salvation—a step that dramatizes the seriousness of sin and the importance of obeying God.

Israel is unique. Notice that by laying out these rituals and rules for

TIMELINE	BIBLE EVENTS	Jewish laws, sacrificial system begin 1440 BC ----				Dates are approximate	
		1500 BC	1400 BC	1300 BC	1200 BC	1100 BC	1000 BC
	WORLD EVENTS	Hindu scriptures (Vedas) begin 1500 BC	People in Canaan (Israel) and Sinai use first known alphabet 1500 BC				Sacrificial altar used in northern Israel 1000 BC

Israel, God is telling the people they are to be holy—a nation separated from sinful practices and devoted to him. In this way Israel becomes a witness to the world, testifying that God is holy and deserves our obedience.

AUTHOR AND DATE

The writer is unnamed, but traditionally considered to be Moses. Much of the book reports on the explicit worship instructions that God gives Moses at Mount Sinai. In fact, nearly all of Leviticus is from the speeches of God; Moses likely provides the quotes.

Like the other books attributed to Moses (the first five in the Bible), Leviticus is probably written during the forty years it takes Israel to reach the Promised Land. Perhaps some of Leviticus is written early in the trip, just after Moses receives the worship instructions from God. Moses would have wanted to implement the rules as quickly as possible, which means he had to teach the priests who would in turn teach the masses.

The book is written to give Israel directions on how to live in peace with God and with one another. Leviticus is not only a book of religious law, but civil law as well. That's because God presents himself as more than Lord at worship time, but as Lord all the time.

ON LOCATION

Israel is camped for a year at the foot of Mount Sinai, while God gives Moses the laws preserved in Leviticus. One mountain long associated with this event is Jebel Musa ("mountain of Moses"), a 7,500-foot-high peak near the southern tip of the Sinai Peninsula (approximate location marked with triangle on the map). In the fourth century AD, Christians built a monastery there to commemorate the meeting between God and Moses.

LEVITICUS OUTLINE

A lamb is sacrificed for sin committed (4:27–35).

God creates an intricate system of animal sacrifice. This gives the people a visible, tangible way of expressing their sorrow for sin and of being assured of God's forgiveness. Like a dramatic object lesson and visual aid, the sacrifice also reminds the people about the seriousness of sin: sin causes spiritual death. This is vividly illustrated by the death of the animal.

The ritual calls for the worshiper to lay a hand on the head of the animal, perhaps as a gesture recognizing that the animal is about to lose its life on his account—because of his sin. "This is because the life of the body is in the blood," God explains. "I have given you rules for pouring that blood on the altar to remove your sins so you will belong to the LORD" (17:11 NCV).

The Jews can eat only select animals (11:1–47).

God tells the Jews they may eat animals that chew the cud and have a split hoof (such as cattle), fish that have fins and scales, and certain insects (such as locusts, crickets, and grasshoppers). But God bans a wide variety of animals, including pigs, camels, shellfish, lizards, and many birds.

God doesn't explain his reason.

Some have theorized God was protecting the Jews from health problems, or from idolatry, since some forbidden animals were used in pagan rituals—especially the pig. But it may be that God was simply providing a visible way of showing Israel and other nations that the Jews were set apart for special service to God.

People who eat non-kosher food become ritually unclean and have to follow certain cleansing rituals before they can worship God.

The nation repents on the Day of Atonement (16:1–34).

The Day of Atonement, known also as Yom Kippur, becomes the holiest day on the Jewish calendar. On this day, each autumn, the high priest offers sacrifices to atone for the sins of the entire nation. First, he sacrifices a bull to atone for the sins of his own family. Then he sacrifices a goat for the sins of the nation. Afterward, he lays his hands on the head of a second goat—called a "scapegoat"—and confesses the sins of Israel. This goat is led into the desert and released to die "so that it can take away their sins." In the New Testament, this image of the scapegoat becomes associated with Jesus "offered as a sacrifice one time to take away the sins of many people" (Hebrews 9:28 NCV).

POINTS TO CONSIDER

Israel's unique laws. Though the 600-plus laws of God recorded in the first five books of the Bible are similar to the laws of other nations during this era, there are some important differences that reveal Israel wasn't simply borrowing from others.

For example, Hammurabi's Code, written several hundred years before Moses, favored the elite. If an upper-class man blinded the eye of another aristocrat, he paid with the loss of one of his eyes. But if he did the same to a commoner, he compensated the injured man only with "one mina [about a pound] of silver." In addition, if a builder constructed a house for a wealthy man and the house collapsed and killed the owner's son, the builder's son could be executed.

Biblical law, however, banned substitutionary punishment. And it treated all citizen offenders the same, regardless of status. Also, the law made special provisions for the disadvantaged. Farmers had to leave part of their crops in the field, as pickings for the poor, widows, orphans, and strangers in the land.

Half sister. One of the many rules God gave Israel was this: "If your father and his wife have a daughter, she is your sister. You must not have sexual relations with her" (18:11 NCV). Yet that's exactly how the Jewish nation began.

Abraham, father of the Jewish people, married his half sister Sarah and then had a son named Isaac. As Abraham explained to King Abimelech, "And it is true that she is my sister. She is the daughter of my father, but she is not the daughter of my mother" (Genesis 20:12 NCV).

Jewish Bible scholars in the Middle Ages, and 16th-century Christian scholar John Calvin, were so uncomfortable with this apparent clash in Scripture that they argued that Abraham and Sarah were cousins. The Bible says they weren't.

The fact is, the marriage of Abraham and Sarah came first. The laws of Moses came later—several hundred years later. So the marriage doesn't show a disregard for the Law; it rather confirms that the story of Abraham comes earlier, as the Bible says.

Sund
Mor
Tues
Wec
Thu
Frida
Satu
Sund
Mor
Tues
Wec
Thu
Frida
Satu
Sund
Mor
Tues
Wec

7:00

8:00

9:00

0:00

1:00

Noon

1:00

2:00

3:00

4:00

5:00

6:00

7:00

8:00

9:00

0:00

FOR FURTHER STUDY

- To discover how New Testament writers build the Christian faith on Jewish traditions, read Hebrews. There, Jesus is shown replacing the sacrificial system, since he offers himself as the ultimate and final sacrifice for sin, "only once and for all time" (Hebrews 7:27 NCV).

Numbers

FORTY YEARS IN THE DESERT

Don't be fooled by the title. Numbers is not just a report from census-takers.

It does include two of these reports (which is how the book earned its name): one census at the beginning of the book, as the Israelites get ready to leave Mount Sinai, and another at the end, as they camp near the border of what is now Israel. But the book is also full of dramatic stories that reveal a lot about what God is like and how he deals with ever-griping, rebellious human beings.

Jews in ancient times knew the book by the name "In the Wilderness." That's a more descriptive title, for that's what most of the book is about: what went on during the forty years it took the Israelites to reach Israel, some 400 miles away—and why it took them so long.

The reason it took so long, in a word, is sin. In fact, one of the main points of the book, and a message for all generations, is that God punishes sin. He gives help when asked. He shows mercy unrequested. He offers love neverending. But when faced with sin, he knows it won't go away if he ignores it. So he doesn't.

Yet even when punishing citizens, leaders, and the entire nation, God gives encouragement and hope. As the apostle Paul noted, "Everything that was written in the past was written to teach us. The Scriptures give us patience and encouragement so that we can have hope" (Romans 15:4 NCV).

BACKGROUND

INFLUENTIAL PEOPLE

Moses, leader of Israel's 40-year trek toward the Promised Land (1:1).
Aaron, high priest and older brother of Moses (1:2).
Miriam, sister of Moses (12:1).
Balaam, sorcerer hired to put a hex on Israel (22:5).
Eleazar, son of Aaron and successor as high priest (19:6).
Joshua, scout who explored Promised Land, successor of Moses (11:28).

THEME

After about a year camped at the foot of Mount Sinai, the Israelites set out for the Promised Land. Traveling through the Sinai desert they face many hardships, including hunger, thirst, and sickness. They are quick to complain but slow to ask for God's help. They don't seem to trust him for the future, though he has only recently come through for them in spectacular ways. Their lack of trust becomes shockingly apparent when they reach the boundary of Canaan, now Israel. They refuse to cross the border. They trust less in God than they do in the report of Israelite scouts who return with terrifying news of massive, fortified cities and of giants "We felt like grasshoppers, and we looked like grasshoppers to them" (13:33 NCV).

Because the people refused to trust that God who saved them from the powerful Egyptians could also save them from the Canaanites, God condemns them to wander in the desert until their generation dies.

TIMELINE	BIBLE EVENTS	Exodus begins 1440 BC	Scouts explore Promised Land 1437 BC	Israelites prepare to enter Promised Land 1400 BC		Dates are approximate	
		1500 BC	**1450 BC**	**1400 BC**	**1350 BC**	**1300 BC**	**1000 BC**
	WORLD EVENTS	Hittite empire begins 1460 BC	Babylonian creation story Enuma Elish written 1450 BC	India produces silk clothing 1400 BC	Nefertiti is queen of Egypt 1380 BC	Tutankhamen (King Tut), age 9, rules Egypt 1361 BC	

POINTS OF INTEREST

Punishment for sin. Notice how quickly God punishes sin. But notice, too, how quickly he forgives this nation of repeat offenders. Time after time they gripe, harshly criticize, and outright rebel. But each time they repent, he forgives. The people do have to suffer the consequences of their actions, but they don't have to suffer alone. God is with them.

AUTHOR AND DATE

Moses is assumed to be the main writer. Numbers 33:2 says he wrote at least part of it. Others may have added to it. For example, it seems unlikely that Moses would write this: "Now Moses was very humble. He was the least proud person on earth" (12:3 NCV).

Moses probably wrote most of Numbers during the nation's desert travels in the 1400s BC. Other knowledgeable writers, such as priests, may have added material and compiled the work into final form after the Israelites settled in the land.

Perhaps the main reason Moses wrote the book is to show that God punishes sin. In fact, the reason the Israelites had to wait forty years before they could go into the Promised Land is because they sinned.

DID YOU KNOW?

• The medical symbol of two snakes on a staff (caduceus) resembles the one described in Numbers. When poisonous snakes enter the Israelite camp, God tells Moses to make a bronze snake and put it on a pole. "When anyone who is bitten looks at it," God says, "that person will live" (21:8 NCV).

• God sentenced Israel to forty years in the desert, one year for every day the scouts explored the Promised Land. Ten of the twelve scouts advised against the invasion—advice that most of Israel accepted.

• The star of David, which has become the national emblem for modern Israel, comes from Balaam's prophecy of a future king of Israel who "will appear like a star" and conquer neighboring desert nation.

ON LOCATION

Numbers is set in the Sinai Peninsula, east of Egypt and south of what is now Israel. This is the sun-parched, rugged land where God condemns the Israelites to spend forty years before entering the Promised Land. The map shows only the first year of their journey.

NUMBERS OUTLINE

Moses takes a census of Israel's fighting men (1:1–54).

After God gives Israel their governing laws during the year they camp at the foot of Mount Sinai, he calls on Moses to get the people ready to leave. Since they will be invading an occupied land, God instructs Moses to take a census and determine how many fighting men he has. Among the twelve families descended from the sons of Jacob, there are 603,550 men of fighting age, twenty and older.

Ark leads the wilderness trek (10:11–36).

A pillar of cloud representing God's presence among the people rises from the tent sanctuary and begins to move. This is the signal that it's time for Israel to break camp and follow. At the front of this migrating nation are priests carrying the ark of the covenant, the chest containing the Ten Commandments. As the ark sets out each day, followed by the long mass of people, Moses says this short prayer: "Rise up, LORD! Scatter your enemies: make those who hate you run from you."

When the people travel by night, the pillar of cloud changes into a pillar of fire.

God provides manna and quail (11:4–32).

When the dew covers the ground in the morning, so does manna, an unknown substance "like small white seeds" that tastes "like bread baked with olive oil." The Israelites eventually grow weary of this one-course meal.

"We remember the fish we ate for free in Egypt," they complain, "We also had cucumbers, melons, leeks, onions, and garlic. But now we have lost our appetite; we never see anything but this manna."

God sends a wind that pushes quail in from the seacoast. The birds cover the ground "three feet deep on the ground, and there were quail a day's walk in any direction." Each person gathers at least fifty bushels; then they begin a feast. What they can't eat right away, they dry in the sun for use later.

Sun
Mon
Tues
Wed
Thu
Frid
Satu
Sun
Mon
Tues
Wed
Thu
Frid
Satu
Sun
Mon
Tues
Wed

Twelve scouts investigate the Promised Land (13:1–14:44).

With the Israelites camping on the southern boundary of Canaan, Moses sends twelve men—one from each family tribe—to scout the land. He wants to know if the towns are fortified with walls, if the soil is good, and if there are trees. The scouts return forty days later. Two men, Joshua and Caleb, show off the grapes, pomegranates, and figs they bring, then urge the people to take the land.

But the other ten scouts argue, "The land that we explored is too large to conquer. All the people we saw are very tall."

The Israelites refuse to go any further. For their lack of faith, God condemns the nation to wander in the desert for forty years—until most of the adults who left Egypt are dead.

Water springs from solid rock (20:1–13).

The Israelites retreat south to Kadesh, an oasis where they apparently spend most of the forty years. There, the water dries us and the people bitterly lament leaving Egypt. Moses and Aaron ask for God's help.

"Take your walking stick," God says, "and you and your brother Aaron should gather the people. Speak to that rock in front of them so that its water will flow from it."

The two men assemble the nation and Moses angrily shouts, "Now listen to me, you who turn against God! Do you want us to bring water out of this rock?" Then he strikes the rock twice with his staff.

Because Moses and Aaron do not speak to the rock as God commanded, so that God gets credit for the miracle, God is angry with them. He tells Moses that he and Aaron will not lead the Israelites into the Promised Land.

Poisonous snakes invade the camp (21:4–9).

The nation of Edom, in what is now western Jordan, refuses to grant safe passage to Israel. This would have given the Israelites a direct path up to the Jordan River crossing into Canaan. So Israel turns south, deep into the desert, to go around Edom. There, again, the people harshly criticize God for making them endure such hunger and thirst.

God sends venomous snakes into the camp, which kill many people. The Israelites repent and ask for deliverance. God tells Moses to erect a pole with a bronze snake at the top. Anyone who gets bitten and looks at the pole will not die.

Centuries later, Jesus will compare this event to his Crucifixion, which provides eternal salvation (John 3:14–15).

Balaam's donkey talks (22:1–24:25).

As Israel turns north and advances toward the eastern border of the Promised Land, they approach Moab in what is now the Dead Sea area of Jordan. The king of Moab becomes frantic. He sends messengers to what is possibly the region of Iraq to hire Balaam, an internationally known prophet and seer. The king wants Balaam to put a hex on Israel.

Balaam loads up his donkey and begins the journey. Somewhere along the way he encounters an angel with a sword. At first only Balaam's donkey can see the divine messenger, so the beast sits down and refuses to go further. The contrast is powerful: a lowly donkey can see what an acclaimed seer can't.

When Balaam beats the donkey, the Lord allows the beast to talk. "What have I done to make you hit me three times?" the animal asks.

Suddenly, Balaam is able to see the angel. This divine being permits Balaam to go to Moab on the condition that he speak only the word of God.

Instead of cursing the Israelites, Balaam blesses them and curses their enemies. Furthermore, he prophesies that "A star will come from Jacob; a ruler will rise from Israel. He will crush the heads of the Moabites and smash the skulls of the sons of Sheth." King David accomplished this in about 1000 BC (2 Samuel 8:2, 11–14).

Joshua is appointed leader when Moses dies (27:12–23).

Before Moses dies, God tells him to commission Joshua as successor. Moses takes Joshua before a massive assembly of the people, puts his hands on him, and appoints him Israel's leader.

Though God does not allow Moses to go into the Promised Land, he lets him see it. Moses climbs a mountain east of the Jordan River. There below him, just across the river, stretches the land "flowing with milk and honey."

There on the mountain, with this marvelous and moving vista before him, Moses dies (Deuteronomy 34:5–6).

POINTS TO CONSIDER

Balaam outside the Bible. The name of Balaam, son of Beor—as he is identified in Numbers—has shown up on a seventh-century BC plaster inscription found among ancient, non-Israelite ruins in Jordan. The words describe Balaam as a "seer of the gods" who received a divine message about a coming disaster.

Inflated population statistics. The census report suggests Israel had at least two million people—more than most nations of the day. This estimate is based on the report that Israel had more than 600,000 fighting men. If each man had, on average, a wife and two children, we're looking at a sea of 2.4 million people wandering around the desert for forty years. And staying alive. We're also looking at 600,000 men only slowly capturing Canaan, a land of city-states with an estimated population of about 200,000. We're also looking at what Numbers says are only 22,273 firstborn sons (3:43). If there were also an equal number of firstborn daughters, each family would have needed more than fifty kids for Israel to have a population of 2.4 million.

Critics point to these unbelievable numbers as evidence that the Bible is not entirely reliable.

In fact, there may have been many fewer Israelites than seemingly reported.

The Hebrew word for "thousand" can also mean "group," "unit," or "family." So in this case, there might have been only 600 units of fighting men—units of unknown size.

Another theory is that scribes who preserved the book on new scrolls later got confused by various categories and merged the numbers. They may have not realized, for example, the difference between trained warriors and untrained militia, so they treated forty-four warriors in Reuben's family as units of thousands, then added them to the 1,500 militia men. The result: 45,500.

Whatever the population, Israel became large enough in Egypt that Pharaoh complained, "There are too many of those Israelites in our country, and they are becoming more powerful than we are" (Exodus 1:9).

The test of an adulteress. Women suspected of committing adultery had to drink a brew of water mixed with dirt from the floor of the tent worship center. If the woman got sick, she was guilty.

Critics ask, "Who wouldn't get sick" The test conjures up images of the cruel, medieval trial by ordeal, in which accused people had to prove their innocence by enduring a fire or boiling water.

In Israel's case, however, God established the test, priests administered it, and the people believed that the God who created earth, water, and humans would control the outcome.

= FOR FURTHER STUDY =

- To find out what happens once the Israelites finally enter Canaan, read the book of Joshua.

- To see the fulfillment of God's promise to reward Joshua and Caleb for being the only two scouts to urge Israel to invade Canaan, read Joshua 14:6–15; 19:49–51. The other ten scouts died from a "terrible sickness" (14:37 NCV).

Sun
Mo
Tue
Wer
Thu
Frid
Satu
Sun
Mo
Tue
Wer
Thu
Frid
Satu
Sun
Mo
Tue
Wer

Deuteronomy

THE LAST WORDS OF MOSES

What do you say to the people you love when you're about to die? And how do you encourage them when you know they'll be facing the greatest challenge of their lives?

The entire nation of Israelites is camped just beyond the eastern border of Canaan, now called Israel. God has promised to give them the land, but they'll have to fight for it; the territory is full of city kingdoms, many protected by stone walls and seasoned warriors.

Moses won't be there to help anymore. He won't part the waters of the sea when they need to escape. He won't draw water from solid rock when they're thirsty. He won't call down quail when they need meat.

He'll be gone. But God won't.

"But don't be afraid of them." says Moses. "Remember what the LORD your God did to all of Egypt and its king . . . The LORD your God will do the same thing to all the nations you now fear" (7:18–19 NCV).

To bolster the people's faith, Moses tenderly reminds them of where they came from, where on the earth they stand, and how they got there.

FAMOUS LINES

- "Listen, people of Israel! The Lord our God is the only Lord" (6:4 NCV). *The creedal statement of the Jewish religion.*

- "Love the Lord your God with all your heart, all your soul, and all your strength" (6:5 NCV). *The words Jesus quoted when asked to identify the most important commandment.*

- "Apple of his eye" (21:10, KJV). *This is the first of several times that the familiar phrase shows up in the Bible. Here, it describes the love God has for Israel.*

BACKGROUND

INFLUENTIAL PEOPLE

Moses, who gives his farewell after leading Israel forty years (1:1).
Joshua, appointed by God to succeed Moses (1:38).

THEME

The Israelites are ready to cross the Jordan River and invade Canaan, the Promised Land. Most adults who escaped Egypt forty years earlier have died. Moses, too, is about to die. The new generation assembled before him is one that grew up during the wilderness trek. They didn't witness the glorious escape. Nor did they stand at the foot of Mount Sinai when their parents promised to obey God in return for guidance, protection, and blessing.

For this new generation, Moses prepares a series of sermons—history lessons that summarize the feats of God and the laws that Israel has vowed to obey. Israel's future, he warns, will be determined by how the people respond to God.

"Today I ask heaven and earth to be witnesses. I am offering you life or death, blessings or curses," Moses says. "Now, choose life! Then you and your children may live. To choose life is to love the Lord your God, obey him, and stay close to him. He is your life, and he will let you live many years in the land, the land he promised to give your ancestors Abraham, Isaac, and Jacob" (30:15, 19–20 NCV).

The question is, will this new generation choose death, as their parents had done?

		Israelites leave Egypt 1440 BC		Moses dies, Israel ready to invade Canaan 1400 BC		Dates are approximate	
TIMELINE	**BIBLE EVENTS**						
		1500 BC	**1450 BC**	**1400 BC**	**1350 BC**	**1300 BC**	**1250 BC**	**1200 BC**
	WORLD EVENTS		Hittite empire begins 1460 BC				Canaanite civilization ends 1200 BC

POINTS OF INTEREST

The book reads like a contract with God. Bible experts say the outline of Deuteronomy follows the format of ancient treaties between kings and their subjects.

In these treaties, such as those of the Hittites in the time of Moses, the king outlines what he expects of the people and what he will give them in return. The treaty also warns the people what will happen if they break their part of the bargain.

Here's the basic outline of ancient treaties, compared to the sections of Deuteronomy that seem to fit the pattern.

1. Preamble, which identifies the rule (1:1–15).
2. Prologue, describing history of the relationship between ruler and servant (1:6–3:29).
3. Rules of the treaty (chapters 4–26).
4. Oath of allegiance, with benefits of keeping the treaty and consequences for breaking it (chapters 27–30).
5. Instructions for observing the treaty, such as periodically reading it in public (chapters 31–34).

The core of Israel's treaty with the King of kings is summed up in the Ten Commandments. Deuteronomy 28:1–14 explains the benefits of obeying God's law: fertile crops, big families, prosperity, pro-

DID YOU KNOW?

• The concept of refuge for the fugitive starts in Deuteronomy, among a nation of former fugitives from Egypt. Moses orders that once the Israelites settle in Canaan, they are to establish six "cities of refuge" scattered around the country. These are cities where people can go after accidentally killing someone. Here they get a fair trial and protection from the victim's avenging relatives and friends. Other law codes from this era order the fugitive returned.

• The idea of a father/child relationship between God and Israel begins here: "And in the desert you saw how the LORD your God carried you, like one carries a child. And he has brought you safely all the way to this place" (1:31 NCV).

• Jesus quotes this book more than any of the other five books of Moses. There are nearly 100 quotes or references to Deuteronomy in the New Testament.

• The old saying, "The heavens are brass," which is a complaint that God doesn't seem to be listening, comes from Deuteronomy's list of warnings about what will happen if Israel breaks its contract with God. "The sky above will be like bronze, and the ground below will be like iron" (28:23 NCV).

tection against enemies, national fame. Deuteronomy 28:15–68 explains the warnings about disobedience: famine, plagues, and invasions ending with the people being uprooted and "scattered to every nation on earth." Some will even be loaded on boats and shipped back to Egypt.

AUTHOR AND DATE

Deuteronomy repeatedly says Moses wrote it. So do other Old Testament books and Jesus. The closing chapter, about the death of Moses, was probably added by Joshua or a priest.

Moses probably wrote the sermons that make up Deuteronomy shortly before he died, about 1400 BC. He delivered these messages to remind the Israelites that they owed their very existence to God, and to urge them to remain faithful to him.

ON LOCATION

The Israelites move out of the wilderness and are camped in what is now Jordan, near where the Jordan River empties into the Dead Sea. Soon they will march west and cross the river into Canaan, the land God has promised them. From Mount Nebo, Moses gets a view of the land.

DEUTERONOMY OUTLINE

Parents teach their children about God (6:1–9).

In one of several farewell speeches before he dies, Moses reminds the Israelites of their rich heritage and of the laws that set them apart from other nations. "These are the commands, rules, and laws that the Lord your God told me to teach you," Moses says, "to obey in the land you are crossing the Jordan River to take."

At the center of the law is this: Israel is to worship God alone.

"Always remember these commands I give you today," Moses says, "Teach them to your children, and talk about them when you sit at home and walk along the road, when you lie down and when you get up."

Renewing the contract with God (29:1–29).

Some forty years after God made a covenant with the Israelites at Mount Sinai, Moses reminds the people about it. "The Lord has made an agreement with you," he says, "and if you keep your part, you will be successful in everything you do."

"We are at this place of worship to promise that we will keep our part of the agreement with the Lord our God," Moses adds. Israel's part is to obey the laws of God.

This contract isn't just for the assembled generation, any more than the contract at Mount Sinai was for the previous generation. "It is also for your descendants," Moses reminds them.

Moses dies (34:1–12).

Moses is 120 years old. His sister and brother, Miriam and Aaron, have already died. So has most of the generation that he led out of slavery in Egypt. Now is the time for Moses to die.

He climbs Mount Nebo, which rises above the rich Jordan River valley and Jericho, the oasis "City of Palms." At the summit, Moses sees the land of promise. And then he dies.

He is buried nearby in an unmarked grave. For a month the people grieve their loss of the one prophet in the Bible who spoke "face to face" with God.

POINTS TO CONSIDER

Hills of iron and copper. Moses told the Israelites that the hills of the Promised Land are filled with iron and copper (8:9). The mountains east of the Sea of Galilee contain iron. And the rugged territory south of the Dead Sea has had rich deposits of both iron and copper. Some of the copper mines in the area date to before the time Israel had kings (starting about 1,000 BC), and were reopened when the Romans arrived. Copper mining has only recently been abandoned there.

Written long after Moses? Many scholars say Deuteronomy was not written by Moses, or even in the time of Moses. They suggest it was compiled centuries later, in the 600s BC, during the religious reform movements sparked by kings Hezekiah and Josiah.

Several clues lead them to believe this. Deuteronomy warns against worshiping sun, moon, and stars, a practice Assyria seems to have introduced to Israel in the 700s BC. The book says God hates it when people "set up holy stone pillars" (16:22 NCV), though this seemed acceptable as late as the time of Joshua (Joshua 24:26). Also, the phrasing and style of the speeches are not found in any Bible book written before the 600s BC.

Scholars who argue that Moses did, in fact, write Deuteronomy counter with several points. Questions about the authorship have surfaced only in the last 200 years. But the earliest Jewish and Christian traditions accept the book's explicit claim that Moses wrote it. In addition, the historical setting seems accurate: the neighboring nations are correctly named, and the structure of the book seems based on treaties common in the time of Moses.

FOR FURTHER STUDY

- To see an elderly Joshua follow Moses' example of a farewell address and a covenant renewal ceremony, read Joshua 24.

- To follow Israel on its conquest of the Promised Land, read the book of Joshua.

- To discover how Israel repeatedly breaks its contract with God, read the book of Judges.

Joshua

ISRAEL'S FIGHT FOR A HOMELAND

This is the story of God delivering on a 700-year-old promise to an old man with no kids.

"Go to the land that I will show you," God told 75-year-old Abraham. "I will make you a great nation and I will bless you" (Genesis 12:1–2 NCV). When Abraham obeyed and arrived near the center of Canaan—now Israel—God said, "Look all around you—to the north and south and east and west. All this land that you see I will give to you and your descendants forever" (Genesis 13:14–15 NCV).

Abraham's grandson, Jacob, led the family to Egypt to escape a famine. There they grew to such numbers that the Egyptians feared the Hebrews could over-run the country, so they enslaved them.

But under God's order, Moses freed them.

And now, under God's order, Joshua was taking them home.

Many scenes in this story are as dramatic as those of the great Exodus. The water of the Jordan River stops flowing so the Israelites can enter the Promised Land. The walls of Jericho sponta-neously collapse before Joshua's army. The sun and moon stand still, so Joshua's soldiers can finish an important battle.

The narrative makes it clear that the conquest of Canaan had little to do with Joshua's military savvy or the Israelites' bravery. It had every-thing to do with a promise God made to an old man with no kids. God delivers on his promises.

FAMOUS LINES

• "When the priests blew the trumpets . . . the people's shout, the walls fell, and everyone ran straight into the city" (6:20 NCV).

• "Choose for yourselves this day whom you will serve . . . As for me and my house, we will serve the Lord" (24:15 NKJV). *Part of the elderly Joshua's farewell to Israel.*

BACKGROUND

INFLUENTIAL PEOPLE

Joshua, leader and military commander of the Israelites (1:1).
Rahab, a Jericho prostitute who hid two Israelite spies (2:1).
Achan, Israelite whose greed cost his nation a battle (7:1).

THEME

After escaping from about 400 years in Egypt—much of that in slavery—and wandering forty years through the Sinai Desert east of Egypt, the Israelites finally arrive on the border of the land God promised them. Their mission is to take the land by force and purge it of the idol-worshiping people who live there.

POINTS OF INTEREST

The land is God's gift, not spoils of war. Just before the invasion, when Joshua must have been plotting his war strategy, God assures his chosen leader that the victories are certain if the Israelites continue to trust him. "I promised Moses I would give you this land," God says, "so I will give you every place you go in the land" (Joshua 1:3 NCV). And before the first trumpet is sounded at the battle of Jericho, God tells Joshua, "Look, I have given you Jericho, its king, and all its fighting men" (Joshua 6:2 NCV). The battle is won before it starts.

God rewards obedience, punishes disobedience. In times of obedience, Israelites watch God level the walls of Jericho, send hailstones to kill enemy soldiers, and stop the sun from setting perhaps to give Israel all the time it needs to defeat the enemy.

But when one man takes some possessions from the dead enemies, against God's order, the Israelites lose their next battle. And when they make a peace treaty without consulting God, they get tricked (see Joshua 9).

TIMELINE	BIBLE EVENTS	Israelites invade the Promised Land 1400 BC		Joshua dies 1375 BC		Dates are approximate
		1400 BC	**1350 BC**		**1300 BC**	**1250 BC**
	WORLD EVENTS		Nefertiti is queen of Egypt 1380 BC	Tutankhamen (King Tut) age 9, rules Egypt 1361 BC		Seafaring Philistines settle in Canaan, along the coast 1300 BC

AUTHOR AND DATE

The book doesn't identify its author. But because of Joshua's starring role in the book named after him, he has traditionally been considered the main writer. The report of his death may have been added by priests Eleazar (Aaron's son) or Phinehas (Aaron's grandson).

Joshua likely wrote the book during the final years of his life, about 1375 BC, and reported on the twenty-five years it took Israel to conquer and begin to settle much of the land God promised them.

He wrote primarily to remind the Israelites, the book's first audience, that they didn't win their homeland through military genius and courage. The land was a gift from God.

ON LOCATION

Most of the story is set in what is now Israel. But the Israelites also conquered and claimed surrounding territory in what is now parts of Jordan, Syria, and Lebanon. After Jericho they moved west, then south (map at left). Only then did they attack the northern area, pressing past the Sea of Galilee (Chinnereth).

JOSHUA OUTLINE

Israelite spies investigate Jericho (2:1–24).

Before leading the Israelites into Canaan, Joshua sends two spies to scout the border town of Jericho just west of the Jordan River. There they learn from Rahab, a prostitute who helps them, that the people have discovered the Israelites are coming and are terrified about it. Jericho citizens have heard the stories about Israel's miraculous escape from Egypt and about how the nation of former slaves defeated the armies that tried to stop their march to the Promised Land.

The spies return with a good report. "The Lord surely has given us all of the land," they say. "All the people in that land are terribly afraid of us."

Israel crosses the Jordan River (3:1–17).

When the Israelites finally enter the Promised Land, after waiting forty years, they do so in miraculous style. Leading the invasion are priests carrying the ark of the covenant, a sacred chest containing the Ten Commandments. When the priests step into the Jordan River, the eastern boundary of Canaan, the river stops flowing. The water begins "piling up at the town of Adam" some twenty miles north.

The Israelites enter the Promised Land much as they had left the land of enslavement: on a path that God makes by sweeping aside a river, as he earlier swept back the waters of the Red Sea.

Jericho walls come tumbling down (6:1–27).

About five miles across the river the Israelites meet their first enemies, who are protected behind the walls of Jericho. For six days the soldiers march around the city, led by seven priests who continually blow ram-horn trumpets. On the seventh day, they march around the city seven times. Then the priests blow the trumpets, the soldiers give a unison shout, and the walls of Jericho collapse. The first of many enemies is defeated.

The Israelites lose the next battle, however. This is because one of their soldiers, Achan, disobeys God's order against taking spoils of war. Achan steals about five pounds of silver, a pound of gold, and a beautiful robe imported from what is now Iraq. For this he is executed. Afterward, the Israelites resume a successful campaign, sweeping south then turning north.

The sun and moon stop in the sky (10:1–28).

When Joshua learns that a coalition army from five cities, including Jerusalem and Hebron, is camped in the hills of Gibeon fifteen miles to the west, he leads an all-night march uphill. As the battle is waged, Joshua asks God to extend the day, perhaps to give Israel time to finish off the enemy. As a result, "The sun stopped in the middle of the sky and waited to go down for a full day."

Eventually, the enemy turns and runs. But when they reach a mountain pass about five miles away, they die in a storm of huge hailstones. "More people were killed by the hailstones than by the Israelites' swords."

Joshua divides the land among twelve tribes (chapters 13–22).

After Joshua's army conquers thirty-one cities in the highlands of Canaan, he divides the land among the twelve tribes of Israel and tells each tribe to finish securing their own territory. Yet to be captured are powerful cities in the coastal plains, such as those being settled by Philistines, who are also newcomers to Canaan.

Joshua's farewell and death (chapters 23–24).

Elderly Joshua calls together the leaders of Israel to bid them farewell. Like Moses before him, Joshua reminds the people of their agreement to worship God instead of the idols that had been so popular throughout Canaan.

At age 110, Joshua dies and is buried in the rugged hills north of Jerusalem.

POINTS TO CONSIDER

Ruins of a city burned by Joshua. The Bible says Joshua's army captured the city of Hazor, north of the Sea of Gailiee, "Then they burned Hazor itself" (11:11 NCV). Archaeological excavations confirm that the city was destroyed by fire during the era when the Israelites were capturing and settling the land.

The Jordan River stopped flowing. When the Israelites crossed the Jordan into Canaan, God arranged for the water to be dammed up several miles to the north, at the city of Adam. Landslides have blocked the Jordan's flow several times in recorded history. An Arab historian writing in 1267 said that "a lofty mound" overlooking the river collapsed and fell into it, blocking the flow for sixteen hours. Earthquakes produced the same effect in 1906 and 1927. The 1927 occurrence, remarkably, took place at Adam. Soil from the 150-foot cliffs tumbled into the river and blocked it for twenty-one hours.

No walls at Jericho? Archaeologists who have explored the ruins of Jericho confirm that the city did have mud brick walls that were violently destroyed. But the scholars don't agree on when the walls collapsed.

Kathleen Kenyon, a noted archaeologist who investigated the ruins in the 1950s, concluded that the city was completely destroyed in about 1550 BC, long before Joshua arrived. But an earlier investigation, in the 1930s, led archaeologist John Garstang to say that the city died a fiery death during the time of Joshua in about 1400 BC. More recently, scholars reviewing Kenyon's work say she misdated the city and that it did, indeed, fall in about 1400 BC. The issue remains hotly contested among biblical scholars.

The sun and moon stood still? Critics argue that if the sun and moon froze in the sky, as the Bible says happened during the Israelite battle at Gibeon, humans would have been thrown off the planet as the rotation lurched to a sudden stop.

Biblical scholars don't know what happened. Perhaps the reference is figurative, and means that the day seemed longer because Israel accomplished so much, or that the sun remained cool and the sky overcast so the Israelites, weary from an all-night march, would not wither in the heat of the day. Some Bible students argue that if God could create the heavenly bodies of the universe, he could certainly put them in a pause mode for a while.

Canaanite holocaust. Before Moses died, he left his people with this seemingly barbaric order: "But leave nothing alive in the cities of the land the Lord your God is giving you" (Deuteronomy 20:16 NCV). Beginning with Jericho, the Israelites "destroyed with the sword every living thing in the city—men and women, young and old, cattle, sheep, and donkeys" (Joshua 6:21 NCV).

What threat could a Canaanite baby pose to the invading Hebrews? And why kill perfectly useful animals, and leave their carcasses to rot?

The only explanation we get comes from Moses: "they will teach you what they do for their gods, and if you do these hateful things, you will sin against the Lord your God." (Deuteronomy 20:18 NCV). Canaanite children adopted by Hebrews would grow up seeking their lost culture and religion. Animals bred for sacrifice to idols would serve as a constant reminder that other gods were available; as the Lord gave help in war, perhaps the rain god Baal would grant help in harvest.

What Moses warned is exactly what happened. Judges, the sequel to Joshua, reports that the Hebrews failed in their mission to rid the land of the Canaanites. Instead, they learned to live alongside them "The Israelites began to marry the daughters of those people, and they allowed their daughters to marry the sons of those people. Israel also served their gods" (Judges 3:6 NCV).

For Further Study

- The book of Judges continues where Joshua leaves off, with the Israelites getting settled in the land.

- If you enjoy the book of Joshua, read Deuteronomy. It, too, calls God's people to devote themselves to the Lord and to trust him for their needs. Among the last words of Moses are these: "The everlasting God is your place of safety, and his arms will hold you up forever" (Deuteronomy 33:27 NCV). Joshua's final speech, a generation later, offers evidence of that promise: "You have seen what the LORD has done to our enemies to help us. The LORD your God fought for you . . . So you must be careful to love the LORD your God" (Joshua 23:3 11–12 NCV).

Judges

HEROES WHO SAVE ISRAEL

Movie producers looking for blockbuster story lines packed with sexual escapades, gruesome violence, and larger-than-life heroes need look no further. The book of Judges has it all.

Among the riveting tales is one about the wife of a religious leader who is gang-raped to death by Israelite men from the tribe of Benjamin. What follows is a bloody civil war that nearly annihilates the tribe of Benjamin.

Then there's Samson, Israel's strongman with a weakness for immoral women. He winds up with an unwanted haircut, strength sapped, eyes gouged out, and dead in a suicide.

These are gut-wrenching, distressing stories of what happened to Israel after Joshua died. What happened, in a word, is sin—followed by rerun after rerun of more sin. Readers often react to these stories in anger. They want to grab Israel by the collective throat and yell into their face, "Don't you remember all God has done for you? Don't you remember your contract to obey him, and what the penalty is if you don't?"

The fact is that they didn't remember.

But God did. He punished them for their sins. Yet no matter what they did, he refused to stop loving them. And whenever they got themselves into deep trouble and called on him for help, he was there.

BACKGROUND

INFLUENTIAL PEOPLE

Samson, strongman and last of Israel's twelve judges (13:24).

Delilah, Samson's fatal attraction (16:4).

Gideon, a farmer turned commander of 300 militia men (6:11).

Deborah, the only female judge (4:4).

THEME

The Israelites have captured and secured most of the highlands in Canaan, now Israel. Joshua has died, leaving them with the charge to continue serving God and to finish the job they started: conquer the land and get rid of all the idol-worshiping Canaanites.

The Israelites do none of the above. They settle into the highlands, learn to live as neighbors with the Canaanites, and begin adopting their religion and way of life. Before long, the lines of distinction between Canaanite and Israelite start to blur.

God punishes the Israelites by sending invaders. Israel endures the suffering for a while, then asks God for deliverance. God sends a leader—called a judge—who saves the people. This plot is rerun over and over twelve times.

DID YOU KNOW?

- The phrase "missed it by a hair" could have come from Judges. The tribe of Benjamin had 700 left-handed warriors "whom could sling a stone at a hair and not miss" (20:16 NCV)

- Most of the twelve judges of Israel weren't legal experts who settled disputes, like judges today. The Hebrew word that best describes these judges means "savior" or "deliverer." Most Israelite judges were military leaders. God chose them to lead regional campaigns against enemies. Samson was the exception; he was a one-man army who led no one. Yet, like the other judges, he is remembered as a military hero. The twelve judges, in the order they appear, are Othniel, Ehud, Shamgar, Deborah, Gideon, Tola, Jair, Jephthah, Ibzan, Elon, Abdon, and Samson.

TIMELINE	BIBLE EVENTS	Joshua dies ┌-- 1375 BC	Gideon's army of 300 1150 BC ----------		Samson fights Philistines 1075 BC ------	Book of Judges written 1000 BC
		1400 BC	**1300 BC**	**1200 BC**	**1100 BC**	**1000 BC**
	WORLD EVENTS	Canaanite civilization ends, assimilated into other cultures 1200 BC ┘	Trojan War ends with fall of Troy 1190 BC --------	China develops postal relay system 1100 BC --------	Mound builders active in North America 1000 BC	Dates are approximate

POINTS OF INTEREST

Repetition. Judges has one basic pattern or plot repeated throughout the book. The Israelites prosper; then they stop worshiping God, face the consequences of punishment, cry out for God's help, and get that help in the form of a leader chosen by God. Notice that by the end of the book, Israel sinks to a new, all-time low.

God's mercy and unrelenting love. Israel breaks its contract, or covenant, with God. For this, they suffer some of the consequences Moses warned about. One in particular: "I will be against you, and your enemies will defeat you" (Leviticus 26:16–17 NCV).

For repeated breach of contract, God has every right to do more: "You will die among other nations and disappear in your enemies' countries" (Leviticus 26:38 NCV). But God stops short of allowing this. For as he had explained through Moses, "But even though this is true, I will not turn away from them when they are in the land of their enemies" (Leviticus 26:44 NCV).

AUTHOR AND DATE

The writer is not named. Samuel the prophet has traditionally been considered the writer. He was Israel's religious leader a few decades after the judges, when many believe that the stories were compiled into a book.

The book covers roughly 300 years, just after Joshua dies in about 1375 BC until just before Saul is crowned the first king of Israel in about 1050 BC. The stories spanning these centuries were probably compiled and preserved in writing sometime after Israel had a king. One strong clue is that the writer repeatedly says the stories take place "before kings ruled Israel" (17:6). The book may have been compiled during the reign of Saul or David, the first two kings. Samuel, the possible author, anointed both men king.

The book was written to preserve an important—though horribly unflattering—slice of Israel's history. The stories vividly show the consequences of disobedience, as well as the never-ending love of God.

ON LOCATION

The stories take place in what is now Israel. The map shows locations where the twelve tribes of Israel settled.

JUDGES OUTLINE

Israel starts worshiping idol (2:6–23).

The people of Joshua's generation do a poor job of passing along the faith to their kids: "their children grew up and did not know the LORD or what he had done for Israel." So the people stop worshiping the Lord and begin worshiping the gods of Canaan. "The LORD was angry with the people of Israel, so he handed them over to robbers who took their possessions."

From time to time, however, the oppression becomes so unbearable for the Israelites that they call on the God of their parents. He answers by sending leaders who rescue Israel from their enemies. "The LORD was with those judges all their lives. But when the judges died, the Israelites again sinned and worshiped other gods. They became worse than their ancestors."

Deborah starts the battle of Mount Tabor (4:1–24).

For twenty-five years the people in northern Israel suffer from a nearby, hostile king further north. When Israel finally calls on God for help, he responds through the prophet Deborah. She tells the people to assemble an army. The odds seem to favor the enemy, for they have a corps of 900 chariots, manned by seasoned professionals. Israel has untrained militia, hastily called to defend themselves.

The Israelites gather at Mount Tabor, a steep hill on which no charioteer would care to fight a battle. But the mountain quickly becomes the least of their worries. Rain suddenly pours from the sky, transforming the valley into a huge mud field that clamps onto the iron wheels of the chariots. The enemies dart from their chariots and run for their lives, but none escape.

Gideon's army of 300 routs thousands (7:1–25).

The Israelites return to their sinful ways. So at harvest time each year, God allows desert raiders on camelback to invade Israel. When the people ask God for help, he calls on Gideon, who replies, "How can I rescue Israel? My clan is the weakest one in Manasseh, and everyone else in my family is more important than I am."

The reluctant Gideon raises an army of about 32,000, but God tells him to reduce the size to a mere 300. In the dark of night Gideon's men secretly surround the enemy camp filled with tens of thousands of invaders. Each Israelite carries a burning torch hidden inside a clay jar. On Gideon's signal they smash the jars, raise the torches, and blow trumpets. The horrified marauders turn for home and run.

Samson meets his match: Delilah (16:4–31).

Samson is like none of the other judges. He doesn't settle disputes among his people, and he leads no one into battle. He's a one-man army who hates the Philistines, for they have killed his new bride and burned her body. So he burns their crops, then slaughters a thousand of their soldiers by using nothing but the jawbone of a donkey.

Samson has incredible strength given by God. He also has a vow to keep—he is never to allow his hair to be cut.

When Samson falls in love with Delilah, the Philistines offer her nearly thirty pounds of silver to find his weakness. After two failed attempts, she succeeds. While he is sleeping, she clips the hair she had earlier woven into seven braids. Then she calls in the waiting Philistines.

Soldiers rush in, capture Samson, gouge out his eyes, then put him to work at a grinding mill. By the time they decide to parade him as a war trophy in front of crowds gathered for a religious festival, his hair has grown. Standing between two pillars, probably made of wooden or stone blocks, Samson prays for strength once more so he can kill more Philistines and die with them. In a powerful surge he breaks the pillars. The roof collapses, killing at least 3,000 Philistines. Samson dies too, the last of Israel's twelve judges.

Israelites worship God and idols (17:1–13).

The book of Judges draws to a close with stories showing that life in Israel can't get much worse. An Israelite man hires a silversmith to craft him an idol. Then he hires a priest to live with him, thinking, "Now I know the Lord will be good to me, because I have a Levite as my priest." Apparently he didn't know the first of the Ten Commandments: "You must not have any other gods except me" (Exodus 20:3 NCV).

In a more disturbing—even sickening—story, an Israelite religious

leader traveling with his wife to the nation's worship center in Shiloh is
attacked by a mob. The mob surrounds a house in which the couple is
spending the night in the territory owned by the tribe of Benjamin.
They demand that the man come out so they can have sex with him.
Instead, the man pushes his wife outside. She is gang-raped all night,
and is dead by morning. The husband cuts her into pieces and sends the
body parts to the twelve tribes of Israel, with a plea for revenge. The
result is a civil war in which eleven of the tribes nearly exterminate the
tribe of Benjamin.

The book ends with this unsettling portrait of anarchy: "In those days
Israel did not have a king. All the people did whatever seemed right in
their own eyes" (NCV).

POINTS TO CONSIDER

Accurate picture of Israel. The stories in Judges match what
has been uncovered about Israelite history during this era.
Israel was not yet a united nation, led by a central leader. It was
a collection of independent tribes, or extended family groups,
that occasionally worked together to fight off invaders. The earliest known nonbiblical reference to the Israelites is inscribed
on a stone from the 1200s BC. The inscription tells of an
Egyptian raid into Canaan.

Why would God choose the likes of Samson? For a hero chosen by God, Samson was surprisingly unrighteous and earthly.
    Endowed with incredible strength, he had a pitiful weakness
for immoral women. In fact, all of his run-ins with the Philistines
started over women: first his bride, then a prostitute, then Delilah.
    Samson had also taken vows, since childhood, to avoid any-
thing ritually unclean, to refrain from drinking wine, and to protect his hair from being cut. He apparently broke all these vows.
He ate honey from a lion's carcass, knowing that touching this
dead animal would render him ritually unclean. Wine flowed
freely at his wedding feast. And he allowed himself to be tricked
into a haircut.
    The book of Judges portrays Samson as a selfish man, driv-
en by his appetites. Even the few prayers he prayed were selfish. His final prayer was for revenge: "Lord God, remember me.
God, please give me strength one more time so I can pay these
Philistines back for putting out my two eyes!" (16:28 NCV).
    Yet as flawed as Samson was, God used him to drive a wedge
between the Philistines and the Israelites. This was important
because at that time the two nations were getting along pretty

well, allowing intermarriage and business dealings. Philistia, however, was the stronger power, and Israel was in danger of becoming assimilated into their culture. Samson made peaceful coexistence much more difficult, helping preserve Israel as a distinct people. About fifty years later, King David finished what Samson started, ending the Philistine dominance in the region.

FOR FURTHER STUDY

- To continue the flow of Israel's story, read 1 Samuel. It picks up where Judges leaves off.

- Hebrews 11 names several of the judges, calling them models of faith.

Ruth

MOTHER OF ISRAEL'S BEST KINGS

The touching story of King David's great-grandmother is one of the most masterfully crafted in all of Hebrew literature. The suspense begins in the first sentence, with a famine driving a family from their home. By the end of the next paragraph, all three men in the family are dead and their widows are destitute.

The suspense doesn't stop until the story reaches its jaw-dropping, surprise conclusion: Ruth—a foreigner—gave birth to Israel's most famous family of kings. Not only is she related to King David, born in Bethlehem; she is an ancestor of the King of kings also born there (Matthew 1:5).

But until the reader reaches this surprise conclusion, Ruth looks cursed by God. In those days, a woman's greatest accomplishment was to have children. Ruth had none. And nearly all of a woman's legal rights depended on her husband—including the right to own property. Ruth had no husband.

> ### FAMOUS LINES
>
> • "Don't beg me to leave you or to stop following you. Where you go, I will go. Where you live, I will live. Your people will be my people, and your God will be my God." (1:16 NCV). *What Ruth told Naomi after both became widowed.*

Also, in the tiny village of Bethlehem, people found acceptance and support in being part of the close-knit Israelite family, the chosen people of God. Ruth was no Israelite.

Ruth was an outsider, but she chose God. And he brought her inside, to the very heart of Israel's faith, transforming her into a model of love and the mother of Israel's most-respected kings.

BACKGROUND

INFLUENTIAL PEOPLE

Ruth, young widow from Moab and great-grandmother of David (1:4).

Naomi, Ruth's mother-in-law, an elderly widow from Bethlehem (1:2).

Boaz, second husband of Ruth (2:1).

THEME

To escape a famine in Israel, a Bethlehem man moves with his wife and two sons to a neighboring country. There, his sons marry local women. Then all three men die, leaving their widows destitute. The matron, Naomi, decides to return to her extended family in Bethlehem. She urges her daughters-in-law to go back to their families as well. One does, but Ruth refuses to abandon the elderly Naomi.

The two widows arrive in Bethlehem in time for the spring harvest of barley and wheat. A kind farmer lets Ruth pick some grain for her and Naomi. Ruth later discovers this man is related to Naomi. Ruth proposes marriage to him, he accepts, and they have a son: Obed, the grandfather of King David.

POINTS OF INTEREST

Salvation. This is the theme of the book. Ruth's life takes one about-

---

DID YOU KNOW?

- Television and film personality Oprah Winfrey was named after Orpah, the daughter-in-law who chose not to stay with Naomi and Ruth. The letters *r* and *p* were switched in Oprah's name.

- The mother of Boaz was Rahab, probably the prostitute who helped the Israelite spies in Jericho. That would make Rahab the great, great-grandmother of King David, as well as an ancestor of Jesus (Matthew 1:5).

- Jews today honor Ruth by reading her story during an annual religious festival at the end of the grain harvest.

		Judges lead Israel in Ruth's era 1375 BC		Saul becomes first king of Israel 1050 BC- - - - - - - - - - - -		David crowned king of Israel 1000 BC
TIMELINE	**BIBLE EVENTS**					Dates are approximate
		1400 BC	**1300 BC**	**1200 BC**	**1100 BC**	**1000 BC**	**0900 BC**
	WORLD EVENTS	Nefertiti is queen of Egypt 1380 BC		Iron tools, weapons used in Israel 1200 BC		China develpes refrigeration,using winter ice 1000 BC

face after another, from hardship to blessing. She is saved from poverty to wealth, widow to wife, childless to mother, and foreigner to Israelite. Her savior is Boaz, a "kinsman-redeemer." According to ancient custom, the closest relative of a widow could agree to redeem her from a life of poverty by marrying her, taking care of her, and giving her children to inherit the dead father's land. Boaz doesn't marry Naomi because she is too old to have children. So he agrees to marry Ruth and take care of both women.

Many Bible scholars see in Boaz an example of God redeeming Israel from slavery and of Jesus later redeeming the world from sin.

Spoken blessings. In every chapter you'll find one person speaking a word of blessing to another. Naomi blesses her widowed daughters-in-law with a prayer that God will treat them kindly and give them new husbands and homes. And when Boaz greets the workers harvesting his grain he says, "The Lord be with you" (2:4 NCV). To which the workers reply, "May the Lord bless you."

The frequency of these blessings suggests that people who believe in God have a right to speak blessings in God's name—and that God hears and responds to those prayers.

AUTHOR AND DATE

The writer is unknown. Jewish tradition says Samuel wrote it. But this seems unlikely since the climax of the book identifies Ruth as the great-grandmother of David, who is crowned king only after the death of Samuel. (Before the people accepted David as king, however, Samuel anointed him as God's choice to succeed King Saul.)

The story takes place in the time of the judges, "Long ago when the judges ruled Israel" (1:1 NCV). The story was then likely passed on by word of mouth for several generations, before being written down sometime during or after the time of David, who began his reign about 1,000 BC.

It's unclear why someone decided to preserve this story. One theory is that it was written to trace the family tree of David, Israel's most popular king. But perhaps there were other reasons as well: to encourage the Israelites to embrace God-loving foreigners (as God embraces Ruth), and to allow future generations to learn from Ruth's example of love for Naomi.

ON LOCATION

The story begins in Bethlehem, then briefly shifts to Moab, Israel's neighbor east of the Dead Sea in what is now Jordan. Within a few paragraphs, the scene switches back to Bethlehem where the rest of the story unfolds. More than a thousand years later, Luke calls this Bethlehem "known as the town of David" (Luke 2:4 NCV) because of family ties going back to Boaz and Ruth.

RUTH OUTLINE

Ruth stays with Naomi (1:1–22).

A famine in Bethlehem drives an Israelite man out of his country. He takes his wife and sons east of the Jordan River into Moab, part of what is now Jordan. There his sons marry Moabite women. But within ten years, all three men die.

Naomi, matron of the family, decides to return to her homeland, perhaps hoping that some family members will take her in. But she urges her two daughters-in-law not to follow. If they return to their own families they might be able to remarry. But for elderly Naomi, it's too late. In a time and culture where women depend on a husband or a son to take care of them, Naomi has neither.

One daughter-in-law leaves, but Ruth adamantly refuses to abandon Naomi. "Don't beg me to leave you or to stop following you," Ruth implores. "Where you go, I will go. Where you live, I will live. Your people will be my people, and your God will be my God. And where you die, I will die, and there I will be buried."

Ruth gleans leftovers in a harvested grain field (2:1–23).

Naomi and Ruth arrive at Bethlehem in the spring, as the barley is being harvested. This is fortunate for them, because the Israelite system of welfare requires farmers to leave some of their crop for their poor, "for foreigners, orphans, and widows" (Deuteronomy 24:19 NCV).

Ruth goes to the field of a man named Boaz and gets permission from the harvesting foreman to glean behind the harvesters. When Boaz finds out that Ruth is the woman who helped Naomi, he instructs his workers to leave extra grain for her. He also invites Ruth to share meals with the group.

Ruth asks Boaz to marry her (3:1–18).

When Naomi finds out that Boaz—a relative of hers—treated Ruth so kindly, she counsels Ruth on the custom of "kinsman-redeemer." Perhaps Boaz will marry Ruth and redeem her and Naomi from poverty.

"Wash yourself, put on perfume, change your clothes, and go down to the threshing floor," Naomi instructs. "Watch him so you will know

Sun
Mon
Tues
Wed
Thu
Frid
Satu
Sun
Mon
Tues
Wed
Thu
Frid
Satu
Sun
Mon
Tues
Wed

where he lies down to sleep. When he lies down, go and lift the cover off his feet and lie down. He will tell you what you should do."

Ruth does as she is told, crawling under the covers after Boaz goes to sleep. Later in the night Boaz awakens to find someone curled up at his feet.

"Who are you?" he asks.

"I am Ruth, your servant girl," she answers, "Spread your cover over me, because you are a relative who is supposed to take care of me."

Boaz is impressed with Ruth's loyalty to her family and to the Jewish traditions. She could marry someone outside the family and abandon Naomi as a troublesome burden. But she doesn't. Boaz agrees to marry her.

Ruth and Boaz have a son (4:13–22).

Boaz marries Ruth and takes Naomi into his care as well. The couple has a son, to the delight of parents and grandmother.

The child is named Obed. He will grow to become the father of Jesse, grandfather of Kind David, great-grandfather of King Solomon, and an ancestor of Jesus.

POINTS TO CONSIDER

Protecting the crops from thieves. The book of Ruth is set in the rough-and-tumble times of the judges, when many Israelites lost sight of God's laws. This setting seems confirmed by the fact that Boaz, a landowner wealthy enough to use hired help, chooses to sleep outdoors beside his grain—apparently to protect it from thieves.

Sneaky Ruth. When Ruth bathes, sprinkles on the perfume, slips into her prettiest robe, then quietly crawls under the covers of Boaz, it looks like she has something other than matrimony on her mind.

But her first words to Boaz when he awakens, and his response, suggest she is following an accepted custom of the day. As a childless widow, she has a right to ask a relative to marry her, take care of her, and help her produce children who can inherit their dead father's property. Women in this culture are not permitted to own property.

Ruth's proposal uses a play on words. She asks Boaz to spread the edge of his "cover" over her. The Hebrew word for "cover" is the same for "wing." When the couple first met, Boaz had said he hoped Ruth would find reward from "the Lord God of Israel, under whose wings you have come for refuge" (2:12, NKJV). Ruth was calling on Boaz to serve as God's wing of protection.

As soon as Ruth is finished speaking, Boaz reveals his respect for her. "The LORD bless you," he says. "This act of kindness is greater than the kindness you showed to Naomi in the beginning. You didn't look for a young man to marry, either rich or poor. Now, my daughter, don't be afraid. I will do everything you ask, because all the people in our town know you are a good woman" (3:10–11 NCV).

FOR FURTHER STUDY

- For stories of other women who win their way into Israel through their own initiative, read about the Canaanite woman Tamar (Genesis 38) and the Jericho prostitute Rahab (Joshua 2; 5:13–6:25).

- Esther is the only other Bible book named after a woman. Like Ruth, she is portrayed as a brave heroine loyal to her family.

- The New Testament story of Mary and Joseph has similarities to the story of Ruth and Boaz. Ruth was an outsider, and that's how Mary would have been treated once her neighbors discovered she had an early baby. Boaz showed compassion for Ruth by agreeing to marry her. Joseph did the same for Mary, though he knew he was not the father of the divine child. Ruth and Boaz raised a family of kings. Mary and Joseph raised the King of kings. You can read the story of Mary and Joseph in Matthew 1–2 and Luke 1–2.

Sun
Mon
Tues
Wed
Thu
Frid
Satu
Sun
Mon
Tues
Wed
Thu
Frid
Satu
Sun
Mon
Tues
Wed

1 Samuel

ISRAEL GETS A KING—AND HIS BAGGAGE

There's a lot more here than the history of how Israel made the switch from a loosely connected group of tribes into a united nation led by a king. There's humanity, flawed to the bone. And there's God, accomplishing his plans in spite of it.

You'll see major personality flaws in all the starring characters, as well as in many of the supporting cast.

Priest Eli didn't seem to have strong parenting skills. His two sons grew up crooked.

Samuel had a similar problem with his boys. Yet he tried to appoint them as the next generation of spiritual leaders. He was deeply hurt when Israel's elders said they'd really rather have a king.

Saul, Israel's first king, seemed clinically depressed much of the time. And when David tried to calm him with the gentle song of a lyre, Saul threw a spear at him. Twice.

> ### FAMOUS LINES
>
> • "Long live the king!" (10:24 NCV). *An Israelite crowd's response to Samuel introducing Saul as the nation's first king.*
>
> • "To obey is better than sacrifice" (15:22, NKJV). *Samuel's criticism of Saul after Saul disobeys God by keeping livestock as spoils of war so he can use them as sacrifices.*

And David, the man who would later become Israel's most respected king of all, had a life-size idol in his house. His wife dressed it in a robe, put goat hair on its head, and slipped it under the bed covers one night to fool Saul's soldiers who were coming to kill David.

These are colorful people, living and learning at a critical moment in Israel's history. What they're learning is the depth of God's love for his people, and the breadth of his resources for proving it.

BACKGROUND

INFLUENTIAL PEOPLE

Samuel, prophet and spiritual leader of Israel (1:20).

Saul, Israel's first king (9:2).

David, Saul's successor (16:1).

THEME

The prophet Samuel becomes the spiritual leader of the nation, serving primarily as a prophet who delivers God's messages to the people and as a judge who settles disputes. When he grows old, the people decide they want a king "just like all the other nations."

But they are not like other nations. That is the point of God's covenant with them. They are God's people, and he is their king. Yet God honors their request. He chooses Saul as their first king. But after Saul repeatedly disobeys, God rejects him as king. God chooses a successor—a shepherd boy named David.

> ### DID YOU KNOW?
>
> • Ichabod Crane, the vain and cowardly man who is terrorized by a man disguised as a headless horseman in "The Legend of Sleepy Hollow," gets his name from a grandson of Eli. When Eli's daughter-in-law gives birth shortly after the Philistines defeat the Israelites, steal the ark of the covenant, and kill her husband, she names that boy Ichabod, which means "the glory is gone."
>
> • The old saying "stay by the stuff" comes from 30:24, "tarrieth by the stuff" (KJV). David was arguing that soldiers who stayed behind to guard the camp deserve a share of the booty taken in battle.

POINTS OF INTEREST

Samuel's birth. Notice that the book tells the story of Samuel's birth, but not the birth of Israel's first king, or even of Israel's most revered king of all time. This is a clue about how important Samuel is to the story. He plays the key role in Israel's shift from a loose coalition of families to a nation ruled by a king. Not since Moses, whose birth story is reported in Exodus, has Israel seen such a charismatic and dynamic leader.

TIMELINE	BIBLE EVENTS	Samuel is born ┌---1105 BC	Saul becomes first king of Israel 1050 BC-----------	David anointed to succeed Saul ┐1025 BC----------	Saul dies 1010 BC----┐	Dates are approximate
		1100 BC		**1050 BC**		**1000 BC**
	WORLD EVENTS	Philistines protect their secret of making iron └--1100 BC	China develops mouth organ └-- 1100 BC	People in eastern North America grow crops 1000 BC	Lyre players painted on Philistine jar └-1000 BC	

Traits that God admires. You'll encounter plenty of human foibles in this book. But notice, too, the character traits that God admires and rewards—Hannah's heartfelt prayer; Eli's confidence in God even when faced with painful news; David's life-on-the-line assurance that God will help him slay a giant.

AUTHOR AND DATE

The two books of Samuel were originally written as one book, by an unknown writer. Because the books give detailed and personal information about Samuel, Saul, and David, it seems likely that the writer had access to records from national leaders. The Bible says such records did exist: "Everything David did as king, from beginning to end, is recorded in the records of Samuel the seer, the records of Nathan the prophet, and the records of Gad the seer" (1 Chronicles 29:29 NCV).

The book was written sometime after Solomon died and Israel split into two nations, in about 930 BC. The writer speaks of the two nations, Israel in the northland and Judah in the south (17:52).

The reason the book exists is to preserve the history of the Israelite nation when they made the change from an association of twelve independent tribes to a unified nation led by a king.

ON LOCATION

The stories take place in Israel. When Saul becomes king, he establishes his capital in Gibeah (identified on this map with the alternative spelling of Geba), the village where he was born, a few miles north of Jerusalem. At this time Jerusalem was still held by the Jebusites; this mountain stronghold had not yet been conquered (see Judges 1:21).

1 SAMUEL OUTLINE

Young Samuel goes to live with the priest (1:21–28).

When Hannah, an infertile woman, asks God to let her have a son, Hannah promises she will let the boy serve God all of his life. Within the year, Samuel is born. As soon as he is old enough to feed himself, perhaps around age three, Hannah takes him to the nation's worship center at Shiloh.

"I am the same woman who stood near you praying to the LORD. I prayed for this child, and the LORD answered my prayer and gave him to me," Hannah reminds Priest Eli. "Now I give him back to the LORD. He will belong to the LORD all his life."

Hannah later has other children, but she never forgets her firstborn. Whenever she comes to Shiloh to worship God, she always brings her boy a new robe.

Young Samuel hears God's voice in the tabernacle (3:1–21).

While sleeping one night, young Samuel hears his name and assumes Eli is calling him. But when he goes to find out what the aged and nearly blind priest wants, Eli says he did not call Samuel. When this happens again, Eli realizes it must be the Lord. So he tells Samuel, "If he calls you again, say, 'Speak, LORD. I am your servant and I am listening.'"

God does, indeed, call again. He tells Samuel that because Eli's two sons are selfish and evil, He will not allow them to become the spiritual leaders of Israel.

The next morning, when Eli hears the disappointing prophecy, he responds with resignation and faith: "He is the LORD. Let him do what he thinks is best."

Philistines capture the ark of the covenant (4:1–10).

When Israelite soldiers begin losing a battle to the Philistines, they send a patrol twenty miles back to Shiloh to get the ark of the covenant, Israel's most sacred object—a gold-covered chest that holds the Ten Commandments. The warriors think it will work as a magical charm to help them defeat the enemy.

The warriors are dead wrong. The battle is lost, Eli's sons are killed in the fight, and the ark is stolen. When Eli hears what happens, he falls backward off his chair, breaks his neck, and dies.

The Philistines put the trophy in their temple, at the feet of a statue of their god. Seven months later they return the ark to Israel, after discovering that it seems to cause diseases.

Samuel becomes the spiritual leader of the people.

Saul becomes the first king of Israel (9:1–10:26).

When Samuel grows old, he appoints his sons to serve as spiritual leaders and judges. But they are as corrupt as Eli's sons were, for they accept bribes. The tribal elders realize this and tell Samuel, "You're old, and your sons don't live as you do. Give us a king to rule over us like all the other nations."

Samuel feels rejected, but agrees to take the matter to God.

God says to Samuel, "Listen to whatever the people say to you. They have not rejected you. They have rejected me from being their king."

God chooses Saul, whom Samuel presents to a crowd that responds with the cheer "Long live the king!"

David kills Goliath (17:1–52).

Every morning and evening during a 40-day standoff between the armies of Israel and Philistia, a Philistine champion named Goliath taunts his enemies: "Choose a man and send him to fight me. If he can fight and kill me, we will be your servants."

No Israelites take him up on the offer, for he stands more than nine feet tall and wears 150 pounds of body armor. The sword he carries can easily slice off a man's head.

When shepherd boy David arrives, bringing food for his brothers in the militia, he hears the challenge and accepts. Using the weapon with which he has driven predators away from his flock—a sling loaded with a stone—David hits Goliath in the forehead. The giant falls facedown in the dirt, and David uses Goliath's own sword to cut off his head.

The Philistines run, chased by the Israelites.

Saul tries to pin David to the wall (18:1–11).

David's popularity soars. People even write songs about him. One song that enrages Saul includes these lyrics: "Saul has killed thousands of his enemies; but David has killed tens of thousands."

Jealous, brooding, and deeply depressed, Saul "prophesied in his house." While David is trying to calm him with the gentle music of a lyre—a technique that has worked in the past—Saul raises the spear he is holding and hurls it toward David. Twice he throws it, and twice David dodges it.

David and his men hide from Saul (24:1–22).

Fearing that David will steal his kingdom, Saul issues the order that David be killed on sight. David becomes a fugitive, with a growing band of followers.

Once, Saul pursues David and his men into an oasis area honeycombed with caves. Saul, unfortunately, chooses to relieve himself in the very cave where David is hiding. A single thrust of a knife may have ended David's problems. Instead, David sneaks up behind Saul and silently cuts of a corner of the royal robe.

After Saul leaves, David burst out of the cave, raising the cloth like a flag. "I won't harm my master, because he is the LORD's appointed king," David shouts. "I did nothing wrong to you, but you are hunting me to kill me."

Humiliated, Saul calls off his soldiers and returns home. But he later renews his irrational quest to kill the giant killer.

Saul consults a medium (28:1–25).

When the Philistine army advances deep into Israelite territory, Saul rushes to engage them, but he is filled with terror. He wants to know what God wants him to do, but there is no one to tell him. Samuel has died of old age. Other prophets have no news. And Saul's own prayers to God go unanswered because of Saul's previous disobedience.

In desperation, Saul visits a nearby medium, asking her to conjure up the spirit of Samuel. To the horror of everyone present, including the medium, the spirit of Samuel appears.

"The Philistines are fighting against me," Saul tells Samuel. "Tell me what to do."

"The LORD has left you and has become your enemy. So why do you call on me?" Samuel replies. "Tomorrow you and your sons will be with me. The LORD will hand over the army of Israel to the Philistines."

7:00

Saul kills himself when the battle is lost (31:1–13).

8:00

Saul returns to camp before daybreak. As Samuel predicted, the Philistines press through the Israelite defenses and begin to close in on Saul and his three sons. One by one the princes fall: Jonathan, Abinadab, Malchishua. Then enemy archers critically wound Saul.

9:00

The king asks his weapons bearer to finish him before the Philistines have a chance to capture and torture him. But the soldier can't do it. Saul props the handle of his sword into the ground and falls on the blade.

0:00

The first king of Israel is dead.

1:00

noon

═══ POINTS TO CONSIDER ═══

1:00

Philistine temple of Dagon. When Philistines captured the ark of the covenant, a golden chest containing the Ten Commandments, they brought it to "Dagon's temple and put it next to Dagon" (5:2 NCV). Archaeologists have found the name of this mysterious deity at several places in the region. One document from the 1300s BC says Dagon is the father of Baal, the Canaanite god of rain and fertility.

2:00

Engedi. David and his men hid from Saul in a cave "in the Desert of En Gedi" (24:1 NCV). The oasis of Engedi would have been a perfect place to hide, for it is concealed in a narrow ravine. Rocky ledges and mounds—pocketed with caves—surround the oasis on three sides. The fourth side opens onto the shore of the Dead Sea. In Bible times Engedi was famous for its vineyards, white henna flowers, and palm trees. *Engedi,* in Hebrew, means "spring of the kid," named after a freshwater spring that plummets from a 300-foot cliff into a refreshing pool.

3:00

4:00

5:00

6:00

Why does God pick a loser like Saul? God chose a shy and humble man to become Israel's first king. Saul was out looking for some of his father's donkeys that had run off when he first came upon Samuel. That's when Samuel broke the news that Saul was about to become Israel's first king. Saul was dumbfounded. "But I am from the tribe of Benjamin, the smallest tribe in Israel," Saul said, "And my family group is the smallest in the tribe of Benjamin. Why are you saying such things?" (9:21 NCV).

7:00

8:00

9:00

0:00

Later, when Samuel was about to introduce Saul to the people, no one could find the reluctant monarch. He was hiding among the pack animals.

Saul had both the potential and the opportunity to faithfully serve God. But like others before and after him, he let power make him into a new and lesser creature. As Samuel later explained to him, "You acted foolishly! You haven't obeyed the command of the LORD your God. If you had obeyed him, the LORD would have made your kingdom continue in Israel always" (13:13 NCV).

FOR FURTHER STUDY

• To read the rest of the story, turn to 2 Samuel. The two books were originally one, but were separated when they were translated from Hebrew into Greek, in about 300 BC. This apparently made the size more manageable, allowing each volume to fit onto a single scroll.

• For the story of another infertile woman who has a son and who promises to let him serve the Lord, read about the mother of Samson. It's in Judges 13.

• For a song in the spirit of Hannah's in 2:1–10, read Mary's song in Luke 1:46–56.

Sun
Mo
Tue
We
Thu
Frid
Satu
Sun
Mo
Tue
We
Thu
Frid
Satu
Sun
Mo
Tue
We

2 Samuel

DAVID: SUPER KING, SORRY FAMILY MAN

A prince falls in love with his half sister, seduces her, rapes her, then hates her. Enter prince number two, the sister's full brother. He kills prince number one, then flees the country and remains an outcast of the family for five years.

These are David's kids.

Like father, like son. For when David catches a glimpse of a married woman taking a bath, he invites her to the palace, gets her pregnant, kills her husband, and marries the woman.

This is David, whom God described as "a man after his own heart" (1 Samuel 13:14 NKJV).

The stories are heart-wrenching, the theology perplexing. These alone make 2 Samuel a captivating book for both casual readers and devoted Bible scholars.

Yet there's more to draw us: a lasting message for everyone who has ever made such a miserable mess of their life that they wondered if God could ever forgive them.

Time and again God forgave David—whenever David asked, no matter what David had done.

FAMOUS LINES

• "I have sinned against the LORD" (12:13 NCV). *David's response when Nathan accuses him of committing adultery with Bathsheba and killing her husband.*

• "My son Absalom . . . I wish I had died and not you." (18:33 NCV). *David's reaction to hearing that his son Absalom has been killed while trying to overthrow him.*

This mercy, as irrational as the love of a father for a rebellious child, is available to everyone. As David put it in a song, "Thank the LORD because he is good. His love continues forever" (1 Chronicles 16:34 NCV).

BACKGROUND

INFLUENTIAL PEOPLE

David, king of Israel (1:1).
Absalom, crown prince who leads a rebellion (3:3).
Nathan, prophet and David's chief advisor (5:14).

THEME

David becomes the new king, replacing Saul. During the forty years of David's reign, he expands the borders of Israel as far north as the Euphrates River into what is now Iraq, and eastward into Jordan. The taxes he gets from these conquered neighbors help lower taxes for the Israelites. But David's reign is not just a success story. Though he secures his borders and throne, thrusting Israel to the top of the heap among Middle Eastern nations, his family lies at the bottom of the barrel. A big chunk of the book is a surprisingly frank set of stories about David's domestic problems—not the least of which is his adultery with Bathsheba, the rape of one of his daughters by one of his sons, and another son's attempted revolution.

DID YOU KNOW?

William Faulkner's novel *Absalom, Absalom*—the tale of a Southern aristocrat who returns from the Civil War to find that his son has disappeared and his plantation is nearly ruined—was inspired by the tragic story of King David and his son.

POINTS OF INTEREST

No sugar-coating. The writer tells it like it is. He doesn't try to make flawless heroes out of flawed human beings. In all of Israel's history, the king most revered is David. And for good reason. He is a godly man who never becomes so brain-damaged by power and prestige that he refuses

TIMELINE	BIBLE EVENTS	David secretly anointed king 1025 BC	David becomes king 1010 BC	Absalom's revolt 975 BC	End of David's reign 970 BC Dates are approximate
		1050 BC	**1000 BC**	**950 BC**	**900 BC**
	WORLD EVENTS	Calendar of farming cycles, oldest example of Hebrew writing 1000 BC	Greeks worship Zeus, Aphrodite, and other gods 1000 BC		Wigs worn by Egyptian aristocrats 950 BC

to acknowledge his sins and repent. But sin he does. His most famous is the adultery with Bathsheba, which he tries to cover up by having her husband killed. But David repents. And God forgives.

David's everlasting dynasty. "But your family and your kingdom will continue always before me. Your throne will last forever," God promises David (7:16 NCV).

The kings that rule in Jerusalem are descendants of David—part of a dynasty that reigns for nearly half a millennium, until Israel is defeated in 586 BC and much of the population is taken away in exile. Afterward, God's promise to David becomes a springboard for the Jewish anticipation of a messiah—a new king from the dynasty of kings.

The New Testament presents Jesus as that messiah. When he rides into Jerusalem on the day that becomes known as Palm Sunday, the people acknowledge this by shouting, "God bless the kingdom of our father David. That kingdom is coming!" (Mark 11:10 NCV).

AUTHOR AND DATE

The unnamed writer is the same person who wrote 1 Samuel. Both books were originally a single volume, but were separated into two books when the Hebrew text was translated for Greek-speaking Jews in about 300 BC. The two books could fit onto a single scroll written in Hebrew because the ancient Hebrew language used no vowels. But Greek used vowels and required about twice as much space.

Like 1 Samuel, the story was written sometime after Solomon died and Israel split into two nations, in about 930 BC. The book was written to preserve the history of David's 40-year rule over Israel.

ON LOCATION

Most of the stories take place in Israel. But some, such as battles, occur in surrounding nations that include Jordan and Syria. The shaded area shows the extent of David's kingdom. After he made Jerusalem his capital, it became known as the city of David.

2 SAMUEL OUTLINE

Tribes gather to confirm David as king (5:1–5).

The disastrous defeat of King Saul and his army leaves Israel in danger of being overrun by the Philistines. Tribal leaders unite behind David, a proven warrior, and install him as the new king. This fulfills the prophecy of Samuel years earlier, and his secret anointing of the shepherd boy.

David rules out of Hebron for seven and a half years. But that's a city within his own family's territory, in the southern part of Israel. David apparently decides that to fully unite the twelve tribes, and to eliminate any hint of favoritism, he needs a neutral capital. He chooses Jerusalem for several reasons. It lies on the border of two tribes, near the center of the nation. And the Israelites haven't yet taken it from the Jebusites who live there.

When David's men capture it, in a daring attack through an underground water shaft, the village becomes known as the City of David, later called Jerusalem.

David brings the ark to Jerusalem (6:1–23).

Since the time of Priest Eli, decades earlier, when the Philistines captured the ark of the covenant, the ark has been out of the spotlight. Though the Philistines returned this chest that holds the Ten Commandments, it sat neglected in a private shrine. David, however, recognizes it as the most sacred object in all of Israel—a symbol of God's presence among his people. He decides to bring it to Jerusalem, in a move that will unite in one location the king's throne and the symbolic throne of God.

In a joyful procession, filled with music and shouts of glee, David dances as he accompanies the ark. His enthusiasm is so unrestrained that his wife, a daughter of King Saul, later criticizes him for acting undignified and "danced with all his might before the Lord. He had on a holy linen vest." But David says he doesn't care what she thinks, he was celebrating in honor of the Lord.

David temporarily puts the ark in a tent, but wants to build a temple. "Look, I am living in a palace made of cedar wood," he says, "but the Ark of God is in a tent."

The Lord, however, says that a tent is good enough for now. "From

Sun
Mo
Tue
We
Thu
Fric
Sat
Sun
Mo
Tue
We
Thu
Fric
Sat
Sun
Mo
Tue
We

the time I brought the Israelites out of Egypt until now I have not lived in a house," God says, through the prophet Nathan. "I have been moving around all this time with a tent as my home." The temple, God says, will come later. It will be built by the next king, one of David's sons.

David watches Bathsheba bathe (11:1–26).

One spring evening when David is apparently having trouble sleeping, he gets out of bed and takes a walk on the roof of his palace. Below he sees a beautiful woman bathing; she's Bathsheba, wife of a soldier away at war. David invites her to the palace, has sex with her, and she leaves. She discovers later that she's carrying his child.

David calls her husband home, hoping the soldier will sleep with Bathsheba and think the child is his. The soldier sleeps outside, since his comrades are suffering on the battlefield. David then arranges for him to fight on the front line, while the troops are pulled back. The soldier dies and David marries Bathsheba.

The prophet Nathan later confronts David about this sin. Though David repents, Bathsheba's son dies. Bathsheba later gives birth to Solomon.

Absalom is killed in a rebellion against his father, David (18:1–33).

Resentment between David and Absalom begins when David fails to punish another of his sons, Absalom's half brother, for raping Absalom's sister. Absalom takes revenge by murdering his half brother and fleeing the county. Three years later David calls his estranged son home, but refuses to meet with him for another two years.

By then, Absalom has decided to overthrow his father. Absalom travels around the country, stirring up resentment, then declares himself king. His following is strong enough that David flees the capital.

The armies of father and son clash in a dense forest. There, Absalom gets yanked off his mule when his long hair becomes tangled in tree branches. The mule runs off, leaving Absalom dangling. Some of David's soldiers surround him and, against the king's order, kill him.

David builds an altar (24:18–25).

David has turned Israel into a powerful fighting nation. He expands his kingdom into an empire that engulfs the Philistines on the Mediterranean coast, and extends eastward into what is now Jordan and northward all the way into Iraq.

In the process, David commits an unspecified sin that God feels obligated to punish. Perhaps David trusts too much on his military might and too little on God. Whatever the sin, God lets David choose the punishment: three years of famine, three months of being chased by enemies, or three days of plague. David chooses the plague, which kills thousands.

When the plague ends, God instructs David to buy the threshing floor on the hilltop overlooking his capital. There, David builds an altar. Later, his son Solomon will build Israel's first temple on that site.

Points to Consider

City of David. On the crest of a ridge just outside the walls of Jerusalem, archaeologists have found the remains of David's capital. The walled fortress that David captured lies between the temple mount, which overlooked his city, and the Kidron valley below.

The city covered about fifteen acres—about half as big as the inside of a large shopping mall—with an estimated population of roughly 2,000. David's son Solomon more than doubled the size and population of the city by adding the hilltop on which he built a magnificent temple.

Were David and Jonathan gay lovers? When David heard that Jonathan, his best friend and Saul's son, had died in battle, he sang a lament that included these words: "Your love to me was wonderful, better than the love of women" (1:26 NCV). This has led many to speculate that the two men were more than best friends; they were homosexual lovers.

This, however, doesn't fit with the Old Testament's repeated condemnation of homosexuality or with David's many heterosexual relationship. The Bible names eight of his wives, and he had many others.

When David spoke of Jonathan's love, he was likely referring to Jonathan's selfless loyalty to him, and to the deep friendship the two men shared.

Why does God kill someone trying to keep the ark from falling? When David decides to move the ark of the covenant to Jerusalem, he suffers a major setback. While transporting it by oxcart, one of the oxen stumbles and the ark begins to fall.

Uzzah, son of the man who has been taking care of the ark for the past twenty years, stops the ark from falling.

"The LORD was angry with Uzzah" for touching the ark, the Bible says, "and killed him because of what he did. So Uzzah died there beside the Ark of God" (6:7 NCV). David immediately changes his plans and stores the chest in someone's home for three months before trying again—successfully.

God's slaying of Uzzah seems more like the kind of capricious behavior we would expect from one of the mean-spirited gods of Greek mythology.

Why did God kill the man? The Bible doesn't say. Even David didn't understand, and "was angry because the LORD had killed Uzzah." It is clear, however, that the ark was not carried as God directed in Numbers 4:4–20.

The ark was the most sacred object in Israel. It represented the presence of God among his people. Only the Kohathites, one branch in the tribe of Levi, were allowed to carry the ark—even then, the ark and other sacred objects of the tabernacle had to be covered "they won't touch the holy things and die" (Numbers 4:15 NCV). Once, when some Israelites tried to sneak a peek inside, God killed them.

Perhaps God killed Uzzah for the flagrant disobedience of transporting the ark improperly and to dramatically remind the onlookers that they should take seriously the warnings of the agreement that their ancestors had made with him.

FOR FURTHER STUDY

- The story of Israel's history continues in 1 Kings. There, the dying David names his surprise successor: passing over his oldest surviving son, David appoints Solomon, his son with Bathsheba.

- To get a feel for the kind of intimate relationship David has with God, read some of the psalms he wrote. Psalm 51 seems to express the kind of sorrow he felt after committing adultery with Bathsheba.

- Psalm 18 conveys the kind of feelings David may have experienced when his son led a coup against him.

1 Kings

THE RISE AND FALL OF ISRAEL

King Solomon orders a baby cut in half so he can watch the reaction of two women who claim to be the mother.

The prophet Elijah challenges 450 prophets of Baal to a contest on Mount Carmel. The deity who sends fire from heaven to consume the sacrifice will be treated by Israel as the only true God.

That's gripping drama. And there's plenty more, thanks in part to the infamous Queen Jezebel. (She executes a farmer who refuses to sell his family's vineyard so the king can turn it into a vegetable garden for his summer palace.)

But there's take-away value in the book as well. You reap what you sow—this message comes through more clearly here, perhaps, than anywhere else in the Bible. Kings who obey God's law reap the benefits listed in the covenant that God made with Israel: rain for the crops, peace in the land, power over invaders. Kings who disobey reap the disasters, which are also listed: disease, famine, overpowering enemies.

Time and again the writer names godly kings and the blessings they reap. And time and again the writer names ungodly kings and the disasters they reap. God, like a loving and savvy father, is consistent in his discipline. But the Israelites, like stubborn and self-willed children, are persistent in their rebellion.

Yet one thing remains certain: "But even though this is true," God has promised their ancestors, "I will not turn away" (Leviticus 26:44 NCV).

> ### FAMOUS LINES
>
> • "Cut the living baby into two pieces" (3:25 NCV). *King Solomon's decision when two women each claim a baby boy belongs to her.*
>
> • "The LORD is God! The LORD is God!" (18:39 NCV). *The response of the Israelites after fire from heaven burns up the sacrifice Elijah offers on Mount Carmel.*

BACKGROUND

INFLUENTIAL PEOPLE

David, elderly and dying king of Israel (1:1).

Solomon, David's son and successor, builder of the temple (1:10).

Elijah, prophet who challenges prophets of Baal on Mount Carmel (17:1).

Ahab and Jezebel, Baal-worshiping king and queen of the northern kingdom (16:28, 31).

THEME

Solomon becomes king after his father David dies of old age. Solomon stretches the wealth and boundaries of Israel to levels never before attained. With the wars of David's reign behind, the Israelites enjoy peace and prosperity as they enter into business deals with surrounding nations. But when Solomon grows old, he begins yielding to pressure from his foreign wives to worship the gods of their homeland. The peace begins to collapse as enemies rise up. When Solomon dies, the nation splits in two and the troubles escalate.

DID YOU KNOW?

• The derogatory phrase "she's a Jezebel," meaning a shameless and immoral woman, comes from 1 and 2 Kings. Jezebel was the Phoenician princess who lived in what is now Lebanon and who married King Ahab. She executed many of God's prophets and imposed on the nation her own religion. She worshiped Baal, a fertility god. Worship included having sex with cult prostitutes—male and female—as a way of persuading Baal to grant fertility to family, flock, and field.

• Legend says the queen of Sheba gave birth to a son by Solomon and that this child became king of Ethiopia. Falashas are a group of Ethiopian Jews who trace their roots to this king. Before the Ethiopian emperor was overthrown in 1974, the nation's constitution said that the royal line descended from the son of "the queen of Sheba and King Solomon of Jerusalem."

TIMELINE	BIBLE EVENTS		Solomon becomes king 970 BC	The temple is finished 960 BC	Israel splits into two nations 930 BC	Ahab begins his reign 874 BC		Dates are approximate
		1100 BC	**1050 BC**	**1000 BC**	**950 BC**	**900 BC**	**850 BC**	**800 BC**
	WORLD EVENTS		Egypt splits in two 1085 BC	Celts of central Europe migrate to France 900 BC	The city of Canton, China is founded 887 BC	Assyrian empire begins expanding 883 BC	Homer writes the Iliad and the Odyssey 800 BC	

POINTS OF INTEREST

The lesson behind the history. This isn't your typical history lesson, for the writer doesn't focus on the most accomplished kings. If he did, he'd be giving more attention to kings like Omri, Ahab's father. Omri was one of the most powerful rulers of the northern nation of Israel—a fact illustrated by ancient records from other nations. But Omri nets a mere six verses in the book.

The writer focuses on kings who are most obedient to God, or least obedient. He's interested in showing what happens when rulers honor the covenant with God, and what happens when they don't.

AUTHOR AND DATE

Like the two books of Samuel and Chronicles, the two books of Kings were originally written as one book, by an unknown writer. They were separated into two books when the Hebrew text was translated for Greek-speaking Jews in about 300 BC. This allowed each book to fit onto one scroll.

The writer drew from a variety of ancient sources, including three that are named: a book about Solomon (11:41), and two books about the many other kings (14:19, 29). The writer may also have had access to records kept by court historians or the prophets: "Everything David did as king, from beginning to end, is recorded in the records of Samuel the seer, the records of Nathan the prophet, and the records of Gad the seer" (1 Chronicles 29:29 NCV).

It's uncertain exactly when the stories were compiled into a single book. Many scholars suspect it was in the mid-500s BC, after the Babylonians had destroyed Jerusalem and dragged off much of the Jewish population into exile. The history recorded in 1 and 2 Kings—which spans the 400 years from the final days of David's reign through the fall of Jerusalem—seems targeted to Jewish readers in exile. The history vividly explains that the Jews got where they are because generation after generation disobeyed God. So the Jews suffered the consequences God had been warning them about since the time of Moses.

On Location

Israel is the center of the action. But other areas in the Middle East add to the setting. To build the temple in Jerusalem, Solomon sends loggers to cut cedar from the forests of Lebanon (Phoenicia on this map). Visiting Solomon, to investigate rumors of his incredible wisdom, is the queen of Sheba, coming from what may have been southern Arabia. The shaded area shows Solomon's kingdom. Trade and transportation routes through the kingdom added to Solomon's influence.

1 KINGS OUTLINE

Solomon decides to cut a baby in half (3:16–28).

Before David dies an old man, he appoints the new king. To everyone's surprise, he does not select his oldest surviving son, Adonijah. The new king is Solomon, David's son with Bathsheba. Early in Solomon's reign, he asks God for wisdom. What follows is astonishing proof that God has granted his request. Two young women come to him, each claiming to be the mother of a newborn son. There are no witnesses to call, so Solomon gives a frightful order.

"Cut the living baby into two pieces and give each woman half," he says.

One woman quickly agrees; the other pleads for him to spare the child.

Solomon points to the pleading woman and says, "Don't kill him. Give the baby to the first woman, because she is the real mother."

Solomon builds the temple (6:1–38).

On a hilltop overlooking Jerusalem, Solomon builds the first of only three temples the Jews have ever had. Stonecutters quarry massive limestone blocks. Craftsmen from throughout the Middle East design furnishings of gold and ivory. Lumberjacks travel to Lebanon to harvest the finest wood available: bug-proof, rot-resistant cedar.

Seven years later, the job is done. Israel has one of the most beautiful and expensive temples in the ancient world—a worship center with golden ceilings, walls, and floors. This white limestone temple is thirty yards long, ten yards wide, and fifteen yards high, shimmering on the Jerusalem hilltop.

Here Jews will offer sacrifices to God for 400 years—until Babylonian soldiers invade the city, strip away the gold, then destroy the building.

The queen of Sheba visits Solomon (10:1–13).

The queen of Sheba, from an Arabian trade nation probably 1,000 miles away, hears about the wisdom and wealth of Solomon. So she assembles a large caravan and goes to investigate.

She is amazed. She says, "What I heard in my own country about your achievements and wisdom is true. I could not believe it then, but now I have come and seen it with my own eyes."

She showers him with expensive gifts: nearly five tons of gold, along with jewels and rare spices. He returns the favor, giving her anything she wants.

Solomon's harem of a thousand (11:1–13).

Solomon makes one big mistake. He grows a harem of 700 wives of royal birth and 300 concubines, or secondary wives. These are mainly political marriages, to secure peace and trade agreements with neighboring kingdoms. But these marriages break a rule that Moses gave several hundred years earlier: a ruler "must not have many wives, or his heart will be led away from God" (Deuteronomy 17:17 NCV).

That's exactly what happens to King Solomon. "As Solomon grew old, his wives caused him to follow other gods. He did not follow the LORD completely as his father David had done" (11:4 NCV).

To punish the king, God raises up enemies who shatter the decades of peace that Israel has enjoyed.

Israel splits into two kingdoms (12:1–33).

By the time Solomon dies, the people of Israel are tired of paying heavy taxes to support the king's enormous household and administration. They're weary, too, of being drafted to build cities, forts, and palaces.

They approach King Rehoboam, Solomon's son and successor, and ask for relief. The rook monarch responds harshly: "My father forced you to work hard, but I will make you work even harder."

The northern tribes secede, start their own nation, and appoint their own king. Only the tribe of Judah, in the south, remains loyal to the descendant of David.

The stories that follow in 1 and 2 Kings reveal that all the kings of the northern nation of Israel "did what the LORD said was wrong" (15:26 NCV). Most kings in the southern nation of Judah, however, are good—with notable exceptions.

Elijah challenges prophets of Baal on Mount Carmel (18:1–46).

Ahab is one of the ungodly kings that blemishes the history of the northern nation. He marries Jezebel, a princess from what is now Lebanon. She kills most of the prophets of God and imports her own prophets of Baal, god of rain.

God punishes Israel with a three-year drought. Then he orders the prophet Elijah to challenge Jezebel's 450 prophets to a contest, while crowds of Israelites watch. Baal's prophets and Elijah are each to offer a sacrificed bull, laid on a pile of wood. The deity that starts the fire on the altar will become the god of Israel.

Baal's prophets pray for hours, but nothing happens. Elijah prays one short prayer, and the fire falls from heaven. The Israelites kill the prophets of Baal, and the drought ends that day.

═══ POINTS TO CONSIDER ═══

Ivory from Solomon's temple. In 1988 the Israel Museum paid a Jerusalem antiquities dealer $550,000 for a 1.68-inch-high ivory decoration shaped like a pomegranate. They paid this hefty sum for a tiny object because they believed the decoration was the head of a scepter used by priests in Solomon's temple.

What led them to this conclusion is a Hebrew inscription written during the 700s BC. It reads: "Belonging to the Temp[le of Yahwe]h, holy to the priests." The letters in brackets represent a guess by scholars, since that part of the ivory is broken off. *Yahweh* is the Hebrew name for God.

Ahab and his father, etched in stone. The Bible doesn't mention the battle of Qarqar in which Ahab led Israel in a multinational force against King Shalmaneser III of Assyria. But Shalmaneser did, in a document called the Monolith Inscription of Shalmaneser. The Bible confirms that Ahab was a warrior king.

The name of King Ahab's father, Omri, shows up in the ancient records of both Moabites and Assyrians. Inscriptions on what has become known as the Moabite Stone, written during the time of Omri in the mid-800s BC, credit him with capturing Moabite territory in what is now Jordan. And long after Omri's death, Assyrian documents continue referring to Israel as "the Land of Omri," in recognition that he was one of Israel's most influential rulers.

King Jehu's portrait. A stone carving from the Assyrian capital of Nimrud shows Jehu bowing before the Assyrian king. Jehu ruled in the early 800s BC. The caption reads: "The tribe of Jehu, son of Omri; I received from him silver, gold, a golden bowl, a golden vase with pointed bottom, golden tumblers, golden buckets, tin, and a staff for a king."

Statues of Baal. The Bible portrays Baal as a fertility god, responsible for the rain that gives life to crops and animals. Ancient statues of Baal show him holding a lightning rod in his hand.

Jereboam's sanctuary for a golden calf. To keep northern Jews from worshiping in Jerusalem, the king of the northern tribes set up two worship centers in the north. The most important was at Dan, where he set up a golden calf. Archaeologists have uncovered the remains of this sanctuary and an altar during excavations that began in 1966.

If Solomon was so wise, why did he marry a thousand women? It was common in ancient times for kings to seal trade and peace agreements with a marriage. The kings would give and receive royal daughters in marriage, hoping this would discourage other parties from breaking the agreement and putting their own daughters in jeopardy.

These marriages, however, chipped away at Solomon's faith. By the time he was an old man, he was worshiping the gods of his foreign wives. Suddenly, the luster of Israel's Golden Age began to fade.

For Further Study

- To read the rest of the story, turn to 2 Kings. The two books were originally one.

- Ecclesiastes, a book that says it was written by a son of David—perhaps Solomon—may reflect the despair Solomon felt after abandoning God. If so, it spotlights the wise conclusion he reached after suffering the consequences of his disobedience: "Honor God and obey his commands, because this is all people must do" (Ecclesiastes 12:13 NCV).

- To read about the return of an Elijah-like prophet who will come just before the Messiah, turn to Malachi 4:5–6 and to the words of Jesus in Matthew 11:7–14, where he identifies John the Baptist as that prophet.

2 Kings

ISRAEL DIES, THE PEOPLE SCATTER

The most tragic event in the history of Israel is vividly, painfully reported in this book.

As a nation, Israel dies.

It's a bit like the Garden of Eden revisited. Adam and Eve are given one rule and are told what will happen if they break it: they'll die. They break it anyhow, and sure enough, they die.

Much later, God enters into a contract, or covenant, with Israel promising to take care of them in return for their obedience. He explains what will happen if they break the covenant: the nation will be scattered abroad. They break the contract anyhow, and sure enough, the Jews of Israel become the Jews of the Diaspora (dispersion).

The negative slant is not the only slant in 2 Kings. There's disobedience and punishment—and plenty of each. But there's obedience and reward too. There are godly prophets accomplishing tremendous miracles. And there are godly kings, whose prayers and righteous living become the difference between life and death for them and the people they govern.

Religion, 2 Kings reveals, is not merely a matter of the heart. It affects history, for better of worse.

FAMOUS LINES

- "You baldhead!" (2:23 NCV). *How some young people taunt the prophet Elisha. Two bears immediately charge out of the woods and maul the youths.*

- "He drives as if he were crazy" (9:20 NCV). *A watchman on a city wall identifies charioteer Jehu by his driving style.*

- "Are you as good a friend to me? . . . If you are, then give me your hand" (10:15 NCV). *Jehu asking a man if he is on Jehu's side. When the man replies he is, Jehu gives him a hand up into the chariot he is driving. Apparently the pedestrian doesn't know what the watchman knows about Jehu's driving.*

BACKGROUND

INFLUENTIAL PEOPLE

Elijah, prophet who rides to heaven in a fiery chariot (1:3).
Elisha, Elijah's successor (2:1).
Naaman, Syrian commander cured of leprosy (5:1).
Jezebel, an evil queen who is murdered (9:7).

THEME

The story of the two Jewish nations of Israel and Judah picks up where 1 Kings leaves off. Elisha becomes Israel's most influential prophet, after his mentor, Elijah, is taken to heaven in a whirlwind. Elisha performs many miracles, even raising a child from the dead and curing an enemy soldier of leprosy. But his efforts to turn the nation's heart back to God seem futile. Assyria destroys Israel in 722 BC. The southern Jewish nation of Judah enjoys more godly leadership and survives 150 years longer. But in 586 BC, it, too, collapses. Jerusalem with its magnificent temple is torn to the ground.

POINTS OF INTEREST

The connection between sin and punishment. The Jews have seen it before, with individuals enduring the consequences of sin, and with the entire nation suffering because of disobedience. But they've never seen punishment as intense as they're about to witness. After generation upon generation heaps disobedience upon disobedience, God invokes the full measure of punishment, according to the terms of his covenant with the Jews. Their nations—first Israel in the north, then Judah in the south—cease to exist.

TIMELINE	BIBLE EVENTS	Elijah's ministry ends, Elisha's begins ----850 BC			Northern nation of Israel destroyed ⌐-722 BC	Southern nation of Judah falls, with Jerusalem 586 BC------------⌐	Dates are approximate
	850 BC	**800 BC**	**750 BC**	**700 BC**	**650 BC**	**600 BC**	**550 BC**
	WORLD EVENTS	Ohio River people build earth burial mounds 800 BC---	First recorded Olympic games --in Greece 776 BC	Rome founded by King Romulus ---753 BC	Chinese philosopher Confucius is born 551 BC----------		

AUTHOR AND DATE

The two books of Kings were originally written as one book, by an unknown writer. They were separated into two books when the Hebrew text was translated for Greek-speaking Jews in about 300 BC. This allowed each book to fit onto one scroll.

The writer drew from a variety of sources, including a book about Solomon, a book about the kings of Israel, and a book about the kings of Judah. The writer may also have had access to records kept by royal historians and prophets.

No one knows for sure when the stories of 1 and 2 Kings were compiled into a single book. Many scholars suspect it was in the mid-500s BC, after Israel and Judah were conquered. They suspect this because the two books seem to target exiled Jewish readers who want to know what they did to deserve such a horrible punishment.

DID YOU KNOW?

• The 1981 Oscar-winning movie *Chariots of Fire,* about a Christian Olympic marathon runner who refuses to run on Sunday, gets its title from 2 Kings 6:17. The verse says that when the prophet Elisha's hometown was surround by enemy invaders, God sent his own army to protect his people. "The mountain was full of horses and chariots of fire" (NCV).

• The phrase "thrown to the dogs" comes from 2 Kings 9:10, 33–34. It describes what happens to Queen Jezebel after she is thrown from her palace window.

• The Lost Tribes of Israel refers to the ten Jewish tribes, descended from ten of Jacob's twelve sons, who seceded from the Jewish nation and were later destroyed by Assyria. Survivors of the invasion were deported to what is now Iraq and eventually lost track of what tribes they belonged to.

• The only woman to rule Judah was Athaliah. After her son, the king, died, she killed all the heirs she could find, then assumed the throne. She was executed several years later when an heir she missed suddenly showed up.

ON LOCATION

The main events take place in the Jewish nations of Israel, in the north, and Judah, in the south. Neighboring empires play important roles. Egypt allies itself with the Jews, while the Assyrians and Babylonians invade and defeat the Jewish nations in spite of the Egyptian alliance. By 650 BC Assyria has overrun Israel and dominates the entire fertile crescent (see map). Less than 100 years later, Babylon is the major power in the area and defeats Judah.

2 KINGS OUTLINE

Elijah's whirlwind ride to heaven (2:1–8).

At the end of Elijah's 25-year ministry as a prophet, he is walking with his young associate, Elisha. At the Jordan River Elijah rolls up his cloak and strikes the water. "The water divided to the right and to the left, and Elijah and Elisha crossed over on dry ground."

"What can I do for you before I am taken from you?" Elijah says.

Elisha asks to take Elijah's place as the leading prophet. Elijah replies, "You have asked a hard thing. But if you see me when I am taken from you, it will be yours. If you don't, it won't happen." Suddenly a flaming chariot pulled by fiery horses takes Elijah up into heaven.

Elisha picks up Elijah's cloak, which has fallen, and returns to the Jordan River. There, he rolls up the cloak, strikes the water, and a path opens—a sign that God has granted his request.

Elisha raises a child from the dead (4:8–37).

A childless woman and her elderly husband provide Elisha with a guest room to use whenever he's in their area. In return, Elisha promises that the couple will have a child. The following year, a son arrives.

Years later the young boy begins to complain of a terrible headache. By noon he is dead.

The woman immediately gets on a donkey and rides to Mount Carmel to find Elisha. She tells him her son has died and convinces him to return with her.

When Elisha arrives, he walks into the boy's room, shuts the door, and prays.

"He went to the bed and lay on the boy, putting his mouth on the boy's mouth, his eyes on the boy's eyes, and his hands on the boy's hands."

The boy sneezes seven times and opens his eyes.

A Syrian commander is cured of leprosy (5:1–27).

Naaman, commander of the Syrian army that God is using to punish Israel for its sin, is a valiant warrior but a man with a dreaded disease—leprosy. A servant girl in his house, captured from Israel, tells Naaman's wife that he could be cured if he would ask Elisha for help.

Naaman goes to Elisha. The prophet gives the commander these simple instructions: "Go and wash in the Jordan River seven times. Then your skin will be healed, and you will be clean."

The commander is furious. He has been expecting some mysterious ritual, not a bath. But with a little encouragement from his servants, he obeys and is cured.

"Look," Naaman says as he reports back to Elisha, "I now know there is no God in all the earth except in Israel."

Jezebel is murdered (9:30–37).

After King Ahab dies in a battle, his son becomes king. Jezebel still wields great influence and "has caused everyone to worship idols." Elisha tells Jehu, an Israelite soldier, that Ahab's family must die and that Jehu is to become king.

Jehu assembles some men and rides to the king's summer palace in the hills of Jezreel. Outside the city he meets the king and kills him. As Jehu continues toward the city, Jezebel learns that he's coming. "She put on her eye makeup and fixed her hair. Then she looked out the window."

Once he does, she yells out, "Have you come in peace, you Zimri, you who killed your master?"

Jehu looks up and asks, "Who is on my side? Who?" Some palace workers catch his eye. "Throw her down," Jehu orders. They do, and Jezebel falls to her death.

Solomon's temple is repaired (12:1–21).

Solomon's magnificent temple, built about 150 years earlier, has suffered from neglect. Baal worship that had grown popular in the northern nation of Israel has also become popular in the southern nation of Judah. The reason is because Ahab of Israel has made a peace treaty with Judah and sealed the treaty by giving one of his daughters in marriage to the crown prince of Judah. When the prince becomes king, Ahab's Baal-worshiping daughter becomes queen.

After her husband dies, she orders the execution of all of David's dynasty, then declares herself queen. One heir survives: her infant grandson Joash, who is secretly raised by a temple priest. About six years later, young Joash is presented as the rightful ruler. The queen is executed. When Joash comes of age, he orders that the temple be renovated.

The northern nation of Israel falls (17:1–41).

Assyria, in what is now Iraq, emerges as one of the most powerful forces in the Middle East. Many nations, including Israel, pay taxes to stay on the good side of the Assyrian rulers. Hoshea, king of Israel, decides to stop payment.

Shalmaneser, king of Assyria, marches into Israel. He surrounds the capital of Samaria for three years and starves the people into submission. The citizens are deported as slaves to several cities in Assyria. Israel is then resettled with Assyrian homesteaders. The ten Israelite tribes that once made up the nation eventually lose track of their tribal identity forever.

"All of this happened," the Bible says, "because the people of Israel had sinned against the Lord their God."

Sennacherib lays siege to Jerusalem, but suffers disaster (18:1–19:37).

Judah has been paying taxes to Assyria, but when the Assyrian king dies, Judah decides to rebel. Judah's King Hezekiah enters into a treaty of mutual support with Egypt, Assyria's rival power.

The army of Sennacherib, the new Assyrian king, captures one Judean city after another before laying siege to Jerusalem.

Standing near the city walls, the Assyrian commander yells out his warnings. "Don't listen to Hezekiah. He is fooling you when he says, 'The Lord will save us.'" he shouts. "Has a god of any other nation saved his people from the power of the king of Assyria? . . . . Neither can the Lord save Jerusalem from my power?"

"That night the angel of the Lord went out and killed one hundred eighty-five thousand men in the Assyrian camp. When the people got up early the next morning, they saw all the dead bodies. So Sennacherib king of Assyria left and went back to Nineveh and stayed there." Jerusalem is spared—for now.

Manasseh sacrifices a son (21:1–18).

Hezekiah, one of Judah's most godly kings, raises a godless son named Manasseh.

This son assumes the throne at age twelve, after his father dies. He rebuilds pagan shrines his father had torn down. And he worships the gods Baal and godess Asherah as well as the sun, moon, and stars. He practices witchcraft, consults fortunetellers, and even sacrifices his own son—all in blatant defiance of God's law.

Jerusalem falls (25:1–26).

The horror that befell Israel 150 years earlier now comes to Judah—but in the form of Babylon, which has conquered Assyria.

Jerusalem suffers a siege that lasts a year and a half, starving many of the people to death. When soldiers of Babylonian King Nebuchadnezzar finally break through the city walls, they make an example of Jerusalem and tear it to the ground. Utterly destroyed is Solomon's temple, the symbol of Jewish national and religious identify.

Many Jewish citizens who survive the battle are deported to Babylon as captives.

The great nation that God promised to make of Abraham's descendants no longer exists.

= POINTS TO CONSIDER =

Hezekiah's tunnel. To provide Jerusalem with water during a siege, Hezekiah tapped into an underground spring by commissioning the construction of "a pool and tunnel" (20:20). This tunnel still exists, cut through nearly 600 yards of solid rock. Miners started at each end and met in the middle, preserving the accomplishment with a brief inscription describing how they did it. The inscription was written shortly before 701 BC, when Assyria invaded Judah and surrounded Jerusalem.

Sennacherib's record. The Bible says Sennacherib led the Assyrians in a siege against Jerusalem, but that he retreated after an unspecified disaster struck his camp and killed many of his soldiers. Sennacherib's own records add credence to the story. He writes about his invasion, and of conquering numerous cities. But he stops short of saying he conquered Jerusalem. "As for Hezekiah, the Judean who did not submit to my yoke . . . I made a prisoner in Jerusalem, his royal residence, like a bird in a cage. I surrounded him with earthwork."

Why did God change his mind about killing Hezekiah? When King Hezekiah became critically ill, the prophet Isaiah arrived with a message from God: "Make arrangements because you are not going to live, but die" (20:1 NCV).

As Isaiah walked away, Hezekiah turned his face to the wall and prayed, "LORD, please remember that I have always obeyed you. I have given myself completely to you and have done what you said was right." Then he cried hard.

Before Isaiah reached the middle of the palace court, God stopped him with a new message for Hezekiah: "I have heard your prayer and seen your tears, so I will heal you. Three days from now you will go up to the Temple of the LORD. I will add fifteen years to your life. I will save you and this city from the king of Assyria; I will protect the city for my sake and for the sake of my servant David."

The Bible doesn't explain why God changed his mind. But it certainly shows that prayer makes a difference.

For Further Study

- The two books of Chronicles cover the same period of history as 1 and 2 Kings. Chronicles was apparently written later to Jews who had returned from exile wondering if they were still God's people, or if the covenant was irreparably broken.

- To read a detailed, eyewitness account of the fall of Jerusalem, turn to Jeremiah 52. And for more background on this era in history, read the story sections throughout Jeremiah. You can skip the prophecy sections, which in many Bible translations are easily recognizable because they are indented like poetry.

- For another view of Hezekiah, read Isaiah 36–39; this section parallels 2 Kings 18–20.

Sun
Mon
Tues
Wed
Thu
Frid
Satu
Sun
Mon
Tues
Wed
Thu
Frid
Satu
Sun
Mon
Tues
Wed

1 Chronicles

THE JEWS COME HOME

The chosen people needed to know if they had become the unchosen.

The Israelite nation was born when Abraham entered into an agreement with God, promising to serve him alone. The nation died after Abraham's descendants shattered the agreement by serving a gallery of gods. Babylon crushed the Jewish defenders in 586 BC, set the cities on fire, and led the masses into exile nearly a thousand miles away.

Decades later, some Jews were allowed to return home. But to what?

Was this still the Promised Land? Was the covenant still valid? Were the Jews still the chosen people?

> ### FAMOUS LINES
>
> • "Thank the LORD because he is good. His love continues forever" (1 Chronicles 16:34 NCV).

The books of 1 and 2 Chronicles answer these questions. Yes, this is still the Promised Land. Yes, the covenant is still in force. And yes, the Jews are still the people chosen by God—though a people who have suffered terribly for their sin.

Evidence of God's favor? The Jews are back in Israel. The temple is rebuilt. The legacy of the priesthood remains intact, with priestly leaders clearly identified. And David's family has been preserved. All of this is God's doing.

He just doesn't give up. That's the good news of Chronicles.

BACKGROUND

INFLUENTIAL PEOPLE

David, king of Israel who makes plans for the temple (2:9).

THEME

The first nine chapters of the book trace the Israelite family tree from Adam, at creation, to Zerubbabel and beyond, after the captivity in Babylon. Then Israel's story picks up with the death of Saul, followed by the crowning of David as king. David secures the nation by defeating Israel's enemies and establishing the capital in Jerusalem. Then he brings into Jerusalem the ark of the covenant, Israel's most sacred relic, which contains the Ten Commandments. Though David is not permitted to build a temple, he receives from God the temple plans that he passes on to his son Solomon. David also begins gathering the construction supplies that Solomon will need later.

POINTS OF INTEREST

What's missing. Notice what the writer leaves out, because this is a clue about the purpose of the book. In telling the story of David, the writer doesn't mention: the conflict with Saul, the adultery with Bathsheba and the murder of her husband, the troubles in the royal family after a prince rapes his half sister, or the attempted coup led by the crown prince.

It's not that the writer is trying to sugarcoat history. He's drawing from a painful history that is already well-known and recorded.

Nor is the writer trying to fill in the missing gaps, to preserve an exhaustive history of Israel. He's trying, instead, to preserve Israel's connection to their ancient covenant with God.

For this reason, he focuses on excerpts of history that show God at work on Israel's behalf.

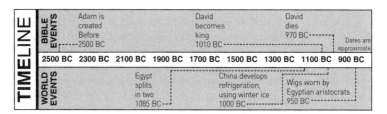

		Adam is created Before 2500 BC			David becomes king 1010 BC			David dies 970 BC		Dates are approximate
TIMELINE	**BIBLE EVENTS**									
		2500 BC	2300 BC	2100 BC	1900 BC	1700 BC	1500 BC	1300 BC	1100 BC	900 BC
	WORLD EVENTS		Egypt splits in two 1085 BC			China develops refrigeration, using winter ice 1000 BC		Wigs worn by Egyptian aristocrats 950 BC		

AUTHOR AND DATE

Ancient Jewish tradition says Ezra wrote 1 and 2 Chronicles along with the books of Ezra and Nehemiah. Ezra was a priest and teacher of Jewish law who returned to Israel after the exile and who led in the rebuilding of the temple. Genealogies listed in 1 Chronicles, and the point at which they end, suggest the book was written about the time Ezra lived.

Whoever the writer was, he apparently used a wide variety of sources. From the Bible, the books of Samuel and Kings provided about half of his material. He also drew from the books of Moses (the first five in the Bible), along with several books of prophets, as well as Psalms. Sources outside the Bible included history books about the kings and records by various prophets.

Like the books of Samuel and Kings, the two volumes of Chronicles were originally one book, later separated so each could fit onto a single scroll.

Chronicles was probably written in the early 400s BC, roughly a hundred years after many of the Jews returned home from exile and rebuilt the temple.

Though the Chronicles repeat some of the same history as the books of Samuel and Kings, the motive is radically different. The earlier books are written for Jews in exile, to show them how they got there. So Samuel and Kings spend a lot of time talking about the sins of Israel. The two books of Chronicles, however, are written for Jews who have returned from the exile wondering if their covenant with God is still in force.

DID YOU KNOW?

• Years ago, some scholars thought that the genealogy in the book was mostly fictional, until archaeologists began discovering that towns were named after many people listed among the tribes of Israel.

• Asaph, author of many of the songs in the book of Psalms, is appointed by David to lead musicians who "worship and giving thanks and praising the LORD, the God of Israel" (16:4 NCV). To read the kind of songs they sang, see Psalm 105.

• There's only one time in the Old Testament that a person is reported to pray to God while seated. It happens when David thanks God for blessing his family and nation: "You made the people of Israel your very own people forever," David prays, "and, LORD, you are their God" (17:22 NCV). A typical posture for prayer in the Old Testament is kneeling. Some people, however, prayed while lying on the ground. Solomon prayed standing, with his hands raised to the sky.

Chronicles focuses less on the sinful history of Israel, and more on the godly heritage on which the nation should build.

ON LOCATION

Most of the story takes place in what is now Israel. David's military victories extend the boundaries of the kingdom (see shaded area on map).

1 CHRONICLES OUTLINE

The Israelite family tree (chapters 1–9).

Beginning with Adam, and continuing all the way through the Jewish exile in Babylon, the writer identifies notable people of God—highlights of the Hebrew family tree.

Nine chapters of names may not seem like a compelling way to draw in readers today. But for the Jews recently back in Israel after decades of exile in Babylon, the list communicates a powerful message: God has not given up on them. Because they have a past with God, they also have a future as the newly restored community of faith.

This genealogy also has the practical value of clarifying who the new leaders are. Among the names of David's descendants, for example, is Zerubbabel. He is the leader who rebuilds the temple so the Jews can reestablish their system of worship. The genealogy also identifies the descendants of Levi, who are to serve as temple priests and assistants.

Saul kills himself when the battle is lost (10:1–14).

After listing the relatively short genealogy of Saul, the writer reports on the final moments of King Saul's life. This becomes a prelude to the man chapters about the accomplishments of King David.

Saul dies during a fierce battle, with Philistine invaders pressing through the Israelite defenses. One by one the princes fall: Jonathan, Abinadab, Malchishua. Then enemy archers critically wound Saul.

The king asks his weapons bearer to finish him before the Philistines have a chance to capture and torture him. Terrified, the soldier can't do it. Saul props the hand of his sword into the ground and falls on the blade.

David brings the ark to Jerusalem (13:1–14; 15:1–16:6).

David becomes the new king of Israel, establishing his capital in Jerusalem. Since the time of Priest Eli, decades earlier, when the Philistines captured the ark of the covenant, the ark has been out of the spotlight. Though the Philistines returned this chest that holds the Ten Commandments, it sat neglected in a private shrine. David, however, recognizes it as the most sacred object in all of Israel—a symbol of God's presence among his people. He decides to bring it to Jerusalem, in a move that unites in one location the king's throne and the symbolic throne of God.

In a joyful procession, filled with music and shouts of glee, David dances as he accompanies the ark.

He temporarily puts the ark in a tent, but wants to build a temple. "Look, I am living in a palace made of cedar," he says, "but the Ark of the Agreement with the LORD sits in a tent" (17:1 NCV).

The Lord, however, says that a tent is good enough for now. "David, you have killed many people. You have fought many wars. You cannot build a temple for worship to me, because you have killed many people. But, you will have a son, a man of peace and rest. I will give him rest from all his enemies around him. His name will be Solomon, and I will give Israel peace and quiet while he is king. Solomon will build a temple for worship to me. He will be my son, and I will be his father. I will make his kingdom strong; someone from his family will rule Israel forever" (22:8–10 NCV).

David prepares building materials for the future temple (chapters 22, 28–29).

David continues to secure his nation so he can establish for his son an era of peace. He does this by defeating the surrounding enemies, including the Philistines who have harassed Israel for several hundred years.

Though David is not permitted to build the temple, God entrusts him with the construction plan. David not only passes this along to his son, he begins stockpiling the supplies that Solomon will need: cedar logs imported from Lebanon, 4,000 tons of gold, 40,000 tons of silver, iron for nails and gateways, precious gems, turquoise, onyx, and marble. David even develops a strategy for managing the work of the priests and the temple support staff, and carefully assigns job responsibilities. Among the temple associates are musicians who sing or play instruments, judges, guard, accountants, and custodians.

With the plans safely in the hands of Solomon, David dies of old age.

7:00
8:00
9:00
0:00
1:00
[oon
1:00
2:00
3:00
4:00
5:00
5:00
7:00
8:00
9:00
0:00

POINTS TO CONSIDER

The family trade. The genealogies speak of clans, or extended families, that work together in a shared trade. It mentions, for example, one family of "experts in weaving cloth" and another of "potter" (4:21–22). This practice of joining the family business was common in the ancient Middle Eastern world.

Why 70,000 innocent people die, while the sinner lives. Chronicles and Samuel each report a perplexing story about King David sinning in some unknown way by counting his fighting men (2 Samuel 24; 1 Chronicles 21). How he sinned is unknown. Perhaps the census was for bragging rights, to highlight his military prowess instead of giving God the credit for Israel's victories.

Whatever the sin, God sent a plague on Israel. David, the sinner, lived. But 70,000 others died.

The Bible doesn't explain why it worked out this way.

But ancient Middle Eastern culture understood better than Western culture today that families and nations share the reward and punishment of their leaders. Ancient societies weren't as individualistic as we are. We see ourselves as responsible for no one but us. The ancients saw things differently. When a family man did something that pleased a king, for example, the man's entire family benefited. But if the man did something wrong, his sons or even his entire family could be executed.

FOR FURTHER STUDY

- Read 2 Chronicles to continue the rest of the story that was originally one book.

- Read 2 Samuel to fill in the details of David's story.

2 Chronicles

SEARCHING FOR GOD
IN A HISTORY LESSON

This is a book about hope.

To people standing beside ash and stone piles that were once their nation, their city, their home, hope is a critical commodity.

After half a century of exile in what is now Iraq, the Jews were given permission to return to their homeland. Many didn't, for they had gotten used to their new life. Many of the Jews who were young and fit enough to make the nearly thousand-mile journey to Israel had never even seen the place. It was not home to them.

But many other Jews, young and old, had preserved the stories of their past. They knew God had promised them the land. So they went back. But they desperately needed to know if this was part of God's plan. Perhaps God had abandoned the Jewish people for their disobedience. Perhaps by now he had found another chosen people.

For Jews struggling with doubts such as these, the writer of Chronicles has a history lesson mingled with a sermon of assurance. He shows them their long history with God. And he implies that they will have a long future too.

What makes Chronicles a class, however, is its timeless message—if there is hope from above for a people who came as unraveled as the Jews, then there's hope for the likes of us.

BACKGROUND

INFLUENTIAL PEOPLE

Solomon, Israel's king and builder of the temple (1:1).

Hezekiah, a godly king who helps Judah survive Assyria (28:27).

Josiah, king and religious reformer (33:25).

THEME

Solomon is crowned king after his father, David, dies. He builds the

temple and rules the nation during a golden era of peace and prosperity. After Solomon dies, the northern tribes reject his son as king when the young ruler threatens to rule harshly. These tribes form a separate nation that is later wiped out by the Assyrians. Survivors are deported, and never return. After about 150 years, the southern nation of Judah is also destroyed, the people deported. These Jews, however, are eventually allowed to return home and rebuild their ruined nation.

POINTS OF INTEREST

The moral behind the history. As in 1 Chronicles, notice that the book is not just a reporting of the history. After all, the history books covering this era have already been written. Chronicles is history from a priest's point of view; it's an attempt to interpret what this history means to Jews who have come back from the exile in Babylon. The moral behind the history is that the Jewish people have a future with God.

TIMELINE

BIBLE EVENTS	Solomon becomes king 970 BC		The temple is finished 960 BC	Israel splits into two nations 930 BC	Northern nation of Israel destroyed 722 BC	Southern nation of Judah falls, with Jerusalem 586 BC
						Dates are approximate
	1100 BC	**1000 BC**	**900 BC**	**800 BC**	**700 BC**	**600 BC**　**500 BC**
WORLD EVENTS	Egypt splits in two 1085 BC	Assyrian empire begins expanding 883 BC		First recorded Olympic games in Greece 776 BC	Rome founded by King Romulus 753 BC	Chinese philosopher Confucius is born 551 BC

Lack of material about the northern nation. The writer almost ignores the northern Jewish nation of Israel, except to acknowledge the monumental events: their seceding from the union and their annihilation.

As far as the writer of Chronicles is concerned, the Lost Tribes of Israel, as they became known, no longer represent the true Israel. Their connection to the covenant of God has been severed. From the beginning of their secession, they worshiped idols. As a result, their nation is destroyed and their surviving citizens dragged into exile—never to return. Those left behind become assimilated into foreign cultures when they intermarry with Assyrian pioneers.

AUTHOR AND DATE

The writer is unnamed. Ancient Jewish tradition says Ezra wrote 1 and 2 Chronicles along with the books of Ezra and Nehemiah. Like the books of Samuel and Kings, the two books of Chronicles were originally one volume that was later separated so each could fit onto a single scroll.

Chronicles was probably written in the early 400s BC, roughly a hundred dred years after many of the Jews returned home from exile and rebuilt the temple.

The stories are carefully chosen to assure the Jews that they have a godly heritage and that their covenant with God is still in force. But the stories also warn them not to repeat the mistakes of the past.

ON LOCATION

Most of the story takes place in what is now Israel. The "golden age" of Solomon's reign ends with his death, and the nation quickly divides in two—Israel in the north and Judah in the south.

2 Chronicles Outline

Solomon asks God for wisdom (1:1–17).

Shortly after Solomon is crowned king of Israel, God speaks to him in a dream, as God has done to Abraham, Jacob, and Joseph in the past.

"Ask for whatever you want me to give you," God says.

"Now give me wisdom and knowledge," Solomon replies, "so I can lead these people in the right way, because no one can rule them without your help."

"You have not asked for wealth or riches or honor, or for the death of your enemies, or for a long life," God says. "But since you have asked for wisdom and knowledge to lead my people." For that, God decides to give Solomon the whole package. "I will give you wisdom and knowledge. I will also give you more wealth, riches, and honor than any king who has lived before you or any who will live after you."

Solomon builds the temple (3:1–17).

On a hilltop overlooking Jerusalem, Solomon builds the first of only three temples the Jews have ever had. He assembles a monumental work force of about 150,000.

Seven years later, the job is done. Israel has one of the most beautiful and expensive temples in the ancient world—a white limestone worship center adorned with golden ceilings, walls, and floors. This elegant temple is thirty yards long, ten yards wide, and fifteen yards high.

Only priests are allowed inside. In the back room, where only the high priest can go one day a year, sits the Ten Commandments inside a gold-covered chest—the ark of the covenant.

In this temple, Jews will offer sacrifices to God for 400 years—until Babylonian invaders destroy the building.

Israel splits into two nations (10:1–19).

By the time Solomon dies, the people of Israel are tired of paying heavy taxes to support the king's administration and his enormous household (he has a thousand wives). They're weary, too, of being drafted to build cities, forts, and palaces.

They ask King Rehoboam, Solomon's son and successor, for relief.

The rookie monarch responds harshly: "He forced you to work hard, but I will make you work even harder. My father beat you with whips, but I will beat you with whips that have sharp points."

The northern tribes secede, start their own nation that they call Israel, and appoint their own king. Only the tribe of Judah, in the south, remains loyal to the descendant of David.

Sennacherib lays siege to Jerusalem but suffers disaster (32:1–23).

The northern nation suffers under godless kings for about 200 years. In 722 BC, Assyria invades and annihilates the kingdom, taking the survivors away as captives.

Like other countries in the region, Judah has been paying taxes to Assyria. But when the Assyrian king dies many years later, Judah decides to rebel.

The army of Sennacherib, the new Assyrian king, captures one Judean city after another before laying siege to Jerusalem. Standing near the city walls, the Assyrian commander yells out his warnings. "No god of any nation or kingdom has been able to save his people from me or my ancestors. Your god is even less able to save you from me."

The Lord sends an angel to the camp of the Assyrians. The next morning the camp is full of dead bodies. Sennacherib returns to Assyria, disgraced.

Jerusalem falls to Babylon (36:9–21).

The southern nation of Judah outlasts its northern brother by about 150 years. This is because Judah has many godly rulers. But some kings lead the people astray.

"The LORD, the God of their ancestors, sent prophets again and again to warn his people, because he had pity on them and on his Temple. But they made fun of God's prophets and hated God's messages." God decides to punish Judah (36:15–16 NCV).

Judah's capital city of Jerusalem suffers a siege that lasts a year and a half, starving many to death. When soldiers of Babylonian King Nebuchadnezzar break through the city walls, they tear the city to the ground. Solomon's glorious temple, the symbol of Jewish national and religious identity, is looted and then destroyed.

Jewish citizens who survive the assault are deported to Babylon as captives.

The nation of Abraham and David no longer exists.

The king of Persia frees the Jews (36:22–23).

About fifty years later, the Persian empire swallows up Babylon, just as Babylon had earlier overpowered Assyria. The new ruler is Cyrus, who, prompted of God, uses the following decree: "The LORD, the God of heaven, has given me all the kingdoms of the earth, and he has appointed me to build a Temple for him at Jerusalem in Judah. Now may the LORD your God be with all of you who are his people."

With this promise, many Jews begin their long trek home.

POINTS TO CONSIDER

Cyrus's policy of releasing captives. Second Chronicles and Ezra both say that Persian King Cyrus let the conquered Jewish people return home to Judah so they could rebuild the temple. A 10-inch-long clay cylinder inscribed with cuneiform writing confirms that Cyrus had a policy of allowing defeated people to return to their homeland.

Known as the Cyrus Cylinder, the document quotes the king as saying he ordered the rebuilding of sacred sanctuaries in holy cities "on the other side of the Tigris . . . I also gathered all their former inhabitants and returned them to their homes."

No 70-year exile. Jeremiah, the prophet who witnessed the fall of Jerusalem in 586 BC, said the exile would last "seventy years" (Jeremiah 29:10). It lasted only about fifty, because Persian King Cyrus released the Jews to return home in about 538 BC, just after Persia defeated the Babylonians (2 Chronicles 36:22).

The 20-year difference remains a puzzle. But there are several possible solutions.

1. Jeremiah had in mind the first deportation of Judeans to Babylon. This happened in about 605 BC, nearly seventy years before Cyrus's decree.

2. The exile extended from the destruction of the temple in 586 BC until its rededication in 516 BC, seventy years.

3. Jeremiah didn't mean seventy literal years. He simply meant a long time. This number was used in this manner on other occasions in the Bible (2 Chronicles 36:21; Daniel 9:24).

━━━━━━━━ **FOR FURTHER STUDY** ━━━━━━━━

- The book of Ezra continues Israel's story, with the Jews returning from exile and starting the job of rebuilding the temple.

- For more details about the era covered in the book, read 1 and 2 Kings.

- To catch a glimpse of what Jesus had in mind when he spoke of "Solomon in all his glory" (Matthew 6:29), review chapter nine, about the queen of Sheba's reaction to Solomon.

Sur
Mo
Tue
We
Thu
Fri
Sat
Sur
Mo
Tue
We
Thu
Fri
Sat
Sur
Mo
Tue
We

Ezra

A SECOND GREAT ESCAPE

Out of the ashes and rock piles of the annihilated Jewish nation emerges a restored Israel.

It's a miracle, reminiscent of the Exodus. But instead of confronting a resistant, stubborn pharaoh who absolutely refuses to let the Jews go—as happened in the days of Moses—we read of three Persian kings who encourage the exiled Jews to return home—and give them gifts and tax breaks as added incentive.

So, nearly a thousand years after the great Exodus, the Jewish nation begins a second exodus. It takes place over several decades, as wave after wave of exiles pack up the families they raised in a foreign land and begin the long, nearly thousand-mile walk northward along the fertile Euphrates River valley in what is now Iraq, then south along the Mediterranean coast, through Lebanon and into Israel.

Pioneers had settled into the land during the Jewish exile. As far as they were concerned, the Jewish homecoming was an unwelcome intrusion.

But with the support of pagan kings, whom the Jews believed were instruments of God himself, they prevailed.

The result is a story that inspires courage and perseverance in anyone facing the intimidating challenge of rebuilding his or her life, home, or faith from the ground up.

BACKGROUND

INFLUENTIAL PEOPLE

Ezra, priest who preaches against Jews marrying non-Jews (7:1).
Cyrus, Persian king who frees Jewish exiles (1:1).

THEME

After fifty years of living in exile, the Jews are free to go home. Persia has defeated Babylon, and Persian King Cyrus has decreed that all Jewish captives may return to their homeland. Furthermore, the king encourages the Jews to rebuild their temple. He even returns the temple furnishings that the Babylonians had taken from Solomon's temple before they leveled it.

> ### DID YOU KNOW?
>
> • Though Ezra preaches a stern sermon against Jews marrying non-Jews, including people from Moab in what is now Jordan, King David's great-grandmother was Ruth, a Moabite. Though foreigners tended to lead Israel away from God and into idolatry, God accepted non-Jews who worshiped him, as Ruth did.

Many Jews return and begin to rebuild the temple in Jerusalem. The job grinds to a halt because of local opposition. But the work begins again, at the urging of the prophets Haggai and Zechariah, who arrive later. Jerusalem's second temple is completed in 516 BC, seventy years after Solomon's temple was destroyed.

Priest Ezra arrives and begins teaching the people from the laws of Moses. His sermons generate nationwide repentance and abruptly end the marriages of many Jewish men to non-Jewish women.

POINTS OF INTEREST

God working through people who don't worship him. Notice that the writer says the temple is rebuilt because of the support of three pagan

TIMELINE	BIBLE EVENTS					
		Jews exiled in Babylon ┌─586 BC	Persia defeats Babylon 539 BC──┐	First wave of exiles return to Jerusalem ┌──538 BC ┌─────┘	Temple rebuilt ┌──516 BC ┌──	Ezra arrives in Jerusalem 458 BC	
							Dates are approximate
		600 BC	**550 BC**	**500 BC**	**450 BC**	**400 BC**
	WORLD EVENTS	Chinese philosopher Confucius is born 551 BC─┘	Cyrus Cylinder confirms return of Jews └─539 BC	Persia conquers Egypt └─525 BC	Buddha, in India, preaches first sermon └─521 BC	Roman republic founded 509 BC	Greek Parthemon in Athens dedicated to goddess Athena 432 BC

kings. (1) Persian King Cyrus issues a formal decree inviting the Jews to return to Jerusalem and rebuild the temple. (2) Decades later, Persian King Darius brushes aside non-Jewish opposition to the continued rebuilding project and tells the Jews to finish their work. (3) Yet another Persian king, Artaxerxes, encourages Jews who have remained in Babylon to return home. He gives money and supplies to any who wish to go.

Copies of official letters. Most of the book, like most of the Old Testament, is written in Hebrew. But Ezra includes some official Persian messages written in Aramaic, the language used in the exile. One example is the memorandum by King Darius in 6:3–12. These are included to give evidence that the Jews had the king's approval to do what they were doing. Some Bible scholars a few decades ago thought these letters were made up. But recently discovered Persian documents reveal that the letters track with Persian policies, and are written in the language of the region, using the formal tone of royal decrees.

AUTHOR AND DATE

The writer is not named. Ancient Jewish tradition says the book was written by Ezra, a priest and teacher who returned from exile about sixty years after the temple was rebuilt. Many believe that the author of Ezra also wrote 1 and 2 Chronicles as well as Nehemiah.

In the earlier editions of the Bible, Ezra and Nehemiah were one book. The first known writer to speak of them as separate was Christian scholar Origen, who lived in the AD 200s. He called them 1 and 2 Ezra.

Like the two books of Chronicles, Ezra was probably written in the early 400s BC, roughly a hundred years after many of the Jews returned home from exile and rebuilt the temple.

The author wrote the book to preserve the good news about what happened when the Jewish exiles were finally freed to return home. What happened is that they began rebuilding their nation by rebuilding their temple. They also made a serious attempt to distance themselves from idol-worshiping foreigners, who could undermine their faith in God.

ON LOCATION

The story takes place in two locations: first in Babylon (modern Iraq), where exiled Jews prepare to return home, then in Jerusalem, where they begin rebuilding the temple. Zerubbabel and the first group of exiles returned to Jerusalem in 538–537 BC. The city walls were not rebuilt until Ezra and Nehemiah led a second wave of Jews back eighty years later.

EZRA OUTLINE

The Jews return from exile (chapters 1–2).

After Persia conquers the Babylonian Empire, Persian King Cyrus issues a magnanimous decree allowing the exiled Jews to return home. He is also encouraging them to rebuild their temple, and is ordering others to donate supplies. He's even returning the sacred furnishings of the temple, stolen by the Babylonians fifty years earlier.

Some 42,000 Jews decide to return, though perhaps most had been born in exile and had never seen the land God promised them.

Once they arrive in Jerusalem, they take up a collection among themselves to begin rebuilding the temple. They produce about half a ton of gold and nearly three tons of silver—a fraction of the nearly 4,000 tons of gold and 40,000 tons of silver that David set aside for the temple built by his son Solomon.

The Jews begin by rebuilding the altar, so they can quickly renew their practice of worshiping God by offering animal and crop sacrifices.

Rebuilding the temple (3:7–13; 6:13–18).

With the sacrificial system back in place, the Jews begin the arduous task of clearing away the rubble of the previous temple and laying the foundation for a new one. When the foundation is complete the people assemble for a service of praise to God. Many are shouting with glee and singing songs that King David had written hundreds of years earlier.

But woven in among the celebrants are disappointed old-timers crying out loud "who had seen the first Temple." Apparently they realize there's no hope of the new temple matching the glory of the first one. What they don't realize, however, is that though the new temple will be smaller and less elegant than Solomon's, it will last nearly a century longer—about 500 years.

The locals manage to get the work halted (4:1–24).

Pioneers who had settled in the land while the Jews were away had started worshiping God, but only as the local god of the land, not as the one and only God of creation. They offer to help rebuild the temple, but the Jews reject the offer.

Insulted, the locals begin causing trouble, threatening the workers and trying to sabotage their efforts. Then, when a new king comes to the Persian throne, they write him a letter and say the Jews are nearly done rebuilding the city. When that happens, the letter charges, "the Jews won't pay any kind of taxes, and there will be less money in your treasury." Furthermore, they add, the Jews have a history of rebelling—a fact they say the king can confirm by checking the records of his ancestors.

The king does check the records and finds that the Jews do have a long record of rebelling. So he orders the work stopped.

For about a decade, the Jews do nothing to rebuild the temple. Then, prodded by newly arrived prophets, they resume their work. When the locals again file their complaint to what has become yet another Persian king—Darius—the king digs out the original decree of Cyrus and allows the rebuilding to continue. About four years later, in 516 BC, the temple is completed and dedicated.

Ezra condemns the marriage of Jews to non-Jews (9:1–10:17).

Upon arriving in Jerusalem, Ezra discovers that many of the Jewish men have ignored the law against marrying non-Jewish women. Even some of the priests and temple workers have broken this law. Ezra goes to the temple courtyard and begins praying and weeping on behalf of the people. He knows that it was Israel's association with non-Jews that led to idolatry, which brought on the exile. And he fears that God will punish the new nation, just as he had punished Judah.

One by one, a crowd of worshipers gathers around him. When they hear his prayers, they begin weeping too. Within three days a vast assembly has gathered there. As rain pours onto the courtyard, Ezra stands to speak.

"You have been unfaithful and have married non-Jewish women. You have made Israel more guilty," he says. "Now, confess it to the Lord, the God of your ancestors. Do his will and separate yourselves from the people living around you and from your non-Jewish wives."

The assembly agrees.

POINTS TO CONSIDER

Cyrus on the record. Inscriptions from the time of Persian King Cyrus confirm that he was tolerant of the religion of conquered people and that he had a policy of allowing the captives to return home and resume their faith. He apparently hoped this would endear him both to the people and to their gods.

In one of his inscriptions he asks, "May all the gods whom I have resettled in their sacred cities ask daily Bel and Nebo [two Babylonian gods] for a long life for me and may they recommend me to Marduk [chief Babylonian god]."

Later Persian kings followed the same policy.

The numbers don't add up. Ezra 2 lists the exiles who returned, as does Nehemiah 7. Both say the total number of people is 42,360. But Ezra's list adds up to 29,818 and Nehemiah's list adds up to 31,089.

There's no clear explanation for the apparent discrepancy.

Perhaps they each took the time to record just a partial list, and added unnamed women to reach the total.

Many Bible scholars, however, think that scribes who preserved the book century after century by copying it from worn-out scrolls onto new scrolls made some mistakes with the numbers. Perhaps some of the numbers on the old scrolls were too hard to read.

Why abandon non-Jewish wives? At what appears to be the insistence of the people, Ezra preached a blunt sermon against Jews marrying non-Jews, then instructed all Jewish men with non-Jewish wives to divorce them and "send away all these women and their children" (10:3 NCV).

The Jews decided on this painful course of action because Ezra reminded them that God's law prohibited such marriages. The law, referring to the Canaanites, said, "Do not marry any of them, or let your daughters marry their sons, or let your sons marry their daughters. If you do, those people will turn your children away from me, to begin serving other gods. Then the Lord will be very angry with you, and he will quickly destroy you" (Deuteronomy 7:4 NCV).

Ezra reminded the former exiles that this is exactly what happened. And the Jews apparently concluded it could happen again. So rather than simply change in the future, they tried to undo the past.

This may not have been how God wanted them to handle it, but it certainly seems to be what they thought God expected of them. Perhaps they believed it was too risky to do anything less. After all, disobedience had recently wiped out their country. They didn't want any chance of a repeat performance.

For Further Study

- To continue the next stage of the story, read Nehemiah, which was originally the second half of the book of Ezra.

- To compare the second and less-magnificent temple of Ezra's day with the first one of Solomon's day, read 1 Chronicles 28–29 and 2 Chronicles 2–7.

- To read the words of prophets who inspired the exiles to rebuild the temple and recommit themselves to God, turn to the books of Haggai and Zechariah.

Sun
Mo
Tue
Wee
Thu
Frid
Satu
Sun
Mo
Tue
Wee
Thu
Frid
Satu
Sun
Mo
Tue
Wee

Nehemiah

REBUILDING JERUSALEM'S WALLS IN 52 DAYS

Sometimes, faith and prayer are not enough to get the job done. Sometimes it takes brains, muscle, and courage. Nehemiah needed it all.

He was a palace servant in Persia when he got word that the former Jewish exiles who had returned to Jerusalem were in trouble. They were both defenseless and disgraced because the city walls were broken and gates burned. Jerusalem held a sacred place in the heart of Jewish people because, since the time of King David nearly 600 years earlier, it had been the spiritual and political center of their nation. Jews without Jerusalem would have been like Americans without America, a congregation without a church, or a family without a home.

The very thought of the city remaining in disrepair plunged Nehemiah into four months of deep depression, which prayer and fasting could not cure. His only remedy was to tackle the insurmountable: to see to it that the walls and gates got repaired. Nehemiah, a palace cupbearer, was going to do this.

The reason the book is a classic is because Nehemiah, the cupbearer, actually did it, with God's help. Nehemiah talked the Persian king into supporting the project, convinced the apathetic Jews to embrace the work, and outsmarted the local opposition.

In accomplishing this, Nehemiah wrote himself into history as a model for tackling God's tough assignments.

FAMOUS LINES

- "Come, let's rebuild the wall of Jerusalem" (2:17 NCV). *Nehemiah's invitation to Jerusalem-area Jews.*

- "The people were willing to work" (4:6 NCV).

- "All the people held up their hands and said, 'Amen! Amen!'" (8:6 NCV). *How the Jews responded to hearing Ezra reading the laws God had given them through Moses.*

- "The joy of the Lord will make you strong" (8:10 NCV).

BACKGROUND

INFLUENTIAL PEOPLE

Nehemiah, Persian palace servant who oversees repair of Jerusalem's walls (1:1).

Sanballat, leader of opposition and possibly governor of Samaria (2:10).

Artaxerxes, Persian king who gives Nehemiah permission to repair the walls (1:1).

Ezra, priest who reads God's Law to the assembled people (8:1).

THEME

Nehemiah, a palace servant who guarantees that the Persian king's wine is not poisoned, is granted a leave of absence so he can oversee the repair of Jerusalem's walls. Despite opposition, and apparent plans to attack the workers and kill Nehemiah, the work is completed in stunningly short order: fifty-two days. Afterward, the priest Ezra reads from God's Law given through Moses, while the Jews listen. Ezra then leads the people in confessing their sins and pledging their allegiance to God.

POINTS OF INTEREST

Faith coupled with action. Notice that Nehemiah "puts feet to his prayers," as the old saying goes. When he hears that Jerusalem's walls need repair, he prays *and* asks the king for a leave of absence and supplies to do the work. Later, when Nehemiah hears of a possible attack against his workers at the walls, he reports, "But we prayed to our God and appointed guards to watch for them day and night" (4:9 NCV).

Leadership qualities. Notice the leadership skills of Nehemiah. He seeks the help of God. Once he realizes what he needs to do, he becomes strong-minded and decisive in pursuing his goal. He uses sound judgment to deal with the sly tactics of his enemies.

TIMELINE	BIBLE EVENTS						Dates are approximate
	Jews exiled in Babylon 586 BC	Persia defeats Babylon 539 BC	Jews start returning to Jerusalem 538 BC	Temple rebuilt 516 BC	Ezra arrives in Jerusalem 458 BC	Nehemiah arrives in Jerusalem 445 BC	
	600 BC	**550 BC**		**500 BC**			**450 BC**
	WORLD EVENTS						
	Chinese philosopher Confucius is born 551 BC	Persia conquers Egypt 525 BC	Buddha, in India, preaches first sermon 521 BC	Roman republic founded 509 BC	Greek philosopher Socrates is born 470 BC	30-year truce between Athens and Sparta begins 445 BC	

AUTHOR AND DATE

The story is compiled from the memoirs of Nehemiah, a Jewish servant in the palace of the Persian king. The book was originally combined with Ezra, so both books were likely written by the same person. Jewish tradition says the author was Ezra, a priest and teacher who returned from exile after the temple was rebuilt. Many believe that the author, whoever he was, also wrote 1 and 2 Chronicles, partly because all these books are set in the time just after the Jewish exile.

Like Ezra and the two books of Chronicles, Nehemiah was probably written in the early 400s BC, shortly after the incidents in the book occurred. This was roughly a hundred years after many of the Jews returned home from exile and rebuilt the temple.

The author preserved the

DID YOU KNOW?

• The Persian city of Susa, where Nehemiah got the disheartening news that Jerusalem's walls were broken, is the same setting for the story of Esther, the next book in the Bible.

• Women helped rebuild the wall (3:12).

• Once Nehemiah repaired the walls of Jerusalem, people apparently didn't want to live there. They had to "cast lots," an ancient version of drawing straws, to see who would be uprooted from the neighboring villages to live inside the city. One in ten drew the short straw and had to move to town. Perhaps one reason for their reluctance to move is that the walls had apparently been torn down only recently, in a previous attack. Maybe they feared an encore attack. Or perhaps they feared the regional leaders who had resisted the renovation project and threatened the workers.

memoirs of Nehemiah to show how this man of action and hero of the faith turned to God in times of need. The book also reminds the Jews not to become careless about honoring their commitment to God.

ON LOCATION

The story begins in Susa, winter capital of the Persian Empire, located along the border of Iraq and Iran. Here, the palace servant Nehemiah is granted a leave of absence to go to Jerusalem, where the rest of the story unfolds. By 500 BC, the Persians completely dominate the region (see map).

Nehemiah Outline

7:00

8:00

9:00

0:00

1:00

Noon

1:00

2:00

3:00

4:00

5:00

6:00

7:00

8:00

9:00

0:00

Nehemiah asks permission to rebuild the walls of Jerusalem (1:1–2:10).

Nehemiah, a Jew living in Persia and working as a palace servant, is paid a visit by his brother, Hanani, from Judah. Nehemiah asks how things are going back in Jerusalem. He's not prepared for what he hears.

"The wall around Jerusalem is broken down, and its gates have been burned," Hanani replies.

This is apparently the result of recent attacks, not of the Babylonian destruction about 150 years earlier. But whatever the cause, the word leaves Nehemiah deeply distressed.

"I sat down and cried," he says. Then for several days he goes without food and prays.

Nehemiah works as the king's cupbearer, the person responsible for making sure the wine is not poisoned. One day when he delivers some wine, the king notices how depressed Nehemiah looks. The king asks what's wrong.

"My face is sad," Nehemiah says, "because the city where my ancestors are buried lies in ruins, and its gates have been destroyed by fire."

The king asks how he can help.

Nehemiah has had about four months to think about this, since that's when he first got the news. He promptly asks for a leave of absence so he can rebuild the walls, and for letters to Persian governors in the west ordering that they supply him with timber for the job. The king grants these request and gives Nehemiah an armed escort of soldiers and cavalrymen.

Rebuilding the walls in fifty-two days (chapters 3–4; 6:15–16).

Several non-Jewish leaders in the area bitterly oppose the renovation project. Perhaps they feel threatened by the proposed fortification. One man, Sanballat, openly ridicules the effort. "What are these weak Jews doing?" he asks. "If a fox climbed up on the stone wall they are building, it would break it down."

When Nehemiah hears that an attack may be in the works, he posts armed guards around the wall and tells all the haulers to keep one hand free to grab a weapon.

As the work speeds on, Sanballat and some of his associates apparently try to set a trap for Nehemiah. They try to schedule a meeting with him. Four times. Each time he refuses.

"But they were planning to harm me," Nehemiah says. "So I sent messengers to them with this answer: 'I am doing a great work, and I can't come down. I don't want the work to stop while I leave to meet you' " (6:2–3 NCV).

Fifty-two days after the repair work begins, it ends—completed. The people in the surrounding nations are astounded. They're also afraid because they realize that since the job got done so quickly, God must be on their side.

Ezra reads the Law (8:1–18).

After the walls are repaired, the Jews meet by one of the city gates and listen to Ezra read some of the laws God gave through Moses. He reads from dawn until noon.

What he reads are possibly selections from the first five books in the Bible, or perhaps Deuteronomy, which is a summary of the Law.

During or after this reading, teachers of the Law walk among the crowd, "explaining the meaning of what Ezra had read." Perhaps they are translating the Law from Hebrew, in which it is written, to Aramaic, the language the Jews learned in exile. Or maybe they are explaining how the people need to apply the Law in their present circumstances, much like Bible teachers and ministers do today.

Religious reform begins (13:4–22).

After the people have heard the Law, Nehemiah begins making changes to bring the community in line with the Law. He notices that merchants are selling their produce on the Sabbath, so he orders the newly built gates closed each Sabbath day—from sundown on Friday until sundown on Saturday.

Nehemiah also observes that the temple is being neglected because temple assistants are working on farms instead. They're at their farms because Jews are not paying the temple tithe, which is to support the temple workers. So Nehemiah tells everyone to start living up to their obligations according to the Law. People from the tribe of Levi are to work in the temple, and Jews throughout the region are to support the Levites by bringing a tenth of their crops to the temple storeroom.

Nehemiah also convinces the people to make a solemn vow not to let their sons and daughters marry idol-worshiping foreigners.

The memoirs of Nehemiah conclude with this request: "Remember me, my God, for this. Do not ignore my love for the Temple and its service."

POINTS TO CONSIDER

Three people on record. Ancient records outside of the Bible identify two of Nehemiah's opponents—Sanballat and Tobiah—as well as Nehemiah's brother, Hanani.

A letter to the Persian-appointed governor of Judah in the 400s BC says Sanballat was governor of Samaria, north of Jerusalem. He led the opposition to the rebuilding of Jerusalem's walls.

Another reference in the same group of documents speak of Hananiah, probably Nehemiah's brother whom Nehemiah called by the shortened nickname Hanani. Hananiah is described as head of Jewish affairs in Jerusalem. The book of Nehemiah says that Hanani of Judah visited the Persian winter capital of Susa and brought news of Jerusalem's broken walls. Perhaps he was there on official business instead of simply visiting his brother.

Several records tell about an important Tobiah family with a genealogy that extends from perhaps 590 BC to 200 BC. One record, written in the 500s BC and found about twenty-five miles from Jerusalem, speaks of a Tobiah as the servant of a king. Other records place some Tobiahs in what is now Jordan, where the Tobiah of Nehemiah's day lived (2:10).

Why did the king give so much help to a mere "cupbearer"? The Bible describes Nehemiah as a cupbearer, the person who brings the king his wine. Yet the king quickly agrees to give Nehemiah: an extended leave of absence, supplies to rebuild the Jerusalem walls and gates, timber to build Nehemiah a house in Jerusalem, and an armed entourage of soldiers and cavalry.

Cupbearers in ancient times often did more than bring the king his wine and taste it to make sure it wasn't poisoned. Many became trusted confidants of the king and wielded considerable influence. Some held other jobs as well. According to Tobit, part of an ancient collection of books known as the Apocrypha, the cupbearer for Esarhaddon, a king of Assyria, was the number two man in the empire: "chief cupbearer, keeper of the signet [royal seal to stamp official documents], and in charge of administrations of the accounts" (Tobit 1:22, NRSV).

FOR FURTHER STUDY

- For the other half of what was originally one book, read Ezra.

- For another book that speaks of faith in action, read James. He says, "In the same way, faith by itself—that does nothing—is dead" (James 2:17 NCV).

Sun
Mon
Tues
Wed
Thu
Frid
Satu
Sun
Mon
Tues
Wed
Thu
Frid
Satu
Sun
Mon
Tues
Wed

Esther

The Queen Who Stops a Holocaust

Esther is one of the best-written short stories in all of Hebrew literature. In fact, it's so well written that some people think it's fiction—just too good to be true.

You've got a queen who refuses to make a command appearance before the king, so the king commands her never to appear before him again. Divorce, Persian style.

You've got a beautiful Jewish maiden who becomes queen and puts her life on the line to save her race from a holocaust.

And you've got a deliciously evil villain, Haman, a high Persian official who seethes with vengeance when a lower official, Mordecai, refuses to bow before him. Haman plots to hang Mordecai on 75-foot-high gallows and slaughter his entire race: the Jews. Instead, Haman winds up paying homage to Mordecai by holding the reins of his horse and walking him

through the capital while Mordecai wears the king's robe and Haman shouts, "This is what is done for the man whom the king wants to honor" (6:11 NCV). If Esther had a laugh track, the volume would be turned up full during this scene.

Later, Haman is hanged from the gallows he built for Mordecai. Happy ending.

Behind this powerful story, which churns up a full platter of emotions from glee to fear, there's an equally powerful message: God looks after His people.

BACKGROUND

INFLUENTIAL PEOPLE

Esther, Jewish queen of Persia who saves the Jews from slaughter (2:7).

Mordecai, Esther's cousin, Persian official who prods her to risk helping the Jews (2:5).

Haman, Persian high official who plots to kill the Jews (3:1).

Xerxes, king of Persia (1:1).

THEME

Persian King Xerxes divorces his queen. To replace her, he chooses a young Jewish orphan named Esther, raised by her cousin Mordecai, a palace official. Mordecai refuses to bow in honor of a higher official, Haman. In retaliation, Haman hatches a scheme to kill all the Jews in the empire. Without identifying who the "troublesome" people are, Haman manages to talk the king into signing an irrevocable order permitting the citizens to slaughter the Jews on a set day. Esther appeals to the king, who is surprised to hear that Haman has targeted the Jews and that Esther is a Jew. He executes Haman, then issues a second order allowing the Jews to defend themselves. The Jews unite, and with the help of Persian nobles defeat their enemies.

DID YOU KNOW?

• Each spring, usually about a month before Passover, Jews celebrate Esther's saving the Jews from a massacre. They do this in the joyous spirit of a Mardi Gras, and call the event Purim (POR-im). Many dress in costumes (especially the children), put on plays, share large meals with family and friends, and give gifts to friends and the poor. *Purim* is an ancient word for the lots, or dice, that Haman used to select which day he would slaughter the Jews.

• When the Jews read aloud the story of Esther during Purim, they boo Haman by stomping, jeering, and rattling noisemakers every time his name appears. This drowns out the sound of his name.

		Xerxes begins 21-year reign as Persian king 486 BC	Esther becomes queen of Persia 479 BC	Slaughter of Jews scheduled to take place 473 BC	
TIMELINE	**BIBLE EVENTS**				Dates are approximate
		500 BC	**450 BC**	**400 BC**	**350 BC**	**300 BC**
	WORLD EVENTS	Persian King Darius builds a canal between the Nile and Gulf of Suez 500 BC	Greeks defeat Persian fleet 480 BC	Hippocrates, the father of medicine, is born 460 BC	Persia falls to Alexander the Great of Greece 332 BC

POINTS OF INTEREST

God. You'll not find him mentioned by name. But if you look closely, you'll see him standing in the wings, directing the action. You'll recognize his work in several places, including in the long string of "coincidences" that end up saving the Jews from mass slaughter.

AUTHOR AND DATE

The writer is unnamed. But the writer's familiarity with the Jewish festival of Purim and with the fact that the Jews had a sense of national identity suggests he was a Jew. His insight into Persian customs, along with the absence of any reference to the Jewish homeland, suggests he lived in Persia—perhaps in the city of Susa, where the story takes place. Among the many possible authors are Mordecai, Ezra, and Nehemiah.

King Xerxes, known also by the Hebrew version of his name, Ahasuerus, ruled Persia from 486 to 465 BC, after his father, Darius. Esther was written sometime during or after this, perhaps near the end of his reign, in the waning years of the Persian Empire.

The book of Esther preserves the marvelous story of how the Jews are delivered from an empire-wide slaughter. It also reveals the reason behind the Jewish celebration of Purim, which Jews still observe.

ON LOCATION

The story takes place in the Persian city of Susa, along today's border of Iraq and Iran, about 100 miles north of the Persian Gulf. The map shows the Persian Empire in 500 BC, when it included Israel.

ESTHER OUTLINE

Esther, a Jew, becomes queen of Persia (1:10–2:20).

At the end of a weeklong banquet, when Persian King Xerxes is "very happy, because he had been drinking much wine," he sends for his queen. He wants her to wear her crown and parade before the male guests so they can all see how beautiful she is.

Queen Vashti, however, is entertaining the female guests at a dinner party. She refuses the command appearance. The king becomes so angry that he strips Vashti of her title and forbids her to ever show her face before him again.

Next, he assigns officials in each of his provinces to search for "beautiful young girls" and bring them to the royal harem. Among these women is a young Jew named Esther. She is an orphan raised by her cousin Mordecai, a Persian official. Like other candidates for the grand title of queen, Esther is led through a one-year regiment of beauty treatments to prepare her to meet King Xerxes. Each woman who spends the night with the king becomes one of his concubines, or secondary wives. But only one will be favored with the title of queen.

Four years after the search began, it is Esther's turn to appear before the king. He falls in love with her. At a dinner party in her honor, and before the leaders of the empire, Xerxes places a crown on her head.

Mordecai won't bow to Haman (3:1–15).

Sometime later, the king appoints his second-in-command, Haman, a descendant of the Amalakites, who were bitter enemies of Israelite settlers in the Promised Land. Though the king orders everyone to bow when Haman walks by, Mordecai refuses. And when Mordecai's colleagues ask why, he responds simply, "Because I am a Jew."

Some officials report this to Haman. He becomes so incensed and decides to wipe out all the Jews in the empire. He meets with the king and tells him, "There is a certain group of people scattered among the other people in all the states of your kingdom. Their customs are different from those of all the other people, and they do not obey the king's laws. It is not right for you to allow them to continue living in your kingdom. If it pleases the king, let an order be given to destroy those people."

To prod the king in the right direction, Haman reminds them that property confiscated from the victims will boost the royal treasury.

Apparently without even asking who these people are, the king approves the plan.

Haman sets the date for the slaughter—eleven months ahead. Meanwhile, he sends couriers throughout the empire to deliver a message translated into every known language. The message says that on the 13th day of Adar (March 7, 473 BC) "to destroy, kill, and completely wipe out all the Jewish people." That meant young and old, women and little children, too.

Esther asks the king to spare her people from a holocaust (4:8–5:8; 7:1–10).

When Mordecai hears about the letter, he asks Esther to go to the king and beg him to have mercy on her people. At this point, the king doesn't seem to know that his ruling is against the Jews, or that Esther is a Jew.

Esther refuses, remind her cousin of the Persian law that allows the king to execute anyone who visits him uninvited.

Mordecai's reply is blunt. "Just because you live in the king's palace, don't think that out of all the Jewish people you alone will escape. If you keep quiet at this time, someone else will help and save the Jewish people, but you and your father's family will all die. And who knows, you may have been chosen queen for just such a time as this" (4:13–14 NCV).

Esther agrees to intercede, on the condition that Mordecai has all the Jews in the city go without eating and drinking for three days, on her behalf. Afterward, Esther goes to the king. Fortunately, he greets her warmly. She invites him to bring Haman to a dinner that evening. There, building the king's anticipation for what she *really* wants, she invites the men to dinner the following day.

By the second meal, Haman is feeling higher and mightier than usual—proud that he has caught the queen's eye. Then Esther tells the king that Haman's plot is against the Jews, which means that both she and Mordecai could die in the slaughter. The king is furious. Adding to his anger is that the night before he had been reminded that Mordecai once warned him of an assassination plot and was never rewarded.

The king orders Haman hanged and promotes Mordecai to fill the vacancy.

The Jews celebrate a holocaust missed (9:1–32).

King Xerxes says that his decree against the Jews, like any other decree bearing his seal, cannot be revoked. But he writes a second irrevocable decree allowing the Jews to assemble into a fighting force and defend themselves. These orders are delivered throughout the empire on swift horses, bred for the king.

When the day of fighting arrives, on the thirteenth of the Jewish month of Adar, Persian nobles and governors lend their support to the Jews. The fighting extends into a second day, with the Jewish forces killing 75,000 throughout the empire. On the third day, the fifteenth day of Adar, the Jews celebrate their survival and victory with a feast.

Every springtime, Jews memorialize the event in a joyful celebration called Purim.

=== POINTS TO CONSIDER ===

The Persian palace uncovered. The Persian palace of Susa, where Esther lived, has been unearthed by archaeologists. It covered more than twelve acres—nearly as big as Jerusalem in King David's day, and about half as big as the inside of a large shopping mall today. The palace had living quarters, along with a smaller section for the king and other officials to conduct the business of the empire. The palace included courtyard gardens, like the one that the Bible says King Xerxes stormed off to when he learned of Haman's plot against the Jews.

No mention of God. Like the Song of Solomon, there is absolutely no mention of God in the book of Esther. Nor is there any mention of prayer, sacrifice, or any other worship practices. The book seems thoroughly secular, and not at all religious.

For this reason, it was one of the last books approved into Hebrew and Christian Bibles. In fact, the most ancient library of Old Testament books, the Dead Sea Scrolls, which date back to the third century BC, contains at least fragments from every book of the Old Testament *except* Esther.

Yet the book was eventually added to the Bible because on closer examination it was judged as thoroughly religious. Though God does not get the spotlight or his name added to the credits, He is directing the events through an incredible string of "coincidences." Esther, a Jew, finds herself catapulted into a position to help the Jews. Mordecai overhears an assassination plot against the king and reports it, endearing himself to the king. The king reads of this and learns he never rewarded Mordecai—and he discovers this the very night before he finds out that Haman has plotted to kill Mordecai and all other Jews.

There are other clues to the religious nature of the book. For example, though Esther doesn't ask the people to pray for her, she does ask them to fast. And Mordecai tells Esther that if she doesn't take a stand for her people "someone else will help" (4:14 NCV)—an apparent reference to the way God has helped the Jews in the past.

Why the writer disguises the religious nature of the book remains a mystery. Perhaps he wanted to draw in secular readers and help them reach their own conclusion that the Jews had help from above.

Fact or Fiction? Some critics charge that Esther is a fictional story. The captivating writing technique seems to portray a story too good to be true. There's the exotic setting, fast-paced action, humor, and sudden reversals with the high and mighty ending up down and dead. There's also the scrumptious irony, balanced events (feasts mingled with fasting), and the happy ending.

In addition, ancient records say nothing of a Queen Esther or Vashti. Historians of Greece, the nation that defeated Xerxes' forces in battle and later conquered Persia, say his queen was Amestris. But Amestris may have been but one of several queens.

The story's accurate reporting of customs and careful attention to names—even of the supporting characters—suggests that the events really did happen. The book also starts the way most ancient histories start, and ends the way they end—even citing sources.

FOR FURTHER STUDY

- For insight into what happens to people like Haman, who "make useless plans" against God and his people, read Psalm 2.

- For another story about a strong-minded woman who did the right thing, read the short book of Ruth, another excellent example of the best in Hebrew literature.

WHY GOOD PEOPLE SUFFER

This is not the story of a man suffering silently, patiently in the night. This is the story of a man yelling at God—a man who wants answers now.

This man is Job. And he has just lost nearly everything he has spent his life working for: his riches, his children, his health.

He has just one quick question for the Creator and Sustainer of the universe.

It's the same question a mother asks after watching her kindergarten son get crushed beneath the wheels of a school bus. It's the question an aging grandfather asks when he finds out he has cancer. It's the question a middle-aged father asks after learning he's been laid off from the company he has dedicated himself to for the past twenty-five years.

Why?

For Job, self-perceived wise men answer the question. But they answer it wrong.

Then for Job, and for us, God answers the question. It's not a complete answer. But it was complete enough for Job.

FAMOUS LINES

• "I was naked when I was born and I will be naked when I die" (1:21 NCV). *Job's reaction after hearing his children have been killed in a windstorm and his vast flocks stolen by raiders.*

• "I have escaped by the skin of my teeth" (19:20 NCV). *Job's analysis of how close he has come to dying.*

BACKGROUND

INFLUENTIAL PEOPLE

Job, a wealthy man who loses his riches, children, and health (1:1).

Eliphaz, the first of three of Job's friends who try to convince him that he sinned (2:11).

Bildad, the second of Job's friends to speak (2:11).

Zophar, the third friend to speak (2:11).

Elihu, a bystander who argues with Job and his friends (32:2).

Job's wife, who tells her husband to curse God and die, so the suffering will end (2:9).

THEME

Job is a rich man who owns thousands of sheep, camels, cattle, and donkeys. He's also blessed with a large family of ten children. But he loses them all one tragic day. Raiders take his herds and kill his servants. A windstorm crushes a house where his children are eating. Then Job breaks out with skin ulcers all over his body. Friends come to comfort him, but add to his misery by insisting he must have committed some horrible sin for which God is punishing him. God sets the record straight and ends Job's torment.

POINTS OF INTEREST

The format. As a kind of road map to the book, notice the three cycles of debates between Job and his three friends. Each cycle runs like this: friend #1 talks, Job replies, friend #2, Job, friend #3, Job. (The one exception comes at the end of the third cycle, when friend #3 doesn't speak. Instead, a bystander adds his thoughts about the matter.) This routine takes up most of the book.

Job's persistence that he is innocent. Like many others in his day, Job

TIMELINE	BIBLE EVENTS		The suffering of Job 2000 BC		
					Dates are approximate
		2500 BC	**2000 BC**	**1500 BC**	**1000 BC**
	WORLD EVENTS	Most pyramids completed 2200 BC	Stonehenge built in England 2000 BC		Three Egyptian stories similar to Job's 1900 BC

believes that health and wealth are signs of God's blessings—disease and poverty are signs of sin. Because Job knows he has done nothing to deserve the horror that has invaded his life, he is left wondering why God is putting him through all this. Bitterness begins to engulf him as he sarcastically complains, "God destroys both the innocent and the guilty. If the whip brings sudden death, God will laugh at the suffering of the innocent" (9:22–23 NCV).

AUTHOR AND DATE

The writer is unknown, though he was probably an Israelite. The writer used the Hebrew name for God, *Yahweh,* a term sometimes translated Jehovah or the Lord.

The story seems to be set sometime in the era of Israel's founding fathers: Abraham, Isaac, and Jacob. Several clues suggest this. As was common in Abraham's day, his wealth was measured by his herds, and he acted as the priest for his family by offering sacrifices to God. In addition, he was raided by Sabeans and Chaldeans, who lived in patriarchal times.

It's uncertain when the story

DID YOU KNOW?

• Aunt Jemima owes her name to Job's oldest daughter, of his second-chance family (42:14).

• "Patient as Job" is a phrase that comes from the story of Job's suffering. Actually, he isn't all that patient. "How I wish that I might have what I ask for," he moans. "There is nothing to hope for so why should I be patient?" (6:8, 11 NCV). "Tenacious as Job" is a better match. In spite of the catastrophes that hit him, and his three nagging friends who insist he's to blame, Job won't budge from his plea of innocence or his faith in God.

• There aren't a lot of references to life after death in the Old Testament. But Job speaks so clearly of a resurrection that he sounds like a New Testament apostle: "I know that my Defender lives and in the end he will stand upon the earth. Even after my skin has been destroyed, in my flesh I will see God. I will see him myself; I will see him with my very own eyes. How my heart wants that to happen!" (19:25–27 NCV)

• The book of Job contains more rare and archaic words than any other book in the Bible. This suggests it was written a long time ago. It has also made the book hard to translate.

was written. It may have been passed down by word of mouth for generations before being committed to writing in the 900s BC. That was the golden age of Israel's wisdom literature, which grew out of the wisdom of King Solomon. Jewish writings from the second century BC speak about the book of Job, showing that it was well respected by then.

Though the writer and the date of the writing remain a mystery, the purpose of the book is clear. It corrects the ancient misunderstanding that suffering is God's punishment. The fact is, as the book of Job dramatically shows, good people are not exempt from suffering.

ON LOCATION

The story takes place in the mysterious homeland of Job, "land of Uz" (1:1 NCV). No one knows where that is. Some guess that it was in Edom, a region southeast of Canaan, along the border of what is now Israel and Jordan. Two clues suggest this: one of Job's friends comes from Teman, and Edomite city; also, Edomites were famous in ancient times for their wisdom—and the book of Job is considered wisdom literature, which seeks answers to practical and philosophical questions of life.

JOB OUTLINE

A desert windstorm kills Job's children (1:13–22).

Job is a godly man who lives near the desert, perhaps east of what is now Israel. He is rich in herds—and servants to tend them. He is also rich in children, with seven sons and three daughters.

Satan, however, decides to test Job's loyalty to God. And God allows the test.

Marauders kill the herdsmen and then steal Job's cattle, donkeys, and camels. A mysterious fire kills the sheep and their shepherds. And a windstorm crushes the home of his oldest son, where all the children have gathered for a meal.

Grief-stricken at the news, Job tears his robe and shaves his head: "The LORD gave these things to me, and he has taken them away. Praise the name of the LORD" (1:21 NCV).

Job suffers with a painful skin disease (2:1–10).

With his wealth and children gone, Job now suffers a third great loss; his health. He becomes infected with a painful skin disease that covers his body with open, festering sores. We can only guess what kind of disease it is: smallpox, chronic eczema, ulcerous boils. What ever it is, it's agonizing.

Job's wife can't stand to see him suffer. "Why are you trying to stay innocent?" she asks. "Curse God and die!" (2:9 NCV).

Job absolutely refuses. "You are talking like a foolish woman," he replies. "Should we take only good things from God and not trouble?"

Three friends come to comfort Job (2:11–13).

Three of Job's friends come and sit silently with him for seven days. Finally Job breaks the silence: "Why was I not buried like a child born dead, like a baby who never saw the light of day?" (3:16 NCV)

One by one, his friends respond. They are certain Job has sinned, and he won't find relief until he repents.

"I have noticed," Eliphas says, "that people who plow evil and plant trouble, harvest it" (4:8 NCV). Bildad asks Job, "Why don't you turn to him and start living right? Then he will decide to rescue and restore you"

(8:5 NCV). Zophar then says to this tormented man who has lost nearly everything, "God has punished you less than you deserve" (11:6 NCV).

In the grueling debate that follows, Job maintains his innocence and retaliates, "You are all painful comforters!" (16:2 NCV). Eventually he turns his attack heavenward: "God has made my name a curse word; people spit in my face" (17:6 NCV).

The Lord answers Job (chapters 38:1–42:6).

A fourth and younger man named Elihu joins the gathering. He takes on the whole group. He's angry with Job for blaming God instead of himself. And he's angry at the three men for not being able to prove Job wrong.

As the youngster drones on, a storm begins rolling in. Suddenly, from out of this storm, God speaks to Job, raising questions no human can answer.

"Where were you when I made the earth's foundation?" (38:4 NCV).

"What is the path to light's home and where does darkness live?" (38:19 NCV).

God's point is clear: there are some things that human beings can't understand. And—sometimes—suffering is one of them.

"Will the person who argues with the Almighty correct him? Let the person who accuses God answer him," God accuses Job. "Would you say that I am unfair? Would you blame me to make yourself look right?" (40:8 NCV).

Job cowers, thoroughly embarrassed. "Surely I spoke of things I did not understand; I talked of things too wonderful for me to know," he admits (42:3 NCV).

Job receives a new family and doubled wealth (42:7–17).

God now turns his attention to Job's friends. "I am angry with you," God says, "because you have not said what is right about me." Then he orders these men to go to Job—the man they had been wrongly accusing—and ask him to pray for them. Otherwise, God warns, he will punish them for their foolishness.

Each man expresses his sorrow to Job and gives him gifts of gold and silver.

In time, Job raises ten more children and produces herds double the

size of those he had before. He lives long enough to see his great-grand-
children have children of their own.

Sun
Mo
Tue
We
Thu
Frid
Satu
Sun
Mo
Tue
We
Thu
Fric
Satu
Sur
Mo
Tue
We

═══ POINTS TO CONSIDER ═══

Ancient stories much like Job's. There are many ancient stories similar to Job's, some written in the time of Abraham, about 2000 BC. But one story is especially similar: *Man and His God,* written in the 1700s BC. It tells of a Job-like man who complains to a god called the "righteous shepherd." The man laments that the god has become angry with him and has allowed enemies to harass him. Then, appealing to the god like son to a father, the suffering man asks how long the god will let this go on. Eventually, this man is delivered from his torment and praises his god.

The story is so much like Job's that the man, who lived in Sumer in what is now southern Iraq, is known as the Sumerian Job.

Stories such as these, along with the mention of Job in other ancient Middle Eastern documents, suggest that Job and his story were widely known.

Surprising scientific insights. Though Job was written perhaps 2,500 years before Columbus sailed the ocean blue, the book doesn't speak of a flat earth. It says God "stretches the northern sky out over empty space" (26:7).

The book also shows that the writer knows a thing or two about the hydrological cycle. "He evaporates the drops of water from the earth and turns them into rain" (36:27–28).

It's a fictional collection of poetry. The book begins and ends with material written in story form. Sandwiched in between is poetry. This had led many to conclude that the events described in the book never happened—that Job is a collection of poems that deal with suffering and that were tied together by the prose introduction and conclusion.

Furthermore, they argue, the prose makes Job out to be a man patiently enduring his calamities, while the poetry shows him challenging God. So the fit seems artificial.

The writing structure, however—poetry surrounded by prose—has shown up in other ancient accounts. And elsewhere the Bible mixes poetry and prose, as when Moses and Miriam sing after the crossing of the Red Sea.

As for the prose and poetry sections revealing a split-personality Job, these two sections present Job at different stages in his struggle.

7:00

8:00

9:00

0:00

1:00

oon

1:00

2:00

3:00

4:00

5:00

6:00

7:00

8:00

9:00

0:00

=== **FOR FURTHER STUDY** ===

- For more evidence that people in Bible times associated suffering with sin, read the story of Jesus healing the blind beggar. The disciples asked Jesus if the beggar was suffering because of his own sins or the sins of his parents. "Neither," said Jesus. "This man was born blind so that God's power could be shown in him" (John 9:3 NCV).

- To read about another man confronting God with tough questions about suffering, read the short book of Habakkuk. There, the prophet Habakkuk asked God why he was going to punish the unrighteous Jews by sending an invasion of the even more unrighteous Babylonians.

- For songs lamenting that God seems to be hiding, read Psalms 10 and 22.

Psalms

SONGS THE ISRAELITES SING

You hear the words as someone reads to a dying loved one, or perhaps as a minister comforts the family beside the grave:

The LORD is my shepherd; I shall not want.
He maketh me to lie down in green pastures: he leadeth me beside the still waters.
He restoreth my soul: he leadeth me in the paths of righteousness for his name's sake.
Yea, though I walk through the valley of the shadow of death, I will fear no evil: for thou art with me (Psalm 23:1–4 KJV).

The choice of words, the images conveyed, even the steady rhythmic pace, seem to generate a consoling, healing power.

FAMOUS LINES

• "Shout to the LORD, all the earth" (100:1 NCV).

• "Your word is like a lamp for my feet and a light for my path" (119:105 NCV).

Psalms is a songbook, direct from the heart of poets who experience the full range of life's sorrow and joy. These inspired writers express in words what the rest of us can only feel. Yet when we read these words of anger, sadness, hope, and praise, they become our own, for they reflect our deepest, and sometimes most private, emotions.

BACKGROUND

INFLUENTIAL PEOPLE

David, the source or inspiration behind nearly half the 150 psalms (18:50).

THEME

This is a collection of songs written over many centuries. There is no plot. There are, however, themes within each song. Surprisingly, the most common songs are those you'd have to file under "complaint." But there are many songs about praise as well, which is why ancient Jews called the book *Tehillim,* meaning "praises."

POINTS OF INTEREST

Repeated thoughts, not sounds. Hebrew poetry doesn't have rhyme or rhythm. Its unique characteristic is repetition of thought, called parallelism. The poet will make a statement in one line, then in a second and perhaps a third line he'll repeat the thought, extend it, or contrast it with an opposite idea. In some Bible translations, the second and third ideas are indented from the first one.

From David's prayer of confession after committing adultery with Bathsheba, here's an example of the second line repeating the thought of the first one:

Take away my sin, and I will be clean.
Wash me, and I will be whiter than snow (51:7 NCV).

Radically different topics. If someone today published a collection of favorite Christian songs, you could expect that the songs would cover a wide range of topics. So does the ancient collection known as Psalms. You'll find songs praising God for his gorgeous universe. And you'll find songs for weddings, worship services, pilgrimages to Jerusalem, the crowning of a king, and soldiers on the march—to name a few.

TIMELINE	BIBLE EVENTS						
	Moses writes Psalm 90 ┌--1440 BC		David writes many songs later preserved in Psalms 1000 BC -----┐		Psalm 137 written in Babylon 550 BC -----┐	Compilation of Psalms is completed 300 BC ----┐	
	1500 BC	**1300 BC**	**1100 BC**	**900 BC**	**700 BC**	**500 BC**	**300 BC**
	WORLD EVENTS Hindu scriptures (Vedas) begin └--1500 BC	China develops mouth organ 1100 BC ---┘		Lyre players painted on Philistine jar └--1000 BC	Plato starts the Academy at Athens, later becoming world's first university 387 BC ----------------┘		Dates are approximate

AUTHOR AND DATE

The book attributes seventy-three songs to David. But the original Hebrew phrase can mean "by David," "dedicated to David," or "in the style of David." Other songs are attributed to Solomon, Moses, and Asaph, chief musician during the reign of David and perhaps Solomon. Some songs remain anonymous.

The psalms were written throughout Israel's history, some from the time of Moses in about 1440 BC, others from the time of King David in about 1000 BC, and others after Babylon defeated the Jewish nation and exiled many of the citizens in 586 BC.

The book exists to give people the words to express their deepest spiritual feelings, privately or in group worship.

DID YOU KNOW?

- The shortest chapter in the Bible, also the middle chapter, is Psalm 117. It has only two verses.

- The longest chapter in the Bible is Psalm 119, with a whopping 176 verses. This poem is so long because it's an acrostic built on the twenty-two letters of the Hebrew alphabet. The poem has 22 eight-verse sections. The first section starts with the first Hebrew letter, *Aleph*. The second section starts with the next letter, *Beth*. And on it goes, clear through the alphabet. Twenty-two times eight equal 176.

- The middle verse in the Bible is this one:
  It is better to trust the Lord than to trust people (118:8 NCV).
- "The Bug Bible," as it became known, was an early English translation of Scripture. It earned its nickname because of a peculiar translation from Psalms. Instead of telling people there's no need to fear the "terror by night" (KJV), it calmed them regarding "bugs by night" (91:5).

- "The Printer's Bible," another early English translation, incorrectly reads, "Printers have persecuted me without a cause." Actually, "princes" were doing the persecuting (119:161).

- Psalms is not only a collection of songs, but it's a collection of five collections. There are five songbooks in Psalms: Book 1 (chapters 1–41), Book 2 (42–72), Book 3 (73–89), Book 4 (90–106), Book 5 (107–150).

ON LOCATION

The songs are set throughout the Middle East, from the Sinai desert where Moses leads the Hebrews, to Israel where David builds a powerful Jewish nation, to Babylon, where the defeated Jews spend 150 years in exile. The composition of the psalms stretched over 1,000 miles (from Egypt to Babylon) and 1,000 years (from the Exodus to the Exile).

PSALMS OUTLINE

The majesty of God's creation (8:1–9).

In a song attributed to David, the onetime shepherd boy who spent a lot of time outdoors, Psalm 8 praises God for creation and expresses dismay that he would entrust such majesty to human beings.

I look at your heavens, which you made with your fingers.
I see the moon and stars, which you created.
Then I ask, "But why are people even important to you?
Why do you take care of human beings?"

LORD *our Lord,*
your name is the most wonderful name in all the earth!
(8:3–4, 9)

The Lord, our shepherd and protector (23:1–6).

In a song expressing deep trust in God—a song that is perhaps the most loved in all of literature—David compares God to a shepherd who protects his flock.

The LORD is my shepherd; I have everything I need.
He lets me rest in green pastures.
He leads me to calm water.
He gives me new strength.
He leads me on paths that are right
for the good of his name.
Even if I walk through a very dark valley,
I will not be afraid,
because you are with me.
Your rod and your shepherd's staff comfort me. (NCV)

Musicians leading worship (33:1–3).

When the Jews assemble to worship God, professional musicians add their support by filling the temple courtyard with the sounds of harps, lyres, horns, flutes, tambourines, bells, cymbals, and metal rattles.

Some psalms are written to be accompanied by certain kinds of instruments. Psalm 4, for example, says it is written for stringed accompaniment. The very name *psalms* comes from the Hebrew word *psalmos,* which means "twanging of strings."

In an anonymous song of thanks, written for public worship, the writer invites worshipers to praise the Lord with music.

> *Praise the LORD on the harp;*
>> *make music for him on a ten-stringed lyre.*
> *Sing a new song to him;*
>> *play well and joyfully.*

Thirsting for God (42:1–11).

In a private, passionate prayer for help, the songwriter expresses deep sorrow because he feels cut off from God. Perhaps he is among the thousands of Jewish exiles forced to live in Babylon, far from home.

> *As a deer thirsts for streams of water,*
>> *so I thirst for you, God. (1)*

> *Why am I so sad? Why am I so upset?*
> *I should put my hope in God*
>> *and keep praising him,*
>> *my Savior and my God.(11)*

Raising hands in praise and prayer (63:4; 134:1–2).

In an uninhibited show of praise to God, or an unrestrained plea for help, the Jews sometimes address him with arms raised.

David, not yet a king and still living in the desert as a fugitive hunted by Saul, expresses his confidence in God:

> *I will praise you as long as I live.*
>> *I will lift up my hands in prayer to your name.*
>> *(63:4 NCV)*

Singing to God (66:1–20).

Though sacrifices and prayer are an important part of worshiping God, so is singing. The people sing about God when they're alone, and when they gather at the temple or synagogue. Sometimes, gathered for worship, they take turns singing to each other. One group will take the first line of song, and the second group will respond with the second line.

In a song for public worship, the writer encourages the whole world to sing to God.

Everything on earth, shout with joy to God!
   Sing about his glory! Make his praise glorious!

Traveling to Jerusalem (84:5).

Three times a year—spring, summer, and fall—every Jew who is able travels to Jerusalem to celebrate important Jewish holidays: Passover and two harvest festivals.

Fifteen songs, Psalms 120–134, are written especially for pilgrims. The songs are called "songs of ascent," perhaps because no matter which way you approach Jerusalem—north, south, east, or west—you have to climb. The city is on a hill, surrounded by hills. Travelers likely sing these songs as they walk to the Holy City. And when they arrive in Jerusalem they may sing one song on each of the fifteen steps leading up to the temple.

Protected by God (91:1–16).

The Jews sing of God's ability to protect them, no matter what the odds. This doesn't mean God will always keep them from harm, but it means he has the power to protect. Yet when suffering comes, he is still in control and will help in ways that human beings can't fully understand.

Those who go to God Most High for safety
   will be protected by the Almighty.
I will say to the Lord, "You are my place of safety and protection.
   You are my God and I trust you." (1–2 NCV)

Studying God's Word (119:1–8).

Just like sacrifices, prayer, and music, studying the laws of God is an important feature of worship. At home and in groups, the Jews read aloud their Scripture and memorize parts of it.

Psalm 119, the longest chapter in the Bible, has 176 verses—every one of which speaks about God's law. Set to music, it becomes a song urging people to nurture their faith by thinking about God's Word.

Lord, you gave your orders

> to be obeyed completely.
> I wish I were more loyal
>   in obeying your demands. (4–5)

A time to cry (137:1–9).

The largest group of psalms are those of people crying to God out of pain or sorrow.

In one such song, written anonymously, a Jewish exile in Babylon paints a vivid and heartbreaking scene about the day the music died.

> By the rivers in Babylon we sat and cried
>   when we remembered Jerusalem.
> On the poplar trees nearby
>   we hung our harps.
> Those who captured us asked us to sing;
>   our enemies wanted happy songs.
> They said, "Sing us a song about Jerusalem!"
> But we cannot sing songs about the Lord
>   while we are in this foreign country! (1–4)

POINTS TO CONSIDER

Golden oldies. In the early 20th century some Bible and history experts were claiming that the psalms were written only about 200 to 400 years before Jesus, even those allegedly written by David and Solomon during Israel's golden age.

Recent archaeological discoveries, however, reveal that the Canaanites, Babylonians, and Assyrians all produced poetry that's incredibly similar to the poetry of the Jews. In fact, scholars today wonder if the Jews of David's time adopted the poetic forms of neighboring cultures to express their unique faith in God.

Songs of hatred. Not all the psalms praise God. Some give him advice. Consider Psalm 140, attributed to David.

Lord, do not give the wicked what they want (8).

Let burning coals fall on them.

Throw them into the fire
  or into pits from which they cannot escape.
Don't let liars settle in the land.

Let evil quickly hunt down cruel people (10–11).

That certainly doesn't sound like a song Jesus would sing.
He said, "love your enemies. Pray for those who hurt you"
(Matthew 5:44 NCV).

Psalms, however, is brimming with the poetry of honest
human emotion. It stands as enduring proof that it's okay to tell
God how we feel even when we haven't gotten over the hurt and
anger of something that has happened. Admitting the pain is
the first step to recovery.

FOR FURTHER STUDY

- To see how New Testament writers use Psalms to identify
  Jesus as the promised messiah, compare Psalm 22:1, 6–8,
  12–13, 28 with Matthew 27:36–46, Luke 23:35–36, and 1
  Corinthians 15:23–24.

- For another Hebrew song, read Habakkuk 3.

Sun
Mo
Tue
We
Thu
Frid
Satu
Sun
Mo
Tue
We
Thu
Frid
Satu
Sun
Mo
Tue
We

Proverbs

Snappy Advice from Wise Old Men

It's certainly not the seamless, fluid writing style that keeps people coming back to Proverbs. This book reads like a lifetime collection of someone's Chinese fortune-cookie messages, scribbled down in the order they came out of the bag.

However disjointed these snappy one-liners and two-liners are, they contain the wisdom of the ages, condensed for the quickly bored.

In the time it takes to read one sentence, we've dished up a life-tested insight on any one of a thick menu of everyday topics: good women, bad women, spoiled kids, lazy slugs, etiquette at dinner meetings, cosigning loans (the advice is, "don't"), controlling that temper, avoiding the wrong crowd.

Lots of great topics. But if you've ever gone to a convention, you probably discovered pretty quickly that you don't choose workshops by their titles. You choose them by who's doing the talking. The primary source for Proverbs is Solomon—the Israelite king about whom God said, "I will do what you asked. I will give you wisdom and understanding that is greater than anyone has had in the past or will have in the future." (1 Kings 3:12 NCV)

He's worth a listen.

Famous Lines

• "If you do not punish your children, you don't love them, but if you love your children, you will correct them" (13:24 NCV). *Source of the old saying, "Spare the rod, spoil the child." This isn't necessarily a command to spank children; it's an encouragement to discipline them in some way. Shepherds carry a long staff, or rod, to reach out and nudge sheep in the right direction—not to club them.*

• "Pride leads to destruction" (16:18 NCV).

• "Trust the LORD with all your heart and don't depend on your own understanding" (3:5 NCV).

• "Train children to live the right way, and when they are old, they will not stray from it" (22:6 NCV).

Background

Influential People

Solomon, reputed to be the wisest king of Israel and author of most of the proverbs (1:1).

Theme

There is none. Most proverbs are two-liners, not arranged according to any noticeable pattern or theme.

Consider these two that follow one another, but have nothing in common:

Guilty people live dishonest lives,
> *but honest people do right.*
It is better to live in a corner on the roof
> *than inside the house with a quarreling wife* (21:8–9 NCV).

Did You Know?

• The 1960 film *Inherit the Wind,* starring Spencer Tracy as a lawyer who argues to let public educators teach the theory of evolution, takes its title from Proverbs "Whoever brings trouble to his family will be left with nothing but the wind" (11:29 NCV).

• "God helps those who help themselves" is not in Proverbs, or anywhere else in the Bible. Neither is "Cleanliness is next to godliness," or "Early to bed and early to rise make a man healthy, wealthy, and wise." These are proverbs that Benjamin Franklin published in *Poor Richard's Almanack* during the mid-1700s.

Points of Interest

General truths, not promises. The proverbs state general principles, not promises from God. For example, it's often true that "A gentle answer will calm a person's anger," (15:1 NCV). But don't count on it every time.

A nine-chapter introduction. Notice that the first nine chapters are different from the rest of the book. They form a poetic essay contrasting wisdom with foolishness. Afterward comes a long string of one-line and two-line maxims, each of which sums up a truth gleaned from life. These truths are universal, not just for God's people. Any person who follows the advice will likely live a better, happier life.

TIMELINE	BIBLE EVENTS		Solomon writes most of Proverbs 950 BC		King Hezekiah's scribes compile proverbs 700 BC	
		1000 BC	**900 BC**	**800 BC**	**700 BC**
	WORLD EVENTS		Calendar of farming cycles, oldest example of Hebrew writing 1000 BC		Homer writes the *Iliad* and the *Odyssey* 800 BC	

Dates are approximate

Poetry. The proverbs follow the characteristics of Hebrew poetry. They don't have rhyme or rhythm, but they have parallel thoughts. The second half of the proverb might repeat the idea in the first, or expand it, or perhaps contrast it. A contrasting proverb:

It is better to eat a dry crust of bread in peace
than to have a feast where there is quarreling. (17:1 NCV)

AUTHOR AND DATE

Proverbs is a collection of pithy sayings from several wise men. Most are attributed to King Solomon, who is reported to have comprised 3,000 proverbs (1 Kings 4:32).

Two otherwise unknown contributors are Agur (30:1) and a king named Lemuel (31:1), who says he is passing along the advice of his mother. Additional proverbs come from a group of sages simply identified as "wise people" (22:17 NCV).

Sages were an important part of Jewish society. They served as consultants to kings, and as teachers to young men. These sages grappled with practical and philosophical problems, while priests and prophets specialized in religious matters.

Many of the proverbs come from Solomon, who reigned from about 970—930 BC. Other proverbs, however, were added as the centuries went by. Some 250 years later, scribes working for King Hezekiah began compiling the proverbs of Solomon (25:1). Still more proverbs were likely added later. It's uncertain when the book was completed, but Bible experts speculate the work may have continued until as late as the 300s BC.

The purpose of Proverbs is clearly stated in the first chapter. The book exists so "They make the uneducated wise and give knowledge and sense to the young." (1:4 NCV) The sayings, in fact, were probably part of the curriculum that sages taught to young sons of aristocrats.

ON LOCATION

Most proverbs were apparently written by Solomon in Israel (shaded area). But some of the other proverbs could have come from anywhere throughout the Middle East. Similar collections of wise sayings from about Solomon's time have been uncovered in both Egypt and Iraq.

Proverbs Outline

Stay faithful to your wife (5:1–23).

The life-savvy sages know that one critical lesson they need to teach their male students is to respect God's command against adultery.

> *The words of another man's wife may seem sweet as honey;*
>> *they may be as smooth as olive oil.*
> *But in the end she will bring you sorrow,*
>> *causing you pain like a two-edged sword. (3–4)*

> *Be faithful to your own wife,*
>> *just as you drink water from your own well.*
> *Don't pour your water in the streets;*
>> *don't give your love to just any woman. (15-16)*

Don't cosign a loan (6:1–5).

Like sex, money is the cause of many troubles in life. So Proverbs is full of advice about money matters. One persistent piece of advice is to avoid debt—especially another person's debt—like a deer avoids the hunter.

> *My child, be careful about giving a guarantee for somebody else's loan,*
>> *about promising to pay what someone else owes.*
> *You might get trapped by what you say;*
>> *you might be caught by your own words.*
> *My child, if you have done this and are under your neighbor's control,*
>> *here is how to get free.*
> *Don't be proud. Go to your neighbor*
>> *and beg to be free from your promise. (1–3)*

Treat people with honesty (11:1–3).

In the long run, say the sages, honesty pays off.

> *The Lord hates dishonest scales,*
>> *but he is pleased with honest weights. (1)*
> *Good people will be guided by honesty;*
>> *dishonesty will destroy those who are not trustworthy. (3)*

Teach your children well (22:6).

Teaching children to behave themselves is a theme that shows up throughout Proverbs.

Train children to live the right way,
and when they are old, they will not stray from it.

Don't be lazy (24:30–34).

Some of the most biting words of the wise men are reserved for lazy people.

I passed by a lazy person's field
and by the vineyard of someone with no sense.
Thorns had grown up everywhere.
The ground was covered with weeds,
and the stone walls had fallen down.
I thought about what I had seen;
I learned this lesson from what I saw.
You sleep a little; you take a nap.
You fold your hands and lie down to rest.
Soon you will be as poor as if you had been robbed;
you will have as little as if you had been held up.

Treasure your wife (31:10–31).

The book of Proverbs ends with a poetic tribute to a good wife. These are the words of a queen mother, passed along to her son, King Lemuel, unknown outside of this one reference to him.

It is hard to find a good wife,
because she is worth more than rubies (10).

She watches over her family
and never wastes her time.
Her children speak well of her.
Her husband also praises her,
saying, "There are many fine women,
but you are better than all of them." (27–29)

Sun
Mo
Tue
Wed
Thu
Frid
Satu
Sun
Mo
Tue
Wed
Thu
Frid
Satu
Sun
Mo
Tue
Wed

=== Points to Consider ===

Proverbs from Egypt. The old age of Proverbs is confirmed by similar teachings from ancient times. In fact, the thirty sayings of the wise men (22:17–24:22) have striking parallels to thirty sections of an Egyptian collection called "The Wisdom of Amenemope," a sage who taught sometime between 1200–1000 BC.

Here, for example, is the first proverb from the wise men:

> Do not abuse poor people because they are poor, and do not take away the rights of the needy in court (22:22 NCV).

Here is a similar saying from the beginning of the Egyptian book:

> Do not steal from the poor
> nor cheat the cripple.

The fine art of manipulating others. Some proverbs seem better suited to a self-help book on getting ahead than to the Bible. Proverbs 23:1–3, for example, shows how to make an impression when dining with a king (don't eat like a pig). And Proverbs 22:1 praises the value of making a good name for yourself.

Advice like this can, in fact, be misdirected and used as a way to gain power and prestige for selfish reasons. But you can also use it to place yourself in a position of service to others.

=== For Further Study ===

- Jesus used proverbial sayings throughout this ministry. For a taste of them, read the Sermon on the Mount in Matthew 5–7, especially the Beatitudes in Matthew 5:3–10.

- Proverbs is practical advice for young men. To read practical advice to young pastors, turn to 1 and 2 Timothy and Titus.

Ecclesiastes

LIFE: WHAT'S THE POINT?

"What is the meaning of life?" That seems like an ethereal, boring question—unless, of course, you've reached midlife and it suddenly dawns on you that someday in the not-distant-enough future when people talk about "ashes to ashes, dust to dust," they'll be talking about you.

When we stand eyeball to dustball with our own mortality—when we suddenly know and feel the full awareness that we will someday die—we begin asking this question that was tackled long ago by the writer of Ecclesiastes.

The first words out of the writer's mouth don't leave us with a great sense of his ability to answer the question.

Nothing makes sense! Everything is nonsense.

"Useless! Useless! Completely useless! Everything is useless." (1:2)

But don't take this as his final word. The final word comes later, after he lays out and analyzes what he has seen in life.

FAMOUS LINES

- "Eat, drink, and enjoy life" (8:15 NCV).

- "There is a time for everything, and everything on earth has its special season" (3:1 NCV).

- "Cast your bread upon the waters" (11:1 NKJV), *which means "be generous."*

- "There is nothing new here on earth" (1:9 NCV).

In the end, he answers the question by pointing directly to heaven. Life, he concludes, is a mysterious gift from God. We should learn to enjoy the gift, and to show our gratitude to the Giver.

BACKGROUND

INFLUENTIAL PEOPLE

Solomon, reputed to be the wisest king of Israel and possible author of Ecclesiastes (1:1).

THEME

The writer seems to be performing an experiment—he's analyzing life. He examines the cycles of life, the chores we run ourselves ragged on, the pleasures we pursue. And he reaches the bleak conclusion that everything "under the sun" is meaningless. Bible experts debate what he means by this phrase, but some say he means "all human endeavor apart from God." That is, without God no one can find lasting satisfaction and meaning in his work, his diversions, or his life.

> ### DID YOU KNOW?
>
> • The name of the book comes from the word the writer uses to describe himself: Teacher or Assembly Leader. In Greek, this word is *ekklesiastes.*
>
> • The Ernest Hemingway novel *The Sun Also Rises* takes its name from Ecclesiastes 1:5, New King James Version.

POINTS OF INTEREST

One man's search for meaning. This will seem like one incredibly convoluted, contradictory book if you read it like a typical essay or a sermon. One minute the writer's saying life is unfair, unfulfilling, and makes no sense whatsoever. The next minute he's saying we should enjoy life, work hard, and obey God.

What you're reading are the honest confessions of a man struggling with doubt, disillusionment, and despair. Fortunately, he works his way through the struggle and finds a sense of comfort worth sharing.

TIMELINE	BIBLE EVENTS	Solomon begins his 40-year reign 970 BC			
					Dates are approximate
		1000 BC	**900 BC**	**800 BC**	
	WORLD EVENTS	Eastern North Americans grow crops 1000 BC		Greek city of Corinth is founded 800 BC	

AUTHOR AND DATE

In the first verse, the writer identifies himself as "the son of David," "king in Jerusalem," and "known to be very wise." Certainly sounds like Solomon, especially when you add a bunch of other clues from chapter 2—such as foreign rulers bringing him "silver, gold, and precious treasures" (as the queen of Sheba did) and his "many wives" (he had a thousand).

Many Bible experts, however, say the style of Hebrew words suggests it was written many centuries later, maybe as late as 300 BC, perhaps by someone trying to approach a vexing issue in the manner that wise King Solomon would. Some passages, in fact, don't sound like something we would expect Solomon to say: 5:8–9 blames the king for overtaxing the poor.

Fragments of the book found among the Dead Sea Scrolls were copied in about 150 BC, suggesting Ecclesiastes was revered at least by then.

If Solomon write this book, he may have done so late in his reign, after he had allowed his foreign wives to coax him away from God and into worshiping their gods. Perhaps Solomon got to the point in his life where he realized that even with all his wealth, power, and wisdom, he was empty without God.

The point of the book—the conclusion the writer reaches after analyzing life—is something he says "can be put into a few words:"

> Honor God and obey his commands, because this is all people must do (12:13 NCV).

ON LOCATION

If Solomon wrote the book, the setting takes place in his capital city of Jerusalem. The numbered areas are the administrative districts in Solomon's kingdom.

Ecclesiastes Outline

What good is hard work? (1:1–18).

Solomon takes a long, hard look at life. And he doesn't like what he sees.

The Teacher says,
"Useless! Useless!
Completely useless!
Everything is useless."
What do people really gain
from all the hard work they do here on earth?
People live, and people die,
but the earth continues forever. (2–4)

The cycle of life rolls on (3:1–22).

God is in control of the life cycle, Solomon says. And there is no amount of hard work we can do to change this.

There is a time for everything, and everything on earth has its special
*   season.*
There is a time to be born and a time to die.
There is a time to plant and a time to pull up plants.
There is a time to kill and a time to heal.
There is a time to destroy and a time to build.
There is a time to cry and a time to laugh.
There is a time to be sad. and a time to dance.
There is a time to throw away stones
*   and a time to gather them.*
There is a time to hug and a time not to hug. (1–5)

What happens now has happened in the past,
and what will happen in the future has happened before.
God makes the same things happen again and again. (15).

Wealth is unsatisfying (5:10–17).

"Whoever loves wealth, will not be satisfied with it." Solomon says. "The more wealth people have the more friends they have to help spend it. So what do people really gain? They gain nothing except to look at their riches" (10–11).

In the end, Solomon says, wealth is worthless to human beings. "People come into this world with nothing, and when they die they leave with nothing. In spite of all their hard work, they leave just as they came" (15).

Life is short. Enjoy! (5:18–20; 9:7–9; 12:13).

After living a long and luxurious life, Solomon concludes that it's the simple things that matter most.

"I have seen what is best for people here on earth." Solomon says. "They should eat and drink and enjoy their work, because the life God has given them on earth is short" (5:18 NCV).

When Solomon's analysis of life is complete, the main conclusion he reaches—the core of everything he has ever been taught—is this:

Honor God and obey his commands,
because this is all people must do (12:13).

= Points to Consider =

Words at least as old as Solomon. Many scholars suspect Ecclesiastes was written hundreds of years after Solomon. Yet a short excerpt, 9:7–9, is remarkably similar to advice that shows up in the Babylonian *Epic of Gilgamesh*, which had been circulating of hundreds of years before Solomon. Parts of this story have survived in several documents, one dating about 300 years before the king, and another about 700 years before him.

Perhaps Solomon, widely known for his international contacts, read the story and drew from it while reflecting on the meaning of life.

Here's a comparison of the two:

Ecclesiastes	*Epic of Gilgamesh*
Be happy and enjoy eating and drinking! God decided long ago that this is what you should do.	Day and night enjoy yourself, eating and dancing.
Dress up, comb your hair, and look your best.	Wear sparkling fresh clothes. Wash your hair and bathe.
Life is short, and you love your wife, so enjoy being with her.	Pay attention to the child who holds your hand. Make sure your wife enjoys being with you.
This is what you are supposed to do as you struggle through life on this earth.	This is what you are supposed to do.

Almost not in the Bible. Ancient Jewish writings say that Ecclesiastes was one of the last books admitted into the canon of Scripture. Many people didn't like it because it seemed so pessimistic.

Why it was eventually added is uncertain. One reason may be because many Jewish leaders believed Solomon wrote it. And another is because it was written in Hebrew, which indicated it was an old book (Greek was the prevailing language when the Hebrew Bible was agreed upon, in the first century AD).

For whatever reasons it found its way into the Old Testament, Ecclesiastes serves up a dramatic reminder that as much as we human beings like to think we're in control, we're not. God is.

For Further Study

- To discover more on fulfillment in life, read the parables of Jesus about the kingdom of heaven. Matthew 13 has several. They help put life on earth in the context of eternal life, and encourage us to give our attention to things of greatest value.

- For still more practical advice about living, read James, often described as the Wisdom book of the New Testament.

Song of Songs

AN INTIMATE LOVE SONG

You can rate this book PG-30. Jews in ancient times did. They wouldn't let a man read it until he was thirty years old. Jewish elders didn't worry about the women because, unfortunately, most of them couldn't read.

This is an erotic poem. The theme is for adults only. As a result, you're not going to hear many sermons from this book because, frankly, it's too frank for kids. You've got a man and woman in love, graphically and explicitly praising the physical features of each other and disclosing their shared fantasy about making love.

Their words are not vulgar or obscene, yet they are unapologetically sensual and intimate.

This is not like any other book in the Bible—not even close. Many godly people, in fact, have argued that it never should have been added in the first place.

But because it's here, we have a beautiful reminder that human sexuality is a gift of God. We also have a model for romance—a reminder that true love feeds on tender words of endearment, whether poetic or plain, spoken straight from the heart.

Background

Influential People

An unnamed woman, from the countryside of Israel (1:2).
An unnamed man, the woman's true love (1:8).
Solomon, king of Israel (1:1).

Theme

This is a poem, full of highly symbolic language. So Bible experts don't agree on the story behind the poem.

There is a host of proposed plots. Here's a sampling.

Solomon chooses a country girl for his bride, but the young lady refuses the king in favor of

> ### Did You Know?
>
> • Like the book of Esther, the Song of Songs doesn't mention God.
>
> • The title of the book comes from the introduction, "Solomon's Song of Songs" (1:1 NCV). So it's called the Song of Songs just as Jesus is called the "King of kings."

her country lover. Or, Solomon and the country lover are the same man. Or, the unnamed country lover is the only man in the story, and when he comes to the woman, she looks upon him as a glorious king—a kind of knight in shining armor.

In ancient times, many Jewish and Christian scholars didn't take the poem literally. Jews saw the poem symbolizing God's love for the Jewish people. Christians later saw it as Christ's love for the church.

Points of Interest

Unrestrained passion. This is a passionate, erotic celebration of love between a man and a woman. Neither the man nor the woman feels the least bit inhibited about expressing their most intimate feelings and desires. The man lovingly, poetically compares the body of his beloved to

TIMELINE	BIBLE EVENTS	Solomon begins his 40-year reign 970 BC		
				Dates are approximate
		1000 BC		**900 BC**
	WORLD EVENTS	Egyptian love songs written 1100 BC	Greeks worship many gods including Aphrodite (goddess of love) 1000 BC	

a garden filled with sweet aroma and brimming with delicious fruit. "Awake, north wind, Come, south wind," the woman replies. "Blow on my garden, and let its sweet smells flow out. Let my lover enter the garden and eat its best fruits" (4:16 NCV). Remember, this was PG-30.

AUTHOR AND DATE

It's uncertain who wrote the book. The Hebrew phrase in verse one that attributes the poem to Solomon can mean it was written by him, for him, or dedicated to him. It is possible Solomon did write it, for he wrote some of the psalms. And he is said to have written 1,005 songs altogether (1 Kings 4:32). But it's also possible that a professional musician wrote the song for one of Solomon's weddings. Or, it may have been written for weddings in general, and dedicated to the memory of the king with a thousand wives.

It's uncertain when the poem was written. If it was composed by or for Solomon, it was probably written sometime during his reign: 970–940 BC.

Though ancient Bible scholars felt strongly that the song was a symbolic expression of either God's love for Israel or Christ's love for the church, modern experts are nearly unanimous in arguing that the poem is a celebration of God's gift of love and sexuality.

ON LOCATION

The setting is Israel. The young woman addresses the "women of Jerusalem." And the two lovers occasionally compare one another to landmarks in Israel. The man says of his beloved, "Your head is like Mount Carmel" (7:5 NCV).

SONG OF SONGS OUTLINE

Beauty, in the eyes of the beloved beholder (1:1–17).

"Kiss me with the kisses of your mouth," a young and beautiful peasant woman tells the man of her dreams. "The smell of your perfume is pleasant, and your name is pleasant like expensive perfume."

These are the captivating, opening lines of a passionate song about sexual intimacy. What follows is an exchange of compliments, in which each lover boldly praises the physical attributes of the other.

"My darling, you are beautiful! Oh, you are beautiful, and your eyes are like doves," the man says.

"You are so handsome," the young woman replies, "my lover, and so pleasant! Our bed is the grass."

The wedding day (3:6–11).

On the day of the wedding, friends of the bride are the first to notice a dust cloud rolling in from the desert. It is the groom, arriving with his procession. This man may actually be Solomon, coming to marry the young woman. Or the poetic description may be a way of saying the young peasant couple is so deeply in love that their humble wedding feels to them like the majestic ceremony of a king and a queen.

The words of love (4:1–5:16).

After the wedding, the groom praises the beauty of his bride by comparing her to some of the most natural beauty he has ever seen. Her hair flows gracefully upon her shoulders, like a flock of goats moving in rhythmic union down a mountainside. Her teeth shine as white as freshly washed wool.

"Your breasts are like two fawns;
like twins of a gazelle, feeding among the lilies.
I will go to that mountain of myrrh and to that hill of incense."

The honeymoon (7:1–8:14).

The bride is just as daring in praise of her husband. She, too, compares him to the natural beauty she has seen: hair wavy and "black like a raven," legs strong as "large marble posts, standing on bases of fine gold."

The passionate compliments continue flowing, as husband and wife praise each other and even more boldly describe their physical desires. The intensity of their expression heats up, crossing the border into sensuality that is neither obscene nor ashamed.

"You are tall like a palm tree," the husband says. "I will climb up the palm tree and take hold of its fruit."

"I belong to my lover," his wife replies.

In what Bible scholars describe as the high point of the poem, the wife gives her husband a bracelet to remember her by. Then she shares with him a remarkable insight into the very nature of love.

It is "as strong as death, strong as the grave. . .

If a man offered everything in his house for love people would totally reject it" (8:6–7).

POINTS TO CONSIDER

Other ancient love songs. It's not at all impossible that the Song of Songs was written in the time of Solomon. Older, similar songs have been recovered from the Middle East. Collections of Egyptian love songs from 1100–1300 BC share similarities with the Song of Songs. Both, for example, were set to music. In both, the lovers refer to one another as "brother" and "sister." And in both, the lovers lavishly praise the beauty of one another and boldly express their shared desires.

Where's God? If you look for any explicit mention of God or religion in the Song of Songs, you won't find it. This is a song about the love between a man and a woman—not just spiritual love that exists within the heart, but physical love as well.

Early on, godly Jews and Christians asked what such a book was doing in the Bible.

How and why the Song made it into the canon of Scripture is uncertain. Perhaps the ancients began revering the poem because they believed Solomon wrote it. Eventually, many felt so uncomfortable treating the poem as a love song between a man and a woman that they began interpreting it symbolically. For the Jews, the husband symbolized God and the wife symbolized Israel. For Christians, the husband was Jesus, and the wife was the church.

More recently, however, Bible experts interpret the song more literally—as a celebration of romantic love that is God's gift to humanity.

For Further Study

- To read about the prophet Hosea wooing back his unfaithful wife, as a symbol of God trying to win back the affection of Israel, turn to Hosea 1–3.

- To see how the New Testament writers speak of the church as the bride of Christ, read Matthew 9:15; 25:1–13; Revelation 19.

7:00

8:00

9:00

10:00

11:00

oon

1:00

2:00

3:00

4:00

5:00

6:00

7:00

8:00

9:00

10:00

Isaiah

HE WROTE AS THOUGH HE KNEW JESUS

It's not just because of the prophet's bizarre escapades—like walking around naked for three years—that his book has become a classic, at the top of the heap among the Bible's seventeen prophetic books. And it's not just because it's one of the thickest books of the lot, nor that its dramatic prophecies came true.

It's a classic because, though Isaiah lived 700 years before Christ, he wrote as though he knew him. Scattered throughout Isaiah's oracles are vivid descriptions and graphic scenes that read as if they flowed from the pen of a poet who saw the miraculous birth of Jesus in Bethlehem, his crucifixion, and his resurrection.

The first disciples of Jesus didn't miss the connection. The Gospels are full of their comments about Jesus fulfilling one prophecy of Isaiah after another.

Jesus didn't miss the connection either. When he stood in his hometown synagogue, in Nazareth, He opened the scroll of Isaiah and read the first two verses of chapter 61.

Then he told his listeners, "While you heard these words just now, they were coming true!" (Luke 4:21 NCV)

As fascinating as this is, however, the book of Isaiah is far more than a sneak preview into the life of Christ. It's a study of sin—of how it slowly destroyed two Jewish nations and of how God will one day wipe it from the face of creation.

FAMOUS LINES

- "Unto us a child is born, unto us a son is given; and the government will be upon his shoulder. And his name will be called Wonderful, Counselor, Mighty God, Everlasting Father, Prince of Peace" (9:6 NKJV).

- "They will make their swords into plows" (2:4 NCV).

- "Here I am. Send me!" (6:8 NCV)

- "Though your sins are like scarlet, they can be as white as snow" (1:18 NCV).

- "Come, let us talk about these things" (1:18 NCV).

BACKGROUND

INFLUENTIAL PEOPLE

Isaiah, prophet whose ministry spans four kings (1:1).
Hezekiah, godly Judean king who usually follows Isaiah's advice (1:1).

THEME

In an astonishing vision, God calls Isaiah to become a prophet during a critical time in Middle Eastern history. Assyria will destroy the northern Jewish nation of Israel, and the southern nation of Judah (Isaiah's country) will face the same threat. Isaiah's job is to deliver God's messages to his fellow Jews.

The prophet warns sinners of both Israel and Judah that God will punish them, using the Assyrians, then the Babylonians. But Isaiah also predicts that when the punishment has ended, God will send a Prince of Peace to restore the nation.

Woven into the plot are intriguing implications about the end of human history, when God punishes the entire world for sin, then makes a new world for the people who have been faithful.

POINTS OF INTEREST

Messages from God in the first person. Isaiah, like the other major prophets, doesn't deliver God's messages in the third person, as a reporter would. Isaiah won't say, for example, "God is sick of your offerings." Instead, he speaks the very words of God: "I am sick of your offerings." Isaiah, however, will introduce most prophecies with the phrase "The Lord has said." This alerts the people that the words they are about to hear come directly from God.

Promises about a coming messiah. You'll find more references in Isaiah to the Messiah than in any other Old Testament book. New Testament writ-

TIMELINE	BIBLE EVENTS	God selects Isaiah to become a prophet 740 BC	Assyria destroys northern Jewish nation of Israel 722 BC	Hezekiah revolts against Assyria 705 BC	Assyria seizes Judah but can't capture Jerusalem 701 BC	Babylon destroys Jerusalem 586 BC	Jewish return to Jerusalem 538 BC
		800 BC	**750 BC**	**700 BC**	**650 BC**	**600 BC**	**550 BC**	**500 BC**
	WORLD EVENTS		First recorded Olympic games in Greece 776 BC	Chinese history confirms solar eclipse 775 BC	King Romulus founds Rome 753 BC	Assyrians choose Nineveh as capital and start rebuilding it 705 BC	Cyrus Cylinder confirms return of exiled Jews 539 BC Dates are approximate

ers often quote Isaiah to show that Jesus fulfilled prophecies about the promised Messiah.

Poetry and prose. In most Bible translations, it's easy to separate the prophecies from the stories. The prophecies are printed in poetic form and are usually indented. The stories and sermons are printed in paragraph form.

Vivid images. Isaiah is a genius of imagery. He's especially fond of treating inanimate objects as though they live and breathe. "Mountains and hills will burst into song" and "trees in the fields will clap" (55:12 NCV). "The moon will be embarrassed and the sun will be ashamed" (24:23 NCV). So don't take all the images literally.

AUTHOR AND DATE

According to tradition, the prophet Isaiah is the author. He is a prominent character throughout the book, and much of the material is written in the first person: "God said to me."

The first thirty-nine chapters are from Isaiah's time. But because

DID YOU KNOW?

• The longest word in the Bible is the name of Isaiah's son: Maher-Shalal-Hash-Baz (8:1). It's a Hebrew phrase that means "invaders are coming soon." Isaiah used this to emphasize that, before his newborn son could say "Mommy" or "Daddy," Assyria would crush Israel.

• Isaiah, the Old Testament book most quoted in the New Testament, is sometimes called the Fifth Gospel. That's because it's filled with prophecies about Jesus. Here are a few of the best known:

> Birth—7:14; 9:6
> Character—11:1–5
> Death—53:1–12

• The book of Isaiah breaks into two main sections: thirty-nine chapters of judgment, followed by twenty-seven chapters of comfort. Coincidentally, the Bible also breaks into two main sections: thirty-nine books called the Old Testament, followed by twenty-seven books called the New Testament.

• Isaiah walks barefoot and naked for three years, to forecast the fate of Egypt and to warn Judah not to join them in a rebellion against Assyria (20:1–6). Instead, Isaiah says, Judah should trust God for protection.

chapters 40–66 refer to Judah's exile in Babylon some 150 years later and the subsequent return home, many Bible experts think the book was written by two or three authors. Others think Isaiah wrote the later chapters by drawing on what God showed him about the future. (See "How many prophets does it take to write a book?" in Points to Consider.)

Isaiah's ministry spanned at least the last four decades of the 700s BC, during the reigns of four kings: Uzziah, Jotham, Ahaz, and Hezekiah. Isaiah apparently lived at least another twenty years because he reports the murder of Assyrian King Sennacherib, who was killed by his own sons in 681 BC.

Jewish legend says Isaiah was sawn in half at the order of Hezekiah's son and successor, Manasseh, who reigned from 696 to 642 BC.

Other prophets during Isaiah's lifetime included Micah, Hosea, and Amos.

The book preserves Isaiah's attempt to convince the Jews to obey God or face the consequences. Tragically, by ignoring him, they chose the second option.

ON LOCATION

Isaiah prophesies in the southern Jewish nation of Judah and probably lives in the capital city of Jerusalem.

Later in the book the setting changes as Isaiah tells about the coming defeat of Judah followed by the people's long exile in Babylon.

ISAIAH OUTLINE

God makes Isaiah into a prophet. (1:1; 6:1–13).

Sometime during the year that King Uzziah died, in about 740 BC, a young man described only as "Isaiah, the son of Amoz" has an incredible, bizarre vision. He sees God seated on a high throne in a temple. Surrounding the throne are glowing, heavenly beings. God asks, "Whom can I send? Who will go for us?"

Isaiah quickly replies, "Send me!"

God tells Isaiah to call the people of Judah back to obedience. But God warns that they won't listen. When Isaiah asks how long the people will disobey, God replies ominously, "Until the cities are destroyed and the people are gone, until there are no people left in the houses, until the land is destroyed and left empty. The LORD will send the people far away, and the land will be left empty" (6:11–12 NCV).

With this promise of failure, Isaiah begins his ministry.

Assyria destroys the northern Jewish nation of Israel (8:1–10).

A few years later, the northern Jewish nation of Israel unites with Syria to fight for freedom from the Assyrian Empire. When Judah refuses to join the coalition, Israel and Syria try to force the issue.

Isaiah tells Judean King Ahaz to stand his ground because God says the kings of Israel and Syria are "like two barely burning sticks that are ready to go out" (7:4 NCV). Ahaz apparently doesn't trust God alone, so he calls on help from Assyria.

The Assyrians come and in 732 BC conquer Syria. Ten years later, they return and destroy Israel, burning the capital city and deporting tens of thousands of the leading citizens.

Judah pays dearly for trusting an alliance with Assyria instead of trusting God's promise: they lose their freedom and must pay taxes to Assyria each year.

"To us a child is born" (9:2–7).

In a prophecy possibly delivered at the coronation of one of Israel's most godly kings, Hezekiah, the prophet Isaiah appears to reflect back on the birth of the king and portray this birth as a sign of hope. New Testament writers also interpreted it as a signpost, pointing to the promised Messiah, Jesus.

"A child has been born to us . . . He will be responsible for leading the people. His name will be Wonderful Counselor, Powerful God, Father Who Lives Forever, Prince of Peace" (9:6 NCV).

When peace comes to stay (11:1–16)

In yet another prophecy that may have been delivered at the coronation of one of Judah's kings, Isaiah speaks of the day when a ruler from the family of King David will lead the nation into an era of enduring peace.

Again, early Christians associated this with the coming kingdom of Jesus, in which God will defeat sin and restore the original beauty of creation. Isaiah describes natural enemies living in harmony, "and a little child will lead them" (11:6 NCV).

The fall of Babylon (13:1–22).

Babylon is still just an emerging power in Isaiah's day, but the prophet foresees a time when it will become powerful and majestic. Yet Babylon will also become a brutal and godless empire—one that will level Jerusalem in 586 BC.

Jewish survivors will lament the sins that caused their downfall, yet criticize God for punishing them with a nation that is even more sinful. Isaiah promises that Babylon will face its own Judgment Day. The devastation will be so thorough that "No Arab will put a tent there," Babylon, sixty miles south of Baghdad, has been completely deserted since the AD 600s.

The Apocalypse (24:1–23)

Before peace comes, however, God will purge the world of sin. This purging begins with the punishment of a long list of nations. Among the many that will suffer are Judah, Assyria, Babylon, Egypt, and Arabia. Then in chapters 24–27, which Bible scholars call the Apocalypse of Isaiah, the prophet says the entire planet will suffer.

"The LORD will destroy the earth and leave it empty; he will ruin the surface of the land and scatter its people," Isaiah says (24:1 NCV).

The devastation is so extensive that it seems God is dismantling his

physical creation. In fact, many experts think Isaiah is speaking about
the end of human history. Yet, after the end comes a new beginning, a
new creation—perhaps the kingdom that Jesus told his disciples he was
preparing (John 14:2–3).

Comforting words for God's people (40:1–31).

After thirty-nine chapters, most of which are warnings about the fall of
Judah and its neighbors, Isaiah does an about-face. Threats of doom
turn to promises of comfort.

The setting moves in fast-forward, 200 years into the future.
Jerusalem is destroyed, and the people of Judah are suffering through
half a century of exile in Babylon.

Our God has said:
"Comfort, comfort my people.
Speak kindly to the people of Jerusalem and tell them
that their time of service is finished" (40:1-2 NCV).

The Suffering Servant (53:1–12).

One of the most captivating prophecies of Isaiah tells about a servant
"hated and rejected by people. He had much pain and suffering." (53:3
NCV).

Jews reading this text in Babylonian exile may have thought Isaiah
was talking about them, the outcast Jewish nation. Perhaps he was. But
the New Testament writers also saw this as a portrait of Jesus (Matthew
8:17). Many phrases seem especially pertinent:
But he was wounded for the wrong we did; he was crushed for the evil
we did.
The punishment, which made us well, was given to him,
and we are healed because of his wounds.
He was beaten down and punished, but he didn't say a word.
He was like a lamb being led to be killed (53:5, 7 NCV).

The new city of Jerusalem (54:1–17).

To a nation grieving over the lost glory of Jerusalem, a city the
Babylonians had reduced to a massive pile of rocks, burned timber, and
shattered pottery, Isaiah paints a glorious picture of the Holy City
restored by God.

Sun
Mo
Tue
We
Thu
Fri
Sat
Sun
Mo
Tue
We
Thu
Fri
Sat
Sun
Mo
Tue
We

Isaiah uses the most lavish images available to describe what this new city will look like: "turquoise stones, . . . foundations with sapphires . . . rubies to build your walls . . . shining jewels for the gates" (54:11–12 NCV).

The first readers of these words may have considered the prophecy fulfilled when the Jews returned from Babylon and rebuilt their nation. But the meaning could reach well beyond this, to a time when God brings salvation to everyone, and once again God can look at his creation and declare, "Their victory comes from me."

POINTS TO CONSIDER

Goodbye, Babylon. "No one will ever live there," Isaiah prophesied. "Wolves will howl within the strong walls, and wild dogs will bark in the beautiful buildings." (13:20, 22 NCV)

This once exquisite, sprawling city along the banks of the Euphrates River now lies in ruins in the rugged and hilly terrain outside of Baghdad. This, the home of Nebuchadnezzar and the capital of the Babylonian Empire, was abandoned by about AD 600.

How many prophets does it take to write a book? Many Bible experts think it took more than one prophet to write the book of Isaiah. Some scholars say the book reflects the work of two or three prophets, writing in different eras. Most of chapters 1–39 are set in Isaiah's lifetime and were probably written by him. But chapters 40–55 seem to be set in Babylon during the exile, 150 years after Isaiah. Chapters 56–66 seem to be set back in Israel, when the Jews are starting to rebuild their country. These last two sections, many scholars argue, were written by two other people, or perhaps by one person who lived during the exile and then returned to Israel.

Experts who say that Isaiah wrote the entire book argue that prophets do sometimes see into the future. They believe that consistency of writing style, choice of words (many of which are unique to the book), and recurring themes argue in favor of a single writer.

The oldest copy of the book, found among the Dead Sea scrolls, was written about 100 BC. It shows no break in the text, treating it all as a single work.

Prophecies don't name names. Isaiah actually names Cyrus—the Persian king who came along 200 years later—as the leader who would "set my people free" (45:13 NCV). This, say some experts, suggests the last half of the book was added long after Isaiah lived, because biblical prophecies aren't usually so specific. This material, they say, was written as history (that is, after the fact), not as a prediction.

Some prophecies in Daniel, however, fit precisely the political jockeying that took place between Egypt and Syria in the time between the Old and New Testament. Of course some scholars argue that these, too, were written after the fact. Yet other scholars argue that God is God and so is fully capable of giving a specific prophecy.

FOR FURTHER STUDY

- For another Judean prophet's perspective on what life was like at the time, read the seven-chapter book of Micah.

- For a glimpse into how New Testament writers interpreted the words of Isaiah as prophecies about Jesus, read these texts: John 12:37–41; Acts 8:26–39; Romans 15:7–21. (There are many more.)

HE PREDICTS DOOM AND LIVES TO SEE IT

The prophet Jeremiah was an eyewitness to the most tragic event in his nation's history. He saw his people slaughtered, with survivors herded up and taken away. He saw Jerusalem burn. He saw his country die.

Actually, he had seen all this coming for 40 years. And he knew it didn't have to end like this. If only he could convince the people to turn back to God—to honor the agreement their ancestors had made with the Lord. If the nation would honor their obligations, which are summed up in the Ten Commandments, God would honor His by protecting and blessing the people. Since they chose to dishonor the covenant, however, God was bound by the agreement to punish them.

Sin had consequences; it was written into the covenant.

Sin still has consequences; it's written into the law of cause and effect, and expressed in wise sayings like "what goes around comes around." It's also repeated in God's Word, in memorable passages like "The payment for sin is death" (Romans 6:23 NCV).

FAMOUS LINES

• "Can a leopard change his spots?" (13:23 NCV)

• "I will put my teachings in their minds. I will be their God, and they will be my people" (31:33 NCV).

• "You are in my hands like the clay in the potter's hands" (18:6 NCV).

• "More than anything else, a person's mind is evil" (17:9 NCV).

Unfortunately, people today—as in Jeremiah's time—have the option of ignoring God's Word.

Jeremiah gives us a chance to learn from the mistakes of his era, for he opens a window that allows us to take a long, hard look at the wages of sin.

BACKGROUND

INFLUENTIAL PEOPLE

Jeremiah, a prophet who witnesses Jerusalem's fall (1:1).
Baruch, the scribe who writes Jeremiah's dictated prophecies (32:12).
Jehoiakim, king who cuts up Jeremiah's first scroll of prophecies (1:3).
Zedekiah, last king of Judah; he takes his army and abandons besieged Jerusalem (1:3).

THEME

The prophet Jeremiah, still a young man, begins his job of delivering God's word during a spiritually upbeat time in Judah's history. King Josiah, a godly ruler, is leading the nation in a revival. But it's too little, too late. The effects won't last, and the Jews will revert to their old ways of worshiping idols and treating each other as if there's no such thing as compassion or the laws of God.

Judgment day is coming in the form of the merciless Babylonian army, and Jeremiah delivers this heartbreaking message. Unfortunately, his is one of the few hearts broken. Most people ignore him, as they do the other prophets.

POINTS OF INTEREST

Poetry, stories, speeches. The prophecies of Jeremiah are easy to spot at a quick glance in most Bible versions; they're indented because they are poems. You'll also find in the book some stories and sermons or speeches, which are written in regular paragraph form.

Poetic repetition. The prophet Jeremiah understands the powerful impact of repeating a striking phrase or idea. This repetition is the most unique characteristic of Hebrew poetry, which does not rhyme or have rhythm.

TIMELINE	**BIBLE EVENTS**	Jeremiah begins his 40-year ministry 626 BC	Babylon invades Judah and takes captives, including prophet Daniel 605 BC	Babylon suppresses Judean rebellion, taking more captives including Ezekiel 597 BC	Babylon destroys Jerusalem and Judean cities, exiling many survivors 586 BC
		650 BC		**600 BC**	**550 BC**
	WORLD EVENTS	Babylon captures Assyrian capital of Nineveh 612 BC	Babylon crushes Egyptian forces 605 BC	Hinduism teaches that at death, the soul moves to another body or animal 600 BC	Founder of Buddhism is born 560 BC

Dates are approximate

Jeremiah's complaints. Scattered throughout the book are complaints and questions Jeremiah raises.

Once he complains, "I am sorry that you gave birth to me since I must accuse and criticize the whole land." (15:10 NCV).

Another time he wonders out loud about God's apparently distorted sense of justice: "Why are evil people successful? Why do dishonest people have such easy lives? You have put the evil people here like plants with strong roots. They grow and produce fruit" (12:1–2 NCV).

AUTHOR AND DATE

The book says Jeremiah dictated the poetic prophecies to his assistant, a scribe named Baruch (36:4). But the prose story sections, say many Bible experts, may have been added by Baruch and other writers.

DID YOU KNOW?

• Jeremiah has more words than any other book in the Bible.

• The prophet acts out many of his messages. For example, on one occasion he wears a yoke to symbolize that God expects the nations of the area to serve Babylon (27:2). Another time God tells him not to attend any funerals or show sympathy to the bereaved. This is to illustrate that God will have not pity on the Jews when it comes time to punish them (16:5).

• The new covenant, which New Testament writers said replaced the hundreds of laws that God gave Moses, is first mentioned here: "Look, the time is coming," declares the Lord, "when I will make a new agreement with the people of Israel and the people of Judah" (31:31 NCV). That time arrived with the death and resurrection of Jesus, says the New Testament (Hebrews 8).

Jeremiah prophesied in Judah for about forty years, from 626–586 BC. He dictated his prophecies, the heart of the book, during the reign of King Jehoiakim (609–598 BC).

The book confronts the Judeans with their sin, gives them a chance to repent, then records the horrifying consequences they suffer when they refuse. Yet throughout, it offers this promise: the nation of Israel will rise again.

On Location

Jeremiah delivers his prophecies in Jerusalem, capital of Judah. When Babylonian invaders conquer the land, they deport much of the population to Babylon, a city near what is now Baghdad. Jeremiah and a group of survivors who remain in Judah later escape to Egypt.

JEREMIAH OUTLINE

7:00
8:00
9:00
0:00
1:00
oon
1:00
2:00
3:00
4:00
5:00
6:00
7:00
8:00
9:00
0:00

Jeremiah visits a potter's shop (18:1–23).

Jeremiah, the son of a priest raised just three miles from Jerusalem, has no desire to become a prophet. When God asks him to speak "as a prophet to the nations," Jeremiah resists. "I don't know how to speak." he replies, "I am only a boy."

"Don't say, I am only a boy," the Lord answered. "You must go everywhere I send you, and you must say everything I tell you to say. Don't be afraid of anyone, because I am with you to protect you" (1:5–8 NCV).

Later, God tells Jeremiah to go to the pottery shop. "Go down to the potter's house," God says, "I will give you my message there."

As Jeremiah and others watch the craftsman at work, they see that when the pottery doesn't shape up well, the potter starts over. Jeremiah, acting on God's instruction, tells the spectators that God can do to the Jewish people what the potter has just done to the clay.

"I am preparing disaster for you and making plans against you," God says through Jeremiah, "So stop doing evil. Change your ways and do what is right" (18:11–12 NCV).

This disaster would come in three waves of Babylonian invasions spread over nearly twenty years. In the first two invasions, the Babylonians would deport leading citizens. In the third invasion, they would destroy all the major cities, including Jerusalem, and deport much of the remaining population.

Someday a godly king will rule (23:1–8).

Jeremiah, speaking God's words, harshly criticizes the unrighteous rulers of Judah. "You have scattered my people and forced them away and not taken care of them. So I will punish you for the evil things you have done!" (23:2 NCV)

Then, in a poetic prophecy, Jeremiah speaks of a coming ruler whom the Jews later associated with the promised Messiah.

"The days are coming," says the Lord,
"when I will raise up a good branch in David's family.
He will be a king who will rule in a wise way;

he will do what is fair and right in the land.
In his time Judah will be saved, and Israel will live in safety (5–6 NCV).

Early Christians would interpret this as a reference to Jesus, who could bring peace to the human heart and who would one day return to rule with wisdom and justice "forever and ever" (Revelation 11:15 NCV).

The sentence: 70 years in exile (25:1–14).

"For these past twenty-three years," Jeremiah says, "I have spoken messages from the Lord to you from that time until today, but you have not listened" (25:3 NCV).

Now their time is up. God will invoke his rights according to the agreement that he and the Jewish people made with each other: "I will scatter you among the nations, and I will pull out my sword and destroy you. Your land will become empty, your cities a waste" (Leviticus 26:33 NCV).

"I will send for all the peoples of the north, along with my servant Nebuchadnezzar king of Babylon," God says through Jeremiah. "That whole area will be an empty desert, and these nations will be slaves of the king of Babylon for seventy years" (25:9, 10–11 NCV).

Jeremiah buys a field (32:1–15).

As Jeremiah had predicted, the Babylonians capture all the major cities of Judah except Jerusalem, which they have now surrounded. Inside is Jeremiah, under arrest in the palace courtyard for speaking out against King Zedekiah's policy of defending the city; Jeremiah had advised surrender.

While the siege is underway, Jeremiah buys a field in his boyhood home nearby. The sale is meant to serve as a symbol to Israel. God tells Jeremiah to put the bill of sale in a clay jar—the ancient version of a safety deposit box—so it will last a long time.

Jeremiah reports what God has told him: "In the future my people will once again buy houses and fields for grain and vineyards in the land of Israel" (32:15 NCV).

The king burns Jeremiah's prophecies (36:1–32).

The story flashes back about twenty years, to when God instructs Jeremiah to write down all the prophecies he has spoken. Jeremiah dictates the prophecies to a scribe, "Baruch, son of Neriah."

Later, Baruch takes the scroll to the temple and reads it to the people. When King Jehoiakim hears the words in a private reading, he is not impressed. As the reader finishes a section, the king reaches over with a small knife, cuts it off, and tosses it in the fire. He does this to the entire scroll.

When Jeremiah hears of this, he vows that since the king threw away the words of God, the king will be killed and thrown out. Jeremiah dictates a second scroll, which becomes the core of the book bearing his name.

Jeremiah imprisoned in a muddy cistern (38:1–13).

Fast-forward back to Babylon's siege of Jerusalem (the chronology of Jeremiah jumps around a bit). Four Jerusalem officials overhear Jeremiah telling some people that if they stay in the city they will die from disease, hunger, or battle. The officials report this to King Zedekiah.

"Jeremiah must be put to death!" they argue, "He is discouraging the soldiers who are still in the city, and all the people, by what he is saying to them."

"Jeremiah is in your control. I cannot do anything to stop you," the king replies.

The officials take Jeremiah to an underground cistern, built to store rainwater. Using ropes, they lower him in, then leave him to die. There's not water in the cistern, but plenty of mud. And Jeremiah sinks deep.

Another official appeals to the king not to let Jeremiah starve down there, and the king relents. Jeremiah is returned to the palace courtyard, under arrest. There, the king calls Jeremiah aside and asks him for advice about the battle.

"If you surrender to the officers of the king of Babylon," Jeremiah says, "your life will be saved. Jerusalem will not be burned down, and you and your family will live."

"I'm afraid," Zedekiah says. He's afraid the enemy soldier will turn him over to the Jews who have sided with Babylon, and that the Jews will torture him.

"Obey the Lord," Jeremiah replies, "Then things will go well for you, and your life will be saved" (38:20 NCV).

Jeremiah survives the fall of Jerusalem (39:1–40:15; 52:1–34).

A year and a half into the siege, the Jews are starving to death. So the king and his army make a break for it under the cover of darkness. The unprotected citizens are left behind.

Babylonian soldiers, however, catch the fleeing king and capture the city. The last memorable scene King Zedekiah sees is the execution of his sons; then he is blinded, locked into chains, and taken to Babylon where he dies a prisoner.

Set afire are the temple, the palace, all the important buildings, and the homes. Then the protective walls of the city are broken down.

The Babylonian commander locates Jeremiah in a string of chained slaves bound for Babylon.

"But today I am freeing you from the chains on your wrists," he tells Jeremiah. Jewish prisoners had apparently spoken of the prophet who tried to convince the king to surrender.

Jeremiah remains in Judea, under the care of the governor that Babylonian King Nebuchadnezzar appoints to rule the area. Sometime later, perhaps as long as four years, the Jews assassinate this governor. Fearing reprisal, they flee to Egypt and force Jeremiah to go with them. There, the Jews take up the worship of the goddess Astarte, "the Queen of Heaven." Jeremiah promises that this remnant of Judah will die in Egypt. Indeed, they disappear from the pages of history, as does Jeremiah.

POINTS TO CONSIDER

The seal of Jeremiah's scribe. In 1975 a clay impression of an ancient seal used to validate official documents was discovered in Israel. The seal is inscribed with the words "Belonging to Baruch son of Neriah the scribe." This is exactly how the Bible describes the associate who helped Jeremiah record his prophecies (32:12). Furthermore, the clay impression was scorched, indicating it had been burned, perhaps in the fire that destroyed Jerusalem in 586 BC.

A second seal impression is also linked to the story of Jeremiah. This one belonged to Jerahmeel, King Jehoiakim's son, who was ordered to arrest Jeremiah and Baruch (36:26).

Letters from a doomed city. Just before the Babylonians conquered Jerusalem, they destroyed the nearby Judean cities of Azekah, then Lachish. Dramatic messages scribbled on broken pieces of pottery—ancient memo sheets—preserve some of the final, frantic military reports.

One message concludes, "We are watching for the fire signals according to the signs my lord has given, because we do not see Azekah."

No 70-year exile. Jeremiah said the exile would last "seventy years" (29:10). It lasted only about fifty, because Persian King Cyrus released the Jews to return home in about 538 BC, just after Persia defeated the Babylonians (2 Chronicles 36:22).

The 20-year difference remains a puzzle. But there are several possible solutions.

1. Jeremiah had in mind the first deportation of Judeans to Babylon. This happened in about 605 BC, nearly seventy years before Cyrus's decree.

2. The exile extended from the destruction of the temple in 586 BC until its rededication in 516 BC, seventy years.

3. Jeremiah didn't mean seventy literal years. He simply meant a long time. This number was used in this manner on other occasions in the Bible (2 Chronicles 36:21; Daniel 9:24).

FOR FURTHER STUDY

- For more on this era in Judah's history, read 2 Kings and 2 Chronicles 34–36.

- For the words of other Judean prophets who lived during Jeremiah's lifetime, read the books of Habakkuk, Zephaniah, and Nahum.

Lamentations

"My Eyes Are Red from Crying"

This may not be the book to read if you're depressed, unless misery loves miserable company. But it's the best place to go in the Bible if you want to understand how people feel when they've suffered an indescribable loss.

"My eyes have no more tears, and I am sick to my stomach. I feel empty inside," the writer moans. "Lord, remember my suffering and my misery, my sorrow and trouble" (2:11; 3:19 NCV).

> **Famous Lines**
>
> • "Great is thy faithfulness" (3:23 KJV).

With good reason. He has lost nearly everything but his life—and he could lose that as quickly as a master could kill a slave.

His country is gone, the cities burned, and the leaders dead or arrested. The citizens are gone, slaughtered by Babylonian invaders or deported to faraway lands. Perhaps many of the writer's friends and close family members are among the dead. And perhaps he's all alone now.

Yet when he reaches deep within himself for a response to all this tragedy, he turns up a surprising, inexplicable revelation. It's obviously not an insight he worked out through his powers of reasoning, for it makes no sense.

"Lord, your loyalty is great," he says. "I say to myself, 'The Lord is mine, so I hope in him'" (3:23–24 NCV).

Most people can't understand an attitude like this, bursting forth from deep despair. But gifts from God are sometimes hard to explain.

BACKGROUND

INFLUENTIAL PEOPLE

Survivors of Judah, a nation defeated and dispersed (1:3).

THEME

This is not a story with a plot, but a sad song about the death of the Jewish nation.

In a collection of five poems, the writer captures the intensity of his feelings about the unspeakable suffering he has witnessed. He knows his nation has sinned, but he can't understand why God has responded so viciously. "Look, Lord," he complains, "to whom you have done this. Women eat their own babies, the children they have cared for. Priests and prophets are killed in the Temple of the Lord" (2:20 NCV).

"Bring us back to you," is his plea. "Make our days as they were before" (5:21 NCV).

> ### DID YOU KNOW?
>
> • This is the saddest book in the Bible, the only book made entirely of mournful song.
>
> • This collection of songs, along with some heart-wrenching songs in the book of Jeremiah, has earned Jeremiah the nickname "the weeping prophet."
>
> • Many Jews today read this book at the Western (Wailing) Wall, where they still lament the destruction of the temple, and pray for the day it will be rebuilt.

POINTS OF INTEREST

Twenty-two-verse chapters. There are five chapters in this book, and all but one have 22 verses. The only exception is chapter 3, which has 66 verses—3 times 22. There's a reason for this. In the 22-verse chapters, each verse begins with a letter of the Hebrew alphabet—starting with *aleph,* followed by *beth,* and continuing through the 22-letter alphabet.

TIMELINE	BIBLE EVENTS	Babylon destroys Jerusalem ⌐---586 BC	Jewish exiles return to Jerusalem 538 BC---------┐	Temple rebuilt 516 BC----------┐
		600 BC	**550 BC**	**500 BC**
	WORLD EVENTS	Babylon crushes Egyptian forces ⌐------605 BC	Cyrus Cylinder confirms return of Jews └-539 BC	Dates are approximate

So each chapter forms an acrostic, using the Hebrew alphabet. Chapter three is a bit different; it begins every three verses with a new letter from the alphabet.

Chapter five is not an acrostic, but it follows the concept by limiting itself to 22 verses.

It took a lot of thought to create these acrostic songs.

Why the writer went to so much trouble is uncertain. Acrostics help people memorize poems and songs. Yet there may be another reason. For when the writer exhausts the entire alphabet, the song also symbolizes fullness. It's as though the writer is saying the Jews have suffered grief from A to Z, many times over.

Poetry with a beat. Lamentations is the one piece of Hebrew poetry in the Bible that breaks the rule that says Hebrew poetry has no rhythm. There's a beat that you can see not only in the original language, but in many English translations as well. The beat is usually 3–2, with three beats in the first line and two beats in the second line. Here's an example:

Our princes were purer than snow, and whiter than milk. Their bodies were redder than rubies; they looked like sapphires (4:7 NCV).

AUTHOR AND DATE

The writer is unnamed but since ancient times has been identified as Jeremiah. This is because the poignant scenes suggest that the writer was an eyewitness to the fall of Jerusalem and the suffering that followed. For example, it seems likely that an eyewitness would report starvation becoming so intense in Jerusalem that "With their own hands kind women cook their own children" (4:10 NCV).

There's also some similarity between Jeremiah and Lamentations in writing style and word choice.

Because the pain is so much on the surface of the writing, and without any clue that relief is in sight, most Bible experts say the songs were written shortly after the fall of Jerusalem in 586 BC, and before the rebuilding of the temple seventy years later.

ON LOCATION

Some songs are set in Israel, as the Jews suffer near-annihilation. Others are set abroad, as survivors are forced to live in exile in Babylon (now Iraq). At least one group of survivors, Jeremiah included, escapes to Egypt.

LAMENTATIONS OUTLINE

Jerusalem is gone (1:1–22).

Somewhere in exile, far from Israel, a homesick poet writes songs about his once-proud Jewish nation, which now lies in ruins.

Jerusalem is a city of rubble, and its people an assembly of slaves "Judah has gone into captivity where she suffers and works hard. She lives among other nations, but she has found no rest. Those who chased her caught her when she was in trouble."

The poet knows that his nation is being punished for its horrible sins, and that if God had not been merciful, we would have been destroyed (3:22). Yet he longs for an end to the torment.

The Jews become like a nation of poor children (5:1–22).

"We are like orphans with no father, our mothers are like widows," the poet writes. "Slaves have become our rulers and no one can save us from them" (5:3, 8).

The poet finds it impossible to understand how God can allow such depth of suffering to go on for so long. He yearns for God to forgive Israel. "But you rule forever, Lord," he says to the Lord. "You will be King from now on. Why have you forgotten us for so long? Bring us back to you, Lord, and we will return" (5:19–21 NCV).

The poet doesn't know how God will respond. But somehow, somewhere he finds a calming, healing assurance: "The Lord is mine, so I hope in him" (3:24 NCV).

POINTS TO CONSIDER

Other songs sung blue. There are other ancient songs written in the despairing spirit of Lamentations. About 1,500 years before a Jew penned his lament about the fall of Jerusalem, another songwriter lamented the fall of Ur, a city in what is now Iraq. "The people lay in heaps," wrote the author of *A Lamentation over the Destruction of Ur*. "Dead bodies, like fat placed in the sun . . . melted away." The author of Lamentations described similar conditions. "People young and old, lie outside on the ground," he wrote. "My young women and young men have been killed by the sword" (2:21 NCV).

In search of an author. Some Bible experts say Jeremiah probably didn't write the book. They argue that ancient copies of the book don't even mention him, some of the language doesn't sound like him, and it's hard to imagine him complaining that Israel's prophets "do not have visions from the Lord" (2:9 NCV). Furthermore, Lamentations speaks of the people that "kept watch from our towers for a nation to save us" (4:17 NCV). Jeremiah preached the opposite—that the people should not look for help from Egypt (Jeremiah 37:7–10).

Other experts, however, say the language *does* sound like Jeremiah's, and that after Jerusalem was destroyed and Jeremiah left the region there *weren't* any prophets remaining to deliver God's message. Regarding the Jews expecting Egypt to save them, the writer may have been expressing not his hope, but the hope of the masses.

What does seem clear is that the author, whoever he was, witnessed the tragedy and shared the heartbreak.

FOR FURTHER STUDY

- For more songs of grief about the fall of Jerusalem, read Psalms 74, 79, and 137.

- Jesus' lament over the impending disaster of Jerusalem fits the pathos of Lamentations (Luke 13:34–35).

- For the history behind Lamentations, read Ezekiel and Zephaniah.

Ezekiel

VISIONS THAT RATTLE THE BONES

This is not a bedtime story. You'll not want to read it alone at night. And you'll certainly not want to read it to your children as you tuck them in.

The book is full of strange and unsettling images. In a vision of the throne room of God, the prophet Ezekiel reports seeing humanoid creatures, each with four faces, four wings, human hands, and calflike hooves. This is part of Ezekiel's story about how God calls him to be a prophet.

Later, Ezekiel tells about his most famous vision: His spirit is transported to a valley filled with the scattered bones of human beings. Right before his eyes, these bones begin to rattle, snapping together to form skeletons. Muscles and skin then erupt onto the bones, quickly spreading and covering them to form lifeless corpses. Finally a wind begins to blow, breathing into the bodies the breath of life. This, God promises, is what he will do for Israel, destroyed by Babylon. As a nation, Jews will be resurrected.

Woven into the book's perplexing scenes are clear and important insights about God. For one, he'd rather forgive than punish. For another, he'll never give up trying to win back the loyalty and love of those who have turned their backs on him.

FAMOUS LINES

- "The daughter is like her mother" (16:44 NCV).

- "Dry bones, hear the word of the Lord" (37:4 NCV).

- "There shall be showers of blessing" (34:26 KJV).

- "The fathers have eaten sour grapes, and the children's teeth are set on edge" (18:2 KJV). *Ezekiel refutes this old adage, saying that God does not punish children for the sins of the parents. People are accountable only for their own sins.*

BACKGROUND

INFLUENTIAL PEOPLE

Ezekiel, Jewish prophet, priest, and prisoner in Babylon (1:1).

THEME

Ezekiel is a 25-year-old priest in Jerusalem when Babylonian soldiers arrive to suppress a rebellion there. They take Ezekiel away as a hostage—one of 10,000 upper-class Judeans enslaved.

Five years later, in a bizarre vision filled with strange-looking creatures from heaven, God calls Ezekiel to become his prophet and to deliver his messages to the Jews in exile. For the next twenty years or more, Ezekiel does just that. First he warns the Jews that their beloved nation and capital city of Jerusalem will fall: "Human, the Lord God says this to the land of Israel: An end!" (7:2 NCV)

> ### DID YOU KNOW?
>
> • The song about the "foot bone connected to the leg bone" comes from one of Ezekiel's strange visions (37:1–14).
>
> • "Son of man" is how God addresses the prophet—about ninety times in all. This title spotlights Ezekiel's humanity and his dependence on God. The prophet Daniel, however, uses the term to describe the future messiah (Daniel 7:13). Jesus used this title more than any other to describe himself.
>
> • The last word in the book of Ezekiel is the symbolic name of the new Jerusalem: "The-Lord-Is-Here."

When the end arrives about eight years after he begins predicting it, Ezekiel radically changes his message, switching from doom to hope. The exiles will return to Jerusalem, the city and temple will be rebuilt, and the nations that hurt Israel will suffer terribly.

TIMELINE

BIBLE EVENTS

Babylon suppresses Judean rebellion and takes Judean hostages 605 BC	Babylon takes 10,000 more hostages, including Ezekiel 597 BC	Ezekiel begins his ministry as a prophet 593 BC	Babylon destroys Jerusalem and other Judean cities, exiling many survivors 586 BC	Persia defeats Babylon 539 BC — Exiles start returning to Jerusalem 538 BC — Temple rebuilt 516 BC

600 BC   **550 BC**   **500 BC**

WORLD EVENTS

Dates are approximate

Babylon captures Assyrian capital of Nineveh 612 BC	Babylon crushes Egyptian forces 605 BC	Founder of Buddhism is born 560 BC	Cyrus Cylinder confirms release of exiled Jews 539 BC

POINTS OF INTEREST

Prophecies acted out. To help people see what he's talking about, Ezekiel sometimes acts out his prophecies.

Once, when his wife dies, he refuses to follow the Jewish mourning customs. He doesn't cry, put on torn and ragged clothing, or cover himself in dirty. When his neighbors ask why, he says the Jews are about to suffer something so horrible that it will leave them in a state of shock; they won't even be able to cry.

Another time, he shaves his head and beard. Some of the hair he burns, some he cuts with a sword, and the rest he scatters to the wind. This, he explains, is what will happen to the Jewish people.

Yet another time, he sleeps on his right side for forty days, to symbolize that the Jews have forty more years to suffer the consequences of their sins.

A lot of vivid symbolism. Don't always take Ezekiel literally. Sometimes it's easy to see he's speaking metaphorically. For example, he'll call Egypt a giant crocodile, and he'll call the seacoast city of Tyre a great ship. But other times it's not as obvious. For example, Ezekiel condemns the king of Tyre by saying he will be thrown out of a garden and cast into a fire (38:11–19). This is a poem in which Ezekiel apparently compares the coming fall of the king to the fall of Satan, who was thrown out of the Garden of Eden.

Don't let the symbolism hide the message. It's supposed to do the opposite. The message is often quite obvious; the colorful images and metaphors are to grab the attention of Ezekiel's listeners and to help them visualize what he's talking about.

Bad news first, good news last. The book divides into two parts. Chapters 1–24 contain Ezekiel's prophecies of warning made before the fall of Jerusalem. Using stern language, he condemns the Jews for arrogantly rebelling against God, and he warns them that judgment day is coming soon.

"I will bring the worst of the nations to take over the people's houses," Ezekiel says on behalf of God. "I will also end the pride of the strong, and their holy places will be dishonored" (7:24 NCV).

After the fall of Jerusalem, Ezekiel's message changes completely. He delivers good news for Judah. First, in chapters 25–32, he pronounces doom on the wicked countries that destroy the Jewish nation. Then in the final 16 chapters, 33–48, he promises the exiles that they will one day return to Jerusalem.

AUTHOR AND DATE

The prophet Ezekiel wrote this book to Jewish exiles living in the Babylonian Empire. He was merely a priest, and not a prophet, until God came to him in a vision. Ezekiel was thirty years old at the time, and five years into his exile that probably began in 597 BC. So the prophecies recorded in this book began in 593 BC, about eight years before the fall of Jerusalem.

ON LOCATION

Ezekiel lives near the Chebar River, close to the Babylonian Empire's capital city of Babylon— about fifty miles south of the modern Iraqi capital, Baghdad. That's nearly a thousand miles from his home in Jerusalem by way of the ancient caravan routes. In chapters 47 and 48 he charts the division of the land after the exile.

EZEKIEL OUTLINE

Ezekiel eats a scroll (2:3–3:3).

While Ezekiel is living in the Babylon area, with other upper-class Jews deported from Judah, God selects him to become a prophet. Ezekiel will deliver God's message to the Jews in exile.

To graphically symbolize that Ezekiel's words will come from God, he is handed a scroll filled with "Funeral songs, sad writings, and words about troubles were written on the front and back."

"Eat what you find; eat this scroll," God says. Afterward, Ezekiel is to go and speak to the people of Israel.

"Then I ate it," Ezekiel reports, "and it was as sweet as honey in my mouth" (2:10–3:3 NCV).

The presence of God leaves the temple (10:1–22).

In a dramatic vision that begins in chapter 8, Ezekiel is transported to the Jerusalem temple. What he witnesses there becomes part of the tragic, unbelievable message he must deliver. The temple represents the presence of God in Israel. The temple's back room, which contains the golden chest that holds the Ten Commandments, represents the earthly throne of God; it is the holiest site in Judaism. The Jews believe that God's presence has been there ever since King Solomon dedicated the temple.

Many Jews cannot conceive of God permitting the destruction of his 300-year-old temple and his holy city of Jerusalem. But what Ezekiel witnesses makes this not only believable, but probable. He sees the dazzling light of God's presence come out the door of the temple and ascend into the heavens.

God is gone.

Invaders from Babylon destroy Jerusalem and the temple (21:1–32).

"Ezekiel," God says, "A sword, a sword, made sharp and polished. It is made sharp for the killing. It is polished to flash like lightning" (21:9–10).

Carrying out God's sword of punishment will be an army of Babylonian soldiers. Ezekiel tells the Jews of his exiled community that

Sun
Mo
Tue
We
Thu
Frid
Satu
Sun
Mo
Tue
We
Thu
Frid
Satu
Sun
Mo
Tue
We

Babylon will build dirt ramps to the top of Jerusalem's walls, invade the city, kill the people, and tear down the walls. The city—and the sacred temple—will smolder in ruins.

The valley of dry bones (37:1–14).

After the messages of doom come messages of comfort. In a vision, Ezekiel is transported to a valley filled with dried-out human skeletons, broken and scattered about. The place looks like the site of a massacre long years ago.

God tells Ezekiel to speak to the bones. He's to say that God will "put muscles on you and flesh on you and cover you with skin. Then I will put breath in you so you will come to life" (37:6 NCV).

Even before Ezekiel is finished speaking, he hears a rattling throughout the valley. Bones snap into joints. Muscles spontaneously grow. Skin envelops them. Then a wind sweeps into the valley, blowing across the corpses and bring them to life. And in a shocking final scene, they all stand up.

"These bones are like all the people of Israel," God explains to Ezekiel. But God instructs the prophet to give this message to the people: "And I will put my Spirit inside you, and you will come to life. Then I will put you in your own land" (37:14 NCV).

A new temple in Jerusalem (40:1–43:27).

In yet another vision, God takes Ezekiel to a mountain. The year is 573 BC (40:1), some thirteen years after the temple was destroyed and fifty-seven years before the Jews would finish and dedicate the replacement temple.

What Ezekiel sees is a new and glorious temple. More importantly, he sees the presence of God returning to this holy place.

"I saw the glory of the God of Israel coming from the east," Ezekiel says. "It sounded like the roar of rushing water, and its brightness made the earth shine" (43:2 NCV).

As Ezekiel bows, he sees the Lord's glory come through the east gate and into the temple, filling it with brilliance. God has returned to his people, and his people have returned to him.

This is a message of deep comfort for a nation living in exile, feeling estranged from God and spiritually dead.

POINTS TO CONSIDER

Ezekiel's the writer. Though Bible experts sometimes disagree about who wrote various books of the Bible, most agree Ezekiel wrote this one. No other prophet in Israel expressed himself in words and actions so distinctly. This unusual brand of writing is easy to recognize throughout the book.

Babylon unearthed. In 1899, archaeologists began digging up the city that Ezekiel and other prophets wrote about. What they found confirms the Bible's account of a massive, beautiful pagan city. Even yet, the full extent of the city is uncertain. A writer in about 400 BC said the total length of the double walls, if arranged in one long line, would stretch out for sixty miles. Some of those walls were 100 yards high and nearly thirty yards thick. Inside the city were massive palaces and several temples to various Babylonian gods.

The eccentric. People reading this book for the first time may wonder if Ezekiel was an eccentric—or worse, crazy. His behavior at times was nothing short of bizarre: shaving his head, refusing to mourn his wife, cooking bread over manure, pretending to tremble as he ate—to name just a few. Yet what Ezekiel did, he did for a reason. And he explained the reasons.

The trembling hands during mealtime, for example, illustrated the fear that would soon overtake Judah; they, too, would eat with trembling hands.

Each of Ezekiel's dramatizations added power to his message. The people might forget the words, but they'd not likely forget the acted-out prophecy. And when the promises were fulfilled a few years later, the people would remember that Ezekiel said it would turn out this way.

FOR FURTHER STUDY

- The prophets Jeremiah and Daniel lived at the same time as Ezekiel—Jeremiah in Judah and Daniel in exile with Ezekiel. Read their books for more insight into the turbulent times.

- Some Bible experts believe that the writer of Revelation borrowed the strange and highly symbolic imagery from the books of Ezekiel and Daniel. Revelation also borrows some of the content. For example, like Ezekiel, Revelation talks about a new Jerusalem.

Sun
Mo
Tue
We
Thu
Frid
Satu
Sun
Mo
Tue
We
Thu
Frid
Satu
Sun
Mo
Tue
We

Daniel

A MEAL THE LIONS SKIPPED

Two of the Bible's most famous stories are reported in this book: Daniel in the lions' den, and the three young Hebrew men in the fiery furnace.

Part of what makes the book a classic is that all four men survived. It wasn't that the lions were stuffed, and the furnace was merely a sauna. The lions were hungry, and proved it the next morning by ravenously eating Daniel's accusers. The furnace was hotter than blue blazes, and instantly broiled the soldiers who pushed the Hebrews inside.

After these and other riveting stories come the lesser-known words of Daniel, in the second half of the book. The prophet tells about some of his incredibly strange visions concerning the future, and of angels explaining what the vision meant.

This short, 12-chapter book was apparently intended to comfort exiled Jews who wondered if God had forsaken them. But if allowed, the book could comfort all people. For through Daniel's stories and visions, God reminds us that he is Lord of creation. He has used his power to invade human history—making appearances in lion dens and kiln furnaces—and he will use that power to direct the future.

In the end, the goodness of his original creation will be fully restored. And when it is, "His rule will last forever" (7:14 NCV).

FAMOUS LINES

• "My God sent his angel to close the lions' mouths. They have not hurt me, because my God knows I am innocent" (6:22 NCV). *Daniel's explanation to the king of how he survived a night in the lions' den.*

• In my vision at night I saw in front of me someone who looked like a human being coming on the clouds in the sky . . . His rule will last forever, and his kingdom will never be destroyed. (7:13–14 NCV) *One of Daniel's end-time visions, which New Testament writers say refers to the second coming of Jesus.*

Background

Influential People

Daniel, Jewish prophet exiled in Babylon (1:6).

Shadrach, Meshach, Abednego, Daniel's friends, who survive the fiery furnace (1:7).

Belshazzar, ruler who sees the handwriting on the wall (5:1).

Theme

As a young nobleman in Jerusalem, Daniel is arrested by soldiers of the world's new superpower, Babylon. With many other Jewish leaders, Daniel is taken to Babylon and forced to live there. The Babylonians quickly realize how intelligent he is, and put him through a three-year training program to become a royal advisor.

With his colleagues, Shadrach, Meshach, and Abednego, he agrees to serve the king. But all four refuse to reject their faith in God. When they're ordered to worship an idol and to stop their daily prayers, they don't comply. This is a capital offense, but God protects them. Daniel's three friends survive a furnace. And Daniel survives a lion's den.

For fifty years or more Daniel serves various kings, first Babylonian, then Persian.

> ### Did You Know?
>
> • The old saying "I could see the handwriting on the wall" comes from Daniel's story of a terrified king watching a disembodied hand write a message on the palace wall (5:5).
>
> • Old Testament writers rarely speak about life after death. But Daniel does, offering the Old Testament's clearest insight into the resurrection: "Many people who have already died will live again. Some of them will wake up to have life forever, but some will wake up to find shame and disgrace forever" (12:2 NCV).

TIMELINE	BIBLE EVENTS	Babylon invades Judea and takes captives, including Daniel 605 BC	Babylon destroys Jerusalem 586 BC	Daniel in the lion's den 539 BC	Jews return to Jerusalem 538 BC
		600 BC	**550 BC**		**500 BC**
	WORLD EVENTS	Temples to Zeus and other gods built in Olympia, Greece 600 BC		Pythagorus invents geometry theories 540 BC	

Dates are approximate

POINTS OF INTEREST

God in control. The dramatic stories and astonishing visions of this book point to one main theme: God is in charge of human history.

At his command, Babylon rises and Babylon falls. When an emperor orders Daniel's friends executed, then another emperor condemns Daniel to death, God overrules. And when the Jews are discouraged, he gives them assurance through Daniel's visions of a glorious future.

Part 1, Part 2. It's easy to spot the end of Part 1 and the beginning of Part 2. The first six chapters are stories about Daniel and his friends. The remaining six chapters are about the mysterious visions of Daniel.

Apocalypse, the genre. Daniel's visions are written in a style that became a genre: apocalyptic. Books of this genre—the most famous of which is the perplexing New Testament book of Revelation—are filled with stories about spirit-world creatures delivering messages to human beings concerning future events.

The symbolism is so thick that even Daniel, a respected sage and trusted interpreter of dreams and visions, needs an angel to tell him what his visions mean. Yet even the explanations of the angel leave questions unanswered. For example, Daniel has a troubling vision about four beasts—a lion, a bear, a leopard, and an unnamed beast with iron teeth. An angel later explains that the four creatures represent four kingdoms that will emerge, one after the other. Neither the angel nor Daniel identifies which kingdoms they are, but many Bible experts speculate they are Babylon, Medo-Persia, Greece, and Rome.

Some Christians look to the apocalyptic writings of Daniel and Revelation for clues about the end of human history and the second coming of Jesus. These people try to make connections between the ancient symbolism and today's headlines. For example, they may associate prophecies about Babylon with modern-day Iraq. But in doing this, these Bible students are trying to explain what wise men like Daniel found unexplainable.

The point of the visions is not to provide a coded road map to the future, but to assure the reader that God's doing the driving.

AUTHOR AND DATE

Many believe Daniel wrote the book sometime after Cyrus defeated Babylon in 539 BC, because that's one of the last events described in the stories about Daniel.

Others say the book was written and compiled centuries later. (See "Looking for the Real Writer" in Points to Consider.)

ON LOCATION

The stories and visions take place in Babylon, capital city of the Babylonian Empire, to which Daniel and his friends are taken after the first Babylonian invasion of Judah in 605 BC.

DANIEL OUTLINE

Daniel's three friends in a fiery furnace (3:1–30).

When Babylon becomes the superpower, it steals some of the finest minds in the Middle East. Among many forced from Judah, with Daniel, are three men: Shadrach, Meshach, and Abednego. In recognition of their intelligence, they are trained to work in the palace.

Later, at a palace event, they refuse to bow in front of a new idol built for the king. As punishment, they are thrown into a furnace so hot that the flames leap out and kill the executioners. Yet inside the furnace, the three men walk around unharmed. With them is a fourth man who "looks like a god."

When the king calls the men back out, they aren't burnt, singed, or even smelling of smoke. The king vows to protect their right to worship God.

The handwriting on the wall (5:1–30).

Years later, a new king throws a banquet for a thousand of his top-ranking officials. He gets drunk and orders drinks served in the sacred cups stolen from the Jerusalem temple. Suddenly a human hand appears and writes these words on the plastered palace wall: "Mene, mene, tekel, and parsin." The king is terribly frightened.

He calls on Daniel, a respected advisor and interpreter of dreams, to explain what the words mean. "God has counted the days until your kingdom will end," Daniel says. "You have been weighed on the scales and found not good enough. Your kingdom is being divided and will be given to the Medes and the Persians" (5:26–28).

That very night, Babylon falls to a coalition of Medes and Persians.

Daniel in the lions' den (6:1–28).

When Daniel rises to become one of the top three officials in the Persian palace, jealous officials plot to kill him. They shrewdly convince King Darius to order the people to pray only to the king for the next thirty days, or face the lions. When the officials catch Daniel praying openly to God, they turn him in. The king is upset and tries to find a way to save Daniel. But his edict is irrevocable.

Daniel spends the night in a den of lions, but is protected by an angel. After a sleepless night, the king rushes to the den to find Daniel alive. The king orders Daniel removed and his accusers thrown in. The death they wished upon Daniel is the death they receive.

POINTS TO CONSIDER

Looking for King Belshazzar. Many Bible experts once wondered if Belshazzar—whom Daniel says was the last ruler of Babylon—was a fictional character. This is because ancient records show that Nabonidus was the Babylonian king overthrown by the Medes and Persians. More recent discoveries of Babylonian records reveal that Belshazzar was the son of Nabonidus, who during the last part of his reign shared power with his son.

This insight into Babylonian history answers another question that had vexed scholars: why Belshazzar asked Daniel to interpret the handwriting on the wall, then offered him not the number two position in the kingdom, but number three (5:7). Belshazzar himself held the second most influential position. The highest position he could offer was the number three spot.

Looking for the real writer. Daniel could not possibly be the writer of the book, some say. They cite many reasons. Here are two of the most frequently mentioned.

1. The book reads as though if were compiled by someone else. The visions are in the first person and might have been written by Daniel. But the stories are in the third person, as though written by someone else reporting Daniel's story. Also, the oldest copies of the book are written in two languages. The opening and closing chapters are written in Hebrew, and the other chapters are written in Aramaic, the language of the Babylonians and Persians.

2. Some of the visions so accurately reflect Middle Eastern history in the second and third centuries BC that they were likely written after those events—not as a prediction, but as history disguised as a prediction. For example, Daniel's description of what took place between the king of the north and the king of the south (chapter 11) matches history's account of what took places as the Ptolemies of Egypt and the Seleucids of Syria fought for control of the region after Alexander the Great died.

Bible experts who content that Daniel *did* write the book say that God is fully capable of empowering his prophets to predict the future.

And though the writing styles and two languages uses remain a puzzle, this doesn't mean that Daniel could not have done the writing at various times during his 50-year ministry. Jesus, in fact, commented about one of the visions "Daniel the prophet" (Matthew 24:15 NCV).

FOR FURTHER STUDY

- The stories of heroic Daniel are in some ways similar to the stories about earlier Israelite heroes Joseph (Genesis 39–41) and Mordecai (Esther). There are dreams and interpretations, and there are Jews being saved from mortal danger brought on by foreign leaders.

- For more of the apocalyptic style of writing, read Ezekiel's visions as well as the visions in Revelation.

- To see how Jesus interprets Daniel's reference to someone committing sacrilege in the temple (9:27; 11:31; 12:11) read Matthew 24:15–28. Jesus tells people to run to the hills when they see this happening. About forty years later, when Romans planted on the temple mount their flagpole-like standards decorated with idols, many Christians left. They escaped the destruction of Jerusalem, when in AD 70 Rome crushed the Jewish rebellion.

Hosea

THE PROPHET AND THE PROSTITUTE

God said, "Go, and marry an unfaithful woman and have unfaithful children, because the people in this country have been completely unfaithful to the Lord" (1:2).

Hosea did. And the story that follows has gripped the attention of people ever since. It's a story of God's persistent love for the Jewish people. Centuries earlier he had entered into a covenant with them. He would be their God, they would be his people. He would take care of them, they would obey the laws he had given through Moses.

God fulfilled his part of the agreement, but Israel didn't. Throughout much of their history, they were not God's people and they did not obey God's laws.

Before invoking the punishment clause in the ancient agreement, God appointed prophets to deliver his messages to the Jews, urging them to come back and warning them about what would happen if they didn't.

But the people treated the prophets with the same disrespect they had shown God and his law. As Jesus put it 700 years later while standing in Jerusalem, "You kill the prophets and stone to death those who are sent to you" (Matthew 23:37 NCV).

Yet the story of Hosea isn't mainly about spiritual rebellion or divine punishment. It's about God's inexplicable, relentless love even for people who treat him like the enemy.

For those who think the Old Testament God is cruel, Hosea reveals a preview of God practicing the compassion that his Son would later preach: "love your enemies" (Matthew 5:44 NCV).

FAMOUS LINES

- "They sow the wind, and reap the whirlwind" (8:7 NIV). *Hosea's way of saying that if Israel doesn't repent, they'll pay for their evil. They'll sow idolatry, and reap annihilation.*

- "Because you are not my people, and I am not your God" (1:9 NCV). *God's complaint about Israel, stated exactly opposite of the wording in the covenant agreement between Israel and God (Leviticus 26:12).*

BACKGROUND

INFLUENTIAL PEOPLE

Hosea, prophet to the northern Jewish nation of Israel (1:1).
Gomer, Hosea's prostitute wife (1:3).

THEME

God instructs Hosea to marry a prostitute as a living reminder that the people of Israel have spiritually prostituted themselves by worshiping the local gods. When Hosea's wife has three children, only the first of whom is clearly identified as her husband's, God instructs Hosea to give them names that symbolize Israel's potential fate: Jezreel, meaning "God Scatters," Lo-Ruhamah, meaning "No Mercy," and Lo-Ammi, meaning "Not My People."

Hosea's wife eventually leaves him and apparently moves in with another man, who treats her as his legal property. Acting on God's order, Hosea buys her back. "Go, show your love to a woman loved by someone else, who has been unfaithful to you," God says, "In the same way the Lord loves the people of Israel, even though they worship other gods and love to eat the raisin cakes" (3:1).

DID YOU KNOW?

• Hosea's name, in Hebrew, is almost identical to the names of Jesus and Joshua. All three mean "God saves." Hosea saves his wife from slavery, Joshua saves Israel from defeat, and Jesus saves the world from sin.

• Hosea is the first of what are known as the Twelve Minor Prophets. They're not "minor" because they have unimportant messages, but because their books are much shorter than those of the Major Prophets: Isaiah, Jeremiah, Ezekiel, and Daniel.

• Hosea was the only prophet from the northern Jewish nation of Israel who ministered to Israel. Amos, who also prophesied in Israel, came up from Judah to deliver God's message.

TIMELINE	BIBLE EVENTS		Jeroboam becomes Israel's king ┌------ 786 BC	Hosea becomes a prophet ┌----- 750 BC	Israel destroyed by Assyria ┌----- 722 BC
	800 BC			**750 BC**	**700 BC**
	WORLD EVENTS		First recorded Olympic games in Greece └------ 776 BC	European nomads invent the saddle 700 BC ------------	

Dates are approximate

Hosea then prophesies that the people will be punished if they don't quickly change their ways. Yet, in spite of their unfaithfulness, God pleads with them to come back by promising, "I will forgive them for leaving me and will love them freely" (14:4 NCV).

POINTS OF INTEREST

Gomer as an example of Israel. Notice the parallels between Gomer, Hosea's wife, and Israel. Both are unfaithful to their beloved. Both become enslaved, Gomer by an unnamed master (3:2), and Israel by Assyria (10:6). Both are sought back in spite of their unfaithfulness and their abandoning the one who loved them.

AUTHOR AND DATE

The book starts by identifying the writer: "Hosea son of Beeri" (1:1 NCV). As is the case with most prophets, very little is revealed about him.

Hosea lived and prophesied during the last twenty years or more of Israel's existence, before Assyria conquered the nation in 722 BC. Hosea said he was called to become God's prophet sometime during the 40-year reign of King Jeroboam II (786–746 BC).

ON LOCATION

Hosea's story takes place in the northern Jewish nation of Israel. The Israelites there seceded from the union about 200 years before Hosea's time, during the reign of King Solomon's son.

HOSEA OUTLINE

Hosea's family portrait (1:1–11).

In one of the most bizarre requests that God has ever made of a Bible character, he instructs the prophet Hosea to marry a prostitute. This marriage is to serve as a living, breathing symbol that Israel has broken its covenant with God and has been unfaithful by worshiping idols.

"I married Gomer," Hosea reports. During the marriage, Gomer has three children: two sons and a daughter. They, too, become part of the living symbol, for Hosea gives them Hebrew names that point to Israel's potential fate: Jezreel, meaning "God Scatters;" Lo-Ruhamah, meaning "No Mercy;" and Lo-Ammi, meaning "Not My People." God's covenant with Israel has a punishment clause for breach of contract. If Israel fails to honor the agreement, God has the right of scatter them among the nations, show them no mercy, and disown them.

Hosea's marriage and family serve as a daily reminder to the people around him about the sins of the nation, and the consequences that the Jews will suffer if they don't change their ways.

Yet, even if Israel fails to repent, God promises that there is coming a day when the people of Israel will be called "Children of the Living God," "My People," and "Shown Mercy." They will return home and enjoy the rich blessings of God.

Hose buys back his wife from another man (3:1–5).

Gomer leaves her husband and family, apparently to return to her trade. For in a poetic lament, God's complaint of Israel seems to parallel Hosea's complaint of Gomer. "Plead with your mother. Accuse her, because she is no longer my wife, and I am no longer her husband. Tell her to stop acting like a prostitute, to stop behaving like an unfaithful wife" (2:2).

God then gives Hosea a second bizarre command. Hosea is to fall in love with Gomer all over again. He's to do this to show that God still loves Israel "even though they worship idols."

By this time, Gomer is living with another man. Perhaps she provides him with income from her prostitution, and he provides her with room, board, and protection. The Bible doesn't say. Whatever their relationship, Hosea needs to buy her back as one would buy a slave. The price is fifteen silver coins and about ten bushels of grain.

In the remainder of the book, Hosea warns that if Israel continues on its current course, God will use Assyria to destroy the nation and lead the people into captivity. But if they give up their idols, Hosea assures them, God will forgive.

POINTS TO CONSIDER

Prostitution an apt comparison. When God told Hosea to marry a prostitute as a living, breathing symbol of Israel's spiritual unfaithfulness, he chose an appropriate metaphor. The people of Israel not only prostituted themselves spiritually, they also did it literally—worship of Canaanite gods involved having sex with temple prostitutes.

Though many people continued to worship God, they also worshiped local gods as a kind of spiritual disaster insurance. The most popular god seemed to be Baal, thought to provide fertility in field, flock, and family. Worshipers believed, for example, that the rain was Baal's semen. And they apparently thought they could stimulate him or at least convince him to honor their request for rain by having sex with his priests and priestesses. Worshipers also entertained him with fertility rites in thanks for good crops, herds, and the birth of a child.

The Hebrew word describing Gomer, however, was a word that usually referred to a street prostitute, not a temple prostitute.

Hosea's marriage, fact or fable? God would not do such a distasteful thing as to order a prophet to marry a prostitute. That has been the conclusion of many respected Jewish and Christian Bible experts throughout the ages, including the famous Christian theologians Martin Luther (father of the Protestants) and John Calvin (theological forbear of Southern Baptists and Presbyterians).

The marriage never happened, some said. It was simply a make-believe story that symbolized Israel's religious adultery. Others suggest Hosea experienced the marriage in a dream or a vision. Still others argue that Hosea was probably married, but his wife was faithful—he portrayed her as a prostitute only to dramatize his point about the strained relationship between God and Israel.

Ancient Jewish commentators, however, had no trouble accepting the story at face value. They believed God told Hosea to marry a prostitute, and he obeyed.

─── **FOR FURTHER STUDY** ───

- For a second opinion into what life was like in Israel during Hosea's day, read the nine-chapter book of Amos. He prophesied just a few years before Hosea.

- Other prophets who lived and wrote in Hosea's time were Isaiah and Micah, though they ministered in the southern Jewish nation of Judah.

- To see how other prophets compare Israel to an unfaithful bride, turn to Jeremiah 2–3 and Ezekiel 16, 23.

- For a New Testament perspective on God's persistent love, read 1 John 4:17–21.

7:00

8:00

9:00

0:00

1:00

oon

1:00

2:00

3:00

4:00

5:00

6:00

7:00

8:00

9:00

0:00

YEAR OF THE LOCUST

The poetry is masterful, the images stark and terrifying.

In the opening scene, locusts swarm in from the desert where predators are few and a single swarm can number into the billions. Starving and aggressive, they devour wheat, barley, figs, grapes, pomegranates—everything an insect can eat. Pastures are grazed to the ground, trees stripped to their naked branches.

As if this isn't bad enough, Joel warns the people that more trouble's ahead: to punish the nation for sin, God is allowing an invasion force to assemble somewhere up north. When it arrives, so does "the Lord's day of judging" (2:1 NCV). But there's hope. "Even now," the Lord says, "come back to me with all your heart" (2:12 NCV).

The choice confronting Israel is the choice confronting all of humanity. Joel says that one day, in "Judgment Valley," God will try the nations of the world and render his verdict. "I will definitely punish them," he promises, "people will live in Jerusalem from now on." (3:21, 20 NCV).

BACKGROUND

INFLUENTIAL PEOPLE

Joel, a prophet of God (1:1).

THEME

Swarm after swarm of locusts invade Israel, devouring the crops and then planting eggs that will hatch and consume the next generation of plants. With harvest and pasture gone, people and livestock go hungry. Water holes lose their shade and dry up. Famine scars the land for years to come.

Joel uses this natural disaster to warn of an even worse catastrophe. Because the people have sinned—Joel doesn't mention how—a monstrously enormous army will invade the land and strip it bare. Joel may be talking about an ancient invasion, an end-time apocalypse, or both.

> ### DID YOU KNOW?
>
> • Swarms of ten billion locusts, an aggressive kind of grasshopper, occasionally invade the Middle East. Eyewitnesses to a 1915 swarm in Israel said the locusts flew around for five days, darkening the sky. Afterward, they ate every plant they saw, then left their eggs behind. The eggs can be killed by plowing the ground.

"Even now," the Lord says through Joel. "Come back to me with all your heart" (2:12 NCV).

If the people do, they can escape a horrifying judgment that Joel simply calls "the day of the Lord."

"He is kind and shows mercy," God assures the people. "He can change his mind about doing harm" (2:13 NCV).

TIMELINE

	BIBLE EVENTS				
		Jeroboam becomes Israel's king ---- 786 BC		Hosea becomes a prophet ---- 750 BC	Israel destroyed by Assyria ---- 722 BC
	800 BC		**750 BC**		**700 BC**
	WORLD EVENTS		First recorded Olympic games in Greece ---- 776 BC	European nomads invent the saddle 700 BC ----	

Dates are approximate

POINTS OF INTEREST

The day of the Lord. This is an important phrase in Joel, repeated five times in the short, three-chapter book. Many prophets use this phrase to talk about any time God does something to a nation or a generation of people—whether to punish or protect.

Joel uses the phrase in both ways. It's a dark and dreadful day when God will punish his enemies, and it's a bright and glorious day when he will save the faithful. Joel also uses the phrase, in chapter 3, to hint of what other prophets and the New Testament describe as a final Judgment Day at the end of human history, when God destroys everything evil. (See "Day of the Lord" in Points to Consider.)

The coming of the Holy Spirit. God says through Joel that there is coming a day when "I will pour out my spirit . . . Then anyone who calls on the Lord will be saved" (2:29, 32 NCV).

That day arrives about two months after the resurrection of Jesus, according to Peter, one of the original disciples. But before Jesus ascends to heaven, he tells the disciples to wait in Jerusalem until the Holy Spirit comes upon them. On the day of Pentecost, a Jewish holiday fifty days after Passover, "They were all filled with the Holy Spirit," (Acts 2:4 NCV). Before a huge crowd of pilgrims from around the world, Peter declares that the prophecy of Joel has today been fulfilled.

AUTHOR AND DATE

The writer is the prophet "Joel the son of Pethuel" (1:1 NCV). He's not mentioned anywhere else in the Old Testament, though there are references to about a dozen other men with this popular name. The only other mention of the prophet Joel comes in a sermon by Peter on the day of Pentecost, when Peter declared that one of Joel's prophecies had just been fulfilled.

There are no solid clues about when Joel lived. His book is preserved among those of the prophets from the 700s BC, just before Assyria destroyed the northern Jewish nation of Israel. Joel does talk about invaders coming from the north—as Assyria did in the 700s BC, Babylon in the 500s BC, and Alexander the Great of Greece in the 300s BC. But Joel doesn't say who the invaders are, so Bible experts are left guessing.

ON LOCATION

It appears that Joel lived in the southern Jewish nation of Judah, which he mentions frequently. But he also speaks of Israel. The name "Israel" could refer either to the northern nation of Israel or to the entire Jewish race, in both Israel and Judah. He may have prophesied in the years before Assyria overran Israel.

JOEL OUTLINE

Invasions of locusts (1:1–20).

"What the cutting locusts have left, the swarming locusts have eaten; what the swarming locusts have left, the hopping locusts have eaten, and what the hopping locusts have left, the destroying locusts have eaten," says the prophet Joel. "Be sad, farmers.

Cry loudly, you who grow grapes. Cry for the wheat and the barley. Cry because the harvest of the field is lost. The vines have become dry, and the fig trees are dried up. The pomegranate trees, the date palm trees, the apple trees—all the trees in the field have died" (1:4, 11–12 NCV).

The food is gone. The rivers are dry. And the livestock wander aimlessly in search of pasture.

As terrible as this is, Joel warns, the worst is yet to come.

Invasion of massive army (2:1–27).

"The LORD's day of judging is coming; it is near," Joel continues his ominous prophecy. "His army is very large! . . . Before them, earth and sky shake" (2:1, 2, 10 NCV).

But it's not too late. The people of Judah can escape the coming disaster if only they will return to God with all their heart. "He is kind and shows mercy," God says. "He can change his mind about doing harm" (2:13 NCV).

Young men and women prophesying (2:28–3:21).

In the years to come, God says he will more than make up for the suffering that Israel has endured because of their sins. "And the threshing floors will be full of grain; the barrels will overflow with new wine and olive oil " (2:24 NCV).

Later, God will give out his spirit to everyone. "Your sons and daughters will prophesy, your old men will dream dreams, and your young men will see visions" (2:28 NCV). On the Jewish holiday of Pentecost, centuries later, Peter stood in the courtyard of Herod's temple and proclaimed that this prophecy had just been fulfilled—the followers of Jesus had been the first to receive the gift of the Holy Spirit (Acts 2:14–21).

Sun
Mor
Tues
Wec
Thu
Frid
Satu
Sun
Mor
Tues
Wec
Thu
Frid
Satu
Sun
Mor
Tues
Wec

That day, 3,000 listeners believed him, were baptized, and received the Spirit.

POINTS TO CONSIDER

Northern army. Joel warns that unless the people stop sinning, God is going to punish them by letting a huge army invade from the north.

Throughout Israel's history, that's where most of the invaders came from. When God decided to punish the northern Jewish nation of Israel, Assyria invaded from the north and conquered the country in 722 BC. When God decided to punish the southern nation of Judah, Babylon invaded from the north several times, eventually destroying Jerusalem in 586 BC.

Later, Alexander the Great invaded from the north in the 300s BC, followed by the Seleucids of Syria in the 200s BC, then the Romans in the 100s BC.

The day of the Lord. This is a waffling sort of a phrase. Over the millennium that it took to create the Old Testament, writers used this phrase inconsistently—sometimes presenting it as doomsday, and other times presenting it as deliverance day.

The single consistency is that it was always a time when God got involved in human history and changed the course of events. Writers described this divine action in many ways, including "that day," "then," and "day of visitation."

Initially the phrase had a positive ring; it was a day the Israelites longed for—when God would deliver them from their enemies, as he had done by freeing the Israelites from Egypt. But later on, the prophets began charging that Israel was the enemy. And like other evil nations that refused to repent of sin, the Jews would die. So the anticipated day of the Lord became the feared day of doom.

Yet the prophets were unwilling to limit the phrase to doomsday, just as New Testament writers were unwilling to limit Judgment Day to the defeat of God's enemies. The prophets said that after punishment comes the restoration of God's people. And the New Testament says that after Judgment Day comes eternal life for the faithful.

The day of the Lord—any day God interrupts human history—is a bad day for the godless and a good day for the righteous.

For Further Study

- To see what Peter said was the fulfillment of Joel's prophecy about the Holy Spirit, read Acts 1–2.

- For what other prophets say about the day of the Lord, read Amos 5:18–27; Zephaniah 1:14–2:3; Isaiah 13:6–14:2. For Jesus' insight, read Matthew 25:31–46.

- Revelation 19:11–21 and 20:11–15 are judgment scenes similar to that in Joel.

Sun
Mo
Tue
We
Thu
Frid
Satu
Sun
Mo
Tue
We
Thu
Frid
Satu
Sun
Mo
Tue
We

Amos

WHEN MONEY TALKS, WHO HEARS THE POOR?

If you want to know what God thinks about a rich society that exploits the poor and lets money do the talking in the courts, read Amos.

Long before advocacy leaders and civil rights organizers, there was a sheepherder named Amos. With vicious honesty, he condemned the wealthy who "they walk on poor people as if they were dirt, and they refuse to be fair to those who are suffering" (2:7 NCV).

Women who mistreat poor servants and beggars, Amos charged, are "fat cows" who will be dragged away by "sharp hooks," like those that butchers used to haul a carcass to the chopping block.

> ### FAMOUS LINES
> • "Get ready to meet your God" (4:12 NCV).
>
> • "Let goodness flow like a never-ending stream" (5:24 NCV).

Amos also condemned leaders, nobles, and merchants who cheat honest people, tax them to death, and twist the face of justice until no one can recognize it anymore.

This criticism did not endear Amos to Israel's leaders. They had two words for him: "Go back!" (7:12 NCV).

But the judgment they imposed on him was the judgment they would face. God wouldn't stand for this kind of *status quo*. He stepped into human history and rearranged Israel's socioeconomic system. Suddenly, with the swooping of an Assyrian invasion force, the rich were on the same level as the poor.

God's concern about social issues didn't end in Old Testament times. Neither did his ability to step into history and change what greedy humans won't.

BACKGROUND

INFLUENTIAL PEOPLE

Amos, prophet, shepherd, and fig farmer (1:1).

Amaziah, a priest who chases Amos off (7:10).

THEME

God calls on Amos, a shepherd and fig grower, to leave his small

village at the desert's edge in the southern Jewish nation of Judah. Amos's task is to deliver a prophetic message to the northern nation of Israel, which is wallowing in prosperity. Amos is to throw the spotlight on the nation's most blatant sins. Wealthy folks are getting richer at the expense of the exploited poor. In court, the verdict goes to the client with the most money. Father and son sleep with the same prostitute. People go through the motions of worship, thinking rituals are enough to appease God.

"I will make you get stuck," God says through Amos (2:13 NCV). Soldiers will invade the land and carry the people away as captives.

A priest named Amaziah replies, "Seer, go back right now to Judah!" (7:12 NCV).

Amos leaves, but not before promising that Amaziah's children will be killed in the war, and the priest will die in a foreign country. As for Israel, Amos leaves the people with a hopeful promise: God will one day restore the nation he has been forced to destroy.

POINTS OF INTEREST

Crimes of injustice. Amos criticizes the people for doing nothing about social injustice running rampant. The poor don't have enough

TIMELINE	BIBLE EVENTS		Amos begins his ministry 760 BC		Northern nation of Israel destroyed 722 BC	Dates are approximate
		800 BC		**750 BC**		**700 BC**
	WORLD EVENTS		Ohio River people build earth burial mounds 800 BC		King Romulus founds Rome 753 BC	Ethiopia starts 50-year rule of Egypt 716 BC

money for food and clothing, and are sold into slavery if they can't pay for a pair of sandals they buy on credit. Merchants regularly cheat people with rigged scales. Judges are bought and paid for. The poor and powerless don't have a chance, unless God steps in.

The mere motions of worship. Many people do nothing more than go through the motions of worship. They think that bringing the appropriate sacrifice is all they need to do to please God. "Come to the city of Bethel and sin; come to Gilgal and sin even more. Offer your sacrifices every morning," Joel says sarcastically (4:4 NCV).

The day of the Lord. This is a phrased used by many Jews of the time. For them, it refers to a day when God will deliver Israel from harm and punish Israel's enemies. But like other prophets, Amos warns that the day of the Lord is nothing for Israel to look forward to: "It will bring darkness for you, not light!" (5:18 NCV).

AUTHOR AND DATE

"These are the words of Amos," the book begins. "One of the shepherds from the town of Tekoa" (1:1 NCV). Amos also tended a grove of fig trees. So he was both a herder and a farmer, living about ten miles south of Jerusalem. He said he was not a prophet, until God gave him this message to deliver to Israel (7:14–15).

His eloquent prose and poetry suggest he was more than a hired shepherd and farmhand. He was apparently an educated man, and perhaps the owner of the flock and grove.

He says he lived when Jeroboam was king of Israel (786–746 BC). The national prosperity that Amos talks about fits the conditions during the later part of Jeroboam's reign, beginning about 760 BC.

ON LOCATION

Amos leaves his hometown and country—Tekoa, ten miles south of Jerusalem in the southern Jewish nation of Judah—and takes God's message to Bethel, a worship center in the northern nation of Israel.

Amos Outline

Sun
Mon
Tues
Wed
Thu
Frid
Satu
Sun
Mon
Tues
Wed
Thu
Frid
Satu
Sun
Mon
Tues
Wed

Amos leaves his flocks to deliver a message (1:1; 7:12–15).

Amos is not someone who earns his living as a prophet, advising national leaders.

"I do not make my living as a prophet, nor am I a member of a group of prophets," he tells his listeners. "I make my living as a shepherd, and I take care of sycamore trees. But the LORD took me away from tending the flock and said to me, 'Go, prophesy to my people Israel.'"

His herds are in a different country, the rival Jewish nation of Judah, in the southland. Acting on God's orders, Amos leaves his work. He also leaves his village of Tekoa, south of Jerusalem, and his country of Judah. He travels twenty miles north of his home to Israel's border town of Bethel, one of the worship centers in the northern Jewish nation.

"I will punish Israel" (2:1–3:15).

The message Amos delivers is blunt. "This is what the LORD says: "For the many crimes of Israel, I will punish them. For silver, they sell people who have done nothing wrong; they sell the poor to buy a pair of sandals. They walk on poor people as if they were dirt, and they refuse to be fair to those who are suffering" (2:6–7 NCV).

For this and more, God says he will "Now I will make you get stuck, as a wagon loaded with grain gets stuck. No one will escape, not even the fastest runner.

Strong people will not be strong enough; warriors will not be able to save themselves" (2:13–14 NCV).

In fact, the nation is strong and prosperous. Optimism is high. So the gloom and doom message of Amos is a bit hard for the citizens to swallow.

Rich people oppress the poor (4:1–13).

You cows of Bashan!" Amos says on behalf of the Lord. A more literal translation calls them "cows of Bashan." In Bible times, cattle from Bashan, in southern Syria, are famous as pampered, prime stock, well fed and well bred.

"You take things from the poor and crush people who are in need,"

Amos accuses these women. "The time will come when you will be taken away by hooks, and what is left of you with fishhooks" (4:1–2 NCV). (Pictures chiseled into stone show Assyrian soldiers leading prisoners on ropes attached to hooks pierced through the noses or lips of captives.)

Amos says God has tried to get their attention, to convince them to return to righteous living. He has withheld rain. He has sent locusts to devour their orchards. He has even killed many people. "Still you," God says, "did not come back to me . . . So this is what I will do to you, Israel; because I will do this to you, get ready to meet your God, Israel" (4:8, 12 NCV).

"Turn back to me, and you will live" (5:1–27).

Even now, at this late date, God gives Israel a chance to mend its ways. "Come to the Lord," Amos pleads, "and live, or he will move like fire against the descendants of Joseph" (5:6 NCV).

Until the Jews stop doing wrong and start doing right, God won't receive their worship. "If you offer me burnt offerings and grain offerings, I won't accept them—You bring your best fellowship offerings of fattened cattle, but I will ignore them. Take the noise of your songs away from me! I won't listen to the music of your harps" (5:22–23 NCV).

What God wants is for his people to "let justice flow like a river, and let goodness flow like a never-ending stream" (5:24 NCV).

God measures Israel with a plumb line (7:1–17).

Israel is a crooked nation. God shows this to Amos in a vision.

"This is what he showed me: The Lord stood by a straight wall, with a plumb line in his hand" (7:7 NCV).

What this plumb line shows is that the people of Israel "don't measure up." The wall is crooked. And like all crooked walls, it must come down.

Both literally and figuratively, the walls of Israel eventually collapse during a war instigated by God. "I will send war," Amos says on behalf of God.

The rebuilding of Israel (9:11–15).

Even if Israel refuses to repent—and refuse they do—all is not lost.

Though God's contract with the Jews, spelled out in the law of Moses, gives him the right to annihilate Israel for breach of contract and to sever all relationship with any survivors, God refuses to do so.

Instead—even before the punishment arrives—God gives Israel a hopeful message. It's the final word he chooses to leave with them. "In that day," he says, "I will set it up again and mend its broken places. I will rebuild its ruins as it was before" (9:11 NCV).

POINTS TO CONSIDER

A prophecy fulfilled. "I, the Lord God, am watching the sinful kingdom Israel. I will destroy it," God said through Amos. "But I will not completely destroy Jacob's descendants," says the LORD. "I am giving the command to scatter the nation of Israel among all nations" (9:8–9 NCV).

Amos predicted this in the mid-700s BC, when Israel's economy and national confidence were riding high. The superpowers of Assyria and Egypt weren't a threat because they were occupied elsewhere.

About a year after Israel's confidence-boosting king died, however, Tiglath-pileser rose to power in Assyria. About forty years after Amos brought his message of doom to Israel, the Assyrians brought the horrifying reality. Israel's capital city of Samaria fell in the winter of 722 BC; many survivors were taken away in chains, never to return.

A prophecy not fulfilled. "I will bring my people Israel back from captivity," God said. "I will plant my people on their land, and they will not be pulled out again from the land which I have given them," says the LORD your God" (9:14–15 NCV). That never happened in biblical times, nor does it seem likely that Israel—or any other nation in modern times—could bank on such a promise.

Some Bible experts say this will take place after the second coming of Jesus, either during a 1,000-year reign on earth or perhaps when all of God's people—Jews and non-Jews—are resettled in heaven.

Hope is an add-on. Some say that the book's hopeful conclusion, beginning at 9:11, was added later, perhaps by Amos after he returned home or perhaps centuries later by someone else. They argue that this conclusion reads like an afterthought and doesn't mesh with the prophet's message of doom.

    But if the words aren't original to Amos, his prophetic book
would have been the only one in the Bible to preach doom
exclusively, without any reference to hope.

For Further Study

• Besides Amos, two other prophets known for their concern
  about the poor and other social justice issues are Micah and
  Isaiah.

• You'll find social justice themes addressed in the New
  Testament by Jesus (Matthew 5–6; 25:31–46) and throughout
  the short book of James.

Obadiah

PAYBACK

We don't like to see the bad guys get away with something. Not in books, not in movies, and certainly not in life—especially our lives. All human beings seem to share a concern for justice.

Obadiah saw injustice about as bad as it gets. He saw what happened after invaders swarmed on Judah. Jewish refugees ran for their lives to the neighboring country of Edom, racial cousins who, like Judah, had descended from Abraham and Isaac. But did Edom embrace their cousins? No, Edom ambushed them. Then Edom arrested them, turned them over to the invaders, and scavenged Judah for anything left behind.

The Jews would not live to see Edom get what it deserved. But the Jews had this promise from God: "The LORD's day of judging is coming soon to all the nations. The same evil things you did to other people will happen to you; they will come back upon your own head" (15 NCV).

> ### FAMOUS LINES
>
> "The same evil things you did to other people will happen to you" (15 NCV). *Obadiah's warning to the country of Edom is the flip side of the Golden Rule: "Do to others what you want them to do to you"* (Matthew 7:12 NCV).

If Obadiah and the other prophets said only one thing about God, they said this: God settles his accounts. And he does it justly. Sooner or later, sometimes later, sin is punished. Always. The story of Edom is just one of many examples in the Bible.

Justice may sometimes be outside our reach. But it's always within God's reach. And in due time, justice will win. The bad guys won't.

BACKGROUND

INFLUENTIAL PEOPLE

Obadiah, a prophet who warns the people of Edom that they'll get the punishment they deserve (1:1).

THEME

Invaders attack and destroy the southern Jewish nation of Judah. Edom, Judah's neighbor south of the Dead Sea, takes delight in this. Edom even arrests the Jewish refugees and turns them over to the invaders. Then Edom raids Judah to steal anything the attackers may have missed.

> ### DID YOU KNOW?
>
> • The Jews and Edomites were related. Jews descended from Jacob. Edomites descended from his twin brother, Esau.
>
> • Obadiah is the shortest book in the Old Testament, with only one chapter and 21 verses.
>
> • Edom was famous for its wise men. One of Job's well-educated friends came from there (Job 2:11).

For this, Obadiah promises, Edom will be wiped out. Judah, on the other hand, will be restored.

POINTS OF INTEREST

Part 1 is doom; Part 2 is hope. Verses 1–14 talk about how God will punish the people of Edom for their cruelty. The rest of the short book (verses 15–21) promises that the Jews will one day return to their land, and will even capture the land of their enemies, including Edom.

TIMELINE	BIBLE EVENTS	Babylon invades Judah and takes captives 605 BC	Babylon suppresses Judean rebellion, taking more captives 597 BC	Babylon destroys Jerusalem 586 BC	Jews start returning to Jerusalem 538 BC
		600 BC	**550 BC**		**500 BC**
	WORLD EVENTS	Temples to Zeus and other gods built on Olympia, Greece 600 BC		Chinese philosopher Confucious is born 551 BC	Dates are approximate

AUTHOR AND DATE

Obadiah is the prophet who wrote this book. We know nothing about him except that he had a common name that means "worshiper of the Lord."

Because Obadiah talks about Edom's treachery against Judah, Bible scholars assume the book was written sometime after 586 BC. That's when Babylon conquered Judah, with support from Edom.

ON LOCATION

The events unfold in the southern Jewish country of Judah, and in Edom south of the Dead Sea. When Babylon conquered Judah, the Edomites collaborated with the invaders, working against their Hebrew cousins.

© 2006 Thomas Nelson, Inc.

OBADIAH OUTLINE

Obadiah's promise: Edom will fall (1–14).

The people of Edom live in mountaintop fortresses, secure in their defenses. "I will still bring you down," God promises, "Even if you fly high like the eagle and make your nest among the stars" (4 NCV).

What God vows to do is wipe them out and give their land to others. The reason? The Edomites, descendants of Esau, celebrate and even contribute to the destruction of Judah, descendants of Esau's twin brother, Jacob.

After invaders—probably the Babylonians—conquer Judah, the people of Edom tour the destroyed Jewish cities "sneering and stealing." Worse, they round up Jewish refugees and turn them over to the invaders.

It's true that God is punishing the Jews for their sins. But that doesn't give Edom the right to gloat or to profit from Judah's disaster. Yet Edom does both.

One day, when the Jews are done suffering the consequences of their sin, God promises to let them return home. When that happens, "The people of Jacob will be like a fire and the people of Joseph like a flame. But the people of Esau will be like dry stalks. The people of Jacob will set them on fire and burn them up" (18 NCV).

══ POINTS TO CONSIDER ══

Rock City abandoned. Obadiah says that though the people of Edom live in a rock fortress, they will be wiped out (3, 9). In Jordan, south of the Dead Sea and near the border with Israel, archaeologists have studied Petra—an Edomite city with homes and temples carved into the solid rock of a hillside.

What they found there and in other Edomite cities is that by the 400s BC Arabs had driven the people of Edom from their land. Ironically, the Edom refugees fled to Judah, where they lived. By the first century AD, King Herod of the Jews was recognized as the ruler of Edom. But in AD 70, when Rome crushed a nationwide Jewish rebellion, the people of Edom disappeared from history.

The ruins of Petra are now a tourist attraction.

Obadiah the plagiarist? Compare verse 1–9 with Jeremiah 49:7–22. They're so much alike that either Obadiah was drawing from Jeremiah's work, or vice versa. Another possibility is that both men drew from the work of yet another prophet.

In our day, this would border on plagiarism. But in ancient times, there were no copyright laws. And besides, both men credited the source of the words: God. Of course, the other possibility is that God simply spoke the same message to two different prophets. After all, he's certainly capable.

Throughout the Old and New Testaments, writers often referred to prophecies and teachings mentioned elsewhere in the Bible. Sometimes, the writers simply quoted the material. Other times, they condensed it or commented on it, in much the same way that preachers do today. Chronicles, for example, expands on some of the events described in Kings.

For Further Study

- Read Jeremiah 49:7–22. The message is nearly identical to Obadiah 1–9.

- For other prophecies against Edom, read Amos 1:11–12; Isaiah 34; and Ezekiel 25:12–14.

Jonah

PROPHET OVERBOARD

This is not your standard book of prophecy.

It's the only book in which a prophet gets swallowed by a fish. And it's the only prophetic book that doesn't have a collection of prophecies. Instead, it serves up a miniscule one-sentence prophecy, which turns out wrong.

God tells the prophet Jonah to go east and deliver a message of doom to Assyria. Instead, Jonah goes west. He boards a ship on the Mediterranean. The Bible doesn't say why he ran. Maybe he was afraid the story would turn out like it did and that he would be mortified when his prophecy didn't come true. Or perhaps he couldn't get enthusiastic about delivering death threats to an empire that thought fine art—suitable for framing on palace walls—was stone carvings that showed captured enemies getting impales on stakes.

FAMOUS LINES

• "The LORD caused a big fish to swallow Jonah" (1:17 NCV).

The Assyrians were ruthless. For entertainment, Assyrian soldiers cut open the stomachs of live prisoners, inserted a live cat, and swiftly sewed the stomach back up. Then they watched the cat claw its way out.

In all of the Bible, Jonah is the only prophet of God whose ministry was not directed to the Jews. Despite his reservations, Jonah took his ministry to Assyria. In Jonah's time there was probably no better way to show that God's love is available to everyone.

BACKGROUND

INFLUENTIAL PEOPLE

Jonah, a Jewish prophet who reluctantly takes God's message to an Assyrian city (1:1).

THEME

God tells Jonah to go to Nineveh, a huge city deep within the feared Assyrian Empire. Jonah's assignment is to warn the citizens that God will destroy their city in forty days.

Jonah apparently fears the Assyrians more than he fears God, so he boards a ship headed in the opposite direction, some scholars think to Spain. A fierce storm erupts. To appease God, the sailors throw Jonah overboard. The prophet is swallowed by a large fish of some kind. Three days later the fish vomits Jonah onto a beach.

> ### DID YOU KNOW?
>
> • The Bible doesn't say a whale swallowed Jonah, only that a "big fish" did.
>
> • In predicting his resurrection, Jesus compares his three days in the grave to the three days Jonah spends inside the fish (Matthew 12:40).

From there, Jonah walks to Nineveh and delivers the message. To his dismay, the people repent and God spares them. Angry that his prophecy hasn't come true, Jonah goes to the desert where he sits and pouts. The book ends abruptly with God explaining that he has a right to show mercy on the 120,000 citizens of Nineveh.

TIMELINE	BIBLE EVENTS		Jeroboam begins his 41-year reign ------ 786 BC		Jonah goes to Nineveh, perhaps before end of Jeroboam's reign ------746 BC Dates are approximate
		800 BC		**750 BC**	**700 BC**
	WORLD EVENTS		Solar eclipse confirmed in Chinese history ------ 775 BC		Assyrians choose Nineveh as capital, and start rebuilding it 705 BC ------

POINTS OF INTEREST

Only one sentence of prophecy. Books by other prophets contain a lot of prophecies. Not Jonah. It has one prophetic sentence: "After forty days, Nineveh will be destroyed!" (3:4 NCV). The rest of this short book tells the story of what leads up to this prophecy, and what happens afterward.

God's compassion extending beyond the Jews. Many Jews in Bible times consider themselves to be not just the chosen people of God, but the only people of God—the only ones who worship him, and the only ones he cares about. But as in the story of Ruth, a woman from Moab, the story of Jonah confirms that God cares deeply about non-Jewish people as well.

AUTHOR AND DATE

We don't know if Jonah wrote the book, or if someone else did. But the story is about "Jonah, son of Amittai," a Galilean prophet from a village near Nazareth. This same "Jonah, son of Amittai" is identified as a prophet who supported King Jeroboam's successful efforts to expand the borders of Israel in the late 700s BC (2 Kings 14:25).

If Jonah wrote the book, he probably did it during the eighth century BC, perhaps during the reign of Jeroboam (786–746 BC). It is possible, however, that someone else—perhaps centuries later—recorded this short, dramatic story that had been passed along by word of mouth for generations. The statement that Nineveh "was" a great city (3:3) would suggest the book was written after Babylon destroyed the city in 612 BC.

ON LOCATION

The story begins in Israel, continues somewhere aboard a ship in the Mediterranean Sea, then inside a fish. It ends in Nineveh, an Assyrian city in what is now northern Iraq.

JONAH OUTLINE

Jonah overboard (1:1–2:10).

When God orders Jonah into the heart of the feared Assyrian Empire, to warn the people of Nineveh that their city is going to be destroyed, Jonah runs away. He books passage on a ship headed in the opposite direction.

God churns up a storm that nearly swamps the ship. Finally, in desperation, the sailors turn to prayer. Jonah confesses that he is the cause of their trouble, and he advises them to throw him overboard. Initially, the refuse and try rowing back to shore. But when they realize it's hopeless, they throw him overboard, and the sea calms down.

Jonah is swallowed by a huge fish of some type. He remains inside for three days, praying a mystifying prayer of thanks to God for rescuing him. Then the fish vomits him up onto a beach.

Jonah preaches in Nineveh (3:1–10).

Jonah walks to Nineveh and delivers the assigned message: "After forty days, Nineveh will be destroyed!" (3:4 NCV).

For some unexplained reason, the Assyrians believe him—a stranger from another country. Yet back in Israel and Judah, the Jews are ignoring God's prophets.

The Assyrians—even the king—stop eating and drinking, dress in ragged clothes, and sit in the dust. They do this to show their sorrow. They won't even let their animals eat or drink.

When God sees this, he has pity and does not destroy them as he had planned.

Jonah is furious that his prophecy doesn't come true (4:1–10).

Jonah is incensed. "When I was still in my own country this is what I said would happen," he complains to God. "I knew that you are a God who is kind and shows mercy. You don't become angry quickly, and you have great love. I knew you would choose not to cause harm. So now I ask you, LORD, please kill me. It is better for me to die than to live" (4:2–3 NCV).

Ironically, Jonah is one of the few prophets in the Bible who is successful. He convinces the people to repent. Yet he considers this anything but success. As far as he is concerned, success requires the annihilation of the 120,000 citizens of Nineveh. Fortunately for Nineveh, God disagrees.

The point of the entire story is that God deeply cares about everyone, and he is eager to show mercy to anyone genuinely sorry for the wrongs they have done. Anyone.

POINTS TO CONSIDER

God cares about non-Jews too. The main point of the story—that God cares about everyone, not just the Jews—is a point repeated throughout the Bible.

When God selected Abraham to become the father of the Jewish nation, God said "And all the people on earth will be blessed through you" (Genesis 12:3 NCV). Later, through the prophet Isaiah, God told the Jews, "I will make you a light for all nations to show people all over the world the way to be saved" (49:6 NCV).

And Paul, writing to Christians in Rome, said that if a person has faith in God it doesn't matter if that person is a Jew or a Gentile. "The same Lord is the Lord of all and gives many blessings to all who trust in him," as the Scripture says, "Anyone who calls on the Lord will be saved." (Romans 10:12–13 NCV).

History or parable? Some Bible scholars say that the story of Jonah never really happened. The story, they argue, is a parable that uses the name of a real prophet, in much the same way that Jesus' parable about Lazarus and a rich man may refer to the Lazarus that Jesus raised from the dead.

The story shares a lot in common with short, dramatic parables that teach a message. For example, the forty-eight verses are packed with captivating miracles—the story's an attention grabber. And it ends abruptly, as soon as the moral is delivered. In addition, Jonah is like none of the other books of prophecy: it's nearly all story, with only one sentence of prophecy. Also, there is no record in Assyrian documents to confirm Jonah's story that Nineveh repented.

Other Bible experts say the story did take place. They argue that Jonah is mentioned in 2 Kings 14:25 and that Jesus compared his own burial with that of Jonah's three days in the belly of the fish (Matthew 12:40).

> But whether Jonah is history or parable, the message remains unchanged. God cares about everyone, and he wants us to do the same.

= FOR FURTHER STUDY =

- For another story about God showing mercy to a non-Jew, read the short book of Ruth.

- For more about God's concern for non-Jews, read Genesis 12:1–3; Isaiah 42:6–7; 49:6; Romans 10–11.

- For background on what life was like in Israel during Jonah's day, read the book of Amos. The two prophets ministered about the same time.

Micah

PAINTING A PORTRAIT OF GOD

Job one for the Bible is to show human beings what God is like. Micah shows there are two sides to God.

There's holiness, which means he's good and just. He takes a stand against us when we become evil and unjust.

And there's love, which means he's like a compassionate father. No matter what we do, good or bad, he loves us.

The book of Micah reads like the flip of a coin. Heads, you've sinned and God will punish you. Tails, he loves you and He'll forgive you. In an ongoing cycle, Micah identifies the sins of the Jews and the consequences they'll have to face. Then he consoles them with the promise that, no matter what, God loves them.

Three times Micah warns the Jews that because of their nation's long-standing sinfulness, the nation will die. Then he promises a saving miracle: one day the nation will be restored. Not because the Jews deserve it for good conduct, but because God loves them and forgives them.

This isn't just a history lesson. It's a glimpse into the character of God. What he did for the Jews, he continues to do for all people. He stands against people who do evil, but loves them nonetheless.

FAMOUS LINES

• "They will hammer their swords into plow blades and their spears into hooks for trimming trees. Nations will no longer raise swords against other nations; they will not train for war anymore" (4:3 NCV).

• "Bethlehem . . . you are one of the smallest towns in the nation of Judah. But the Lord will choose one of your people to rule the nation" (5:2). *Because of this verse, some Jews in ancient times believed the Messiah would be born in Bethlehem, birthplace of Jesus.*

• "He has told you what he wants from you: to do what is right to other people, love being kind to others, and live humbly, obeying your God" (6:8 NCV).

BACKGROUND

INFLUENTIAL PEOPLE

Micah, a rural Judean prophet who criticizes the leaders of Israel and Judah (1:1).

THEME

This is not a story, but a collection of prophecies written as poetry. Micah denounces corrupt officials—religious and political—in both the northern Jewish nation of Israel and the southern nation of Judah. Judges take bribes, priests teach God's Word only for money, and prophets tell fortunes for profit. Rulers mislead the people, nobles take advantage of the poor, and the masses take their pleas to idols.

For this, Micah says, God will destroy both nations. Assyria, in fact, destroys Israel during Micah's lifetime, in 722 BC. Assyria also overruns Judah about twenty years later, stopping short of destroying it. But another nation, Babylon, decimates Judah in 586 BC.

Micah promises however, that a time will come when the Jewish nation will be restored and worship God.

POINTS OF INTEREST

A pattern of doom and salvation. The prophecies are arranged in an obvious pattern: doom (1:1–2:11), salvation (2:12–13), doom (3:1–12), salvation (4:1–5:15), doom (6:1–7:7), salvation (7:8–20).

Old Testament prophets have an earned reputation as messengers of doom. But no book of prophecy in the Bible is without hope. Like the other prophets, Micah warns that sin has consequences and is punishable

> ### DID YOU KNOW?
>
> • Like Isaiah, Micah may have walked around naked for a time. This was to graphically show the fate of future prisoners who would be stripped and deported (compare 1:8 with Isaiah 20:1–4).
>
> • Micah may have personally known several famous prophets who lived when he did: Isaiah, Jonah, Hosea, Amos.

TIMELINE	BIBLE EVENTS		Micah begins several decades of ministry	Israel is destroyed by Assyria	
			---- 742 BC	---- 722 BC	Dates are approximate
		750 BC		725 BC	700 BC
	WORLD EVENTS		Ivory carvings popular in Samaria Phoenicia, Egypt	Merchants in Greece prosper, farmers starve	
			---- 750 BC	---- 725 BC	

by God. But Micah also assures that punishment is not the last word. God still loves the people, and when the punishment is over, He will prove it.

Charges of injustice. Micah, like the prophet Amos, who lived at the same time he did, criticizes the leaders and nobles for misusing their power.

"Listen, you rulers of the nation of Israel" God says through Micah. "You should know how to decide cases fairly, but you hate good and love evil. You skin my people alive and tear the flesh off their bones. You eat my people's flesh and skin them and break their bones; you chop them up like meat for the pot, like meat in a cooking pan" (3:1–3 NCV). Using this kind of stark, symbolic imagery, Micah attacks the rich and powerful for wallowing in wealth and self-indulgence. Not only do they leave the helpless to fend for themselves, but the leaders make dishonest decisions against the poor. They cheat families out of homes and land. They worship wealth, not God. They revere power, not justice. They admire achievement, not mercy.

AUTHOR AND DATE

The prophecies are from Micah, a rural prophet who lived in a small village about twenty-five miles southwest of Jerusalem.

Verse 1 says that his ministry took place during the reigns of three Judean kings: Jothan, Ahaz, and Hezekiah. These men reigned between 742 and 687 BC. Decades later, the prophet Jeremiah quoted Micah, confirming that during the days of Hezekiah, Micah predicted "Jerusalem will be plowed like a field. It will become a pile of rocks" (Jeremiah 26:18 NCV; compare to Micah 3:12). Micah lived to see the Assyrians destroy Israel.

ON LOCATION

Micah delivers his prophecies in the southern Jewish nation of Judah. But he criticizes both Judah and the northern Jewish nation of Israel, often addressing them by the names of their capital cities: Jerusalem (Judah) and Samaria (Israel).

MICAH OUTLINE

Once Samaria, a capital city, now a vineyard (1:1–16).

For their many sins against God and each other, both Jewish nations will be destroyed.

"So I will make Samaria a pile of ruins—a place for planting vineyards," Micah prophesies. "I will pour her stones down into the valley and strip her down to her foundations. All her idols will be broken into pieces" (1:6–7 NCV).

What happens to Samaria and the entire northern Jewish nation of Israel will also happen to Jerusalem and the southern nation of Judah. "Because Samaria's wound cannot be healed. It will spread to Judah; it will reach the city gate of my people, all the way to Jerusalem" (1:9 NCV).

Among the host of charges that God levels against the Jewish nations are these: "you who hate fairness and twist what is right. You build Jerusalem by murdering people; you build it with evil. Its judges take money to decide who wins in court. Its priests only teach for pay, and its prophets only look into the future when they get paid" (3:9–11 NCV).

A ruler will be born in Bethlehem (5:2–5).

God refuses to abandon the Jewish people because of their sins. They *will* have to face the consequences of their sinful choices, but not forever. In the future, Micah prophesies, the Jewish people will repent of their sins, stop doing evil, and return to God. In return, God will bless them by sending a chosen leader—a messiah—who would lead into peace, like a shepherd leads sheep to quiet waters.

"Bethlehem Ephrathah," Micah says, "though you are too small to be among the army groups from Judah, from you will come one who will rule from days long ago." (5:2 NCV).

Seven hundred years later, wise men from an eastern nation followed a light to Israel because they believed that unusual astronomical events such as comets were signs that a future ruler had been born. When they arrived in Jerusalem and asked King Herod if they could see the child who had been born king of the Jews, Herod was upset. *He* was the king of the Jews, and he had no newborn son. Furthermore, he had already killed his brother to secure the throne. He would kill this newborn threat too, if he could. Herod turned to the religious leaders and asked them where the messiah would be born. They turned to the book of Micah and found their answer: Bethlehem.

POINTS TO CONSIDER

Born in Bethlehem. About 700 years before Jesus was born in Bethlehem, Micah prophesied that the Messiah would come from this tiny village on the outskirts of Jerusalem.

Today, pilgrims go to Bethlehem to visit the oldest church in the world, built over a cave believed to be the birthplace of Jesus. The first known reference to the cave comes from Justin Martyr, a Christian who was born about the time the apostle John died, around AD 100. John took care of Mary after the Crucifixion. It seems reasonable that Mary told John where Jesus was born, and that the site was known and revered among Christians living in the Jerusalem area.

In AD 135, Roman Emperor Hadrian destroyed all sacred sites. He replaced them with shrines to Roman gods. Over a cave stable in Bethlehem, he built a temple to the god Adonis—ironically, known for his death and resurrection. Each winter, Adonis is said to go to the underworld. Each spring, he returns to earth.

Two centuries later another Roman emperor, Constantine, replaced the shrines with churches. The Church of the Nativity was built in about AD 325 to commemorate the birth of Jesus. It stands today.

Two themes, two writers. Some suspect the book was written by two writers—one who penned the words of doom, and another who wrote the words of hope. As the theory goes, one of the writers or perhaps a later editor compiled the prophecies into their current pattern, alternating the themes of doom and salvation.

The presumption here is that one writer couldn't write in two styles. But even today, writers can and do jump from style to style, genre to genre.

FOR FURTHER STUDY

- Amos was another prophet concerned about social problems.

- Read Matthew 2:1–16 to see how the Jews of Jesus' day interpreted Micah's prophecy about a Jewish leader coming from
  Bethlehem (5:2).

- To read more about the two kinds of God—judgment and
  mercy—turn to Nahum.

- For more about the kind of social concern that Micah
  expressed in 6:8, read Isaiah 1 and the Sermon on the Mount
  (Matthew 5:1–7:29).

Sur
Mc
Tue
We
Th
Fri
Sat
Sur
Mo
Tue
We
Th
Fri
Sat
Sur
Mo
Tue
We

Nahum

MIDDLE EASTERN
REIGN OF TERROR TO END

It seems an odd coincidence that Nahum, a prophet whose name means "comfort," delivers a message that sounds entirely vindictive.

At first glance it looks as though the Jews are supposed to take comfort in hearing the good news that God will soon annihilate Assyria, an empire that has too long terrorized the entire Middle East.

"Nineveh," Nahum says, addressing the Assyrian capital, "you will be drunk, too. You will hide; you will look for a place safe from the enemy" (3:11 NCV).

The language of Nahum is strong and staccato, like the rapid-fire jabs of an avenger. Yet the prophecy, written as a poem full of emotional symbolism, was not meant to condone revenge and violent retaliation. It was written to assure the Jewish people that Assyria's reign of terror was almost over.

Evil is real. The Jews knew that all too well. But so is the justice of God. Sooner or later, but always in God's timing, evil is stopped and the guilty are punished. It's in the deliverance from evil—not the punishment of the guilty—that the Jews found comfort.

In the meantime, throughout the suffering, the Jews could take heart in knowing that "the LORD is good, giving protection in times of trouble" (1:7 NCV). We can take comfort in that too. This doesn't necessarily mean we'll escape unharmed, or even with our physical lives intact. But we will endure, and evil won't.

BACKGROUND

INFLUENTIAL PEOPLE

Nahum, Judean prophet who vows that God will punish Assyria for its cruelty (1:1)

THEME

For centuries the Assyrian Empire, headquartered in what is now northern Iraq, has been terrorizing the Middle East. At will, they crush nations. One of the victims is the northern Jewish nation of Israel, wiped out in 722 BC. Many survivors are deported to central Assyria—especially craftsmen, teachers, and other skilled people who can make a valuable contribution to the empire.

Roughly 100 years later, while Assyria is still bullying the Mediterranean world, the Jewish prophet Nahum has a vision about the empire. He sees its savagery and its defiance of God. And he hears what God says he will do to Assyria: "I will make a grave for you, because you are wicked . . . I will stop you from hunting down others on the earth " (1:14; 2:13 NCV). Nahum delivers this message to the people of his nation, who are currently being forced to serve the empire by paying taxes to it.

POINTS OF INTEREST

Assyrian terror. Nahum describes an empire so vicious and brutal that it epitomizes evil. When the Assyrians capture a city, they are merciless. Holding babies by the ankles, they swing them like clubs and dash

DID YOU KNOW?

• English poet Lord Bryon (1788–1824) in his poem The Destruction of Sennacherib portrays the fierceness of the Assyrian army: The Assyrian came down like the wolf on the fold, and his cohorts were gleaming in purple and gold.

• About 100 years before Nahum, the prophet Jonah told Nineveh it would be destroyed in forty days. The people repented and were spared.

TIMELINE	BIBLE EVENTS			
		Earliest possible date of Nahum's vision ------ 663 BC		
				Dates are approximate
	700 BC		**650 BC**	**600 BC**
	WORLD EVENTS	Assyria sacks Thebes, Egypt 663 BC	Assyrian empire begins to crumble when King Ashurbanipal dies 630 BC --------	Nineveh— Assyrian capital— destroyed 612 BC

them against stone walls. Members of enemy royal families are auctioned off to the highest bidder, or tortured and executed. (See "Vicious Assyria" in Points to Consider.)

Poetic justice. Nahum uses poetry and graphic symbolism to describe the coming destruction of Assyria. Don't read the descriptions literally. They are meant to express the seriousness of Assyria's crimes and the satisfaction that the Jews and the rest of the world will get when they find themselves freed from this international bully.

AUTHOR AND DATE

"I am Nahum from Elkosh," the book begins. We know nothing else about him. He is not mentioned in any other book of the Bible. Even the location of Elkosh remains a mystery.

Nahum probably had the vision described in this book sometime between 663 and 623 BC. He said Thebes Egypt had already fallen (3:8–10); it fell to Assyria in 663 BC. And he predicted the fall of Nineveh, which Babylon and coalition forces captured in 612 BC. This time frame places Nahum alongside two other prophets: Zephaniah and a young Jeremiah.

ON LOCATION

The Assyrian Empire, centered in what is now Iraq, is the target of Nahum's prophecy. But the message seems in-tended for the people of Judah, to assure them that God will soon put an end to Assyria's tyranny.

NAHUM OUTLINE

Nineveh falls (2:1–13).

To Assyria's complete surprise—but as Nahum had prophesied—the combined forces of Babylonians and Medes strike at the heart of the empire. Nineveh falls.

Assyria had been the evil superpower of the Middle East for centuries—taking whatever it wanted, whenever it wanted. It had taken the northern Jewish nation of Israel in 722 BC, swallowing it whole and deporting the citizens. Afterward the empire had allowed the southern nation of Judah to survive, but only if Judah joined other countries in annually feeding money into the Assyrian treasury at Nineveh.

It must have been hard for the Jews to believe what Nahum predicted: "Nineveh is robbed, ruined, and destroyed (2:10 NCV).

For Assyria's long history of cruelty, God promised he would send an army to destroy them. The Babylonians and Medes arrived at Nineveh's doorstep in 612 BC. Nahum had said that when this happens, "The river gates are thrown open" (2:6 NCV)—perhaps a reference to the Khoser River that ran through the city to the nearby Tigris River. The writer of the ancient book *Babylonian Chronicles* says a flood washed away some of the walls. Perhaps the invaders broke a dam for this very purpose.

" 'I am against you, Nineveh,' says the LORD All-Powerful," Nahum said several years before the attack. "I will stop you from hunting down others on the earth, and your messengers' voices will no longer be heard" (2:13 NCV).

Nineveh is so utterly destroyed that its massive ruins do not resurface until 1845, when archaeologists finally uncover them.

POINTS TO CONSIDER

Vicious Assyria. Nahum and other Bible prophets paint Assyria's portrait with dark and bloody colors. Assyria invaded nations as a source of income, slaughtered the young and old alike, then mutilated and tortured to death the leaders. Entire countries—such as the northern Jewish nation of Israel—were deported, and their homeland resettled with Assyrian pioneers.

The findings of archaeologists confirm that Assyria was as

Sun
Mo
Tue
Wed
Thu
Frid
Satu
Sun
Mon
Tue
Wed
Thu
Frid
Satu
Sun
Mon
Tue
Wed

brutal as the Bible says. In laying siege to a city, Assyrian soldiers would impale captured enemies on wooden spikes as thick as a fencepost. Some Assyrian kings ordered the corpses stacked like cord wood beside the city wall. Assyrian king Shalmaneser III built a pyramid of decapitated heads in front of a besieged city.

Assyrian kings bragged about their battlefield ferociousness by hiring artists to re-create the grisly scenes in stone carvings mounted on the palace walls.

Vengeful book, vengeful God. Some say Nahum reads like a book solely about revenge, starring the god of vengeance. In fact, they say, it reads like the exact opposite of Jonah, a story about God showing mercy to the Assyrians.

"I will pull your dress up over your face," God tells the Assyrians through Nahum, "and show the nations your nakedness and the kingdoms your shame. I will throw filthy garbage on you and make a fool of you. I will make people stare at you" (3:5–6 NCV).

This vicious-sounding poetry is not a portrait of the character of God; it's a mirror held up to the Assyrians. For treating others like trash, God was going to allow invaders to attack and defeat Assyria.

Pulling up Assyria's skirt is a metaphor that means this proud empire would suffer international humiliation. In ancient times, people publicly humiliated prostitutes and adulteresses by stripping them or by lifting their dresses (Ezekiel 16:37–39). "Nakedness" was perhaps a Hebrew play on words, since it sounds much like "exile," which is what the Assyrians did to many captured enemies.

The message behind the evocative poetry is that though it looks like no one can stop Assyria from terrorizing the world, God can and will.

For Further Study

- To see God showing compassion to Assyria, read Jonah.

- To read more about the two sides of God—judgment and mercy—turn to Micah.

- Just as Nahum portrays God as a divine warrior who will rescue His people from tyranny (1:2–10), so does the prophet Habakkuk (3:3–15).

Habakkuk

WHERE IS GOD WHEN PEOPLE SUFFER?

Why does God sit by and do nothing when good people suffer at the hands of the wicked? That's Habakkuk's question for God.

Judah had become a moral sewer. It bred extortion, violence, and swarms of criminals out for blood. Habakkuk wanted it to stop.

So what does God do? He decides that Judah should suffer at the hands of the Babylonians. Judah was a nation of saints compared to the Babylonians. Sure, the Judeans ignored the laws of God, sold debtors into slavery, and cheated the poor into starvation. But the Babylonians didn't even pretend to worship God, they stole entire countries, and raped the women and girls to death.

Habakkuk thought a follow-up question was in order: Why the Babylonians, of all people?

God didn't give a direct answer. He did assure Habakkuk that the Babylonians would eventually face their own judgment day. But essentially God left the prophet with this terse response: "The LORD is in his Holy Temple—all the earth should be silent in his presence" (2:20 NCV).

When you can't understand what's going on, God was telling Habakkuk, understand this: the Lord is in control.

That was all this prophet needed to hear. Already—some 2,600 years ago—God had a reputation for knowing what he was doing.

FAMOUS LINES

• "The just shall live by his faith" (2:4 KJV). *God's expressed desire that people learn to trust him. Martin Luther zeroed in on this idea, as paraphrased in Romans 1:17, to launch the Protestant movement. Luther argued that people are saved by faith in God, not by performing church rituals.*

• "Fig trees may not grow figs, and there may be no grapes on the vines . . . But I will still be glad in the Lord; I will rejoice in God my Savior" (3:17–18 NCV).

Background

Influential People

Habakkuk, a prophet in Judah who asks God why He's not punishing the wicked (1:1).

Theme

Habakkuk has a vision of engaging God in a two-way conversation. The prophet begins by asking God why he's allowing Judah to go unpunished for "wrong things . . . destroying things and hurting others in front of me; they are arguing and fighting" (1:3 NCV). God answers that he will punish Judah by sending the Babylonians to destroy the nation "their prisoners are as many as the grains of sand" (1:9 NCV).

Habakkuk protests that God shouldn't use the Babylonians to punish the Jews. "How can you be quiet when the wicked swallow up people who are better than they are?" Habakkuk pleads (1:13 NCV).

God replies that he will punish the Babylonians later. But in the meantime, he wants his people to learn to trust him. Habakkuk responds with a masterful and moving song of confidence in God.

> ### Did You Know?
>
> • A legend recorded in *Bel and the Dragon*, a book of the Apocrypha, reports that Habakkuk took a bowl of stew to Daniel in the lions' den. An angel reportedly transported Habakkuk from Judah to Daniel's location in Babylon, then home again.
>
> • Among the ancient library known as the Dead Sea Scrolls is a commentary on Habakkuk. The author, who lived when Rome occupied Israel, said Habakkuk's references to Babylon stood for Rome. In fact, as Babylon destroyed Jerusalem in 586 BC, so did Rome in AD 70.

TIMELINE	BIBLE EVENTS	Habakkuk predicts the fall of Jerusalem (earliest likely date) 612 BC	Babylon invades Judah, takes captives 605 BC	Babylon suppresses Judean rebellion, taking more captives 597 BC	Babylon destroys Jerusalem and other Judean cities 586 BC Dates are approximate
		625 BC	**600 BC**		**575 BC**
	WORLD EVENTS	Athens gets a code of laws 621 BC	Babylon begins 70-year dominance of Middle East 612 BC		Babylon defeats Egypt at battle of Carchemish 605 BC

POINTS OF INTEREST

A prophet talking with God. This is an unusual book of prophecy. Prophets usually deliver God's message to human beings. But here, the prophet is questioning God. So the book is not so much an oracle from God or a story about the life of a prophet as you'll find in other books of prophecy. It's a record of the dialogue between Habakkuk and God.

A song of trust in God. The third and final chapter in this short book is a song of confidence in God. Though Habakkuk is shaken by the news that Babylon will conquer his homeland and destroy the holy city of Jerusalem, he praises the miracle-working God of creation and pledges unwavering allegiance to him. This son, like those of Psalms, is later set to music and sung or recited in worship services. As indicated in the closing note to the music director, the song was once accompanied by stringed instruments.

AUTHOR AND DATE

"I am Habakkuk the prophet," the book begins. Habakkuk is not mentioned by name outside this book. But several times the New Testament quotes the phrase from Habakkuk that would later launch the Protestant Reformation: "But those who are right with God will live by faith" (2:4 NCV; compare this with Romans 1:17; Galatians 3:11; Hebrews 10:38).

Habakkuk likely prophesied in the years just after Assyria had fallen (612 BC) but perhaps before the Babylonians had defeated Egypt (605 BC) to assume the role of top superpower in the Middle East. Babylon defeated Judah three times in the next twenty years, carrying off hostages each time: 605 BC, 597 BC, and 586 BC, when Jerusalem was leveled.

Other prophets that Habakkuk may have known are Jeremiah, Zephaniah, and Nahum.

ON LOCATION

Habakkuk's conversation with God takes place "at the tower," probably somewhere along the walls of Jerusalem (2:1 NCV). It is here he gets word that the nation of Judah will fall to Babylonian invaders who "laugh at all the strong, walled cities" (1:10 NCV). Judah becomes absorbed into the Babylonian Empire and many of its citizens are located.

HABAKKUK OUTLINE

Awaiting the invasion of Babylon (3:1–19).

Our LORD, how long must I beg for your help? Habakkuk pleads (1:2). His country of Judah is hopelessly bogged down in sin: "So the teachings are weak, and justice never comes. Evil people gain while good people lose; the judges no longer make fair decisions" (1:4 NCV).

"I will use the Babylonians," God replies. "those cruel and wild people who march across the earth and take lands that don't belong to them" (1:6 NCV).

This isn't the kind of help Habakkuk has in mind. "How can you be quiet when the wicked swallow up people who are better than they are?" the prophet implores (1:13 NCV).

God assures Habakkuk that after the Babylonians finish their job of punishing Judah, they will be punished for their own sins. In the meantime, the job of the righteous is to "live by faith" (2:4 NCV)—to trust God.

"I have heard the news about you," the prophet answers (3:2 NCV). On this basis, Habakkuk promises that no matter what happens he will trust in God. And if the Babylonians take everything—stripping vineyards, groves, and fields, and stealing all the livestock—Habakkuk will lean on God. "The Lord GOD is my strength. He makes me like a deer that does not stumble so I can walk on the steep mountains" (3:19 NCV).

POINTS TO CONSIDER

Arguing with God: a biblical tradition. When Habakkuk argued with God, he wasn't breaking new ground. He was joining a town hall meeting filled with inquisitive, respected biblical leaders.

Moses argued that he wasn't a good enough speaker to confront Pharaoh. Gideon couldn't believe God was calling him to lead an army, so he asked for—and god—miracles to prove that God would help him. Job insisted that he didn't deserve the horrors that had robbed him of his children, flocks, and health. Jeremiah resisted becoming a prophet, arguing that he was too young.

God dealt patiently with each of these men, as he did with Habakkuk.

Sun Mor Tues Wec Thu Frid Satu Sun Mor Tues Wec Thu Frid Satu Sun Mor Tues Wec

Using evil to do good. Habakkuk fully expected God to punish Judah for becoming such a sinful country. But he was shocked when God told him that Babylon would do the punishing. Babylon was more godless than Judah. This was like assigning Hitler to executed a convicted war criminal, or Charles Manson to run a halfway house for celebrity stalkers.

But one of the Bible's many revelations about God is that he has the power to use evil to do good. For example, after Joseph's brothers sold him to slave traders, Joseph ended up in Egypt, second in power to the king. There, he was responsible for keeping the people from starving during a famine. When his brothers came to Egypt for grain, Joseph told them not to fear him: "You meant to hurt me, but God turned your evil into good to save the lives of many people, which is being done" (Genesis 50:20 NCV).

God uses people and nations—good and evil—to accomplish his goal of saving humanity from sin and restoring his creation to the paradise that was lost when sin contaminated it.

FOR FURTHER STUDY

- Habakkuk's description of God's power (chapter 3) is much like the description in Nahum 1:2–8.

- For insights from other prophets of the day, read the books of Jeremiah, Zephaniah, and Nahum.

- To see how the New Testament interprets Habakkuk's phrase, "but those who are right with God will live by faith" (2:4, NCV), read Romans 1:17; Galatians 3:11; Hebrews 10:38.

Zephaniah

GOOD-BYE, HUMAN RACE

This is probably not the book to turn to for comfort on the brink of a nuclear attack or as a monster asteroid speeds toward earth.

Hear the word of the Lord—the first words out of the mouth of the prophet: "I will sweep away everything from the earth," says the Lord" (1:2 NCV). That's a promise from God.

Zephaniah lived in a day when most Jews didn't worship God any longer. They worshiped gods of other nations, and even sacrificed their children to appease the idols. They cheated one another to accumulate wealth for themselves. They showed nothing but disdain for the people whom God repeatedly told them to take care of: the poor, the widows, the orphans.

God gave the Jews centuries to change their ways. He sent prophet after prophet to warn them about the consequences of their sins—consequences clearly written into the laws of Moses. Now, God had seen enough. Zephaniah said the Lord would punish the Jewish nation and ultimately bring an end to life on this planet.

Yet, the end is not the end.

The prophet also said that God will gather up the faithful to live in a mysterious time and place where sorrow is no more. Zephaniah's last words are that those who love the Lord can trust him, even when they can't trust anyone else.

> ### FAMOUS LINES
>
> - "I will remove human beings from the earth" (1:3 NCV). *God's promise of a coming judgment. Some scholars see this as extravagant exaggeration, common in ancient poetry, and say it refers to the imminent decimation of Judah. Others take it more literally, saying it refers to the end of humanity, when the faithful are gathered into heaven.*

BACKGROUND

INFLUENTIAL PEOPLE

Zephaniah, a prophet who predicts the destruction of Judah and the surrounding nations (1:1).

THEME

The three-chapter book of Zephaniah is not a story with a plot, but a prophecy written as a poem. Punishment for sin is the theme.

Judah will be defeated and plundered for a multitude of sins. But the wrath of God doesn't stop there. Zephaniah names countries to the north, south, east, and west of Judah—perhaps symbolizing the four points of the compass—and declares that the Lord will destroy them all. The graphic descriptions read like those of an end-time apocalypse.

> ### DID YOU KNOW?
>
> • God sings. Zephaniah says God "he will sing and be joyful about you" (3:17 NCV). This may be only a poet's way of describing God's joy. On the other hand, it doesn't seem too far-fetched to believe that the one who inspires so many songs could also sing them.
>
> • Zephaniah was probably a prince. He's identified as the great-great-grandson of Hezekiah—likely *the* Hezekiah, former king of Judah (1:1).

Yet the prophet speaks of an assembly of righteous survivors living joyously in a restored Jerusalem. It's unclear if Zephaniah is referring to the city that the Jews rebuilt after their tragic defeat and exile, or to a heavenly city, or both.

TIMELINE	BIBLE EVENTS	King Josiah begins 31-year reign 640 BC	Zephaniah delivers his prophecy 630 BC	Jerusalem destroyed by Babylonians 586 BC *Dates are approximate*
		650 BC	**600 BC**	**550 BC**
	WORLD EVENTS	Japan founded, says a legend 660 BC	Assyrian Empire begins to crumble when King Ashurbanipal dies 630 BC	Horse racing becomes Olympic sport 624 BC

POINTS OF INTEREST

Doom. Tagged by God for destruction are Judah and nations surrounding her on four sides: Philistia (to the west), Moab and Ammon (modern Jordan, east), Ethiopia (south), Assyria (Iraq, north). The "day of the Lord" devastation—brought on by sin—seems to engulf the entire planet. In fact, the prophecy reads like the reversal of the Creation story. For God had created fish, birds, land animals, and human beings, in that order. But now he is going to destroy people and animals, birds and fish (1:3).

To the ancient student to Jewish scriptures, the prophesied doom may have conjured up images of destruction as cataclysmic as the Flood. This next catastrophe, however, would apparently come by means of "fire that will burn up the whole world" and leaving the land "like Sodom and Gomorrah" (1:18; 2:9 NCV).

Joyful survivors. Like all other prophets in the Bible, Zephaniah adds a message of hope. After the punishing destruction, God promises to gather up the scattered survivors who are his true worshipers. United, the people of God will celebrate the end of sorrow, violence, and injustice.

Poetic symbolism. Zephaniah writes in a poetic style that draws from vivid and, at times, exaggerated images. This makes it hard to interpret the words as precisely as we might like. It's clear that he's talking about God punishing the southern Jewish nation of Judah for turning its back on him and worshiping idols. It's also clear that Zephaniah foresees God punishing the surrounding nations. But whether or not the prophet is also foreshadowing the end of human history and the beginning of a new age in a celestial "Jerusalem" is less certain.

AUTHOR AND DATE

Zephaniah is the prophet behind this book. The unusual, four-generation genealogy in the first verse adds credibility to the theory that Zephaniah carried the royal blood of King Hezekiah.

The prophet says he received his message from God during the reign of King Josiah (640–609 BC). Josiah assumed the throne at age eight, and by age twenty began making religious reforms, such as tearing down pagan altars (2 Chronicles 34:3). Because Zephaniah describes the rampant idolatry in Judah, he probably prophesied before the reforms began in about 628 BC. It's quite possible that Zephaniah's warning of a global disaster may have been a catalyst for the spiritual reform.

Zephaniah predicted the fall of Nineveh, so he apparently delivered his message before 612 BC, when this prophecy was fulfilled.

On Location

Zephaniah delivers his prophecy in the southern Jewish nation of Judah, perhaps in the capital city of Jerusalem.

ZEPHANIAH OUTLINE

The end of all life on this planet (1:2–3).

I will sweep away everything from the earth," says the LORD. "I will sweep away the people and animals; I will destroy the birds in the air and the fish of the sea. I will ruin the evil people, and I will remove human beings from the earth" (1:2–3 NCV).

This is the jaw-dropping lead of Zephaniah's prophecy. Zephaniah goes on to describe the doomed fat of his own country of Judah, along with the surrounding nations. All are destined for destruction. Judah will be demolished and plundered for abandoning God and worshiping the stars and idols. The other nations will be wiped out for worshiping their own pride, threatening the Jews, and mocking God.

Yet somehow, after God has destroyed the earth in his "fiery anger," he brings together "scattered people . . . true worshipers" who have apparently survived the holocaust (3:8, 10 NCV). And with this, a new age dawns. The people who survive "won't do wrong or tell lies; they won't trick people with their words. They will eat and lie down with no one to make them afraid" (3:13 NCV).

━━━━━ POINTS TO CONSIDER ━━━━━

Judah's tragic fall. Zephaniah's description of the fall of Judah, which took place about forty years after the prophecy, accurately portrays what happened.

"Princes and the king's sons and all those who wear foreign clothes" were punished (1:8 NCV). King Zedekiah was forced to watch his sons executed. Immediately afterward, his eyes were gouged out.

God's anger flared up "like a fire" (1:18 NCV). Babylon torched the cities after looting them.

The streets of Jerusalem and other Judean towns were "are ruined; no one lives there at all" (3:6 NCV). The Babylonians knocked over the buildings and walls, then deported the surviving citizens.

The end is near. "The LORD's day of judging is coming soon; it is near and coming fast," Zephaniah said (1:14 NCV). Within a few decades, Judah was overrun and burned to the ground. But other aspects of "the great day" do not appear to have happened yet—2,600 years later.

All human and animal life on the planet has not been snuffed out (1:2). Nor has a mysterious group of survivors assembled to celebrate the end of sorrow (3:14, 18).

Old Testament prophecies, however, sometimes had two meanings: one referring to the immediate future, and another referring to the distant future. Jesus used the same technique when he gave signs about "the end of the world" (Matthew 24). Parts of the prophecy were fulfilled forty years later, when the Romans destroyed Jerusalem. Other aspects are still unfulfilled, and many believe will unfold only at the second coming of Christ.

FOR FURTHER STUDY

- To learn about what Judah was like during Zephaniah's day, read 2 Kings 21–23 and 2 Chronicles 33–35.

- For more about "the day of the Lord," a Judgment Day theme central to Zephaniah, read the book of Joel, which also emphasizes this idea.

- For more prophecies about what appears to be the end of human history, read Isaiah 24–27, a passage known by Bible experts as the Apocalypse of Isaiah.

Haggai

RELIGION ON HOLD FOR EIGHTEEN YEARS

If religion has taken a backseat to other things in your life, like making a living, the prophet Haggai has a word from the Lord for you.

Haggai lived about 2,500 years ago at a time when one of the most important ways that the Jews expressed their faith—especially Jews in the Jerusalem area—was to worship God at the temple. There they would sing praises, listen to the instruction of the priests, and offer sacrifices in thanks for God's goodness, or in sorrow for their sins.

But there was no temple anymore. The Babylonians had destroyed it, along with the rest of Jerusalem, before deporting the Jewish citizens. Some fifty years later the Persians defeated the Jews and freed them to go home. Once back in Jerusalem, one of the first things they did was to lay the foundation for a new temple. But opposition from outsiders forced them to stop. For the next eighteen years the Jews went about their private business abandoning the temple.

> ### FAMOUS LINES
>
> • "Is it right for you to be living in fancy houses while the Temple is still in ruins?" (1:4 NCV). *God's complaint to the Jews returned from exile.*
>
> • "The LORD says, 'I am with you." (1:13 NCV).

But along comes Haggai with a message from God for the Jews, and for us. Don't neglect the Lord. Don't exclude him from your life. Talk to him. Sing to him. Offer him expressions of your gratefulness and your sorrow. Worship him with an assembled community of believers.

BACKGROUND

INFLUENTIAL PEOPLE

Haggai, prophet who urges Jews returned from exile to rebuild the temple (1:1).

Zerubbabel, Persian-appointed governor of Judah and descendant of King David (1:1).

Joshua, high priest, not *the* Joshua, who led the Israelites into the Promised Land (1:1).

THEME

After the Jews return from exile, they lay the foundation for a new temple. But neighboring communities convince Persian leaders to order the work stopped. Almost twenty years pass, and nothing more has been done to rebuild the temple, even though a new Persian king supportive of various religions has been on the throne for more than a year.

At the end of an apparently weak harvest season, Haggai tells the high priest and the governor of Judah that the reason the people have been suffering from crop shortages is because the temple has not been rebuilt. God will bless the people again, Haggai says, once they resume work on the temple.

> ### DID YOU KNOW?
> • Haggai is the second shortest book in the Old Testament, after Obadiah.
>
> • If this book reports all the prophecies of Haggai, his ministry covered less than four months.

About three weeks later, the rebuilding begins.

Though Haggai does not report the completion of the project, perhaps because he does not live to see it finished, Ezra says it takes about three and a half years (Ezra 6:15). The new temple is dedicated in the spring of 516 BC, seventy years after Solomon's temple was destroyed.

TIMELINE	**BIBLE EVENTS**	King of Persia decrees the exiled Jews can return home 538 BC	Jews complete the foundation of the temple 536 BC	Haggai urges the Jews to complete the temple 520 BC	The temple is completed 516 BC *Dates are approximate*
		550 BC		**525 BC**	**500 BC**
	WORLD EVENTS	Cyrus of Persia conquers Babylon 539 BC	Actor Thespis wins first prize in a tragedy competition in Athens 534 BC	Darius succeeds Cyrus as king of Persia 522 BC	Buddha, in India, preaches his first sermon 521 BC

POINTS OF INTEREST

Connection between obedience and prosperity. In no uncertain terms, Haggai bluntly tells the religious and civic leaders of Judah that the people are suffering from a bad harvest and a sour economy because the temple hasn't been rebuilt. Within about three weeks, construction begins. For such obedience, God tells the people through Haggai, "Do you have seeds for crops still in the barn? Your vines, fig trees, pomegranates, and olive trees have not given fruit yet. But from now on I will bless you!'" (2:19 NCV).

The Bible as a whole doesn't teach that obedience guarantees prosperity. The story of Job dramatically proves that suffering can come to the most godly of people; for a time, Job was obedient *and* broke. But there are occasions—as Haggai reports—when God reserves the right to punish the disobedient with financial hardship and to reward the obedient with rich blessing.

Emphasizing a point. Haggai emphasizes key points by raising questions and by repeating important phrases.

One critical question he asks is this: "Is it right for you to be living in fancy houses while the Temple is still in ruins?" (1:4 NCV).

Repeated phrases, as translated in the New International Version, include the following: "Give careful thought" (1:5, 7; 2:15, 18), "I will shake the heavens and the earth" (2:6, 21), and "I am with you" (1:13; 2:4).

AUTHOR AND DATE

The prophecies are from Haggai, a Jewish prophet whose name means "festival," suggesting he was born on one of the Jewish holidays. Another prophet, Ezra, said that Haggai and Zechariah both urged the Jews to rebuild the temple (Ezra 5:1; 6:14).

Haggai may have been an old man by the time he delivered this message, perhaps over seventy. He implied that he remembered how glorious Solomon's temple once looked (2:3); it had been destroyed sixty-six years earlier, in 586 BC.

Haggai delivered several prophecies from August through December in 520 BC, "This message came in the second year that Darius was king, on the first day of the sixth month" (1:1 NCV). Darius reigned from 522 to 486 BC. The dating is unusually precise because Haggai reported the month and day of each prophecy, as well as the date that the Jews resumed work on the temple.

ON LOCATION

The story takes place in Jerusalem.

Haggai Outline

Sur
Mc
Tue
We
Th
Fri
Sat
Sur
Mc
Tue
We
Th
Fri
Sat
Sur
Mc
Tue
We

Laying the foundation of the new temple (1:1–15; 2:18).

Nearly two decades after the first wave of Jews returned from exile, many are living in expensive homes. Yet there is no temple for the Lord. For this spiritual negligence, Haggai reports, the people have been suffering from mildew, mold, and hail that have devastated the crops. This announcement comes in late August, near the end of a pitiful harvest.

Within about three weeks the Jews have organized a workforce and begin laying a new foundation. Cutting and transporting monster blocks, they finish the foundation before winter.

Pleased with their progress, Haggai assures the people that in the seasons ahead God will bless them with abundant harvests. Furthermore, Haggai adds, there is coming a day when nations will bring their treasures to Israel, the new temple will more glorious than Solomon's, and peace will reign in Jerusalem.

══ Points to Consider ══

Darius's autobiography. Sources outside the Bible confirm that Darius was king of Persia, as Haggai reported. In fact, Darius had the story of his rise to power inscribed in three languages on a cliff wall in Iran. Archaeologists used this inscription to decipher cuneiform languages.

Darius was also open-minded about other religions, as the story of Haggai implies. Though Darius worshiped Persian gods, ancient records also say he rebuilt Egyptian temples.

Zerubbabel was no messiah. Haggai's closing prophecy suggests that Zerubbabel, who led the first wave of Jews back from exile, would also become the promised messiah who would destroy Israel's enemies and restore the nation to glory.

"Tell Zerubbabel, the governor of Judah," God instructs Haggai, "I am going to shake the heavens and the earth. I will destroy the foreign kingdoms and take away the power of the kingdoms of the nations . . . I will make you important like my signet ring, because I have chosen you!' says the LORD All-Powerful" (2:21–22, 23 NCV).

Furthermore, God told Haggai that the temple whose construction Zerubbabel supervised would be greater than Solomon's.

None of these prophecies was fulfilled in Zerubbabel's day. In fact, Zerubbabel disappeared from history even before his comparatively Plain Jane temple was finished. This has fueled speculation that he was executed for leading a movement to free Judah from Persian domination and to become king.

Was Haggai wrong?

Old Testament prophecies sometimes had both immediate and future meanings. This appears to be the case with Haggai's prophecy. Zerubbabel was God's chosen ruler, through whose leadership the temple was rebuilt. Five centuries later, King Herod renovated and expanded this temple to one much more spectacular than Solomon's. as for the kingdoms of earth falling, perhaps the fulfillment lies in the future.

For Further Study

• For more about the rebuilding of the temple, read the books of Ezra and Zechariah.

Zechariah

JEWS REBUILD THEIR TEMPLE

The people of Jerusalem needed a shot in the arm, big time. They were back home from exile, but home to what? After nearly twenty years, they were still bankrupt spiritually, financially, and politically. Their temple lay in ruins. So did their harvests. So did their independence; Israel had been swallowed up by the latest and greatest superpower: Persia.

What could the Jews possibly do to turn all this around?

Nothing. That's the bad news.

The good news is that God is in control. That's the inspiring, motivating message of Zechariah, expressed in visions and prophecies. Furthermore, Zechariah said, God is going to see to it that the temple is rebuilt, prosperity returns to the land, and Israel is ruled by the king of peace.

Strangely enough, when the people started to believe this, they suddenly found themselves with the strength and determination to load a bundle of future history on their backs and carry it in the direction God intended it to go.

That's exactly what happened in Jerusalem. It's still happening among those who believe that God is the sovereign Lord over all creation.

FAMOUS LINES

- "Kill the shepherd, and the sheep will scatter" (13:7b NCV). *Jesus quoted this to describe what would happen to him and his disciples (Mark 14:27).*

- "Rejoice greatly, people of Jerusalem! Shout for joy, people of Jerusalem! Your king is coming to you. He does what is right, and he saves. He is gentle and riding on a donkey, on the colt of a donkey" (9:9). *A verse the New Testament says is fulfilled on Palm Sunday, when the crowds cheer as Jesus rides into Jerusalem (Matthew 21:2– 9; John 12:14–15).*

BACKGROUND

INFLUENTIAL PEOPLE

Zechariah, a Jewish prophet and priest born in exile, in Babylon, but among the first Jews freed to return to Israel (1:1).

THEME

The book is not a story with a plot. It's a report of Zechariah's eight visions and his prophecies for the Jews who have returned to Israel, after enduring several decades of exile in Babylon.

The Jews have been back for almost twenty years, yet they have not rebuilt the temple. They had started the project right away, with the Persian king's blessing. But they abandoned it when local opposition convinced a new king that if the Jews rebuilt the city, they would rebel.

Now, however, yet another king is on the throne. And he's supportive of different religions. In this setting, Zechariah and the prophet Haggai both urge the people to finish what they started.

> ### DID YOU KNOW?
>
> • "Never again" is a phrase that many say in response to the Holocaust. God uses this phrase to describe a future age, perhaps after his people are assembled in heaven: "No one will hurt my people again" (9:8 NCV).
>
> • Though Zechariah has only fourteen chapters, it's the longest of the twelve minor prophets.

Zechariah's visions encourage the people to trust that God will help them rebuild not only the temple, but the nation. The prophecies in the second half of the book, chapter 9–14, are messages of punishment for the ungodly and salvation for the faithful. The closing prophecy looks forward to an end-time age when God defeats evil and reigns unopposed as the king of creation.

TIMELINE	BIBLE EVENTS	Zechariah and other Jewish exiles return to Jerusalem 538 BC	Zechariah's first reported message from God 520 BC	Jerusalem temple rebuilt 516 BC Dates are approximate
		550 BC	**525 BC**	**500 BC**
	WORLD EVENTS		Temple of Artemis built in Ephesus 550 BC	Darius succeeds Cyrus as king of Persia 522 BC

POINTS OF INTEREST

The Messiah. This fourteen-chapter book talks more about the Messiah than any other Old Testament book, with the exception of the massive, sixty-six-chapter book of Isaiah. New Testament writers, and Jesus himself, often quote Zechariah to show that Jesus fulfilled what was predicted. Here's a partial review of the prophecies, and the New Testament fulfillment:

Ruler on the throne (2:10–13)—Revelation 22:1–5

> Holy priesthood (3:8)—1 Peter 2:5
> Heavenly high priest (6:12–13)—Hebrews 8:1–2
> Riding a donkey (9:9–10)—Matthew 21:4–5
> Betrayal price: thirty pieces of silver (11:12–13)—Matthew 26:14–15
> The money is used to buy potter's field (11:13)—Matthew 27:9
> Body is pierced by spear (12:10)—John 19:34, 37
> Good shepherd killed, sheep scattered (13:6–7)—Matthew 26:31

Angels. Angels appear to Zechariah in all eight of his visions, reported in chapters 1–6. These angels serve as God's messengers who help the prophet understand what each vision means. As elsewhere in the Bible, the angels aren't portrayed as figurative apparitions, but as living beings.

Part 1, Part 2. This book divides into two sections that are so different from each other that some say they are the work of two writers. Part 1, chapters 1–8, deals primarily with the visions of Zechariah concerning the rebuilding of the temple. Part 2, chapters 9–14, contains prophecies about God punishing Israel's enemies and rescuing Israel.

AUTHOR AND DATE

As stated in the first verse, the book was written by the prophet Zechariah, beginning in October or November of 520 BC.

We arrive at this date because Zechariah said the word of God came to him in the second year and eighth month of Persian King Darius's reign. The eighth month on the Jewish calendar covers the end of October and the beginning of November. Zechariah's ministry spans at least two years, because his prophecy beginning in chapter 7 is from the fourth year of Darius's reign (518 BC).

Haggai was prophesying at the same time, in the same place (Jerusalem).

ON LOCATION

Zechariah ministers at Jerusalem in Judah. Though Judah was once a nation, now it's just a small province in the growing empire of Persia.

ZECHARIAH OUTLINE

Rebuilding the temple (1:1–17).

In a series of visions given to the prophet Zechariah, God motivates the Jews who have returned from exile in Babylon to finish rebuilding the temple. This is a job the Jews had started eighteen years earlier, but one they halted because of local opposition.

"My Temple will be rebuilt," God reveals in the first of eight visions, "and the measuring line will be used to rebuild Jerusalem" (1:16 NCV).

Jerusalem becomes a thriving city again (1:17–2:5).

Tied to God's assurance that the temple will be rebuilt is his promise that the cities of Judah will prosper again—especially the city of Jerusalem, his "chosen city."

Eventually, God says, the population will expand beyond the walls: "Jerusalem will become a city without walls, because there will be so many people and cattle in it. I will be a wall of fire around it,' says the LORD. 'And I will be the glory within it" (2:4–5 NCV).

Zechariah's message, with that of the prophet Haggai, must have struck a nerve. The people began rebuilding the temple, and saw it through to completion four years later.

The king of peace riding on a donkey (9:9–10).

In the most famous of his prophecies, Zechariah looks even deeper into the future—more than 500 years deep, to the time of Jesus.

"Everyone in Jerusalem, celebrate and shout! Your king has won a victory, and he is coming to you. He is humble and rides on a donkey . . . I will bring peace to nations, and your king will rule from sea to sea."

Matthew and John both say this prophecy is at least partly fulfilled on the Palm Sunday when Jesus rides a donkey into Jerusalem, while crowds cheer his arrival as the promised Messiah (see Matthew 21:9; John 12:13–15).

Though God's kingdom of peace is not fully established then, it is started. And Zechariah promises that what God has started, he will finish.

Sun
Mon
Tue
Wed
Thu
Fri
Sat
Sun
Mon
Tue
Wed
Thu
Fri
Sat
Sun
Mon
Tue
Wed

Points to Consider

Messiah arrives. Zechariah said that a Good Shepherd—a leader and deliverer sent from God—would replace the bad ones that had plagued Israel. The New Testament writers saw Jesus as the unmistakable fulfillment of Zechariah's many prophecies about this messiah. They saw it in the prophet's references to the leader riding into Jerusalem on a donkey, the thirty pieces of silver, suffering the pierce of a spear, and being killed. (See "The Messiah" in Points of Interest.)

Author, author. Most Bible experts agree that Zechariah wrote chapters 1–8. But some suspect that a later writer, perhaps one or more of Zechariah's disciples, wrote the remaining six chapters. These scholars argue that the second half of the book—which they call Second Zechariah—is radically different in writing style, choice of words, and message.

In fact, the message at times seems opposite of First Zechariah. For example, chapters 1–9 paint a picture of national restoration, but chapters 9–14 reflect disillusionment with the restoration, and speak of warfare coming before peace. In addition, the later chapters say nothing of the Persians, but mention the Greeks—who defeated Persia in 332 BC.

Scholars who contend that Zechariah wrote the whole book argue that the differences make sense: the first part of the book is prose—a reporting of visions, and the second part is poetry—prophetic messages from God about the future, both near and distant.

Whether or not Zechariah wrote the prophecy, New Testament writers as well as Jesus cited them as authentic messages from God.

For Further Study

- For another perspective on what was happening in Jerusalem during Zechariah's day, read the two-chapter book of Haggai, a prophet who lived and ministered alongside Zechariah. The 10-chapter book of Ezra also reviews the history, though Ezra lived a generation or so later.

- Zechariah's sixth vision speaks about an evil woman. This concept is expanded in Revelation 17:1–19:4.

Malachi

FRAUDS AND FREELOADERS IN GOD'S HOUSE

Malachi is the final word in the Old Testament—the last message left stirring in the minds of people through the 400 years until Jesus was born.

For such an important location in the Bible—the finale of the First Testament—you'd be right, though it might not look that way to you at first.

He tells the people to stop sacrificing sick, crippled animals. We don't sacrifice anymore, so this might not seem to apply to us. But if we go through the motions of worshiping God, without worshiping in a spirit of sincerity, the words do apply.

He tells the people to bring ten percent of their harvest and herds to the temple, as Jewish law required. Most of us aren't farmers, we don't worship in a temple, and we're not obliged to observe Jewish customs. But God's work goes on, and we can be a part of it.

FAMOUS LINES

• "Goodness will shine on you like the sun, with healing in its rays" (4:2 NCV). *Malachi implies that in a future age, God will heal the sin-damaged creation by defeating evil and restoring justice.*

Malachi also tells the people that the Lord is coming, bringing justice and healing. The message of the New Testament is that the Lord has come. He invites us to join his followers in seeking justice for the helpless and healing for the spiritually sick.

Background

Influential People

Malachi, a prophet who condemns insincere worship (1:1).

Theme

A century after the Jews have returned from exile in Babylon, they are again losing respect for God. They still go through the mechanics of offering sacrifices. But these sacrifices come from the bottom of the barrel—with a stamp of approval from the priests.

Did You Know?

• When Jews eat the *Seder* Passover meal, some leave the door cracked open and set out an extra glass of wine called the "Elijah cup." They do this in anticipation that Elijah will someday return, as Malachi predicted, announcing the good news of salvation.

• Jewish law required the people to give to the temple ten percent of their harvest and of the increase in their herds.

"I wish one of you would close the Temple doors," God says through Malachi, "so that you would not light useless fires on my altar!" (1:10 NCV).

Malachi urges the people to treat God with the respect due him. They're to treat each other with respect too: not cheating in marriage, or lying in court, or taking advantage of employees, or ignoring the poor, or swindling foreigners.

In the end—and Malachi says the end is coming—God will settle all scores.

Points of Interest

Insincere worship. Throughout this short book, Malachi complains that the people go through the motions of worship as though it's the motion that God wants.

TIMELINE	BIBLE EVENTS			
		Temple is rebuilt ┌--- 516 BC		Malachi begins his ministry ┌----- 440 BC Dates are approximate
	525 BC		**475 BC**	**425 BC**
	WORLD EVENTS	Persia begins century-long rule over Egypt └-- 525 BC	Socrates is born 470 BC ---------	Sparta and Athens begin 30-year truce └-- 445 BC · Plato is born └-- 428 BC

They miss the point: God wants the motions to flow out of an inner sense of devotion and love. These people don't feel devoted. They feel obligated. Instead of bringing God the best they can, they bring the least they think they can get by with: crippled bulls, blind sheep, stolen goats.

Elijah. Malachi is the only prophet to announce that God will send the prophet Elijah as a messenger to prepare the way for the Lord's arrival, and the salvation to follow (3:1; 4:5). Jesus later explains that John the Baptist fills that role (Matthew 11:7–14; see also "Elijah's return" in Points to Consider).

Judgment day. Malachi vows "there is a day coming that will burn like a hot furnace" (4:1 NCV). When it does, justice comes with it. Evil is trampled and the righteous " will jump around, like well-fed calves" (4:2 NCV).

AUTHOR AND DATE

"I am Malachi," the book begins. Nothing more is known about this prophet. Some Bible experts think "Malachi" is a title, not a name. The word means "my messenger." (See "Malachi who?" in Points to Consider.)

The book was written sometime after the temple was rebuilt (516 BC). Malachi's description of a decaying sacrificial system and his concern about Jews marrying non-Jews seems to fit the conditions around the time of Ezra and Nehemiah, roughly 450 BC.

ON LOCATION

The prophet is one of several who addressed Jews in Jerusalem.

MALACHI OUTLINE

Offering damaged goods to God (1:6–2:3).

God is insulted. He has allowed the Jewish people to return home from exile and to rebuild their temple and capital city. Yet, after some 100 years, they are becoming lax in their worship. They're bringing damaged offerings even though Jewish law requires them to sacrifice animals without any kind of defect (Leviticus 22:18–23).

"Isn't it wrong," God asks rhetorically, "when you bring blind animals as sacrifices, that is wrong. When you bring crippled and sick animals, that is wrong. Try giving them to your governor. Would he be pleased with you? He wouldn't accept you" (1:8 NCV).

Priests are as guilty as the others, for they permit this to go on.

God, through the prophet Malachi, says, "honor my name," says the Lord All-Powerful. "If you don't, I will send a curse on you and on your blessings" (2:2 NCV).

Bringing the tithe to the temple (3:8–12).

Should a person rob God?," the Lord says. "But you are robbing me.

"You ask, 'How have we robbed you?' "You have robbed me in your offerings and the tenth of your crops" (3:8 NCV).

The Jews were supposed to bring a tenth of their harvest and herd to the people. This was distributed as salary to the temple workers, as funds to maintain the temple facilities, and as charitable gifts to people in need.

"Bring to the storehouse a full tenth of what you earn so there will be food in my house," God says. "I will open the windows of heaven for you and pour out all the blessings you need" (3:10 NCV).

The book—and the Old Testament—concludes with the promise that the Lord is coming, on the heels of a messenger who will prepare the way for him. Then the New Testament picks up the story of God's work among the human race. Jesus is born. And when he grows up, his ministry follows that of John the Baptist—the prophet who described himself as "voice of one calling out in the desert, 'Make the road straight for the Lord' " (John 1:23 NCV).

POINTS TO CONSIDER

Elijah's return. The concluding book of the Old Testament ends with the promise that the prophet Elijah will appear as a forerunner of the Lord's arrival—to prepare the Lord's way. The New Testament begins with the birth of Jesus, and tells of John the Baptist's ministry, which prepared the way for Christ's ministry.

John didn't realize he was the "Elijah" that Malachi was talking about. Even though John said he came to prepare the way for someone whose sandals he wasn't worthy to untie, when priests asked him if he was Elijah or perhaps the messiah, John replied, "No, I am not" (John 1:21 NCV).

Jesus knew better. He said, "John is Elijah, whom they said would come" (Matthew 11:14 NCV).

Malachi who? Malachi might not have been the writer's name. Many scholars think the word was used as a descriptive title instead of a proper name.

Malachi means "my messenger," which was a common way of referring to God's prophets. In fact, the first Greek translation of the Old Testament—in about 250 BC—translated the term as a title, not a name.

The writer's choice of the word malachi to describe himself may also have been a way of pointing toward the book's unique prophecy: "The LORD All-Powerful says, I will send my messenger (3:1 NCV)—a reference to the prophet who would prepare the way for the Lord's arrival.

Whatever the author's name, New Testament writers quote the book with authority and respect—as does Jesus.

FOR FURTHER STUDY

- Malachi quotes God as saying, "I hate divorce" (2:16 NCV). For more on God's feeling about divorce, read the words of Jesus in Matthew 19:3–9.

- To see how the New Testament portrays John the Baptist as the promised Elijah, turn to Matthew 17:1–13.

- For more about the Jewish law of tithing, read Leviticus 27:30–32 and Numbers 18:21–24.

Sun
Mo
Tue
We
Thu
Frid
Satu
Sun
Mo
Tue
We
Thu
Frid
Satu
Sun
Mo
Tue
We

Matthew

JESUS AND HIS TEACHINGS

Matthew is the first of four New Testament books about Jesus. Like any collection of stories about one person, each version is different. And there's something unique enough about Matthew's story to inspire Christian leaders long ago to put his ahead of all others in the New Testament.

Like the three other books about Jesus, Matthew is called a Gospel, meaning "good news." More than any other Gospel, Matthew zeroes in on exactly what that good news is, for he concentrates on the words Jesus spoke. He records accusing words (23:24), comforting words (28:20), and motivating words (5:9).

In Matthew, you'll not find as much dramatic action as you'll discover in Mark, or as many spotlights on compassion as you'll see in Luke, or as much proof of the deity of Jesus as you'll uncover in John. But in Matthew, you'll find the most complete record of what Jesus taught. And you'll learn how his teachings grow out of Old Testament scriptures.

FAMOUS LINES

- "Do to others what you want them to do to you" (7:12 NCV). *The Golden Rule, from what has become known as Jesus' Sermon on the Mount.*

- "Man shall not live by bread alone" (4:4 KJV). *Jesus' response when Satan asks him to prove he is the Son of God by turning stones into bread.*

- "Blessed are the meek: for they shall inherit the earth" (5:5 KJV). *One of several "Beatitudes" from the Sermon on the Mount.*

- "They will name him Immanuel," which means "God is with us" (1:23 NCV). *Matthew's citation of Isaiah 7:14, given as one of many evidences that Jesus fulfills prophecies about the Messiah.*

Reading Matthew is as close as any of us can get to finding a soft clump of grass on a Galilean hillside, and sitting down to listen with thousands of others while Jesus teaches as though we, alone, are with him.

BACKGROUND

INFLUENTIAL PEOPLE

Jesus, God's son in a human body, and the Messiah that prophets said God would sent to Israel (1:1).

Twelve apostles, working-class men whom Jesus recruits to become his disciples (4:18; 10:1–4).

THEME

Jesus, a descendant of Abraham and King David, is born to a virgin. Astrologers arrive, saying they have followed a star they believe is a sign that the future king of the Jews has just been born. Herod, current king of the Jews, fears the child may be the Messiah, a king and deliverer promised by the prophets. Herod kills all the children ages two and under in the vicinity of Bethlehem. Jesus, however, escapes when his family flees to Egypt and stays there until Herod dies.

At about age thirty, Jesus begins his ministry by being baptized, then by preaching and calling twelve men to join him as disciples. For perhaps three or four years he preaches and performs astonishing miracles in Galilee, his home region in what is now northern Israel. His most famous sermon, recorded only in Matthew, is called the Sermon on the Mount, a masterful summary on how to live as a citizen under God's government on earth.

Predicting his death, Jesus goes south to Jerusalem, healing people and teaching as he goes. In Jerusalem he faces the combative Jewish scholars entrenched in their traditions. When Jesus reveals that some of these traditions have no basis in Scripture, and—worse—that the leaders are hypocrites misleading the people, they become infuriated. They plot to kill him, but realize they have to do it secretly because he has a large following of people who believe he is either the Messiah or another great prophet.

						Dates are approximate
TIMELINE	**BIBLE EVENTS**	Birth of Jesus 6 BC ----	King Herod dies 4 BC -------		Jesus begins ministy AD 26 ------	Jesus crucified AD 30 -------
	30 BC			**AD 1**		**AD 40**
	WORLD EVENTS	Cleopatra and Mark Antony commit suicide 31 BC	Cultures noted for wood crafts live on North American Pacific Coast AD 1 ------		Tiberius begins 23 years as Roman emperor AD 14	Rome invades Britain AD 43 ----

During his prayer time one Thursday evening, Jesus is arrested, interrogated throughout the night, and tried the next morning by Pilate, the Roman governor. Reluctantly, Pilate gives in to the wishes of the assembled Jews and sentences Jesus to death. The execution is carried out immediately, and Jesus is dead before sundown.

On the following Sunday morning, he rises from the dead and appears to women who have come to his tomb. Later he meets with His remaining disciples and gives them what is now called the Great Commission: "So go and make followers of all people in the world" (28:19 NCV).

POINTS OF INTEREST

The Jewish angle. This is the most Jewish Gospel of all, written to convince Jews that Jesus is the Messiah that the prophets said was coming. That's one reason it comes first in the New Testament, right after Malachi, which ends with the promise of the Lord's coming.

> ### DID YOU KNOW?
>
> • In the family tree of Jesus are four women with tarnished backgrounds—not the kind of people Jews expect in the family tree of the great Messiah. There's Rahab, a pagan prostitute; Bathsheba, an adulteress; Ruth, a non-Jew who sneaks under the covers of a prospective husband; and Tamar, who becomes pregnant by her father-in-law. These memories of scandal would challenge the too-rosy memory of Jews conceited about their pedigree. And they would also counter attacks on the virgin Mary by reminding Jews that women with bad reputations are in the family tree of the great King David, forebear of the Messiah.

More than the other Gospels, Matthew quotes Old Testament prophecies about the Messiah, to show that Jesus fulfilled them. Matthew cites the Old Testament no fewer than fifty-seven times, compared with thirty in the runner-up, Mark.

A lot of comments on the death of Jesus. In all the Gospels, but especially in Matthew, look for a lot of material about the suffering and death of Jesus. The Gospel writers know they have a lot of explaining to do because the execution of Jesus, as a common criminal, is not what conventional wisdom says will happen to the Messiah. In reading the prophecies, most Jews expect the Messiah to restore the glory of Israel and the kingship of the nation. Jesus, however, is crowned with thorns and nailed to a cross, beneath a mocking sign that calls him king of the Jews.

The Gospel writers take the Jews back to the prophets to read other passages, which portray a humble Messiah, rejected by leaders, and sacrificed for the sins of others. Prophecies about a victorious, ruling Messiah, many believe, point to the second coming of Jesus.

Five teaching sessions of Jesus. The book seems woven around five sets of teachings by Jesus. Some scholars believe these teachings were the original core of the book, provided by Matthew, and that the story line was added later.

These teachings are the Sermon on the Mount (chapters 5–7), commissioning the twelve disciples as ministers (10), parables revealing what the kingdom of heaven is like (13), guidelines on how to live as citizens in God's kingdom (18), and warnings about the end of the age and judgment day (24–25).

The kingdom of heaven. "The kingdom" refers to God's saving revolution on earth and to life set free by his government. Both the miracles and the teachings of Jesus show that God's reign applies not only to heaven and the future, but also to earth right now. God is revolutionizing "life as usual" through Jesus' ministry and wherever people embrace the policies of his government. Think of the Sermon on the Mount (5–7) as an Inaugural Address a U.S. president gives at the beginning of his term. In it Jesus, God's King for Jews and "all nations," outlines the policies of God's administration, showing people how to live as citizens of this kingdom.

Different responses to Jesus. Despite his astonishing miracles and compassionate teachings and manner, not everyone embraces his ideas. Many do, and crowds follow him. But his insights and unique interpretation of Old Testament Jewish laws make him seem like a threat to Jewish traditionalists who stubbornly cling to their understanding of what God expects from people.

AUTHOR AND DATE

Both the author and date are uncertain. The writer is not named in the book, but Christians writing in the second century said the book was written by Matthew, a tax collector who became one of the twelve original disciples of Jesus.

Clues within the book suggest it was written near the end of the first century, sometime after the Romans destroyed the Jerusalem temple in AD 70. Without the temple, there was no need for priests because there was no place to offer sacrifices. So the Jewish scholars, called Pharisees, rose to prominence. The book seems written especially to a Christian Jewish community trying to define and defend itself against traditional Judaism that—before the century was over—excommunicated Christian Jews from all synagogues. One clue that the Christian Jews faced such persecution appears in Matthew 23:34 NCV, which says the Jews "will kill and crucify. Some of them you will beat in your synagogues and chase from town to town."

ON LOCATION

The story of Jesus unfolds in what is now Israel, beginning in his hometown region of Galilee, and continuing southward through Samaria and into Judea, where he dies and is resurrected in the city of Jerusalem.

Matthew Outline

Wise men visit Jesus (2:1–12).

Within about two years after Jesus is born, wise men from an unnamed country in the east arrive in Jerusalem. Ironically, these non-Jews become among the first in Matthew's Gospel to testify that Jesus is the long-awaited Messiah. "Where is the child born to be king of the Jews" they ask. "We saw his star in the east and have come to worship him." Many in this day believe that a unique event in the sky, such as the arrival of a new star or comet, is a sign that a great leader has been born.

King Herod, who has killed his own brother to protect the throne, is instantly worried. Consulting Jewish scholars, Herod learns that the Messiah will be born in Bethlehem. He reveals this to the sages, asking them to report back after they find the child, so he can "worship him too."

The wise men find Jesus, but in a dream are warned not to return to Herod. When Herod realizes the men aren't coming back, he orders all the boys executed who are two years old and under, living in the Bethlehem area. Jesus and his family escape to Egypt.

The story of the wise men probably troubles many orthodox Jews because they do not expect God to entrust such important news to pagan astrologers. But God does not allow human expectations to limit the good things he does for this world.

Baptism of Jesus (3:13–17).

John the Baptist, identified as the promised forerunner of the Messiah, reluctantly baptizes Jesus after expressing his hesitation: "I need to be baptized by you!"

John baptizes people as a symbol of their spiritual cleansing after repentance. Jesus is baptized to endorse John's ministry and, as a representative of all humanity, to be an example of humble obedience to God. Unlike all others, Jesus "did not sin" (Hebrews 4:15 NCV). Yet his baptism is clearly appropriate, for the sky opens and a voice from heaven says, "This is my Son, whom I love, and I am very pleased with him."

Afterward, Jesus goes into the desert where he is tested by Satan.

Some Bible experts see in these scenes echoes from the Exodus, which helps Jews see Jesus as a living example of the child God wanted Israel to be. Like the Jews, Jesus is called out of Egypt (after Herod dies), he passes through the water, and he is tested in the desert. Only after passing the test does his ministry begin.

Sermon on the Mount (5:1–7:29).

The Gospel of Matthew spends most of its time revealing what Jesus taught—not what he did or where he went. The most famous sermon of Jesus is called the Sermon on the Mount, delivered somewhere on a hillside possibly near the Sea of Galilee, where many of his disciples had worked as fishermen.

This sermon may actually be a collection of highlights from many sermons, for it succinctly captures the essence of what Jesus teaches. Here are the famous Beatitudes, which show that God's kingdom is not full of the high and mighty, but of people who are poor in spirit, humble, sorrowing, pure in heart, persecuted. Here, too, are Jesus' insights about criticizing others, adultery, divorce, revenge, loving our enemies, helping the needy, prayer, worry, judging others—to name a few.

Instead of giving detailed rules for people to follow. Jesus gives broad principles that make it incredibly difficult to find loopholes. When in doubt about what to do, Jesus says, "just as your Father in heaven is perfect" (5:48 NCV). For those who don't know how God acts, Jesus shows them.

Jesus heals a "sleeping" girl (9:18–26).

One day while Jesus is teaching, a government official rushes to him and, kneeling, says, "My daughter has just died. But if you come and lay your hand on her, she will live again."

When Jesus arrives at the man's house, a crowd of mourners has already gathered. Jewish custom requires speedy burial, usually the same day. Jesus tells the people to leave. "The girl is not dead," he says. "Only asleep."

Suddenly, cries of sorrow erupt into heckling laughter. The people eventually leave the house nonetheless. With that, Jesus takes the girl by the hand and helps her up.

News of this miracle worker quickly spreads throughout the region, producing mixed reviews. Many people are drawn to his message that points to the intent of the Jewish law: obedience to God. These supporters praise God for the miracles of healing they see Jesus perform. But others, including some Jewish scholars who don't agree with his interpretation of scripture, charge that he gets his power from "the prince of demons" (9:34 NCV).

Jesus sends out the Twelve (10:1–42)

In the second of Jesus' five major teaching sections, he gives his twelve original disciples instructions for a mission they are to undertake. Jesus, like other ancient rabbis, has selected a small group of men to live and travel with him during his ministry, receive his teaching, watch his actions, follow His instructions, and continue his work when he is gone. The twelve—apparently symbolizing the twelve tribes, or extended families, of Israel—are working-class men such as fishermen. Matthew is a tax collector, a profession hated among the Jews. Tax collectors in Israel at the time are usually Jews who collaborate with the Roman occupying force by assessing and collecting taxes, often overcharging and keeping the extra money.

The mission of the disciples, apparently short-term and perhaps a trial run for the ministry they will perform when Jesus is gone, is to do what Jesus has been doing: teach about the kingdom of heaven, as well as heal the sick, exorcise demons and even raise the dead. They are to take no pay. And when they aren't welcomed, they are to leave and "shake its dust off your feet" (10:14 NCV).

"Don't be afraid of people," Jesus says. "Who can kill the body but cannot kill the soul" (10:28 NCV).

Parable of weeds among the wheat (13:24–30, 36–43).

Jesus often teaches by using parables—short stories that are easy to picture and that communicate a spiritual meaning. Matthew says that Jesus' teaching method is yet another fulfillment of prophecy because the psalmist spoke of one who would teach with parables (compare Psalm 78:2 with Matthew 13:35). Matthew also says Jesus uses these stories to let his followers in on "the secrets about the kingdom of heaven."

The several parables in chapter 13 reveal mysteries about God's kingdom. The parable of the tall-growing mustard seed and of the yeast show that the kingdom will emerge suddenly in the world. The parables about the hidden treasure and the pearl show that people have to decide whether or not to become citizens of the kingdom. And the parable of the weeds in the wheat field reveal that people will be rewarded for choosing the kingdom and punished for rejecting it.

In this parable, Jesus compares himself to a farmer sowing good seeds that produce "all of God's children who belong to the kingdom. The weeds are those people who belong to the Evil One." At harvesttime—an expression of end-time judgment—the wheat is gathered in. But the weeds are separated and burned.

Jesus feeds the 5,000 (14:13–21).

In a memorable scene told in all four Gospels, Jesus and his ministry-weary disciples sail away from the crowds for a rest. But the people on shore keep the boat in sight and follow it. When Jesus and his men arrive at a remote sin, they are met by thousands—5,000 men, not counting the women and children.

As tired as he is, Jesus is still moved with compassion and heals everyone who is sick.

When the disciples suggest dispersing the crowd so they can get food, Jesus asks, "You give them something to eat."

All that the disciples manage to round up is one boy's lunch: five pieces of barley bread and two small fish. Jesus takes it, looks to heaven and gives thanks for it, then hands it to the disciples to distribute. The people eat their fill, and the disciples collect twelve large baskets of leftovers.

Peter recognizes Jesus as the Son of God (16:13–20).

While in Caesarea Philippi, north of the Sea of Galilee and near Mount Hermon, Jesus asks the disciples who people say he is. They reply that some speculate he is the spirit of John the Baptist, who was recently beheaded. Others say he is the spirit of Elijah, Jeremiah, or some other Old Testament prophet.

When Jesus asks who the disciples think he is, one disciple boldly replies, "You are the Christ, the Son of the living God."

Jesus gives this disciple, Simon, the new name of Peter, which means "rock." Then Jesus says, "On this rock I will build my church, and the power of death will not be able to defeat it" (16:18 NCV). Later, on the day of Pentecost, when God sends the Holy Spirit to empower the disciples after the ascension of Jesus, it is Peter who preaches the first sermon (Acts 2).

Jesus transfigured into a being of light (17:1–13).

After Jesus begins preparing the disciples for his coming death and resurrection, he takes his three closest disciples—Peter, James, and John—to a hilltop. There they see Jesus changed into his glorified, heavenly form: "His face became bright like the sun, and his clothes became white as light" (17:2 NCV).

Suddenly, the prophets Moses and Elijah appear, also as beings of light, talking with Jesus. A glowing cloud rolls overhead, and from it a voice says, "This is my Son, whom I love, and I am very pleased with him. Listen to him!" (17:5 NCV).

When the disciples hear this, they drop to the ground, terrified. But Jesus tells them not to be afraid. When the men look up, Jesus is alone. He tells them to say nothing about this until after His resurrection.

Jesus' triumphal entry into Jerusalem (21:1–11).

Jesus arrives in Jerusalem on what becomes the first Palm Sunday, just before his Friday crucifixion. Crowds who had heard of him cheer, welcoming him as the long-awaited Messiah who would save them from their enemies and restore righteousness to Israel.

Jesus is riding a donkey—just as the prophet Zechariah said the Messiah would arrive in Jerusalem (Zechariah 9:9). The people respond by paving the path with a carpet of palm branches and cloaks, befitting the arrival of a king.

"Praise to the Son of David!" they shout. "God bless the one who comes in the name of the Lord." These words from Psalm 118:26, together with the actions of the crowd, reveal that many believe they are witnessing the arrival of the Messiah.

Jesus cleanses the temple (21:12–17).

When Jesus enters the temple courtyard—the worship area for non-Jewish believers—he sees the place filled with merchants selling sacrificial animals and exchanging foreign currencies for the Hebrew coins required in temple offerings.

Angrily, he flips their tables, quoting Isaiah: "It is written in the scriptures, 'My Temple will be called a house for prayer.' But you are changing it into a 'hideout for robbers'" (21:13 NCV).

Some ancient sources suggest that Jewish merchandising was later moved outside the temple area. But Jesus may be symbolizing what he later prophesies—the destruction of the temple. Romans level it in AD 70, while crushing a Jewish revolt. This ends the Jewish sacrificial system; they haven't had a temple sin.

A parable about Judgment Day (25:31–26).

As Jesus and his disciples leave Jerusalem, to stay in nearby Bethany, they stop en route and rest on the Mount of Olives. There Jesus warns them about the coming fall of Jerusalem and the later end of the human age, saying he will return to take the citizens of God's kingdom to their eternal home.

No one knows when this will happen, Jesus says, so everyone needs to live in a state of readiness.

To illustrate the judgment that will follow his second coming, Jesus tells a story about sheep and goats, animals easily separated. The sheep, symbolizing godly and compassionate people who help the needy, are rewarded with "eternal life." The goats, representing the godless and selfish, "will be punished forever."

The Last Supper (26:17–30).

The high priest and other members of the Sanhedrin, the top Jewish ruling body, plots strategies for arresting and executing Jesus because of his unorthodox interpretation of Scripture. The night of the arrest, Jesus arranges to eat a final meal with his disciples.

This meal is rich with symbolism that endures in the rite of Communion, or the Eucharist. He breaks bread and tells the men that it represents his body, which will soon be broken. Then He gives them wine and says it represents his blood, "poured out, so that many people will have their sins forgiven."

After singing a hymn, the group goes to a garden on the Mount of Olives to pray. There Jesus is arrested, betrayed for unknown reasons by Judas, who leads officers to him. The disciples scatter. Peter waits outside the home of the high priest, but vigorously and repeatedly denies knowing Jesus—as Jesus predicted he would do. Judas hangs himself.

7:00

8:00

9:00

0:00

1:00

oon

1:00

2:00

3:00

4:00

5:00

6:00

7:00

8:00

9:00

0:00

Pilate sentences Jesus (27:11–26).

The Sanhedrin convene an emergency session and spend the night interrogating Jesus. After lying witnesses fail to give enough evidence to warrant execution, the high priest, in frustration, asks Jesus, "tell us if you are the Christ, the Son of God" (26:63 NCV). Jesus confirms he is. The court charges him with blasphemy and takes him to the governor, Pilate, who alone has authority to order an execution.

Pilate finds no cause to execute Jesus, but eventually gives in to the early-morning crowd of Jesus' opponents, viciously screaming, "Nail him to a cross!" Pilate publicly washes his hands, saying he is innocent of this man's blood. Then he orders Jesus crucified.

The execution of Jesus (27:33–66).

Soldiers given custody of Jesus know that he claims to be the Messiah, king of the Jews. They dress him in a robe of scarlet, the color of royalty, then make him a crown from branches of a thornbush.

After beating him, they force him to make a humiliating march through the city, carrying the crossbeam on which his hands will be nailed. The vertical beam is fixed at the execution site outside the city walls.

Once crucified, Jesus hangs between two criminals. Above his head is a sign that reads, "This is Jesus, the King of the Jews."

With this execution, Jewish leaders hope to prove that Jesus is no messiah. Anyone "whose body is displayed on a tree is cursed by God" (Deuteronomy 21:23 NCV). And that, they believe, includes Jesus.

Yet when Jesus dies, his last words quote the beginning of a song about a servant of God who suffers and is later proven righteous (compare 27:46 with Psalm 22). Instantly, the earth shakes so violently that a soldier exclaims, "He really was the Son of God!"

Because Jesus had claimed he would rise on the third day, the Jewish leaders convince Pilate to seal the tomb and post a guard. This way, they argue, Jesus' disciples can't steal the body and claim he rose from the dead.

Resurrected Jesus greets women at the tomb (28:1–20),

Early Sunday morning, when Sabbath is over, several women followers of Jesus go to the tomb to finish preparing his body for burial. There was no time for this Friday afternoon, as dusk and Sabbath approached.

But by this time, an angelic being of light had appeared and rolled back the stone, then sat on it. The guards were so terrified they passed out. When they came to, they reported to the Jewish priests, who bribed them to keep quiet.

When Mary Magdalene and at least two other women arrive, the angel is still there. "Don't be afraid!" the angel says. "I know that you are looking for Jesus, who has been crucified. He is not here. He has risen from the dead as he said he would" (28:5–6 NCV).

As the women turn to leave, Jesus greets them. "Go and tell my followers to go on to Galilee," He says. "They will see me there."

Jesus meets his disciples in Galilee. There, he gives them what has become known as the Great Commission. "So go and make followers of all people in the world," He says. "I will be with you always, even until the end of this age."

POINTS TO CONSIDER

Jesus fulfills prophecies. More than any other Gospel, Matthew tries to prove to Jewish readers that Jesus is the Messiah they've been anticipating—the Messiah that, for hundreds of years, prophets have been saying God would send.

Many of the prophecies are especially convincing because they could not have been artificially fulfilled. On the basis of what the prophet Micah said in 5:2, for example, the Jews believed the Messiah would come from Bethlehem, hometown of their greatest king, David. Jesus was born there.

Isaiah 53, known as the Suffering Servant passage, reads almost like an eyewitness account of the suffering and death of Jesus: "He took our suffering on him and felt our pain for us . . . he was wounded for the wrong we did; he was crushed for the evil we did . . . The punishment, which made us well, was given to him . . . The LORD has put on him the punishment for all the evil we have done' (4, 5, 8, 10).

Zechariah described the beginning of the messiah's kingdom: "Rejoice greatly, people of Jerusalem! Shout for joy, people of Jerusalem! Your king is coming to you. He does what is right, and he saves. He is gentle and riding on a donkey, on the colt of a donkey" (9:9 NCV). Matthew reveals that this prophecy is fulfilled in the Triumphal Entry, on the first Palm Sunday (21:1–9).

Jesus doesn't fulfill all prophecies. Though Jesus fulfills many prophecies about the Messiah, other prophecies seem yet unfulfilled. For example, Isaiah says that when the Messiah, "he will be fair in his decisions for the poor people of the land . . . Then wolves will live in peace with lambs, and leopards will lie down to rest with goats" (11:4, 6 NCV). This utopian era of peace did not follow the donkey-riding Jesus into Jerusalem. Nor did Jesus reestablish the great kingdom of David, as many prophecies said he would.

But as Jesus told Pilate, "My kingdom does not belong to this world" (John 18:36 NCV). Many believe that the prophecies about a glorious kingdom and everlasting peace will be fulfilled when the Messiah returns in a Second Coming, to take the citizens of heaven home (1 Thessalonians 4:13–17).

Jesus doesn't speak kindly of non-Jews. "Don't go to the non-Jewish people," Jesus told his disciples, when sending them on a tour of ministry throughout Galilee. "But go to the people of Israel" (10:5 NCV)

And later, when a non-Jewish woman asked Jesus to heal her demon-possessed daughter, Jesus replied, "God sent me only to the lost sheep, the people of Israel When the woman pleaded, Jesus replied, "It is not right to take the children's bread and give it to the dogs" (15:24, 26 NCV).

It sounds as though Jesus was calling non-Jews "dogs." Yet the woman apparently sensed something else in the tone of His voice, or perhaps glimpsed a twinkle in his eye. For she argued that even dogs deserve crumbs. "Woman," Jesus replied, "you have great faith! I will do what you asked" (15:28 NCV).

The ministry of Jesus did, in fact, seem to focus primarily on the Jews. And why not? He was a Jew and the Messiah that Jews, not Gentiles, had been waiting for. The Gospel of Matthew stresses Jesus' Jewishness and his mission first to his own people, to fulfill the promises God made to them, beginning with Abraham. Yet non-Jews are also included in the reach of the good news, as the beginning, middle, and ending of Matthew show: pagan astrologers are led by God to worship Jesus, the child-king (2:14); later, Jesus praises a Roman centurion who showed more faith than anyone else He had met (8:10); finally, he directs his followers to make disciples out of "all people in the world" (28:19).

===== **FOR FURTHER STUDY** =====

- The Gospels of Mark and Luke are similar to Matthew's. John's Gospel is more theological, emphasizing the divinity of Jesus more than retelling the highlights of his life's story. But all three Gospels add depth to Matthew's portrait.

- Read some of the Old Testament prophecies that Matthew says Jesus fulfilled. For example: Jesus is Immanuel, God with us (1:23; Isaiah 7:14); born in Bethlehem (2:6; Micah 5:2); a healer of diseases (8:17; Isaiah 53:4). For more, see "Jesus fulfills prophecies" in the Points to Consider section.

- Read Acts to find out what happens after Jesus ascends into heaven, leaving the disciples behind.

Sun
Mo
Tue
We
Thu
Frid
Satu
Sun
Mo
Tue
We
Thu
Frid
Satu
Sun
Mo
Tue
We

Mark

THE MOST ACTION-PACKED STORY OF JESUS

It comes second in the New Testament, but it's probably the first Gospel worth reading—for many reasons.

In short—the shortest of the four Gospels—and it's action-packed, jumping from one miracle of Jesus to another, and from one confrontation to another; silencing demons, feeding thousands, calming storms, walking on water, dying, rising to life.

When Matthew and Luke sat down to write their Gospels, they had probably already read Mark. Their works show signs of borrowing from the book.

One thing Mark helps us appreciate about Jesus, better perhaps than any other Gospel, is what Jesus suffered on our behalf. Some forty percent of this short book lays out details of the final, traumatic week of Jesus' life. And the earlier part of the book throws the spotlight on the pain Jesus endured from the very beginning of his ministry: confrontation with hostile spiritual forces and with human beings intent on humiliating and then killing him. He even suffered the rejection of his family and his lifelong friends.

Words alone can't convey all that Jesus went through to help us understand how much God loves us. But the words of Mark are the place to begin.

FAMOUS LINES

- "Many who are now first will be last, and many who are now last will be first" (10:31). *Jesus tells his disciples that in the afterlife, some of this world's most respected people will be humbled, and the least respected will finally receive the honor due them.*

- "I will make you fishers of men" (1:17 NIV). *What Jesus said to Peter and Andrew, fishermen he was inviting to become his disciples.*

- "Give to Caesar what is Caesar's and to God what is God's" (12:7 NIV). *The answer Jesus gives to Jewish leaders trying to trick him into a traitorous quote by asking if Jews should pay taxes imposed by the Romans.*

BACKGROUND

INFLUENTIAL PEOPLE

Jesus, God's Son, who has come to earth in human form (1:1).

Twelve apostles, men Jesus invited to join his ministry as disciples (1:16; 3:14–19).

THEME

Surprisingly, Mark skips the childhood of Jesus altogether, beginning instead with John the Baptist preaching in the desert. This is a logical place to start, because John fulfills the Old Testament prophecy of the messenger who is to prepare people for the Lord's arrival.

Jesus arrives, is baptized by John, then retreats into the desert, where he overcomes several temptations offered up by Satan. Immediately afterward, Jesus begins his ministry in Galilee (northern Israel) by choosing four fishermen as the first of twelve disciples. Then comes a flurry of miracles—casting out demons, healing the sick—followed by calling the remaining disciples.

Jesus' ministry of teaching and healing continues, with dramatic results. Crowds, captivated by his new insights into Scripture and astonished by his miracles, follow him by the thousands. But mingled in among the admirers are skeptics—Jewish scholars and religious leaders who don't agree with his nontraditional interpretation of Scripture. Repeatedly they try to humiliate him with trick questions, but each time they walk away humiliated themselves. By the third chapter, Mark reveals that these leaders intend to kill Jesus.

When Jesus turns south, taking his ministry to Jerusalem, he knows that the end is near—yet his disciples can't imagine a suffering Messiah. Everything they've heard about the promised Messiah is that he will reign in glory as a king with the stature of David.

TIMELINE	BIBLE EVENTS	Birth of Jesus r--6 BC		Jesus begins ministy AD 26 --------	Jesus crucified AD 30 -----------	Dates are approximate
		10 BC	**AD 1**			**AD 40**
	WORLD EVENTS		Trials by combat used among German tribes AD 1 -----------		Cremation prefered burial method by wealthy Romans AD 30 -----------	Nero is born AD 37

Jesus enters Jerusalem on a Sunday, amid cheering crowds who give him a royal welcome. Five days later, by 9 a.m., he is nailed to a cross. By about 3 p.m., he is dead. But come Sunday morning, his tomb is empty, and an angel dressed in white is declaring that Jesus is alive and preparing to visit his devastated disciples.

> ### DID YOU KNOW?
> • More than 1,000 years after Jesus, knights of the Crusades search Israel for the Holy Grail—the cup of wine over which Jesus spoke the words "This blood is poured out for many" (14:24 NCV). People in the Middle Ages collect sacred relics, which they believe have mystical power. Any trace of the blood of Jesus, they think, will be the most powerful relic of all.

POINTS OF INTEREST

Less talk, more action. Mark focuses on what Jesus did than what he taught. In fact, this Gospel contains fewer teachings of Jesus than any of the four Gospels.

Like other action-packed stories, the pace is frantic. Mark jumps from one scene to the next, often saying that the subsequent scene happens "immediately." This conveys the image of a perpetually busy Jesus, and it leaves the reader empathizing with the weariness that he and his disciples must have experienced.

A suffering Jesus. There are only sixteen chapters in this short book, and the last six are devoted to the final week of Jesus' life: his suffering and crucifixion.

There are perhaps two important reasons why Mark emphasizes this.

First, the Jews of Jesus' day cannot conceive of a suffering Messiah. They expect a king. That's why the disciples argue over who among them should be permitted to sit at the right and left of Jesus' throne, after he becomes king (10:37, 41). They argue this even after Jesus tells them—three times—that he is going to be executed. The Old Testament prophets have spoken of a suffering servant sent from God, but the Jews apparently don't associate these passages with the Messiah. Instead, they latch onto prophecies about the Messiah's glory days, which are yet to come.

Second, the suffering of Jesus has an important implication for the early Christians reading this Gospel. The book seems to have been written about thirty years after the time of Jesus, during the AD 60s. It is in AD 64 that Rome catches fire and Emperor Nero decides to lay the blame on Christians. This begins an empire-wide persecution of Christians. Many are martyred in ghoulish coliseum games. Others are executed. Peter and Paul are probably both killed during this holocaust of Christians. The followers of Jesus, during the days of Nero, have to be prepared to follow Jesus to the death.

Jesus keeping secrets. Apparently to keep his already imposing opposition to a minimum, to allow him time to complete his ministry, Jesus repeatedly tells the people not to say anything about who he is or what miracles he has done.

When a demon addresses him as "God's Holy One," Jesus orders the spirit to "Be quiet! Come out of the man!" (1:24–25 NCV). Jesus forces other demons to do the same (1:34). And when Jesus heals a man of leprosy, he urges the man to tell no one (1:44). Mark is full of other similar examples.

Jesus also uses parables as coded messages to followers—messages hidden from his opponents, who are perplexed by the symbolic stories (4:10–12).

So what's the big secret? Jesus himself. He is the Messiah, God's Son, and revealer of the kingdom of God. And this mystery of Jesus and the kingdom is revealed only to those who have the key that unlocks the door: faith.

Son of Man. This is Jesus' favorite way of describing himself. He uses it fourteen times in Mark.

By applying this term to himself, Jesus suggests that he intends to fulfill the prophecy of Daniel 7:13–14 NCV: "I saw in front of me someone who looked like a human being coming on the clouds in the sky. He came near God, who has been alive forever, and he was led to God. He was given authority, glory, and the strength of a king. People of every tribe, nation, and language will serve him. His rule will last forever, and his kingdom will never be destroyed."

This image of a royal, victorious Messiah—which the disciples associated with Jesus—is one that many Christians believe will unfold only at the Second Coming, when Jesus returns to earth (Matthew 24:30).

Author and Date

The writer is unnamed, but Christian leaders in the early second century said it was written in Italy by John Mark and was based on the memories of Peter. John (his Hebrew name) was also called Mark (his Latin name). It's unclear whether he ever met Jesus (see 14:51–52), but he was well-acquainted with the apostles. It was to the home of John Mark's widowed mother that Peter went, after an angel released him from prison one night (Acts 12:12). Her home was a meeting place for Christians, and a group was praying there when Peter arrived.

Most Bible experts say Mark was the first Gospel written and that the writers of Matthew and Luke had access to Mark's manuscript, and borrowed from it. Matthew, for example, repeats 601 of the 678 verses in Mark. Most believe Mark was written in Rome by the early 60s. The story does contain Latin terms, and it explains Israel's geography and some Aramaic words, both of which would have been familiar to people living in Israel. The biblical evidence and early Christian writers indicate that both Peter and John Mark were in Rome during the Christian persecution of the 60s.

ON LOCATION

The story takes place primarily in what is now Israel, though some of the scenes show Jesus ministering east of the Jordan River, in what is now northern Jordan. The early part of Jesus' ministry takes place in his hometown region of Galilee, in northern Israel. His last week takes place in the Jerusalem area, in the region of Judea. (See map in Matthew, page 311.)

MARK OUTLINE

Jesus calls fishermen (1:14–20).

Before Jesus begins his ministry, he is baptized by John the Baptist, whom he recognizes as the Messiah's forerunner, prophesied in the Old Testament. Then Jesus goes into the desert for a time of prayer. The public opposition he will soon face is paralleled by the spiritual opposition he faces here. Satan tempts him, trying to get him to abandon his mission, but Jesus proves himself stronger than Satan. He eventually leaves the desert to begin his work.

To learn from him and carry on the work after he is gone, Jesus assembles a group of twelve men. The first four he calls are fishermen who work on the Sea of Galilee. As Jesus is walking along the shore, he sees the brothers Andrew and Simon (whom Jesus later renamed Peter), casting a net.

"Come follow me," Jesus says. "I will make you fish for people" (1:17 NCV). Both men join him immediately, perhaps because they've already heard his preaching and witnessed his power.

Further down the shore Jesus invites another team of brothers, James and John, bold men Jesus later nicknames "Thunderbolts." They, too, leave their nets and follow.

Later, Jesus selects his remaining apostles: Philip, Bartholomew, Matthew, Thomas, James son of Alphaeus, Thaddaeus, Simon, known as the Eager One, and Judas Iscariot, who would later betray him.

Jesus casts out an evil spirit (1:21–28).

Even before Jesus faces opposition from human beings, he faces it from cosmic, spiritual forces. While Jesus is teaching in a synagogue at Capernaum, a seaside fishing village in Galilee, a demon-possessed man storms into the service and interrupts.

"Jesus of Nazareth!," the demon yells, "What do you want with us? Did you come to destroy us? I know who you are—God's Holy One!"

"Be quiet!" Jesus replies, "and come out of this man!"

The evil spirit shakes the man, screams, and departs. Jesus has overpowered the cosmic opposition, just as he will later overpower his human enemies.

All the people who witness this dramatic encounter are bewildered and wonder where Jesus gets his power. News of Jesus spreads quickly through the town and beyond, and people begin coming to him for healing. Lepers, lame, blind, demon-possessed—Jesus heals them all.

Picking grain on the Sabbath (2:23–3:6).

One Sabbath, the disciples of Jesus pick some heads of grain as they follow him through a field.

A group of Pharisees, a strict Jewish sect, sees this and confronts Jesus. The Pharisees believe that plucking even a few heads of grain is harvesting, which is work, which the Ten Commandments forbid on the Sabbath. Jesus disagrees and tells them the Sabbath was made to benefit people, not deprive them.

Later, Jesus does more "work" on the Sabbath by healing a man with a crippled hand. Rather than marveling at Jesus' obvious power, the Pharisees become so incensed that they start making plans to kill Jesus.

Parable of the sower (4:1–20).

Jesus knows that not everyone will accept his teachings. He reveals this in a clever story about a farmer sowing seeds.

Some seeds fall on the road and are taken by birds. These seeds symbolize people who hear Jesus' message but are snatched away by Satan. Some seeds land in shallow dirt resting on stones; the seeds spring up quickly but die. These are people who accept the message but don't develop spiritual roots. Some seeds land among thorns and get choked. These are people who accept the message but let it get squeezed out by preoccupation with other things, such as making money. Finally, some seeds land in good soil and produce a great harvest. These are people who accept Jesus' message and pass it on.

Through parables like this, Jesus is able to reveal mysteries about the kingdom of God to his followers, for they have the faith in him that it takes to understand the symbolism. But his opponents, who have nothing but contempt for him, often remain mystified by these stories.

Healed by touching Jesus' robe (5:21–34).

While Jesus is walking in a crowd, a woman who has been suffering from menstrual bleeding for twelve years decides that even touching the robe of Jesus will bring her healing. When she touches him, Jesus feels a release of power.

"Who touched my clothes" he asks. Ridiculous question, the disciples think, for they're all in a crowd. Jesus tells her.

Throughout his ministry, faith is the response Jesus looks for. Through faith, strangers and non-Jews are healed. But without faith, even Jesus' family and the Jewish leaders experience nothing. In Jesus' hometown, lack of faith limits his healings (6:5–6).

Jesus feeds 4,000 (8:1–10).

As Jesus had earlier fed 5,000 people, he again feeds a crowd of 4,000. Earlier, he had five patties of bread, probably pita-style, and two small fish. Here he has seven patties of bread and a few fish. But the result is the same: the people eat their fill, and the disciples collect many basketfuls of leftovers.

Showing an utterly amazing lack of insight about who Jesus is and what he can do, the disciples later suspect he is upset with them for bringing only one loaf of bread on a trip they're taking.

"Why are you talking about not having any bread?" Jesus asks. "You have eyes, but you don't really see. . . How many baskets did you fill with leftover pieces of food" (8:17–19 NCV).

Jesus calls Peter "Satan" (8:27–33).

"The Son of Man must suffer many things," Jesus says, speaking of himself. "And that he would be rejected by the Jewish elders, the leading priests, and the teachers of the law. He told them that the Son of Man must be killed and then rise from the dead after three days" (8:31 NCV).

The disciples believe Jesus is the Messiah; Peter has already expressed this (8:29). But they can't conceive of a suffering Messiah—only a victorious one. When Peter advises Jesus to stop talking like this, Jesus responds, "Go away from me, Satan! You don't care about the things of God, but only about things people think are important."

Jesus then tells the men that if they are to be his followers, they have

Su
M
Tu
We
Th
Fri
Sat
Su
M
Tu
We
Th
Fri
Sat
Su
M
Tu
We

to be willing to give up their lives. But he assures them that in so doing, they will preserve their souls. Six days later, Jesus gives Peter, James, and John a glimpse into the afterlife by allowing them to see him in his glowing, heavenly body as he talks with Moses and Elijah (9:2–8).

Little children with Jesus (10:13–16).

While Jesus is teaching, some parents come forward, hoping to have Jesus bless their children. The people in Bible times believe that blessings, like prayers, can unleash a power that otherwise remains untapped.

When the disciples tell the parents to stop bothering Jesus, he quickly seizes the moment to teach his disciples two lessons. Blessing the children, he shows the kind of compassion he wants them to imitate. Then, calling attention to the trusting nature of children, he reveals how to become a citizen of God's kingdom.

But the disciples don't yet understand that God's kingdom is a spiritual one, not a physical one. They argue over which disciples deserve the honored seats beside the Messiah's throne (9:33–37; 10:35–45).

The first Palm Sunday (11:1–11).

At least three times Jesus has told the disciples he will die, yet it hasn't seemed to sink in. The jubilant scene as Jesus enters Jerusalem on Sunday gives the disciples all the more reason to anticipate a happy ending. Jesus rides in on a donkey, just like Zechariah 9:9 says the Messiah will arrive.

Crowds welcome Jesus with a carpet of palm branches and cloaks, while cheering him as the Messiah descended from King David: "Praise God! God bless the One who comes in the name of the Lord! God bless the kingdom of our father David!"

But this joyous scene begins the painful and predominant theme of Mark: the suffering and death of Jesus.

Immediately following this scene, Mark sets the stage for the final battle between Jesus and the Jewish leaders—and for God's rejection of the people who reject his Son. God's rejection of the unrighteous is symbolized first by a fig tree that Jesus kills with a curse, and second, by Jesus' prediction that the temple will be destroyed—a prophecy fulfilled forty years later. Neither the tree nor the temple provide what God intends they provide, so they are destroyed. Likewise, God will reject people who do not exhibit faith in Jesus.

Jesus is anointed at Bethany (14:1–11).

Wednesday, the day before Jesus is arrested, he becomes the honored guest at a meal in Bethany, just outside of Jerusalem and across the ridge called the Mount of Olives. Back in Jerusalem, Jewish leaders are trying to figure out how to catch Jesus away from his admiring crowds so they can arrest him without starting a riot, then quickly execute him.

But in Bethany, an unnamed woman opens a sealed, stone flask full of expensive perfume—worth a year's salary. This kind of perfume is used on special occasions, such as to anoint the body of a loved one who has just died. The woman pours this on the head of Jesus. Some of the guests quickly begin mumbling to each other about what a waste this is, since the woman could have sold the perfume and given the money to the poor.

Jesus silences the critics. "Leave her alone!" he says. "This woman did the only thing she could do for me; she poured perfume on my body to prepare me for burial."

Afterward, Judas goes to the Jewish priests and offers to help them arrest Jesus. Why he does this, we don't know. Luke says only that Satan enters his heart (Luke 22:3). The following night, while Jesus is praying in a secluded place on the Mount of Olives, Judas leads temple officers to arrest him.

Jesus is executed (15:21–47).

When the high priest learns that Jesus is in custody, he calls an emergency session of the Sanhedrin, a 70-member legislature-court of priests, scholars, and respected elders. They find Jesus guilty of blasphemy after he acknowledges that he is both Messiah and Son of God.

This is a capital offense, so at dawn they take him to Pilate, the Roman governor who alone has power to order an execution. Pilate sees no reason to kill Jesus, but the Jews are screaming their insistence. A politician with a knack for survival, Pilate yields to the will of the people and orders Jesus crucified.

At about 9 a.m., Roman soldiers nail Jesus to a cross.

Pleased with their success, Jewish leaders mock, "If he is really the Christ, the king of Israel, let him come down now from the cross. When we see this, we will believe in him" (15:32 NCV).

At noon the sky turns black and stays that way until 3 o'clock. About

Sun
Mo
Tue
We
Thu
Fri
Sat
Sun
Mo
Tue
We
Thu
Fri
Sat
Sun
Mo
Tue
We

this time, Jesus dies. In that moment, an earthquake rips through the land, strong enough to tear the sacred curtain inside the temple. At the foot of the cross a soldier proclaims what the disciples of Jesus still do not seem to believe: "This man really was the Son of God!"

Women at the tomb of Jesus (16:1–8).

The body of Jesus is taken down before dusk, when Sabbath begins. There is no time to carefully prepare the body by anointing it with oil, as is the custom. But the corpse is wrapped in linen and placed in a tomb cut from solid rock. The entrance is sealed with a huge, disk-shaped stone that rolls along a stone-chiseled groove on the ground.

Sunday morning, three women who have followed Jesus walk to the tomb to properly prepare his body for burial. They're worried how they're going to move the heavy stone by themselves. They needn't be. The stone is rolled away. Inside the tomb is a white-robed young man, instead of Jesus.

"Don't be afraid," the man says. "You are looking for Jesus from Nazareth, who has been crucified. He has risen from the dead; he is not here" (16:6 NCV).

It's uncertain what the writer intends to say next, because there are several conclusions that show up in ancient manuscripts (see "The book's uncertain ending" in Points to Consider). But whatever happens next is enough to convince even the spiritually imperceptive disciples that Jesus is both the Messiah *and* the Son of God. Fifty days later, on the day of Pentecost, they boldly proclaim this at the temple.

That very day, some 3,000 place their faith in these words—and the church is born.

Points to Consider

Old Testament signs pointing to Jesus. Mark told the story of Jesus much as the disciples must have told it after the Resurrection. He builds on the foundation of Old Testament promises about the Messiah, beginning exactly where Malachi—the last book of the Old Testament—ends. He starts by introducing John the Baptist as the promised forerunner to the Messiah.

When the disciples ask Jesus why he speaks in perplexing parables, Jesus shows that he is fulfilling the prophecy of Isaiah 6:9-10 (Mark 4:10-12). And when Jesus warns the disciples that they will scatter when he is arrested, he confirms this by citing the prophet Zechariah (13:7; Mark 14:27).

The temple falls, as Jesus predicted. One day as Jesus was leaving the temple, one of his disciples expressed wonder at the beauty of the architecture. Jesus replied, "Do you see all these great buildings? Not one stone will be left on another. Every stone will be thrown down to the ground" (13:2 NCV). Jesus then went on to talk more about the coming destruction of Jerusalem.

About forty years later, in AD 70, Rome crushed a Jewish rebellion. They burned the city and leveled the last temple that the Jews have ever had.

The book's uncertain ending. It's a mystery how the writer intended to conclude his book, for there are several endings to choose from. The oldest Greek manuscripts end the book with three women running away from the empty tomb of Jesus, "they did not tell anyone about what happened, because they were afraid" (16:8 NCV).

More recent manuscripts add endings that better match the other Gospels, with the women eventually reporting the news to the disciples, as the angel had told them to do (16:7).

It's possible that the writer died before he completed the book, since he apparently wrote in Rome when Nero was slaughtering Christians. Or perhaps the ending was torn off the original scroll, and other writers added what they knew to be the rest of the story.

Clashing facts. When you read the Gospels side by side, you'll notice some apparent discrepancies. For example, Mark reports that there were three women at the tomb of Jesus on resurrection Sunday, while Matthew speaks of only two. And Mark quotes Peter as declaring that Jesus is the Messiah, while Matthew quotes the apostle declaring Jesus is the Messiah and the Son of God.

If four members of a band wrote stories about life on the road with a famous musician, we would expect a lot of overlap, but also some variation. People see the same things differently. And they tend not to have tape recorders running, so their recollection of memorable quotes may not be word-for-word as spoken.

The core issue is whether or not the Gospels witness truthfully in answering the question: Who is this Jesus? The Gospels are early written witnesses to Jesus: they express the testimony of those who had been with Jesus during his ministry, after his resurrection, and (after his ascension to heaven) through the outpoured Holy Spirit. Through all their differences, the Gospels agree that Jesus rose from the dead and is now "both Lord and Christ" (Acts 2:36). And they agree that how people respond to this Jesus determines whether they live or die, eternally.

FOR FURTHER STUDY

- For more insights about Jesus, read the other three Gospels: Matthew, Luke, and John. For the Gospel least like Mark, begin with John.

- Read Acts to see how the disciples respond to their newfound faith that Jesus is the Son of God.

Luke

A Tender Physician's Story of Jesus

The Gospels seem so redundant—pretty much the same stories, some miracles. Why not drop one? Luke, for example?

If early Christians had cut Luke from the canon, we'd miss some of the best-loved stories in the Bible. Luke, a physician, is the only one who reports the birth of Jesus in such moving detail that listening to his version has become as much of a Christmas tradition as listening to carols: "And she gave birth to her first son. Because there were no rooms left in the inn, she wrapped the baby with pieces of cloth and laid him in a feeding trough" (Luke 2:7 NCV).

There's the story of the loving shepherd, leaving his ninety-nine safe sheep to look for the lost one. And the story of the prodigal son, squandering his share of the family wealth, then returning home to the open arms of a loving father. And the story of the good Samari-

Famous Lines

- "Our Father which art in heaven, hallowed be thy name" (Luke 11:2 KJV). *The first sentence of the Lord's Prayer.*

- "Glory to God in the highest, and on earth peace, good will toward men" (2:14 KJV). *The praise of angels in a shepherd's pasture on the night of Jesus' birth.*

- "Physician, heal thyself" (4:23 KJV). *The words of Jesus, anticipating the command of his hometown critics, wanting to see him perform in Nazareth the miracles they hear he has done elsewhere.*

- "I am sending you out like lambs among wolves" (10:3 NIV). *The warning of Jesus to seventy-two followers he is sending on a mission of preaching and healing.*

tan, a half-breed who shows compassion to an injured man after blue-blood Jews, supposed men of God, walk on by.

Fourteen such stories of Jesus are told only in Luke. There are six miracles, including the one of Jesus healing ten lepers, and only one coming back to say thanks.

But perhaps what we would miss most is the word *Savior.* Though it shows up once in the Gospel of John (4:42), it's center stage in Luke, from beginning to end. From the choir of angels above a Bethlehem pasture to Jesus' resurrection and ascension, we are invited to witness God's salvation.

BACKGROUND

INFLUENTIAL PEOPLE

Jesus, God's Son, who has come to earth in human form to offer salvation from sin, and eternal life to everyone who has faith in him (1:31).

Twelve apostles, men Jesus invites to join his ministry as disciples (5:10; 6:13–16).

THEME

The angel Gabriel makes dramatic appearances to announce the coming births of two men who will change the course of history: John the Baptist and Jesus. Gabriel tells Zechariah, John's future father, that his son will "go before the Lord in spirit and power like Elijah" (1:17 NCV). This foreshadows John's role in announcing the arrival of the Messiah. A month later, Gabriel tells Mary, a teenage virgin from a low-income family, that she will miraculously give birth to Jesus.

Both children are born. John begins his ministry, urging people to repent of their sins and then be baptized to show their devotion to God. Jesus is baptized and begins his ministry. A short time later, John's ministry ends when he is arrested and beheaded for criticizing the governor's marriage to a niece.

Jesus teaches and heals throughout his home region of Galilee for several years, establishing a following of people who believe he is the Messiah. But he draws the ire of Jewish leaders insulted that he doesn't share their interpretation of Scripture on many key points, such as how

TIMELINE	BIBLE EVENTS					Dates are approximate
		Birth of Jesus 6 BC --------------		Jesus begins ministy AD 26 ----------	Jesus crucified AD 30 -----------	
	40 BC			**AD 1**		**AD 40**
	WORLD EVENTS	Rome names Herod the Great king of Jews ---- 40 BC	Druids in Britain believe they are decended from a supreme being AD 1 ------------		Romans make first known reference to diamonds -------- AD 16	

to show respect for the Sabbath. They keep close tabs on him, like religious police.

As he turns south, toward Jerusalem, his ministry is drawing to a close. But he continues preaching and healing, even among non-Jewish groups such as the Samaritans. When he finally arrives in Jerusalem, boisterous crowds welcome him as the promised Messiah-king. Yet Thursday evening, while praying, he is arrested and rushed to the Jewish leaders, who try him all night, condemn him to death, then at daybreak on Friday, they insist that the Roman governor issue the death sentence.

That same morning, Jesus is nailed to a cross. By early afternoon, he is dead. On Sunday, however-er, he is raised to life and later appears several times to the disciples. Some time afterward, on the Mount of Olives, the disciples watch him ascend into the sky.

DID YOU KNOW?

• Luke is believed to be the only non-Jewish writer of Scripture. His literary contribution of the Gospel of Luke and its sequel, Acts, amounts to nearly one-fourth of the New Testament.

• Legend says Luke was an artist, and that in AD 590 Pope Gregory the Great used one of Luke's paintings to lead a procession that stopped a plague. An angel is said to have appeared, sheathing its bloody sword, ending the plague. Luke, at least, was a painter of vivid word pictures that inspired many artists.

• John the Baptist and Jesus were related, though the Bible doesn't say how (1:36).

POINTS OF INTEREST

The way of salvation. The one fact that drives this Gospel is that Jesus is the savior of the human race. What Luke chooses to report about Jesus—events, miracles, and teachings—all point to this single truth, which angels reveal to shepherds: "Today your Savior was born in the town of David. He is Christ, the Lord" (2:11 NCV).

The most comprehensive story of Jesus. Luke covers Jesus in more detail than any other Gospel, from the announcement of his birth to the report of his ascension into heaven. There's so much carefully reported detail that many Bible scholars refer to the author as the first Christian historian.

Good news for everyone. Luke uses many techniques to show that salvation through Jesus is available to everyone.

1. Throughout the book, Luke reveals that Jesus came not just for the Jews but also as a "light for the non-Jewish people," adding that "all people will know about the salvation of God!" (2:32; 3:6 NCV).

2. Unlike Matthew, Luke traces Jesus' genealogy back to Adam, father of all people, instead of stopping with Abraham, father of the Jews.

3. Luke reports Jesus' parable of the good Samaritan, which commends a race that many Jews hate.

4. Luke identifies a remarkable number of women, who in ancient times are usually treated as insignificant. The birth of Jesus, for example, is told from Mary's point of view—not from Joseph's, as is done in Matthew. And most of the male characters in Luke have female counterparts.

A non-Jewish audience. The book seems written by a non-Jew, especially for non-Jews. The writer makes comparatively few references to the Old Testament, which would have been unfamiliar to Gentiles. Luke is also the only New Testament author who refuses to describe Jesus as a rabbi. Instead, Luke uses the Greek equivalent, a word meaning "master."

Jesus' compassion for the needy. Luke's Gospel is full of stories showing how much Jesus cares about the poor and the social outcasts.

He announces that he has come "to tell the Good News to the poor . . . to free those who have been treated unfairly" (4:18 NCV). "You people who are poor are blessed," Jesus says, "the kingdom of God belongs to you." Then Jesus quickly adds, "But how terrible it will be for you who are rich, because you have had your easy life (6:20, 24 NCV).

Jesus is drawn to the sinners, and even eats with tax collectors—people shunned as profiteering Jewish traitors who collaborate with the Roman enemy.

The prayer life of Jesus. Prayer is important to Jesus. He prays throughout this Gospel, including after his baptism, before selecting disciples, and before dying. He also teaches the disciples how to pray and tells the crowds several stories about the importance of taking requests to God (11:5–9; 18:1–8, 9–14).

AUTHOR AND DATE

Luke, a physician and an associate of the apostle Paul, is traditionally considered the writer of this Gospel, as well as its sequel, Acts. Though the book never names its writer, Christian leaders in the second century attributed the work to Luke. Certainly it makes sense that a physician would write the book that reports more healing miracles than nay other Gospel. And leave it to a physician to give the most dramatic account of the birth of Jesus.

Both the Gospel and its sequel are addressed to "Honorable Theophilus," perhaps a Roman official who asked for information about Christianity. In response the writer produces an eloquent composition, drawing from material gathered from a variety of sources, including eye-witnesses.

The book may have been written as early as the late 50s, before the execution of Luke's companion, Paul. But emphasis on Jesus' prophecy about the fall of Jerusalem, fulfilled in AD 70, suggests the book was written in the closing decades of the first century.

ON LOCATION

The story takes place primarily in what is now Israel, with some scenes east of the Jordan River, in what is now northern Jordan. Much of Jesus' ministry takes place in his hometown region of Galilee, in northern Israel. His last week takes place in the Jerusalem area, in the region of Judea. (See map in Matthew, page 311.)

LUKE OUTLINE

Shepherds visit newborn Jesus (2:1–20).

After the angel Gabriel tells the virgin Mary that both she and her elderly relative Elizabeth will soon give birth to sons (Jesus and John the Baptist), Mary travels south to visit Elizabeth. There, Mary and Elizabeth's husband—the two who received Gabriel's messages—express their praise in what have come known as Mary's song (also called the *Magnificat,* which means "glorifies") and Zechariah's Song.

Each hymn expresses themes that Luke will highlight throughout the book. "He has filled the hungry with good things," Mary sings, "and sent the rich away with nothing" (1:53 NCV). "Now you, child," Zechariah sings, "will make his [God's] people know that they will be saved by having their sins forgiven" (1:76–77 NCV).

The moving story of Jesus' birth reveals that the first to visit the Savior were not wealthy rulers or prestigious Jewish leaders, but humble shepherds guarding their sheep near Bethlehem. They got an invitation they couldn't refuse: angels filled the night sky with the brightness of God's glory. "Today your Savior was born in the town of David," an angel said. "He is Christ, the Lord. This is how you will know him: You will find a baby wrapped in pieces of cloth and lying in a feeding box."

The shepherds rush to the place and tell Mary and Joseph what the angel said.

Young Jesus debating at the temple (2:41–52).

Luke gives us the Bible's only glimpse of Jesus as an adolescent.

Each spring, Mary and Joseph take Jesus and their other children to Jerusalem, to celebrate the Passover festival that commemorates Israel's freedom from slavery in Egypt during the time of Moses. One year, when Jesus is twelve, he accidentally gets left in Jerusalem after the festival. Mary and Joseph are traveling with a group of family and friends, and incorrectly assume Jesus is among the caravan.

Once they discover he is not, they frantically rush back to Jerusalem and begin searching throughout the city, which is crowded with holiday visitors. After three days they find their boy sitting in the temple courtyard, talking with sage teachers who are astonished at the lad's insight.

When Mary asks her son why he stayed behind and caused her such terrifying worry, Jesus replies, "Why were you looking for me? Didn't you know that I must be in my Father's house?" (2:49 NCV).

Jesus grows wise and strong. "People liked him, and he pleased God."

Jesus rejected in his hometown. (4:14–30).

At roughly thirty years of age, Jesus is baptized and begins his ministry of teaching and healing. Clearly and dramatically, he explains his mission by opening a scroll and reading a prophecy from Isaiah. On hand to hear this inaugural address, in his hometown of Nazareth, are family and friends who have shared a lifetime with him.

"The Lord has put his Spirit in me, because he appointed me to tell the Good News to the poor. He has sent me to tell the captives they are free and to tell the blind that they can see again. God sent me to free those who have been treated unfairly" (4:18 NCV).

Jesus closes the scroll and reports, "While you heard these words just now, they were coming true!"

The people can't believe their ears. As far as they are concerned, Jesus is Joseph's son—not the Messiah. Furious at his blatant blasphemy, they try to throw him from a cliff, but he slips through the crowd and leaves town.

Jesus heals a paralyzed man (5:17–26).

The miracles of Jesus, and his unique insight into Scripture, quickly begin to draw huge crowds. One day as he is teaching in a house, some men can't get their paralyzed friend through the swarm of people. So they remove the roofing tile and lower their friend through the ceiling.

Jesus is so impressed by this show of faith that he says, "Friend, your sins are forgiven" (5:20 NCV).

When Jewish scholars instantly object, saying only God can forgive sins, Jesus asks which is easier—to heal the man or forgive his sins. Jesus says he has the power to do both.

"Take your mat, and go home," Jesus tells the now-healed paralytic. The man does just that, to the astonishment of everyone present.

Luke uses stories like this to allow Jesus himself to answer critics who, decades later, would raise the same objections that an earlier generation of Jewish scholars had expressed.

A soldier's faith (7:1–10).

A Roman soldier who is not a Jew but who worships God convinces some Jewish friends to do him a favor. They ask Jesus to heal a servant of his who is deathly sick. Jesus agrees and begins walking to the soldier's home, but he is intercepted by others bearing a second message from the officer.

The message is that Jesus need not trouble himself by coming, but can heal the servant from a distance.

Jesus says, "I tell you, this is the greatest faith I have found anywhere, even in Israel" The servant is healed by the time the messengers get home.

Jesus calms the storm (8:22–25).

One evening Jesus decides to leave Galilee and sail across the lake, called the Sea of Galilee, to an area where mostly non-Jews live. In a remarkable story that emphasizes both his humanity and divinity, Jesus has become so weary that he falls into a deep sleep. He isn't even awakened by a sudden squall that terrifies the disciples—many of whom are seasoned fishermen.

"Master, Master!" they scream. "We will drown!"

Now awakened, Jesus asks, "Where is your faith?"

He tells the storm to be quiet, and the wind and waves fall placid.

Parable of the good Samaritan (10:30–37).

After Jesus one day tells a Jewish scholar that the two most important laws are to love God and to love your neighbor, the scholar asks who is our neighbor. Jesus replies with this famous story, reported only in Luke.

A man walking the deserted, 15-mile path from Jerusalem to Jericho is attacked by robbers, stripped, beaten, and left for dead. Later in the day, a priest approaches, but walks right on by. Then comes another temple worker, but he walks by also. Finally a Samaritan arrives, helps the man, takes him to an inn, and pays the innkeeper to take care of the victim until he recovers. Samaritans are considered by Jews as hated half-breeds—descendants of Jews who intermarried with Assyrians and who mangled the Jewish faith by adding elements from pagan religions.

"Which one of these three people was a real neighbor?" Jesus asks.

"The one who showed him mercy," the scholar replies.
"Then go and do what he did," Jesus says.

The Lord's Prayer (11:1–4).

Jesus frequently goes off by himself to pray. After one such session, one of his disciples asks that he teach them all how to pray. Jesus responds with an example that has become known as the Lord's Prayer, repeated in the Sermon on the Mount (Matthew 6:9–13).

"Father, may your name always be kept holy. May your kingdom come. Give us the food we need for each day. Forgive us for our sins, because we forgive everyone who has done wrong to us. And do not cause us to be tempted."

Parable of the prodigal son (15:11–32).

Jesus has what Jewish leaders believe is a terribly bad habit: He associates with known sinners. "Even eats with them," they grumble (15:2 NCV).

In response, Jesus tells three stories to show that the reason he came to earth is to find and save the lost. He tells a story about a lost sheep, a lost coin, and finally the beloved story of a lost son.

In this story, a son asks for and is given his share of the family property. He promptly leaves home and spends all the money in wild living. Broke, he finds himself eating pig fodder to survive. He decides to go home and ask his father for a job, since even the servants are better off than he.

On the son's last stretch home, his father spots him a long way off and takes off running, arms wide open.

This, Jesus is teaching, is how the Lord welcomes each sinner home to the kingdom of God.

Zacchaeus the tax man (19:1–26).

The story of Zacchaeus is a great example of what the Jewish leaders are talking about. Here Jesus associates with a tax collector—a Jew who collects Roman-imposed taxes from fellow Jews. Tax collectors routinely overtax and keep the extra money.

As Jesus is passing through Jericho on his way to Jerusalem—and to his inevitable crucifixion—a crowd meets him and begins walking with him.

Like others, Zacchaeus has heard and wants to get a look at him. But Zacchaeus is too short. So he runs ahead and climbs a tree. When the crowd approaches the tree, Jesus stops, looks up, and says he'd like to stay the night at Zacchaeus's home.

By the time Jesus leaves Jericho, Zacchaeus is a changed man. He offers to give half his money to the poor and to repay everyone he has cheated—four times the amount.

A widow's offering (21:1–4).

Jesus arrives in Jerusalem on what later becomes known as Palm Sunday, because cheering crowds welcome him with a carpet of palm branches. Sometime before his Thursday evening arrest, he stands with his disciples in one of the temple courtyards. There, they watch people dropping their offerings into temple collection boxes.

Some donors are rich, and make the size of their gifts as conspicuous as possible. When Jesus sees a poor widow give what he knows is all she has, he turns to the disciples and says, "This woman is very poor, but she gave all she had to live on."

Jesus prays in Gethsemane (22:39–46).

On Thursday evening, Jesus eats a final meal with his disciples. Then he leads them to the Mount of Olives, where he prays passionately for God to spare him from the crucifixion. Yet Jesus quickly adds, "Do what you want, and not what I want."

Led by Judas, a corps of temple guards arrive and arrest Jesus. They take him to the home of Caiaphas, the high priest, who convenes an emergency session of the Sanhedrin, a 70-member legislature-court of priests, scholars, and respected elders. After an all-night trial, they convict Jesus of blasphemy for claiming to be the Son of God.

At daybreak, the assembly leads Jesus to Pilate, the Roman governor, who alone has the authority to condemn a local prisoner to death. When Pilate refuses, not agreeing that blasphemy is a capital offense, the Jews charge that Jesus is an insurrectionist, stirring up crowds for a possible revolt. Pilate remains unconvinced, as does Herod, governor of Galilee, who is also in town. But Pilate eventually gives in to the persistent assembly and orders Jesus executed immediately.

Jesus is crucified (23:26–56).

As Jesus is nailed to a cross he prays, "Father, forgive these people! They don't know what they're doing."

Some in the crowd hurl insults at him. One of the two criminals hanging beside him snaps, "Aren't you the Christ? Then save yourself and us." The other man, however, tells him to show some respect for God. Jesus replies by promising that the second man will join him this day in paradise.

Jesus dies about 3 p.m. and his body is entrusted to a Sanhedrin member who had objected to the council's sentence. Jesus is buried in this man's newly cut tomb, but by Sunday morning he is raised from the dead.

Jesus on the road to Emmaus (24:13–35).

On the day of his resurrection, Jesus joins two dejected travelers on their way to Emmaus, a village seven miles from Jerusalem. The two men don't recognize the Lord. They tell him about how the Crucifixion has dashed their hopes in Jesus, whom they had thought was the Messiah. But Jesus, without revealing his identity, replies, "They said that the Christ must suffer these things before he enters his glory." Then he teaches them a Bible lesson, proving his point by quoting the books of Moses and the words of the prophets.

Only later, as he breaks bread for them during a meal, do they recognize who he is. Then he disappears.

Luke and the other Gospels report that Jesus appears to his followers many times after the Resurrection. In his final appearance to the remaining eleven disciples—Judas has hanged himself—Jesus tells them to remain in Jerusalem "until you have received that power from heaven" (24:49 NCV). After this, they are to tell others what they experienced in their few short years with Jesus.

The book of Acts reports the arrival of heaven's power some fifty days after the crucifixion, followed by the birth of the church on that very day.

POINTS TO CONSIDER

The Galilee boat. During an Israel drought in 1986, the Sea of Galilee shoreline receded dramatically. Two men who lived nearby noticed in the mud below what looked like the outline of a boat. When they looked closer, it became clear that this was an ancient boat. Rains had recently returned, and the level of the lake was rising, so a team of archaeologists began working in 24-hour shifts to excavate the ancient treasure.

Within a few days they retrieved what they later discovered was a small fishing boat from Jesus' century—perhaps one much like Jesus and the disciples sailed on the evening they got caught in a sudden storm (8:23).

Buried in the mud, the boat was remarkably well preserved with the hull intact. Measuring nearly 27 feet long, 8 feet wide, and 5 feet high, it could carry at least fifteen passengers. It would take at least four rowers and a helmsman to propel the craft.

The sudden storm. The squall that caught the disciples off guard one night is like many that still happen on the Sea of Galilee. Actually a freshwater lake, the sea rests in a deep basin 700 feet below sea level, almost completely surrounded by hills. Storms erupt when hot air trapped in this basin rises and collides with cool air blowing in from the Mediterranean Sea and pouring down the ravines.

The virgin birth. Many people, including some Christians, doubt what Matthew and Luke report as the virgin birth of Jesus.

In fact, Matthew's reference to Isaiah's prophecy, "The virgin will be pregnant" (Matthew 1:23 NCV) translates into Greek a Hebrew word that means "young woman," not necessarily a "virgin." The translation that Matthew and Luke used is not unique to them. Jewish scholars translating Isaiah into Greek in the 200s BC also used "virgin," apparently wanting to stress what they believed would be God's supernatural involvement in the coming birth of a messiah.

Though Isaiah's prophecy may not point directly to a virgin birth, the reports of Matthew and Luke both say this is how Jesus was born.

Beyond criticizing the translation, some add that a virgin birth implies there is something dirty and sinful about human sexuality—sinful enough that God felt compelled to spare Jesus from any guilt by association. Yet Jesus spent his lifetime in close association with sinners, repeatedly taking flak from Jewish leaders for getting too cozy with the disreputable. And his first miracle in the Gospel of John is at a wedding. Jesus was no prude.

Many Christians view the virgin birth as one more piece of miraculous evidence pointing to what Jesus and the early Christians taught: Jesus is both fully human and fully divine—which, of course, takes us from one mystery to another: How could he be 100 percent both? This question leaves us standing on the foundation that Jesus taught was the most firm of all: faith in God.

FOR FURTHER STUDY

- Acts shows how the disciples boldly continued the work Jesus began, starting the Christian church.

- Matthew and Mark are two similar accounts of the life of Jesus. John also focuses on Jesus, but emphasizes primarily the teachings and miracles that show he is the Son of God.

Sun
Mor
Tues
Wed
Thu
Frid
Satu
Sun
Mor
Tues
Wed
Thu
Frid
Satu
Sun
Mor
Tues
Wed

John

A Deep Thinker's Story of Jesus

John is the cerebral Gospel for thinking humans—perhaps too cerebral for some.

If the action-packed Gospel of Mark was written for shorter attention spans, John has the opposite end of the spectrum in mind: people who enjoy peeling off layer upon layer of dramatic, insightful symbolism, and people who want nothing more than extensive, detailed teaching sessions led by the Master Teacher.

Ironically, the Gospel of John exists for one reason: to convince us to have faith in what he cannot possibly explain. The unexplainable is that Jesus and God are one, and that when Jesus lived on earth, he was both truly God and truly human.

John doesn't even try to explain how this could be. He simply reports that it is. He provides testimony from an intriguing array of witnesses, including Jesus himself. And he leaves us with a convincing string of miracles that bear the unmistakable signature of God.

Then John leaves us with a deep and sincere hope that we will have faith enough to believe.

Famous Lines

- "I was blind, and now I see" (9:25 NCV). *A man's response to Jewish leaders who hope to prove that Jesus hasn't cured any blindness.*

- "For God so loved the world, that he gave his only begotten Son, that whosoever believeth in him should not perish, but have everlasting life" (3:16 KJV). *Jesus' explanation of why he has come to earth.*

- "I am the bread that gives life" (6:35 NCV). *Jesus' claim to be the source of spiritual nourishment that produces eternal life.*

BACKGROUND

INFLUENTIAL PEOPLE

Jesus, God's Son, who was present at the Creation of the world and who has come to earth in human form to offer eternal life to everyone who has faith in him (1:17).

Twelve apostles, men Jesus invites to join his ministry as disciples (1:40–45).

THEME

Instead of starting with the birth of Jesus or at the beginning of his ministry, John takes us all the way back to Creation. Jesus was there, John says. He was "with God, and the Word was God" (1:1 NCV). This launches the driving theme of the book: Jesus is not just a prophet or the Messiah—though he is certainly both—he is part of the Godhead. He is the Son of God, who has come from heaven and has taken the form of a human being to show people what God is like.

This stated, John introduces the promised predecessor of the Messiah—John the Baptist—who calls Jesus "the Lamb of God who takes away the sin of the world!" (1:29 NCV).

Jesus selects twelve disciples to learn from him, help him in ministry, and continue his work after he returns to heaven. Jesus then begins his work, engaging in detailed teaching sessions about who he is and why he has come, and performing miracles that convince many people he is both the Messiah and the Son of God. Most Jewish leaders, however, remain unconvinced that he is anything but a fraud who gets his power from the devil.

The second half of the book tells about the final week in the life of Jesus. He rides into Jerusalem amid cheering masses, washes the feet of the disciples at the Last Supper, then is arrested, tried all night long, and

					Dates are approximate
TIMELINE	**BIBLE EVENTS**	Birth of Jesus ------- 6 BC	Jesus begins ministy AD 26 --------	Jesus crucified AD 30 ------------	
	10 BC		**AD 1**		**AD 30**
	WORLD EVENTS	Druids in Britain believe they are decended from a supreme being AD 1 --------		Pilate begins 10-year rule as governor AD 26 ------------	Tiberius' 16th year as Caesar Ad 30 ----

nailed to a cross the next morning. Two days later, Sunday morning, he is resurrected from the grave and is talking again with his disciples.

The book concludes by ex-pressing the hope that readers will believe Jesus is the Son of God, and that through faith they will enter into the kingdom of God and live forever.

POINTS OF INTEREST

Jesus portrayed as God. John takes Jesus all the way back—to the beginning of Creation. This startling introduction presents Jesus as part of the Godhead. In words reminiscent of the Creation story, John begins his book: "In the beginning there was the Word. The Word was with God, and the Word was God" (1:1 NCV). Word is from the Greek term logos,

which means different things to different people. The Jews think of it as the power of God, for all God has to do is speak the words "Let there be light" (Genesis 1:3 NCV) and there is light. The Greeks think of it as cosmic reason, the well-designed frame on which the universe is built.

Jesus is both of these—the power of God, and the one whose signature is stamped on the universe. But John takes the term further. Just as a word reveals a thought, Jesus is the expression of God, physically revealing the invisible, spiritual presence of God.

Jesus is God who "became a human and lived among us" (1:14 NCV).

The book's purpose. The author himself explains why he wrote the book. "These [stories] are written so that you may believe that Jesus is the Christ, the Son of God. Then, by believing, you may have life through his name" (20:31 NCV).

What's missing. Notice what John leaves out. You'll not find a single parable. Nor will you find anything about the birth of Jesus, his baptism, temptation, the Last Supper, his agonizing prayer on the night of his arrest, or his ascension into the sky.

John, probably written last of the four Gospels, does not repeat most of the stories that have been circulating for decades. Instead, it focuses on Jesus' deity, using carefully selected miracles and teachings that propel this theme.

Seven miracles. John reports seven miracles of Jesus, which he calls "signs" that prove Jesus is God.

1. Jesus turns water into wine (2:1–12). This shows he is the source of physical life who can take one substance and make it into a new creation.

2. He heals a soldier's son by long-distance (4:46–54), showing he is not limited by geography.

3. He heals a lame man on the Sabbath (5:1–17), revealing he is not limited by time.

4. He feeds 5,000 people (6:1–14), then declares he is the bread of life—the source of both physical and spiritual nourishment.

5. He walks on water (6:16–21), as Lord of nature.

6. He heals a blind man (9:1–41), proclaiming himself the light of the world that can overpower any form of darkness.

7. He raises Lazarus from the dead (11:17–45), revealing his power over death.

Seven "I am" descriptions of Jesus. Jesus describes himself with seven revealing statements. All begin with "I am," the phrase God used to describe himself to Moses: "I am who I am. When you go to the people of Israel, tell them, 'I am sent me to you' " (Exodux 3:14 NCV).

1. "I am the bread that gives life!" (6:35 NCV). Manna from heaven kept the Israelites from starving in the desert. Jesus says he is the source of spiritual nourishment: "Whoever comes to me will never be hungry."

2. "I am the light of the world. The person who follows me will never live in darkness but will have the light that gives life" (8:12 NCV).

3. "I am the door for the sheep" (10:7 NCV), the only entrance into God's eternal kingdom.

4. "I am the good shepherd . . . I give my life for the sheep" (10:14–15 NCV).

5. "I am the resurrection and the life. Those who believe in me will have life even if they die" (11:25 NCV). The body will die, but the soul that trusts in Jesus will live forever.

6. "I am the way, and the truth, and the life . . . The only way to the Father is through me" (14:6 NCV).

7. "I am the true vine" (15:1 NCV). Anyone cut off from him will wither and die, like pruned branches.

Seven layers of meaning. John's language is rich in symbolism, often with more than a single meaning.

For example, when Jesus calls himself "the bread that gives life," early Christian readers probably envision many images. They think first of wheat or barley bread, one of their staple foods. They think also of the manna that God sent from heaven to keep the Israelites from starving, for Jesus comes from heaven. They think of the bread they eat each Passover to commemorate how God saved them from slavery, for Jesus offers freedom from slavery to sin. And they certainly think of the Last Supper, when Jesus breaks a loaf of bread and tells his disciples that this represents his body, which will be offered as a sacrifice for the sins of humanity. This Gospel invites readers to scan all of the Old Testament's library of images while pondering the meaning of Jesus.

AUTHOR AND DATE

The author is probably the apostle John, one of Jesus' three closest disciples. John is not mentioned in this Gospel, but he is named in the other three. His conspicuous absence here, along with the book's many references to a "follower Jesus loved" (13:23 NCV), suggest he was the writer. When the book was published, probably near the end of the first century, the church accepted it as the authentic testimony of the apostle John.

It's uncertain exactly when the Gospel was written. Some believe John write it around the middle of the century, perhaps the same time some of the other Gospels were written. Others suggest John wrote it late in the century, AD 85 or later, to supplement the other Gospels. Some Christian writers in the second century say this is exactly what happened, that an elderly John wrote it in Ephesus, a coastal city in western Turkey.

ON LOCATION

The story takes place primarily in what is now Israel, with some scenes east of the Jordan River, in what is now northern Jordan. Much of Jesus' ministry takes place in his hometown region of Galilee, in northern Israel. His last week takes place in the Jerusalem area, in the region of Judea. (See map in Matthew, page 311.)

JOHN OUTLINE

Jesus at Creation (1:1–18).

Describing Jesus as the Word—the expression of God, in the way a word expresses a thought—John begins his gospel by placing Jesus alongside God at the beginning of time. "He was with God in the beginning. All things were made by him" (2,3 NCV). Yet this Word "became a human and lived among us" (14 NCV). In this way, Jesus "has shown us what God is like" (18 NCV).

Since humanity first sinned, contaminating God's good creation, God has been working his plan to purge this contamination—to remove sin and its destructive effects. By associating Jesus with the first Creation, John also portrays Jesus as the one who will establish the New Creation, the kingdom of God.

Jesus turns water into wine (2:1–11).

Jesus attends a wedding at the small village of Cana. When guests drink the last of the wine, Jesus' mother reports this to him, as though she expects him to remedy the problem.

He instructs the household servants to fill with water six stone jars—each jar holds 20–30 gallons. Then he tells them to dip some out and take it to the reception coordinator. The coordinator says this new wine is the best wine of the feast.

This miracle is the first of seven "signs" or proofs that John reports. These signs are intended to convince people that Jesus is God in the flesh. By turning the natural substance of water into the new creation of wine, Jesus shows he is the source of creation and the sustainer of life.

Jesus talks with a Samaritan woman (4:1–42).

While traveling home from southern Israel, Jesus arrives in a small town in Samaria. Tired and thirsty, he sits beside the village well, waiting for someone with a bucket. The disciples have gone to buy food.

When a woman arrives, Jesus asks for a drink of water. But she says she can't understand why he's talking to her, since Jews and Samaritans don't get along.

"If you only knew the free gift of God and who it is that is asking you for water," Jesus replies, "you would have asked him, and he would have given you living water" (10 NCV).

Before the visit is over, this woman has brought the entire village to Jesus, and the people have declared, "We know that this man really is the Savior of the world" (42 NCV).

Jesus feeds 5,000 people (6:1–59).

As Jesus continues his ministry of healing and teaching, huge crowds are drawn to him. One day, 5,000 people approach him in an isolated field along the shores of the Sea of Galilee. When they grow hungry, Jesus miraculously feeds them, using only five small loaves of barley and two fish. Everyone has plenty to eat, and the disciples gather up twelve large baskets of leftovers.

That evening, Jesus leaves the area. But by the next day, some of the people have tracked him down. Jesus accuses them of coming back not to learn, but to eat. They should be seeking spiritual bread from heaven.

"I am the bread that gives life!" He says. "Anyone who eats this bread will live forever" (48, 51 NCV).

Lazarus returns from the dead (11:1–44).

The final and most dramatic of Jesus' seven miracles is the resurrection of Lazarus. As Lazarus lies dying, his sisters send word to their friend Jesus, expecting him to come quickly. But Jesus delays telling his disciples that Lazarus's illness "to bring glory to the Son of God" (11:4 NCV).

By the time Jesus arrives, Lazarus has been dead four days. Jesus orders the tomb opened. And as the group of mourners watch, Jesus shouts, "Lazarus, come out!" Lazarus emerges, "his hands and feet wrapped with pieces of cloth, and a cloth around his face."

This graphically shows the power of Jesus over death. It also foreshadows his own Resurrection, perhaps a couple of weeks later.

Jesus washes the feet of his disciples (13:1–17).

Before eating the Last Supper, Jesus performs the humble chore of washing the feet of his disciples. It is something servants do for guests, or disciples for their rabbi.

This is not just an object lesson in humility, with deity teaching humanity how to behave. It's also a symbol of the spiritual cleansing that Jesus makes available to everyone. When Peter objects to the washing, Jesus gives a stern reply. "If I don't wash your feet," he says, "you are not one of my people" (8 NCV).

Years later, when Paul converts, he, too, must be cleansed. "Wash your sins away," he is told, "trusting in him to save you" (Acts 22:16 NCV).

Peter denies knowing Jesus (18:15–27).

At the Last Supper, shortly before his arrest, Jesus predicts that Peter will three times deny knowing him—this very night, before the rooster crows.

When officers arrest Jesus and take him to the high priest, Peter stands outside the priest's home with soldiers and servants, warming himself by a fire. One by one, throughout the night, people ask Peter if he is a disciple of the man inside. And one by one, Peter denies it. At the moment of the third denial, a rooster begins to crow.

By now, Jesus' trial is over and he is condemned of blasphemy. All that the Jews need is the Roman governor's order of immediate execution.

Jesus is crucified (19:28–42).

Pilate, the governor, tries to talk the Jews out of the execution. "Do you want me to crucify your king?" he asks.

"The only king we have is Caesar," they reply (15 NCV).

This is a powerful, deeply symbolic moment. There was a time when God was Israel's king, but the Israelites demanded that Samuel choose them a human king. Though this made Samuel, God's prophet, feel like a failure, God consoled him: "They have rejected me from being their king" (1 Samuel 8:7 NCV).

When the Jews reject Jesus, once again they reject the kingship of God.

Doubting Thomas sees Jesus (20:24–31).

On Sunday morning, a resurrected Jesus appears to his disciples, who are hiding behind locked doors. For some reason, Thomas is not there. Later, when the disciples tell him they've seen Jesus, Thomas says he'll believe it when he can touch the spear wound in Jesus' side and the nail scars on his hands.

A week later, Jesus returns. This time, Thomas is there.

"Look at my hands," Jesus says. "Put your hand here in my side. Stop being an unbeliever and believe" (27 NCV).

Needing no more convincing, Thomas replies, "My Lord and my God!"

Jesus gently rebukes Thomas for needing proof—after all he has seen. And he commends those in years to come "who believe without seeing me will be truly blessed."

POINTS TO CONSIDER

The anti-Semitic Gospel? John is more hostile to "the Jews" than any of the other three Gospels. When the other Gospels talk about the opponents of Jesus, they specify Jewish leaders, such as priests or scholars. But John simply calls them "the Jews" (5:16 NIV).

John reports Jesus going so far as to say the Jews didn't descend from Abraham: "Your father the devil" (8:44 NCV). Physically, they came from Abraham. But spiritually, there was no resemblance.

Not all Jews, however, opposed Jesus. In fact, Jesus was a Jew. So were all of his twelve disciples. So were the vast majority of his many other followers.

In the Gospel of John, "the Jews" is a technical term that means the opponents of Jesus, not all people who are racially Jews.

John probably wrote his Gospel in the last quarter of the first century, shortly after Jewish leaders had grown so weary of Jewish Christians worshiping with them that they expelled them from the synagogues. If so, this book was written during the height of an us-them, Christian-Jew antagonism. Many of the Christians were Jews, racially. And many continued to honor Jewish traditions, such as the Sabbath and Jewish holidays. But more and more they were also beginning to think of themselves as distinct. Religiously speaking, they were followers of Jesus. The Jews still worshiping in the synagogue, however, were not.

How many Gods are there? The Gospel asserts that the Word, Jesus, was truly God (1:1). Jesus also said he was the Son of

God, and one with the Father (14:10). Yet when asked what the most important law was, he cited the creed of the Jewish people, first expressed in Deuteronomy 6:4: "Listen, people of Israel! The Lord our God is the only Lord. Love the Lord your God with all your heart, all your soul, all your mind, and all your strength" (Mark 12:29–30 NCV).

The Lord is one. Not two, not three.

So how can the Lord be one, as Jesus admitted, and yet seem to be more than one, with the Son on earth praying to the Father in heaven?

The Gospel of John doesn't explain how, but the Prologue clearly asserts that the Word-Son-Jesus is God, yet distinct from God the Father (1:1–18). And the end of the book includes another testimony to Jesus' unique identity. After he touches the wounds of the risen Jesus, Thomas exclaims "My Lord and my God!" (20:28 NCV). In telling us who Jesus is, John stresses both identity (Jesus is the Lord God) and distinction (the Son is closely related to but not identical with the Father or the Holy Spirit). The earliest Christians lived with this complex relationship but left it to theologians in later centuries to explain the complex oneness of God in the doctrine of the Trinity.

FOR FURTHER STUDY

- Other New Testament books traditionally attributed to John are the short letters of 1, 2, and 3 John and the mysterious end-time prophecy of Revelation.

- Read Matthew, Mark, and Luke for additional details about the life and ministry of Jesus.

- Acts begins where the ascension of Jesus ends, with the disciples boldly reporting what Jesus taught them.

Acts

THE CHURCH IS BORN

It's strange that the second book in a series should be so full of firsts.

Acts, a sequel to the Gospel of Luke, tells of Jesus' ascension into heaven, then proceeds to report on the first sermon by a disciple, the first miracle by a disciple, the first steps toward organizing the Christian movement, the first orchestrated persecution of believers, the first Christian martyr, the first non-Jewish convert, and the first missionary trip.

It's also strange how quickly the original disciples of Jesus become lost in the picture, like a dozen golden stems of wheat blurred amid a harvest field. The disciples are revered throughout their lifetimes as leaders of the movement, because of their intimate association with Jesus and the eyewitness stories and divinely illumined insights they often speak about. But other leaders quickly rise, eclipsing the ministry of the disciples who are seldom mentioned in the rest of the Bible.

The book of Acts introduces these wonder-working, charismatic leaders, the most famous of whom is Paul. Acts also reminds us where this wonder-working power and spiritual vigor come from; at each bend in the road, early believers turn for guidance to the Holy Spirit. And like Jesus, the Holy Spirit never misleads.

God's Spirit making bold witnesses out of ordinary people is the reason behind the phenomenal success of the first-generation church. He'll also be the reason behind any successes of the 21st-century church.

FAMOUS LINES

- "It is more blessed to give than to receive" (20:35 KJV). *Paul quoting a proverb of Jesus' that does not appear in any of the Gospels.*

- "Then anyone who calls on the Lord will be saved" (2:21 NCV). *Peter announcing that this prophecy of Joel's is now fulfilled.*

- "But when the Holy Spirit comes to you, you will receive power. You will be my witnesses—in Jerusalem, in all of Judea, in Samaria, and in every part of the world" (1:8 NCV). *The last words of Jesus to his disciples, spoken as he ascends to heaven.*

BACKGROUND

INFLUENTIAL PEOPLE

Paul, one-time Jewish persecutor of Christians, who converts to become missionary and advocate for non-Jewish Christians (13:9; in 7:58 by his Hebrew name, Saul).

Peter, leader of the twelve original disciples, who preaches the first sermon after Jesus' resurrection (1:13).

Stephen, the church's first martyr, killed by a Jewish mob (6:5).

Barnabas, Paul's missionary colleague (4:36).

THEME

The story picks up where the Gospel of Luke leaves off, with the ascension of Jesus into heaven. As Jesus rises into the clouds, he gives a final instruction to his disciples. He tells them to wait in Jerusalem for the Holy Spirit, who will fill them with power. Afterward, they are to tell everyone what they have witnessed during their few years with Jesus.

Ten days later, the Holy Spirit arrives with dramatic fury, filling the house with the sound of a powerful wind. Suddenly, the Holy Spirit enables the disciples to praise God in languages they have never learned. This amazes the throng of Jewish pilgrims in town from all over the Roman Empire for the holy day of Pentecost, a harvest festival of thanksgiving. Peter preaches the first sermon of the newborn church, and 3,000 people become followers of Jesus.

The believers begin to organize, selecting leaders to help the apostles. But the Jewish council that arranged for the execution of Jesus becomes alarmed at the growth of what they believe is just another heretical Jewish movement. They begin persecuting the believers, trying and imprisoning them. During the trial of Stephen, a newly elected church leader, the Jews become so furious that they drag him outside and stone him to death. Many Christians flee Jerusalem, taking the gospel with them.

TIMELINE	BIBLE EVENTS	Jesus ascends to heaven AD 30	Stephen martyred AD 35 Paul converts AD 35	Paul's missionary journeys begin AD 46	Paul imprisoned at Rome AD 60		Dates are approximate
		AD 30	**AD 40**	**AD 50**	**AD 60**	**AD 70**	**AD 80**
	WORLD EVENTS	Gamaliel is leading rabbi of Pharisees AD 30	Emperor Claudius begins 13-year reign AD 41	Buddhism of India introduced to China AD 58	Rome burns; Christians blamed, persecuted AD 64	Jews in Israel revolt AD 66	Mount Vesuvius erupts, burying Pompeii AD 79

One Jew named Saul tries to hunt them down. But on a search-and-arrest trip to Damascus, he meets Jesus and converts to Christianity. Sometime later Paul (Saul's Roman name) becomes a leader of a predominantly non-Jewish congregation in Syria. From there, at the prompting of the Holy Spirit, he and Barnabas are sent on a preaching tour to cities throughout the Roman Empire.

He is eventually arrested in Jerusalem and sent to Rome for an imperial trial that may have ended in his execution. As the book draws to a close, Paul remains under house arrest in Rome, bravely teaching others about Jesus.

DID YOU KNOW?

• The term *Christian* didn't surface until about a decade after Christ, perhaps as a demeaning term like "Moonie," used to describe a member of Sun Myung Moon's Unification Church. The earliest Christians called themselves followers of "the Way," short for "the Way of Jesus" (24:14 NCV).

• Though Acts is the first known history of the church, written as early as thirty years after the Resurrection, it is probably not the first Christian document. Most of Paul's letters were written even earlier, some as early as twenty years after the Resurrection.

• The two books of Luke—the Gospel of Luke followed by Acts—make up nearly one-fourth of the New Testament.

POINTS OF INTEREST

The acts of Paul. Though the book is called Acts of the Apostles, the original disciples of Jesus quickly disappear from the scene. By chapter 6, the book begins introducing other leaders of the rapidly expanding movement. And by chapter 13, Paul emerges as the book's main character and as leader in the ministry among the fastest-growing segment of the church: non-Jews. Though the church starts among the Jews, over the years the Jews increasingly reject the church and its message that Jesus is the Messiah and Son of God.

"We had to tell God's message to you before we told it to anyone else," Paul explains to a synagogue full of Jews. "But you refuse to listen. You are judging yourselves not worthy of having eternal life! So we will now go to the people of other nations" (13:46 NCV).

God keeping his promises. One of the main points that Luke makes, in both the Gospel of Luke and in Acts, is that God keeps his promises. In the Gospel, Luke points out how Jesus fulfills Old Testament prophecies about the Messiah. And in Acts, Luke reports in meticulous detail of the apostles, Paul, and other godly men fulfilling Jesus' commission to the church: "You will be my witnesses—in Jerusalem, in all of Judea, in Samaria, and in every part of the world" (1:8 NCV).

The story begins in a strictly Jewish setting, during the harvest festival of Pentecost in Jerusalem. There, the Holy Spirit–empowered church picks up where the ministry of Jesus ends. The apostles and others then take the news of Jesus outside the capital city, to the surrounding region of Judea. Next they start house churches in Samaria, the region to the north. And by the end of the book, the church has scattered across thousands of miles and is welcoming people of all cultures and nations.

The job of the Holy Spirit. Just as the Holy Spirit—the third person of the Godhead—fills Jesus at the beginning of his ministry (Luke 4:1), the Spirit also fills the apostles and other followers of Jesus, giving them supernatural power that helps convince many about the truth of their message (2:4, 43, 47).

The spirit continues filling believers from all walks of life, not only performing wonders through them but also helping them make important decisions (15:28; 16:6–7).

God's surprise attacks on barriers to the gospel. Notice how God continues to surprise church leaders—even the apostles—by knocking down one barrier after another that would restrict the expanding kingdom of God. Here are three examples.

Customs fall. Jewish Christians argue that all Christians need to observe Jewish dietary laws restricting what people can and cannot eat. To Peter's astonishment, God shows him a vision that repeats what Jesus had taught earlier: under God's new covenant with humanity—which replaces the old covenant with Israel—all food is kosher (Mark 7:19; Acts 10).

Racism falls. The gospel is extended to the Samaritans, a race of Jewish half-breeds that pure-blooded Jews hate (8:14–17).

Vengeance falls. Citizenship in the kingdom of God is extended to enemies of Israel, Roman soldiers occupying the land. Though independence-loving Jews will revolt in AD 66, Christians are to embrace Roman believers as brothers in Christ (chapter 10).

AUTHOR AND DATE

Luke, a physician and an associate of the apostle Paul, is traditionally considered the writer of this book, as well as its Gospel predecessor—

Luke. Though neither book names its writer, Christian leaders in the second century attributed both to Luke.

The two books share a unique writing style and are both addressed to "Theophilus," perhaps a Roman official who asked for information about Christianity. In response, the writer produces an eloquent composition, drawing from material gathered from a variety of sources, including eyewitnesses and perhaps his own travel diary (sometimes when reporting about Paul's ministry the writer refers to "we," as in Acts 16:10).

The book may have been written in the early 60s, before the execution of Luke's companion, Paul, perhaps during Nero's persecution of Christians beginning in AD 64. But emphasis in the Gospel of Luke on Jesus' prophecy about the fall of Jerusalem, fulfilled in AD 70, suggests to many experts that both books were written later.

ON LOCATION

The story covers the first thirty years of Christian history, beginning in Jerusalem. There, the apostles witness the ascension of Jesus into heaven. Ten days later, when the promised Holy Spirit arrives and fills them with power and boldness, the men immediately start preaching the good news about Jesus. Thousands convert. The church quickly expands beyond Jerusalem into most of the Roman Empire. Within three decades Christians are worshiping in house churches throughout what is now Israel, Syria, Turkey, Greece, and even Rome, some 2,000 miles away.

ACTS OUTLINE

Jesus ascends to heaven (1:1–11).

Jesus remains with his disciples forty days after the Resurrection. Then he leads them to the Mount of Olives, across the valley from Jerusalem. Don't leave Jerusalem yet, he says. "Wait here to receive the promise from the Father which I told you about."

"Then," Jesus says, "You will be my witnesses—in Jerusalem, in all of Judea, in Samaria, and in every part of the world." With this, Jesus rises into the sky and out of sight.

The disciples stare into the clouds, perhaps feeling abandoned. But two angels suddenly appear with this comforting message: "Jesus, whom you saw taken up from you into heaven, will come back in the same way you saw him go."

The Holy Spirit fills the disciples (2:1–13).

The disciples return to Jerusalem and select Matthias to replace Judas, who had betrayed Jesus and then hanged himself. After about ten days the Spirit arrives, flooding the room with the sound of a mighty wind. Above each person's head hovers a flame, perhaps symbolizing the presence of God.

The Spirit's arrival marks a turning point in the way God communicates with human beings. Until now, God has sent the Holy Spirit to only select individuals, such as prophets who conveyed God's instructions to the people. But today, the promise God had made to Joel comes true: "I will pour out my Spirit on all kinds of people" (Joel 2:28 NCV). All who call on the Lord personally receive the presence of God. With this the mission of Jesus is transferred to the apostles, then to the converts.

Three thousand converts in one day (2:14–47).

When the Holy Spirit arrives, the disciples are mysteriously enabled to speak in different languages. This is a timely miracle, since foreign-speaking Jews from all over the world are in town to celebrate the harvest festival of Pentecost.

At 9 a.m. Peter boldly addresses the crowd, which includes Jewish leaders who fifty days earlier had executed Jesus. Instead of denying that he knows Jesus—as he did the night of Jesus' trial—Peter proclaims that Jesus is Messiah and Lord, and that "Jesus is the One whom God raised from the dead."

Some 3,000 believe what they hear, perhaps because Peter's words are backed up by miracles. The converts repent of their sin, are baptized, then spend time with the apostles learning more about Jesus.

The church is born.

A husband and wife die (5:1–10).

Compassion for the needy becomes a trademark of the fledgling Christian movement. When someone has a need, others sell property and possessions and bring the money to the apostles, who oversee the compassionate ministries.

A man named Ananias and his wife, Sapphira, decide to sell some property, give part of the money to the apostles, and keep the rest. Appearing before Peter individually, they each lie and say they have donated all the money from the sale. When Peter replies that they have lied to God, the accusation strikes them like a blow, and they drop dead. The Bible doesn't state the cause of death. But believers realize the power of the Holy Spirit is not to be trifled with.

Stephen becomes the first Christian martyr (7:1–60).

Among several Spirit-filled men that the apostles choose to help them is Stephen. He is such a compelling speaker that some Jews have him brought up on charges of "speaking against this holy place and the law of Moses" (6:13 NCV).

Standing before the same Jewish council that tried Jesus, Stephen doesn't defend himself. He reminds the tradition-minded Jews that God is not confined to any temple built by humans and that their ancestors killed the prophets who spoke of the coming Messiah. Then Stephen has a vision: "I see heaven open and the Son of Man standing at God's right."

Enraged, a mob drags Stephen from the courtroom and stones him to death. Standing nearby, holding the cloaks of the executioners is Saul, better known by his Roman name, Paul.

Philip takes the gospel to Samaria (8:4–8).

That very day, Jews begin hunting down and imprisoning people who believe as Stephen did. Many believers leave town, taking their teachings about Jesus with them throughout the territories of Judea and Samaria. Philips, who like Stephen is one of seven chosen to help the apostles, travels north to Samaria, a region Jews tend to avoid. Many Jews believe Samaritans are physical and spiritual half-breeds—former Jews whose blood and religion have been contaminated by foreigners.

Despite this prejudice, Philip invites them to become citizens in the kingdom of God. Many accept, prompted by healing miracles that Philip performs.

Paul's conversion (9:1–19).

Among Jews committed to chasing down these heretics is Saul, whose Roman name is Paul. As he nears Damascus, a brilliant light from the sky strikes him, driving him to the ground. As he trembles in the dirt a voice asks, "Saul, Saul! Why are you persecuting me?"

"Who are you, Lord?" Saul replies.

"I am Jesus."

The Lord tells Saul to go on to Damascus and wait for instructions. When the light disappears, Saul is blind. His traveling companions escort him into the city, where he refuses to eat or drink.

God directs a believer living in the city to go to Saul and to pray for his healing. Before Saul leaves town, he is telling others about Jesus, perhaps even quoting the sermon of Stephen.

Peter's strange vision of animals (10:9–23).

At noontime one day, Peter goes to his rooftop to pray. There he sees a vision. Animals prohibited from the Jewish diet since the days of Moses are lowered from heaven.

"Get up, Peter;" says a voice. "kill and eat."

The apostle refuses to break the Law of Moses. But the voice replies, "God has made these things clean, so don't call them 'unholy'!"

Peter is baffled by this vision. While he's still thinking about it, messengers from a Roman soldier arrive and ask him to come with them. Peter goes, and the soldier's entire household is converted. When these

Sun
Mo
Tue
We
Thu
Fri
Sat
Sun
Mo
Tue
We
Thu
Fri
Sat
Sun
Mo
Tue
We

non-Jews (often called Gentiles) receive the Holy Spirit and praise God in other languages, Peter realizes what the vision means: God's new covenant with Jesus' followers now embraces the entire world.

Saul begins his missionary trips (13:1–3).

Saul is invited to help lead a growing congregation in Antioch, Syria, about 100 miles from his hometown of Tarsus. Most of the believers are non-Jews, drawn to this new religion teaching that you don't have to be a Jew or observe Jewish customs about diet and circumcision before God will accept you.

While Paul is there, the congregation and leaders alike feel impressed by the Holy Spirit to send him and Barnabas on a ministry tour to other cultures.

The men board a ship and set sail for the island of Cyprus, where Barnabas was raised. There, Saul converts a high Roman official, Sergius Paulus. From then on the Bible identifies Saul by his Roman name: Paul. Perhaps Paul employs this name to honor the Roman, or perhaps it shows that he has stepped out of the Hebrew culture to minister almost exclusively to the Greek-speaking world.

The journey continues into western Turkey, where the men start tiny congregations in one city after another. Before Paul dies, he will make several such missionary trips, covering about 10,000 miles, planting churches from Turkey to Italy, and earning a reputation as God's apostle to the non-Jews.

Paul argues against making non-Jews follow Jewish laws (15:1–21).

The church's first big controversy is over whether or not to make non-Jews observe the laws of Moses, especially laws about circumcision and diet, which have kept many people from converting to Judaism.

Peter stands and tells the group about his earlier vision and about the Spirit filling the household of a Roman soldier. Peter argues that this shows God has invited non-Jews to join his people. Paul and Barnabas reinforce this argument by reporting miracles they saw among non-Jews during their recent missionary trip.

In what is apparently a split decision, the council decides against ordering non-Jews to obey Jewish laws. This ruling confirms what many Jewish Christians like Paul have long been teaching: you don't have to be a Jew to be a Christian.

Paul and Silas in prison (16:16–40).

On a second missionary trip, Paul and his colleague Silas arrive in Philippi, a city in northern Greece. There, Paul exorcises a demon from a slave girl. This infuriates her owners, who have been making money from her demon-powered ability to tell the future. The businessmen convince city leaders to beat and imprison the two strangers for disturbing the peace.

About midnight, as Paul and Silas are singing and praying, a powerful earthquake breaks open the prison doors. The jailer prepares to kill himself because jailers are usually executed when prisoners escape. Paul stops him, calling out that no one has left.

The jailer apparently recognizes the authenticity of their faith, for he takes the two home, treats their wounds, and is baptized as a new believer. The next morning, Paul and Silas are released and escorted out of town.

Riot at Ephesus (19:23–41).

During this third and final missionary trip, Paul arrives in Ephesus, a bustling city in western Turkey. Ephesus is famous as the worship headquarters for Artemis (the Romans called her Diana), goddess of the hunt, harvest, and childbirth. Her huge temple here is one of the seven wonders of the ancient world.

Paul's preaching winds up cramping the business of craftsmen who make silver statues of Artemis. The craftsmen call a town meeting in the theater, then work the city into a riot by claiming that Paul's teaching is not only hurting the economy, but also undermining the worship of Artemis.

When Paul hears about this, he wants to defend himself before the crowd. But believers convince him not to go near the theater. When the uproar is over, he slips out of town, leaving behind a committed core of Christians.

Paul on trial before the governor (24:1–27).

When Paul leaves Ephesus, he returns to Jerusalem, where he anticipates arrest. With him he carries an offering he has collected among non-Jewish congregations for poverty-stricken Jewish Christians. Paul hopes this will help ease tensions between Jews and non-Jews. It does not. His presence at the temple sparks a riot that results in Roman soldiers taking him into protective custody and whisking him off to the regional government headquarters in Caesarea, fifty miles away.

In a trial before the Roman governor, Felix, Jewish priests charge Paul with instigating riots and desecrating the temple by bringing in a non-Jew. Apparently unconvinced that Paul has done anything wrong, Felix placates the Jews by holding Paul in prison for two years, until Festus is appointed governor. After two more indecisive trials, one before Festus and one before Agrippa, Roman-controlled ruler of the Jews, Paul appeals his case to the emperor's court in Rome.

Paul is shipwrecked (27:1–44).

Late in the year, when sailing can be treacherous, Paul is put aboard ship in the care of a sympathetic Roman officer transporting several prisoners to Rome. After approaching the island of Crete in the hopes of finding a safe winter harbor, they get caught in a two-week storm that blows them 600 miles west. The ship eventually breaks apart in shallow water near Malta, an island south of Italy and Sicily. Miraculously, everyone survives.

Three months later they set sail on a ship that wintered in Malta. By spring, Paul arrives in Rome.

Paul preaching, under house arrest at Rome (28:16–31).

For two years Paul waits for his case to come to trial. Although under arrest and constantly accompanied by a guard, he is free to teach any who come to him. Paul also writes letters to encourage congregations he helped start, such as those in Ephesus and Colossae.

Oddly, the book ends without reporting what happens at the trial. This may be because the case hadn't been tried yet, or because the tragic fate of Paul is so well-known that Luke decides to leave the reader with a scene that he believes Paul would like to be remembered by.

Early Christian writers say Paul was beheaded in Rome. The execution may have taken place after this trial. But Clement of Rome, a Christian leader writing in the late AD 90s, says Paul was martyred on his second trip to Rome after going to the "extreme limit of the west" (probably Spain, the western extent of the empire).

POINTS TO CONSIDER

Bold disciples confirm the resurrection. Once you've read the early chapters of Acts and compared them to the closing chapters of any of the Gospels, you can't help but notice the radical change in the disciples. On Passover weekend, in early spring, they run for their lives when Jesus is arrested. They are afraid to stand with him when he faces death. Peter, the lead disciple, won't even admit to household servants that he is a disciple.

Fifty days later, each disciple is willing to face death alone on behalf of Jesus. In the temple courtyard, within the viewing of Jewish leaders who plotted the execution of Jesus, they speak the same words that got Jesus killed: they proclaim him Messiah and Son of God.

Something happened during those fifty days to change the disciples—something that wiped away their fear of death.

They had seen the afterlife. They talked with the resurrected Jesus and ate fish with him along the seashore. Months before they had heard his words "Don't be afraid of people, who can kill the body but cannot kill the soul" (Matthew 10:28 New International Version). But now they believed him. And then the Holy Spirit fell upon them, making them bold to witness to the risen Jesus, who is Lord over all.

Fearless of death, they witness to Jesus by continuing his teachings and actions. Eventually, early Christian writers report, this costs them their lives. But, Jesus would quickly add, not their souls.

Why did God change his mind about dietary laws? God himself told Moses what kind of animals the Jews could and could not eat. The list is in Leviticus 11. Cattle, sheep, and even grasshoppers are kosher. Pigs, rabbits, and shellfish are not.

Suddenly Jesus comes along and declares all meat edible (Mark 7:19). And God confirms this in a vision to Peter (Acts 10:9–16).

The dietary laws were part of God's agreement, or covenant, with Israel. If the Jews obeyed the laws given through Moses—some of which seem to have served no purpose other than to function as a badge of distinction, marking the Jews as a unique race set aside to serve God—Israel would be protected and blessed by God. Repeatedly, the people broke even the most basic laws, expressed in the Ten Commandments (Exodus 20). "Look, the time is coming, when I will make a new agreement," God said through the prophet Jeremiah (31:31 NCV). In this new covenant, New Testament writers explain, God writes his most fundamental laws onto the human heart, so we know right from wrong. This new agreement is for Jews, but also for "people who believe in . . . God's Son" (John 3:16, 18 NCV).

Sun
Mo
Tue
Wed
Thu
Frid
Satu
Sun
Mo
Tue
Wed
Thu
Frid
Satu
Sun
Mor
Tues
Wed

God's plan was to entrust the Jews with a mission: "I, the Lord, called you, a light to shine for all people" (Isaiah 42:6 NCV). Through Jesus, a Jew, God accomplishes just that.

For Further Study

- Read the Gospel of Luke. This is Part One in the two-part work of the writer, and the volume referred to in Acts 1:1,2 NCV: "To Theophilus. The first book I wrote was about everything Jesus began to do and teach until the day he was taken up into heaven."

- The 21 New Testament letters that follow, especially letters by Paul, fill in details about events described in the last half of Acts.

:00
:00
:00
:00
:00
oon
:00
2:00
3:00
4:00
5:00
6:00
7:00
8:00
9:00
0:00

Romans

PAUL EXPLAINS WHAT CHRISTIANS BELIEVE

Second to Jesus, Paul is the most influential Christian of all time. That's primarily because of the legacy he left in the letters he wrote. Romans, his letter to a congregation in Rome, is Paul's masterpiece—a skillfully crafted summary of many important Christian beliefs.

Paul writes the letter as a seasoned minister, twenty years deep in the faith. Out of all he has experienced and witnessed, he shares what he believes are some of the most important lessons of life.

Lesson one: Everyone has sinned and stands in the need of God's forgiveness (3:23).

Lesson two: God not only wants to forgive us, but he sent his Son to make forgiveness available to everyone. If we simply have faith in Jesus, Paul explains, God sets "free from sin through Jesus Christ" (3:24 NCV).

Lesson three: We should live as if we're taking our cue from God, not from the devil. "So brothers and sisters, since God has shown us great mercy," Paul says, "I beg you to offer your lives as a living sacrifice to him. Your offering must be only for God and pleasing to him" (12:1–2 NCV).

Romans is not a light read. Though the letter ends with a few chapters of easy-read-

> ### FAMOUS LINES
>
> • "The wages of sin is death, but the gift of God is eternal life" (6:23 KJV).
>
> • "All have sinned, and come short of the glory of God" (3:23 KJV).
>
> • "All things work together for good to them that love God" (8:28 KJV).

ing, practical advice about everyday living, the earlier chapters are thick with theology, a word that means "God talk." But this theology is important because it explains why Christians believe and behave the way they do. Christians who understand the reasons behind their faith are better motivated, more effective servants of God. History is full of examples (see Did You Know?), the future will be, as well.

BACKGROUND

INFLUENTIAL PEOPLE

Paul, a formerly ultraconservative Jew who becomes the early church's leading minister to non-Jewish Christians (1:1).

THEME

This is a letter with a theme—salvation—not a story with a plot. But the letter has a background that helps us understand what is on Paul's mind as he writes.

Two decades into his ministry, Paul is near the end of his third and final missionary trip. He feels he has done about all he can in the eastern Mediterranean. So he's going to deliver an offering he has collected for poverty-stricken Jewish Christians in Jerusalem. Then he hopes to take his teachings about Jesus to Spain, the western perimeter of the Roman Empire. On the way, he'll stop in Rome to meet believers there.

So before returning to Jerusalem—where he will be arrested—he writes the Romans to tell them of his plans and to solicit their help. Because Paul wants them to know who they will be helping, he tells them about his beliefs.

Paul says that everyone—Jew and non-Jew alike—has sinned and needs the forgiveness and salvation of God. Without these, people remain covered in guilt, unfit to stand in the presence of a holy God. So God is forced to condemn them to an eternity of separation from him. But Paul says it doesn't have to be this way. God has provided forgiveness and salvation through the sacrificial death of Jesus. All that human beings need to do to receive both of these is to have faith—an attribute with a long Jewish tradition dating to the time when elderly Abraham, father of the Jews, trusted that God would give him a son and make their descendants into a nation.

TIMELINE	BIBLE EVENTS		Conversion of Paul ---- AD 35	Paul's missionary journeys begin AD 46 ----		Paul's missionary trips end AD 57 -----------	Dates are approximate Paul imprisoned at Rome AD 60 --
	AD 30	**AD 40**			**AD 50**		**AD 60**
	WORLD EVENTS	Jews expelled from Rome over "Chrestus" controversy AD 49 -----------			China, Rome conduct trade via 4,000-mile-long Silk Road AD 50		Claudius poisoned, Jews return to Rome AD 54

When people are saved, Paul says, the Holy Spirit makes himself at home inside them. The Spirit empowers people to live a godly life—to say no to evil desires that once controlled them like domineering bosses, and to pursue sacred opportunities they would not otherwise have seen.

POINTS OF INTEREST

The reason Paul writes the letter. Paul has never been to Rome and was apparently not involved in starting the congregation there. But he writes "Now I have finished my work here. Since for many years I have wanted to come to you, I hope to visit you on my way to Spain. After I enjoy being with you for a while, I hope you can help me on my trip" (15:23–24 NCV). In this last sentence Paul appears to hint that he would appreciate it if believers in Rome would help back his trip, with prayer and funds.

Romans is like an ambassador's letter of introduction, identifying who Paul is ("a servant of Jesus Christ," 1:1 NCV) and what message he intends to preach in Spain, in order to prepare the way for a good reception when he arrives.

An introduction to basic Christian beliefs. In short order, Paul's words stop sounding like a letter and start sounding like a textbook for Christianity 101. Paul's thesis is this: "I am not ashamed of the Good News, because it is the power God uses to save everyone who believes— to save the Jews first, and then to save non-Jews" (1:16 NCV).

Paul then explains what this good news is: "If you declare with your mouth, "Jesus is Lord," and if you believe in your heart that God raised Jesus from the dead, you will be saved" (10:9 NCV). Paul goes on to talk about the radically new life of such a person, carefully explaining religious ideas that are sometimes hard to understand: sin, grace, faith, justification, redemption, salvation, sanctification, death, and resurrection.

DID YOU KNOW?

• Romans has been a life-changing read for many. After Martin Luther read in it that salvation is through faith and not church rituals, the Protestant Reformation was born. Woman-chasing, pleasure-loving Augustine was converted after reading Romans 13:13–14, a passage about turning from reckless living and embracing Jesus. Methodist founder John Wesley felt "strangely warmed" after studying the book. A revival in England followed.

• Romans is the first letter in the New Testament because it's the longest of the letters. The letters were originally arranged from longest to shortest, but that order changed a bit over time.

Of sanctification, for example, a word that means holiness, Paul says that the Holy Spirit makes "Gentiles into a holy offering" (15:16). This doesn't mean they become morally perfect. It means that God has seen their faith and he has separated them from the faithless. "Holy" means reserved for God's purpose. And it's God who makes the reservation, not on the basis of our behavior but on the basis of our faith, which inevitably changes our behavior.

Four big ideas. Paul has created, in Romans, a study filled with deep theological insight. So Bible experts have broken the work down into many possible outlines—the raw frame on which they believe Paul built the letter. Here's one of many outlines.

After introducing himself, Paul shows that everyone has sinned and needs salvation (1:18–3:20). He explains how God has made salvation available through Jesus (3:21–8:39). Next, Paul assures everyone that there's ample room in the kingdom of God for Jews (9–11). Paul closes with lessons about how to behave (12–15), followed by a chapter of personal notes concerning many individuals.

AUTHOR AND DATE

Paul wrote the letter in about AD 57, possibly in Corinth, Greece, near the end of his third and final missionary journey.

"Now I am going to Jerusalem," he writes, "the believers in Macedonia and Southern Greece were happy to give their money to help the poor among God's people at Jerusalem . . . After I am sure the poor in Jerusalem get the money that has been given for them, I will leave for Spain and stop and visit you" (15:25–28 NCV).

Unfortunately, Paul was arrested when he got to Jerusalem and imprisoned for two years. When he finally does arrive in Rome, in about AD 60, he is a prisoner waiting for trial in the emperor's court. It is unclear if Paul is executed after this trial, or if he is released, only to be executed following a later trial in the city after returning from Spain.

ON LOCATION

Paul addresses a Christian congregation in Rome, capital of the Roman Empire. Paul has ministered throughout the eastern Mediterranean, in what is now Israel, Syria, Turkey, and Greece. (See map in Acts, page 362.) Now he hopes to visit Rome on his way to taking the gospel to Spain, at the western edge of the empire.

ROMANS OUTLINE

Christians worshiping in Rome (1:1–17).

After twenty years of ministry in the eastern Mediterranean, Paul feels he has done all he can there and that it's time to move on.

"I want you to know that I planned many times to come to you," Paul writes to the congregation in Rome. "But this has not been possible. I wanted to come so that I could help you grow spiritually as I have helped the other non-Jewish people.

I have a duty to all people—Greeks and those who are not Greeks, the wise and the foolish. That is why I want so much to preach the Good News to you in Rome" (1:13–15 NCV).

After spending time in Rome, Paul says he hopes the believers there will help send him on to Spain. But because most people in the congregation know Paul only by reputation, he writes a letter introducing himself and his beliefs. Most likely, the letter is read aloud during one of the meetings, which are often held in the larger homes of the more wealthy church members. Because Paul's letter is such a masterfully crafted summary of important Christian beliefs, it is probably copied and circulated among churches throughout the empire.

Abraham, an example of faith (4:1–25).

A hallmark of Paul's beliefs is that people become acceptable to God through faith—not through making sacrifices or observing Jewish customs, such as circumcision, dietary restrictions, and annual religious holidays.

This is great news to people from non-Jewish backgrounds. Many of them have worshiped God, but have stopped short of converting to Judaism because of the seemingly harsh requirements. On the other hand, most Jews—even Jewish Christians—believe that their traditions come from God and are sacred. They don't believe that mere faith can save anyone.

To prove that faith is enough, Paul reminds his readers that God singled out Abraham to become father of the Jews because of Abraham's faith—not because he followed the rules. Most of the rules, in fact, didn't arrive until several centuries later, in the time of Moses.

"People cannot do any work that will make them right with God," Paul writes. "So they must trust in him, who makes even evil people right in his sight" (4:5 NCV).

As convincing as Paul could be, age-old traditions die hard. And throughout Paul's lifetime and beyond, this remained a touchy topic for Jewish and non-Jewish Christians worshiping together, as they likely did in Rome.

Adam brings death, Jesus brings life (5:12–6:14).

Everyone has sinned and fallen short of God's glorious standard," Paul writes, "and all need to be made right with God by his grace, which is a free gift. They need to be made free from sin through Jesus Christ" (3:23–24 NCV).

Paul explains what the story of Genesis reveals, that sin and death entered the world when Adam and Eve disobeyed God and ate forbidden fruit. God's good creation became contaminated. "Sin came into the world because of what one man did, and with sin came death," Paul explains. "This is why everyone must die—because everyone sinned."

The problem is that a holy God cannot coexist with sin. The sin must be cleansed, or the sinner removed from the presence of God. In Old Testament times, God set up the sacrificial system as a way to allow people to find cleansing and forgiveness. The death of the animal graphically reminded everyone of the deadly seriousness of sin. Later, God sent Jesus as the ultimate and final sacrifice, launching a new means of spiritual cleansing. In a way that we can't fully understand, Christ's sacrifice and resurrection provided a way for individual human beings to correct the damage done by Adam. We correct the damage when we have faith that Jesus is the remedy for sin and death.

"One man disobeyed God, and many became sinners," Paul says. One good act that Christ did makes all people right with God. And that brings true life for all" (5:19, 18 NCV).

Jews and non-Jews become children of God (9–11).

The church gets its start among Jews who believe Jesus came to earth as the Messiah and Son of God. But as time passes and the church realizes that this means the prophesied age of the new covenant has arrived, and the age of the old covenant had ended—with all of its laws about circumcision, diet, and rituals—Jews become increasingly hostile toward Christianity. By the end of the century, Jews will prohibit Jewish Christians from worshiping in synagogues.

Paul realizes that non-Jewish believers might begin looking down on Jews, including Jewish Christians. But Paul reminds his mostly non-Jewish readers that God has carefully cultivated the Jewish people, just as a farmer cultivates and purposefully prunes an olive tree.

"You non-Jewish people are like the branch of a wild olive tree," Paul says, which has been grafted to the "first tree" (11:17 NCV).

Paul's point is clear. The roots of Christian faith are Jewish. For it is the Jews who have long been drawing spiritual nourishment from God. And it is through Jews—such as Jesus, the disciples, and Paul—that God extends salvation to the rest of the world.

Even though most Jews reject God, Paul says, "they are still God's chosen people, and he loves them very much" (11:28 NCV). In the end, Paul adds, Israel will return to God and be saved.

Behaving like children of a loving God (12:1–21).

Paul explains that when Jesus sacrificed himself for the sins of the human race, this rendered the Jewish sacrificial system obsolete. In practice, Romans ended it forty years later when they destroyed the temple. Since AD 70 the Jews have not had a temple for making sacrifices. A 1,300-year-old mosque now sits on the temple hilltop.

Instead of offering animal sacrifices, Paul urges the people to offer their bodies "as a living sacrifice to him. Your offering must be only for God and pleasing to him, which is the spiritual way for you to worship. Do not be shaped by this world; instead be changed within by a new way of thinking. Then you will be able to decide what God wants for you; you will know what is good and pleasing to him and what is perfect" (12:1–2 NCV).

This letter makes such an impression on the Romans that when Paul finally arrives in Italy, as a prisoner on his way to court, many of the congregation travel forty miles to meet and accompany him on the last leg of the journey (Acts 28:15).

=== **POINTS TO CONSIDER** ===

Tension between Christians and Jews. Paul talks a lot about Jews having the right to membership in the church, as though he's addressing a predominantly non-Jewish congregation that wonders if Christianity is big enough for both.

First-century Roman history Suetonius says that in AD 49 there was such an uproar among Jews over "Chrestus," probably Christ, that Emperor Claudius expelled the Jews from Rome. They weren't allowed to return until Claudius died in AD 54, just a few years before Paul reminded the mostly non-Jewish church of Rome that in God's eyes there's no difference between Jew and non-Jew: "Anyone who trusts in him will never be disappointed, because there is no difference between those who are Jews and those who are not," Paul writes. "The same Lord is the Lord of all and gives many blessings to all who trust in him. Anyone who calls on the Lord will be saved" (10:11–13 NCV).

Politically incorrect about homosexuality. Some describe Paul as homophobic. He says homosexuality is "not natural," even "shameful." He stops only a hair shy of name-calling when he implies that practicing homosexuals are perverts: receiving "punishment for those wrongs" (1:27 NCV).

Creative Bible interpreters say that when Paul spoke of "unnatural" sexual behavior he was condemning homosexual acts by heterosexuals. But this interpretation doesn't come from Paul. It comes from the prevailing belief today that homosexuality is natural for some people.

As politically incorrect as it may be, when Paul says homosexual acts are unnatural, he means they're sinful, they're contrary to God's plan. Paul is repeating what God revealed to Moses more than a thousand years earlier. For along with prohibiting adultery, incest, and having sex with animals, God said, "You must not have sexual relations with a man as you would a woman. That is a hateful sin" (Leviticus 18:22 NCV).

Even if homosexual tendencies are determined by genetics or by events in life, and therefore we are not responsible for our sexual desires, we are responsible for our actions. And though it would seem unfair for God to place such a burden on human beings, people in the sin-damaged world carry a wide variety of burdens.

"Come to me, all of you who are tired and have heavy loads," Jesus once said, "I will give you rest. Accept my teachings and learn from me, because I am gentle and humble in spirit, and you will find rest for your lives" (Matthew 11:28–29 NCV).

Whatever the burden, Jesus promises to help us carry it and learn from it.

FOR FURTHER STUDY

- Read Galatians for another in-depth, but more freewheeling, emotion-packed glimpse into Paul's beliefs.

- For more about how Christianity grows out of the Jewish faith, and fulfills it, read Hebrews.

Sun
Mo
Tue
Wed
Thu
Frid
Satu
Sun
Mo
Tue
Wed
Thu
Frid
Satu
Sun
Mo
Tue
Wed

1 Corinthians

PAUL'S LETTER TO A FRACTURED CHURCH

There's no such thing as a perfect church when human beings are on the roll. Never has been, never will be, until the roll is called up yonder.

Consider the church founded by the most notable, influential, successful Christian minister of first-generation believers. Paul didn't stay in Corinth only a few days or weeks, as he did in most cities. He stayed for two years, training and nurturing the spiritual infants. Several years later, however, the Corinthians were still behaving like disobedient, rebellious kids.

They were arguing over who in the church was most important, suing each other in court, turning a blind eye to incest among the congregation, and showing that they were thoroughly confused about key Christian beliefs such as the Resurrection.

In a blunt though loving letter, Paul replies to an array of practical questions the Corinthians raised in a letter to him. But he also confronts issues they were apparently too embarrassed to mention.

This is not a boring letter.

First Corinthians is gripping because of the deeply emotional issues Paul tackles. And it's timely because, unfortunately, there's a little bit of Corinth in every church—a lot of Corinth in some.

FAMOUS LINES

- "Let us eat and drink, because tomorrow we will die" (15:32 NCV). *Paul quotes a Greek proverb to suggest what our attitude should be if Christ was not raised from the dead.*

- "O death, where is thy sting? O grave, where is thy victory?" (15:55 KJV). *A praise of believers who realize that, like Jesus, they, too, will be resurrected.*

- "But you can trust God, who will not permit you to be tempted more than you can stand" (10:13 NCV).

- "You should know that your body is a temple for the Holy Spirit who is in you" (6:19 NCV). *Paul's reminder to the Corinthians to take good care of their bodies.*

BACKGROUND

INFLUENTIAL PEOPLE

Paul, a leading minister to the non-Jewish world, and founder of the church at Corinth, Greece (1:1).

THEME

A couple of years after leaving the church he started in Corinth, Paul receives troubling news. Messengers arrive with a letter from the congregation asking for his help in solving a number of divisive problems. Not all the bad news is in the letter. The messengers and other sources report additional problems: power struggles among the leadership, cliques in the congregation, an I-don't-want-to-get-involved attitude about church members involved in illicit sex, Christians suing Christians.

Paul begins his letter by dealing with these problems first, since they reflect a deep-seated misunderstanding about what it means to be a Christian. Only then, beginning with chapter 7, does he address the questions that the Corinthians asked—questions about more practical issues of everyday living and worship service. Questions such as, "It is good for a man not to have sexual relations with a woman" (7:1 NCV). And is it okay to eat "meat that is sacrificed to idols" (8:1 NCV), which priests sell wholesale to meat vendors who resell it at a profit in the meat markets?

In all of Paul's advice, he urges the believers to act in unity and love. If they can do this, he teaches, their other problems will wither and die.

POINTS OF INTEREST

A power struggle in the church. The congregation is breaking into factions that prefer one of at least three leaders: Paul, Peter, or Apollos (1:12). Apollos, mentioned in Acts 18:24–28, is an Old Testament scholar

TIMELINE					
BIBLE EVENTS	Paul starts church in Corinth AD 50	Paul writes 1 Corinthians AD 55	Paul's missionary trips end AD 57		Dates are approximate
	AD 40	**AD 45**	**AD 50**		**AD 55**
WORLD EVENTS	London founded AD 43	Some Jews expelled from Rome move to Corinth (Acts 18:2) AD 49 / Romans learn about soap, from Gauls (France) AD 50		Isthmian Games held at Corinth AD 51	Claudius poisoned by wife, Jews return to Rome AD 54

and a charismatic speaker. Peter, one of the original disciples of Jesus, may have appealed to Jewish Christians at Corinth. Paul, founder of the church and advocate for non-Jewish believers, maintained a loyal core of supporters.

"Agree with each other," Paul advises. "Christ has been divided up into different groups! Did Paul die on the cross for you? No!" (1:10, 13 NCV).

Christians behaving badly. Besides the power struggle, there are other problems in the church—

> **DID YOU KNOW?**
>
> • First Corinthians isn't Paul's first letter to the church at Corinth. It's just the first one that survived. In 1 Corinthians Paul refers to "my earlier letter" (5:9 NCV).

many stemming from Christians behaving as if they have a license to sin. There is a man who has married his stepmother, in defiance of both Roman and Jewish law that considers this incest (Deuteronomy 27:20). Paul is shocked that the congregation lets this man remain in the church, as though he is doing nothing wrong.

Though God judges people outside the church, Paul says, Christians have an obligation to judge and discipline their members. Paul advises the Corinthians to stay away from professing believers who blatantly "sin sexually, or are greedy, or worship idols, or abuse others with words, or get drunk, or cheat people" (5:11 NCV). In even sterner advice Paul adds, "You must get rid of the evil person among you" (5:13 NCV).

Another example of bad behavior is Christians suing each other by "judges who are not right with God" (6:1 NCV).

"Are you not able to judge small cases as well?" Paul asks. "If you have ordinary cases that must be judged, are you going to appoint people as judges who mean nothing to the church?" (6:2, 4 NCV).

Practical advice about life and worship. In chapter 7 Paul starts answering a variety of questions the church has asked him.

Here's a sampling of the topics.

Marriage. Paul apparently expects Jesus to return soon, so he advises people not to get married, but he concedes "It is better to marry than to burn with sexual desire" (7:9 NCV).

Eating food offered to idols. Paul says this issue is not particularly important, since all food comes from God. Paul does say, however, that Christians should be sensitive to other believers who have scruples against eating such food (8:1–13).

Dressing for worship services. People should dress appropriately, Paul says, not as trend-setters calling attention to themselves or as lures for the opposite sex (11:1–16).

The Lord's Supper. This is a shared celebration of the death and resurrection of Jesus, Paul explains. But Corinth has turned it into a segregated potluck, where rich members cluster in cliques to eat rich folks' food, while the poor eat comparative crumbs (11:20–33).

Spiritual gifts. God gives different abilities to different people, Paul says. Each gift is important and useful in God's work (12:1–31).

A beautiful hymn about love. One of the most famous chapters in the Bible is Paul's lyrical message about love. The poem comes immediately after Paul has talked about other gifts from God, to emphasize that all talent is useless if it doesn't flow from a heart of love. "I may speak in different languages of people or even angels," Paul asks. "But if I do not have love, I am only a noisy bell or a crashing cymbal" (13:1 NCV).

The ability to love others, Paul argues, is the greatest gift of all—greater than hope, and even greater than faith (13:13). This is a powerful message especially in Corinth, a city famed for its great temple of Aphrodite, goddess of love.

AUTHOR AND DATE

"I, Paul, am writing this greeting with my own hand" (16:21 NCV). This conclusion, along with the introduction, "From Paul," (1:1 NCV), clearly identifies who the writer is.

Early church leaders included this letter in the New Testament because they believed it came from the pen of Paul, the most influential minister among first-generation Christians.

Paul wrote the letter from Ephesus in about AD 55, two or three years after leaving Corinth. Some five years earlier Paul first arrived in the city and started the church during the second of his three missionary trips throughout the eastern Mediterranean. Paul didn't usually stay in a town longer than a few weeks, but he made an exception for Corinth, a busy port full of international travelers who might hear his message and take it home with them. Paul stayed in Corinth for two years, then returned after writing 1 Corinthians, during his third missionary trip.

ON LOCATION

Paul's letter is addressed to Christians in a young church he started a few years earlier, during his second missionary journey (shown on the map), at Corinth, perhaps the busiest city in ancient Greece. Located south of Athens, Corinth is near a four-mile-wide land bridge separating the Aegean Sea in the east and the Adriatic Sea in the west.

Eastern trade ships carrying products destined for Rome and other western cities would often stop in Corinth. If the ship were small enough, it could be hauled up onto a huge wagon, wheeled across the isthmus, then launched into the Adriatic. This saved merchants a 200-mile trip around the tip of Greece, sparing them from storms and pirates. Larger ships unloaded their cargo and had it hauled to other ships waiting at the Adriatic port. Nero started a canal in AD 66, but the project was stopped after engineers doubted it could be done and Corinthians complained that a canal would keep travelers from stopping in the city. The project was completed in 1893 and is still used.

1 CORINTHIANS OUTLINE

Sun
Mo
Tue
Wei
Thu
Frid
Satu
Sun
Mo
Tue
Wei
Thu
Frid
Satu
Sun
Mo
Tue
We

Christians quarrel over who's in charge (1:10–31).

A few years after Paul leaves the church he founded in Corinth, continuing his preaching trips throughout the eastern Mediterranean, the congregation splits into squabbling factions. Some prefer the guidance of their founding minister. Others prefer the interpretations of Peter, who is still observing many Jewish customs and probably living in Jerusalem. Others gravitate to Apollos, a brilliant scholar and dynamic speaker living in Corinth.

Paul begs the Corinthians to stop arguing, since only Christ is the leader of the church. "Did Paul die on the cross for you?" Paul asks. "Were you baptized in the name of Paul?" (1:13 NCV).

All three leaders are merely servants of God, Paul says. "Paul and Apollos and Peter all belong to you" (3:22 NCV). Comparing God's spiritual kingdom to a garden, Paul says, "I planted the seed, and Apollos watered it. But God is the One who made it grow" (3:6 NCV).

Immorality in the church (5:1–13).

Paul is shocked to find out that a member of the church has married his stepmother, and the church has taken no action to discipline him. By both Roman and Jewish standards, the man has committed incest.

"I wrote you in my earlier letter [before 1 Corinthians] not to associate with those who sin sexually," Paul says. "But I did not mean you should not associate with those of this world who sin sexually, or with the greedy, or robbers, or those who worship idols. To get away from them you would have to leave this world" (5:9–10 NCV). Paul explains that God judges those outside the church, but believers have a responsibility to protect the name of Jesus by disciplining those who call themselves Christians.

Paul's advice: "You must get rid of the evil person among you" (5:13 NCV). This harsh judgment is not to condemn the man to everlasting banishment, but to bring him to his senses so he will repent and return to Christ and the church.

7:00
8:00
9:00
0:00
1:00
oon
1:00
2:00
3:00
4:00
5:00
5:00
7:00
8:00
9:00
0:00

Christians suing Christians (6:1–11).

Bickering among the church gets so bad that Christians start taking one another to court. "How can you bring yourself to go before judges who are not right with God?" Paul asks. "Surely there is someone among you wise enough to judge a complaint between believers."

Roman courts operated without the notions we cherish today: fairness and justice being blind. Roman judges were expected to decide in favor of the wealthier, more influential party. The poor and other persons of low social standing feared being hauled into court, because—guilty or innocent—their misery would surely be multiplied if their accuser were higher class or wealthier. In prohibiting lawsuits between believers, Paul protects the socially weaker members and calls the whole church to its responsibility to apply God's wisdom to disagreements among themselves.

More of a segregated feast than a Lord's Supper (11:17–34).

In many churches, Corinth included, when believers observe the ritual of the Lord's Supper by eating bread and drinking wine that represents the body and blood of the crucified Jesus, they also eat a full meal called a "love feast."

A problem develops.

"You are not really eating the Lord's Supper," Paul writes. "This is because when you eat, each person eats without waiting for the others. Some people do not get enough to eat, while others have too much to drink" (11:20–21 NCV).

The love feast is apparently like a potluck, held at a large meeting place, often the home of wealthy members. Church members cluster in socioeconomic cliques—rich folks eating fancy food together and poorer families and slaves eating the meager morsels they can bring.

This dishonors Christ, Paul says, and it divides people who should be united in gratitude for what Jesus did for them on the cross.

Paul advises the people who are hungry to eat before they come to worship, so they can concentrate on the ritual meal and thank Jesus for the gift of salvation and the promise of a resurrection.

God's greatest gift: the ability to love (13:1–13).

Paul writes that God has entrusted to the people of Corinth a wide variety of talents, or gifts: prophecy, healing, teaching, speaking in other tongues. All of these are important because they allow Christians to help others. But Paul says the greatest gift of all—the gift that channels our talents in the right direction—is the gift of love.

"I may have the gift of prophecy. I may understand all the secret things of God and have all knowledge" Paul asks. "But even with all these things, if I do not have love, then I am nothing."

Compassionate love—inspired by Christ's death for humanity—produces a selfless people who are kind and patient, not boastful or easily angered, always supportive and hopeful, never keeping a record of the wrongs that others do.

Christians don't start out this way, Paul says. "When I was a child, I talked like a child, I thought like a child, I reasoned like a child. When I became a man, I stopped those childish ways" (13:11 NCV).

Growing Christians cultivate an attitude of love above all others. Among the three most noble traits—faith, hope, and love—Paul says "the greatest of these is love."

The resurrected Jesus meets with his disciples (15:1–58).

Some Corinthians are confused about the resurrection of Jesus and what it has to do with them. Some apparently don't believe that bodies will be resurrected. Instead, these people have adopted the Greek understanding that only the soul is immortal. Paul teaches that Jesus—soul and glorified body—was both resurrected and witnessed by hundreds.

"And if Christ has not been raised, then your faith has nothing to it," Paul explains. "But Christ has truly been raised from the dead—the first one and proof that those who sleep in death will also be raised. Death has come because of what one man did, but the rising from death also comes because of one man. In Adam all of us die. In the same way, in Christ all of us will be made alive again" (15:17, 20–22 NCV).

Paul reveals that some day, in an instant, "those who have died will be raised to live forever." Our former bodies made from dust will become like that of "the man of heaven."

When this happens, Paul says, the prophecies of Isaiah and Hosea will

Sun
Mo
Tue
We
Thu
Frid
Satu
Sun
Mo
Tue
We
Thu
Frid
Satu
Sun
Mo
Tue
We

be fulfilled, and people will praise God, saying, "Death is destroyed forever in victory. Death, where is your victory? Death, where is your pain?" (Isaiah 25:8; Hosea 13:14 NCV).

POINTS TO CONSIDER

Erastus was here. Erastus is identified in the New Testament as a colleague of Paul (Acts 19:22; 2 Timothy 4:20) and as the Corinth city treasurer (Romans 16:23). These references may have been about two people. Even if that's so, both were Christians, and the Erastus of Corinth was a member of the church there.

Archaeologists working in the ruins of ancient Corinth found a block of pavement stone with this inscription, written in the Roman language of Latin: "Erastus, commissioner of public works, bore the expense of this pavement."

The inscription may be identifying the same Corinthian Christian and city treasurer that Paul wrote about.

Isthmian Games. The Isthmian Games, an athletic competition second in popularity only to the Olympics, were held in Corinth every four years—including AD 51, when Paul was in town. The Isthmian Games featured a wide variety of races by runners, horsemen, and charioteers.

Probably not coincidentally, Paul's first use of athletic imagery appears in his letter to the Corinthians. Comparing Christians to runners in a race, Paul says, "You know that in a race all the runners run, but only one gets the prize. So run to win!" (9:24 NCV).

"All those who compete in the games use self-control so they can win a crown. That crown is an earthly thing that lasts only a short time," Paul adds, "but our crown will never be destroyed" (9:25 NCV). In fact, winners' crowns at the Isthmian Games were woven from withered stalks of celery.

Women, keep quiet in church. Sometimes Paul comes across as the first liberationist. After all, he's the one who said, "In Christ, there is no difference between Jew and Greek, slave and free person, male and female. You are all the same in Christ Jesus" (Galatians 3:28 NCV). Unfortunately, to many readers Paul looks more like a chauvinist in 1 Corinthians: "As is true in all the churches of God's people, women should keep quiet in the church meetings . . . If they want to learn something, they should ask their own husbands at home" (14:33–35 NCV).

On the topic of women, Paul can be puzzling. On the one hand, he commends Phoebe as a church deacon (Romans 16:1) and even describes a woman named Junias by using the rare and highest church leadership title of "apostle" (Romans 16:7). Yet in other letters he insists that men should be in charge (1 Corinthians 11:2–16) and that women should be subject to men in everything (Ephesians 5:24).

How could Paul say all these things? Some scholars suggest that Paul struggled between male-female equality in Christ and the traditional female subordination of his day. Some think that Paul affirmed that men and women are equal in worth before God but are given different roles within that equality. God made men responsible for leading, but he requires them to lead as Christ leads the church. Other scholars say that Paul restricted women's activities only in the churches where women were abusing leadership.

FOR FURTHER STUDY

- Read Paul's follow-up letter: 2 Corinthians.

2 Corinthians

PAUL FIGHTS A HOSTILE TAKEOVER

Ministers and congregations have a long history of not getting alone. The first case on record is of Paul and the church he started in Corinth. Paul plants the church like a seedling, then stays for two years and nurtures it. Eventually, he moves on to start other churches. That's when trouble starts.

Arguments break out in Corinth about who's in charge, how Christians should behave, and how they should worship. By long-distance courier and by a personal visit, Paul addresses these problems. Then, within the year, another crisis strikes. Others who claim to be apostles arrive in Corinth and begin wooing church leaders away from Paul's leadership. Second Corinthians doesn't say exactly what these fraudulent apostles teach, but Paul accuses the intruders of repackaging the gospel with "another Jesus," "a spirit or gospel that is different" (11:4 NCV).

Paul refuses to back off. He fights for the hearts and minds of the Corinthians. It's a battle he knows he might lose. If he were concerned about his personal pride and reputation, he'd walk away and turn his energy to the many other churches that appreciate him more. But Paul cares about the Corinthian people. He's willing to endure whatever heartache and humiliation it takes to win them back to the true Jesus, the true spirit, and the genuine message.

BACKGROUND

INFLUENTIAL PEOPLE

Paul, leading minister to the non-Jewish world, and founder of the church at Corinth, Greece (1:1).

Titus, Paul's associate who carries a letter to Corinth that tries repairing the damaged relationship between Paul and the congregation (2:13).

THEME

Shortly after the Corinthian Christians receive Paul's letter known to us as 1 Corinthians, some outsiders arrive. Paul doesn't say who these people are, but clearly their take on Christianity differs from his. Paul calls the intruders "workers who lie" who "look like apostles of Christ" (11:13 NCV). They apparently represented Jewish Christianity, yet 2 Corinthians says nothing about observing such Jewish matters as circumcision, food restrictions, and religious holidays.

The relationship between Paul and the Corinthians already was badly strained. The church itself had started fracturing into cliques and arguing over lifestyles and worship practices. After writing 1 Corinthians, Paul makes a visit to the church. But this only aggravates the tension.

Intruder alert.

Gifted in the art of persuasion, the newly arrived intruders lob charge upon charge at Paul. All we know of the charges is what we can infer from Paul's defense, preserved in 2 Corinthians. But the outsiders seem to attach his authority and motives. In response, Paul presents himself as an honest and sincere minister of Christ who cares deeply about the Corinthians.

POINTS OF INTEREST

Verbal attacks against Paul. Religious teachers arrive in town, saying

					Dates are approximate
BIBLE EVENTS	Paul begins missionary trips ⌐--- AD 46	Paul starts church in Corinth ⌐--- AD 50	Paul writes 1, 2 Corinthians AD 55 -------¬	Paul's missionary trips end ⌐-- AD 57	
AD 45	**AD 50**		**AD 55**		**AD 60**
WORLD EVENTS	Famine strikes Jerusalem sometime within L--- next 7 years AD 46		Some Jews expelled from Rome move to L-- Corinth (Acts 18:2) AD 49	Claudius poisoned by wife, Jews return L-- to Rome AD 54	

TIMELINE

they are Christians. They quickly show they are opponents of Paul, because they begin turning the church against their founding minister.

Here are what seem to be several main points of attack, along with excerpts of Paul's defense.

1. Paul is a self-appointed apostle, not one personally commissioned by Jesus, as were the original disciples. "When I was with you, I patiently did the things that prove I am an apostle—signs, wonders, and miracles" (12:12 NCV).

2. Paul is self-promoting. "We do not preach about ourselves, but we preach that Jesus Christ is Lord" (4:5 NCV).

3. Paul can't be trusted, since he didn't come to Corinth when he said he would. Paul replies by saying that his last visit was so painful that he decided a cooling-off period was in order. "So I decided that my next visit to you would not be another one to make you sad . . . I did not write to make you sad, but to let you know how much I love you" (2:1, 4 NCV).

4. Paul is pocketing money collected for the poverty-stricken believers in Jerusalem. "We do not sell the word of God for a profit as many other people do" (2:17 NCV). Paul implies that the intruders are seeking donations for themselves from the Corinthians. Paul had refused to do this (12:13). Instead, he earned his keep by working as a tentmaker (Acts 18:3).

5. Paul barks boldly in his letters, but in person he's a coward who has nothing worth saying (10:10). "When we are there with you, we will show the same authority that we show in our letters" (10:11 NCV).

Paul's reluctant bragging about his sufferings. Bible experts call 11:16–12:13 the "Fool's Speech" because Paul says ", accept me as you would accept a fool. Then I can brag a little, too" (11:16 NCV). Paul feels uncomfortable bragging about anything except the Lord. But he feels that his back is to the wall and his ministry in Corinth will be over if he doesn't speak up.

The Fool's Speech might look like self-defensive bragging, but it's not. It's a parody on ancient speeches and letters that commend a person. This is an appropriate defensive technique because the intruder-critics in Corinth have come with letters of commendation.

In a sarcastic reversal of typical commendations, Paul begins bragging about experiences that show him as a victim—a loser by the world's standards. Paul reports suffering one tragedy after another—all because he is doing God's will and on behalf of the Corinthians.

The readers can't help but be reminded of how Jesus suffered for the same reason.

For many Corinthians, this speech likely generates a renewed sense of gratitude for what Paul and Jesus have endured on their behalf.

Paul's "thorn in the flesh." In describing what he has suffered throughout his ministry, Paul speaks of a "painful physical problem" that torments him and keeps him from getting conceited (12:7 NCV).

Paul shows himself to be weak in that, though he asks God three times to remove the "problem," God refuses. Jesus, too, asked to be spared the suffering of the cross. Because Jesus suffered, Paul is willing to do the same—even if it makes him look weak in the eyes of the world.

Paul never says what the "problem" is. Bible experts have many theories, including some kind of physical problem such as malaria or poor eyesight (he writes in big letters, Galatians 6:11), or his never-ending persecutions, or his rejection by the Corinthians.

Personal information about Paul. This letter reveals more autobiographical information about Paul than any of his other letters. Much of this comes in chapters 11–12, where he talks about how he suffered as a minister; beatings, jailings, shipwrecks, stoning, public humiliation. The list goes on. He also describes what sounds like a vision or an out-of-body experience in which he caught a glimpse of the afterlife (12:1–6).

An impassioned fund-raising letter. Surprisingly, in this letter that includes a defense against charges that he's preaching for profit, Paul asks for money.

But the money is not for him. In fact, he makes it a point to remind the Corinthians that during the two years he lived among them, he did not accept their money. The donation he is now requesting is for the poverty-stricken Christians in Jerusalem. This is a special offering Paul has been collecting from churches throughout the eastern Mediterranean.

Paul applies some gentle pressure by telling the Corinthians that he has bragged about their generosity. "I know you want to help. I have been bragging about this to the people in Macedonia [a comparatively poor province to the north] telling them that you in Southern Greece have been ready to give since last year. And your desire to give has made most of them ready to give also . . . But I am sending the brothers to you so that our bragging about you in this will not be empty words" (9:2–3 NCV).

AUTHOR AND DATE

The letter is "From Paul, an apostle of Christ Jesus" (1:1 NCV), along with his associate Timothy.

Paul wrote the letter a few months after writing 1 Corinthians, during his third and final missionary trip. Drawing on clues from the text, some Bible experts speculate that he wrote 1 Corinthians in the spring while staying at Ephesus, then 2 Corinthians in the winter while in Macedonia.

ON LOCATION

Like 1 Corinthians, Paul's letter is addressed to Christians in a young church he started a few years earlier at Corinth, Greece. Located south of Athens, Corinth is near a four-mile-wide land bridge separating the Aegean Sea in the east and the Adriatic Sea in the west. (See map in 1 Corinthians, page 384.) Paul apparently assumes that other churches in the region will read circulated copies of the letter, since he also addresses "all of God's people in Achaia," the Roman province that is now Greece.

2 CORINTHIANS OUTLINE

Roman conquerors in a victory march (2:14–17).

Paul begins his emotional letter by saying how glad he is that God always comforts us when we suffer. This is an apt introduction since Paul is going to spend much of the rest of his letter talking about the torment he has endured from the Corinthian church and from others.

Paul says that followers of Christ in this generation—and especially ministers—should expect hardship, opposition, and rejection because these are what Christ got. To illustrate two extremes in the way people react to the gospel, Paul draws on an image familiar to citizens of large cities in the Roman Empire. It's the scene of a Roman procession: soldiers marching in a victory parade after a battle. On display are the prisoners of war who will be executed for the emperor's pleasure or sold as slaves. Along the roadway, citizens cheer and fill the air with the sweet smell of burning incense. To the conquerors, this perfumed scent is fragrant and welcome. To the captives, the smell means death.

Paul then paints a picture of himself and other Christian ministers marching in a victory parade led by Jesus. To "us as captives," he says, "we are the sweet smell of Christ among those who are being saved and among those who are being lost. To those who are lost, we are the smell of death that brings death."

Some people welcome the gospel and its messengers. But many reject both and resist them with a vengeance.

Human bodies are like tents: temporary (5:1–10).

Paul is amazed that God would entrust a message as important as the gospel to frail human beings.

"We have this treasure from God, but we are like clay jars that hold the treasure," Paul says. "We have troubles all around us, but we are not defeated. We do not know what to do, but we do not give up the hope of living. We are persecuted, but God does not leave us. We are hurt sometimes, but we are not destroyed. We carry the death of Jesus in our own bodies so that the life of Jesus can also be seen in our bodies. We are alive, but for Jesus we are always in danger of death so that the life of Jesus can be seen in our bodies that die" (4:7–11 NCV).

Paul doesn't have an inordinate fear of death because he believes the only thing to die will be the body, which God will replace with an eternal body.

"We know that our body—the tent we live in here on earth—will be destroyed," Paul writes. "But when that happens, God will have a house for us. It will not be a house made by human hands; instead, it will be a home in heaven that will last forever."

A collection for the poor at Jerusalem (8:1–9:15).

Torment stalks Paul like a predator everywhere he goes. Many Jewish Christians, for example, vehemently disagree with the Jerusalem council's decision, years earlier, to allow non-Jewish believer to join the church without having to observe long-standing Jewish laws such as those about circumcision, kosher food, and religious holidays (Acts 15). So they follow Paul, who is famous as a minister to non-Jews, and try to undo the damage they believe his preaching has done.

To help defuse this tension, Paul tries to unify Jewish and non-Jewish factions of the church with a tangible expression of concern: he collects an offering from his predominantly non-Jewish churches for poverty-stricken Jewish Christians in Jerusalem. Actually, Paul says this isn't his idea, but that it comes out of the Jerusalem council meeting (Galatians 2:10). Yet Paul gets 100 percent behind the suggestion and promotes the offering throughout his travels, as shown by references in Acts, 1 and 2 Corinthians, and Romans.

The Bible doesn't say how the Jerusalem believers got poor. One theory is that the spirit of generosity that started at Pentecost spurred many believers to give away nearly everything they owned (Acts 4:32–37). Another suggestion growing out of Scripture is that a famine hit the regions sometime after Paul began his first missionary trip in about AD 46 and before Emperor Claudius died in AD 54 (Acts 12:27–30). Yet another reason may be because older Jews often move to Jerusalem to spend their final days in the Holy City and be buried there. The church may have had to bear the brunt of caring for women whose husbands preceded them in death.

Whatever the reason for the poverty, the offering for Jerusalem is important to Paul. He pleads with the Corinthians to be generous.

"You should not be sad when you give, and you should not give because you feel forced to give," he adds. "God loves the person who gives happily" (9:7 NCV).

Paul later delivers the offering in person, fully aware that he may be arrested and tried for heresy by the same Jewish legislative body that tried Jesus. In fact, Paul is arrested and eventually transported to Rome for trial in the emperor's court. That's the last the Bible says of Paul. Christian writers at the end of the century report that Paul was executed.

Paul escapes Damascus in a basket (11:16–33).

In the closing chapters of his letter, Paul grapples with the biggest problem now threatening the Corinthian church: "workers who lie" who have arrived with letters of commendation and who are winning control of the church (11:13 NCV).

Paul takes an incredibly creative approach to winning back his congregation. Instead of bragging about his spiritual power and influence—as the intruders have done about themselves—Paul writes a sarcastic parody on self-promotion; he brags about his weaknesses and the humiliations he has suffered.

Once, he admits, he had to sneak out of Damascus like a criminal, lowered over the city wall in a basket. This took place shortly after his conversion. Jews had posted guards at the city entrance and had planned to kill him as a religious traitor when he came out (Acts 9:20–25).

In this humiliating litany, Paul shows what great dangers and hardships he has endured out of love for God and for the Corinthians.

"Five times the Jews have given me their punishment of thirty-nine lashes with a whip. Three different times I was beaten with rods. One time I was almost stoned to death. Three times I was in ships that wrecked, and one of those times I spent a night and a day in the sea. . . I have been in danger in cities, in places where no one lives, and on the sea. And I have been in danger with false Christians" (11:24–26 NCV).

The climax of this parody comes when Paul reveals that Jesus, too, suffered terribly because of the gospel message. "He was weak when he was killed on the cross," Paul says, but now Jesus "lives now by God's power."

The Corinthians should see how only Paul—not the crowd-pleasing latecomers—fits the pattern established by Jesus and is therefore their genuine apostle.

POINTS TO CONSIDER

Paul wasn't much to look at. The Bible gives only scant hints of what Paul looked like, but those hints mesh with the earliest surviving description of him, preserved in a second-century book.

Writing in the *Acts of Paul*, the Christian author describes Paul as "a man of middling size, and his hair was scanty, and his legs were a little crooked, and his knees were far apart; he had large eyes, and his eyebrows met, and his nose was somewhat long."

Paul quoted his critics as saying, "Paul's letters are harsh and powerful. But in person, he is a weakling" (10:10). The New International Version translates "weaking" as "unimpressive," while the New Revised Standard Version puts it this way: "his bodily presence is weak." Whatever the description meant, it was no compliment.

Paul didn't deny that he appeared weak to people who evaluated him by worldly values. On the contrary, he admitted it, then built on it by reminding the Corinthians that Jesus was crucified in weakness.

"It is true that he [Jesus] was weak when he was killed on the cross, but he lives now by God's power. It is true that we are weak in Christ, but for you we will be alive in Christ by God's" (13:4 NCV).

In other words, the Lord has a remarkable capacity for turning weakness into power. "So I am very happy to brag about my weaknesses," Paul adds, "Then Christ's power can live in me" (12:9 NCV).

More than one letter. Second Corinthians is a cut-and-paste job drawing from two or more of Paul's letters, some scholars say.

The letter is anything but smooth-flowing literature, seamlessly blending one topic into the next. Reading it is like taking a ride in a four-wheel-drive vehicle. One moment your chauffeur is cruising you down the expressway, chatting about how fulfilling his job is. The next moment he has ripped into a cornfield and is suddenly talking politics.

Abrupt sidetracks, radical changes from pleasant tones to harsh tones, and the variety of topics—rebukes, fund-raising, sarcasm (to name just a few)—lead some Bible experts to conclude that 2 Corinthians is a composite of two or more letters. One theory is that the intense, heartbreaking letter Paul mentions in 2:4 is at least partly preserved in chapters 10–13 and has been tacked onto the letter that came after it: 2 Corinthians 1–9.

Other scholars, however, see 2 Corinthians as a single letter that addresses the many-faceted problems in Corinth. These scholars suggest that Paul's gentle tone at the beginning, followed by the stern tone at the end, shows that Paul was trying to mend bridges before crossing over to confront the big problem: fake apostles trying to take control of the church.

Early church leaders treated 2 Corinthians as a single letter. And none of the earliest Greek manuscripts show evidence that the letter was pieced together.

FOR FURTHER STUDY

- Read Paul's earlier letter to the church: 1 Corinthians.

- For another emotional defense of Paul's ministry, read his letter to the church in Galatia.

- Philippians is another letter in which Paul's gentle tone changes abruptly. In strong language he condemns people who argue that non-Jews must observe the rite of circumcision.

Sun
Mo
Tue
We
Thu
Frid
Satu
Sun
Mo
Tue
We
Thu
Frid
Satu
Sun
Mo
Tue
We

Galatians

THE CHURCH THAT ENRAGES PAUL

This is the most emotionally charged book of the Bible. As you read it, you can almost see the thick purple veins popping out on Paul's neck as he unloads on the misguided Christians of Galatia.

"I am shocked," Paul begins.

He has taught them God saves them by trusting in Christ alone, not in doing religious things. And now he gets word that they don't believe this anymore. Instead they believe some newly arrived missionaries who teach that Christians have to obey the Jewish laws.

Paul is adamant that the Law has nothing to do with salvation now that Jesus has come. And with fervent emotion he reminds the Galatians of the miracles and the gift of the Holy Spirit they experienced when Paul was still in the area. "How did you receive the Holy Spirit?" Paul asks. "Did

> ### FAMOUS LINES
>
> • "People harvest only what they plant" (6:7 NCV).
>
> • "I have been crucified with Christ; it is no longer I who live, but Christ lives in me" (2:20 NKJV). *Paul's declaration that Jesus is in charge of every aspect of his life.*

you receive the Spirit by following the law? No, you received the Spirit because you heard the Good News and believed it" (3:2 NCV).

Frankly, it's hard to understand the rage and intensity that drives Paul to say what he does, the way he does. This holy apostle uses some of the most vehement language in Scripture. Yet in an oddly familiar way, when he detonates his anger all over the Galatians and the people leading them in the wrong direction, he sounds like a furious but loving parent reading the riot act to a child who just did something incredibly stupid and nearly got killed.

Sometimes love is silent. But sometimes love is a vein-popping scream, calling one back from the brink of disaster.

BACKGROUND

INFLUENTIAL PEOPLE

Paul, an apostle famous for his ministry among non-Jews; founding minister of churches throughout Galatia (1:1).

Peter, leader of the twelve original disciples, who draws a sharp rebuke from Paul for avoiding non-Jewish Christians (1:18).

THEME

While traveling throughout Galatia, in western Turkey, Paul had told the Jews and non-Jews living there that they needed only faith in Jesus to become Christians. Many had accepted his teachings, which were backed up by miracles.

Now, several years later, Paul gets word that other Christian teachers have arrived in the area and are contradicting him. These teachers, Jews who accept Jesus as the Messiah, insist that all non-Jews (Gentiles) must trust Jesus *and* obey the laws given by Moses. This is a controversial issue previously argued and supposedly settled in Paul's favor at a Jerusalem summit meeting of Christian leaders in about AD 49 (Acts 15).

Paul writes an eloquent, sometimes bitterly harsh, defense of his teaching and his authority as an apostle commissioned by God to "tell the Good News about him to those who are not Jewish" (1:16 NCV). He tells of his miraculous conversion while en route to arrest Christians, of seeing Jesus, and of the struggles he faced defending the gospel. He appeals to the example of Abraham, a man who lived before the time of the Jewish laws, to show that God accepts people because of their faith, not because of their obedience to rules.

The Jewish law, Paul argues, was intended to serve only until the Messiah arrived (3:19). With the sacrificial death of Jesus, God established a new covenant that liberated humanity from the law. Instead of

		Paul starts churches in Galatia on first missionary trip AD 46	Jerusalem council grants Gentiles waiver from Jewish laws — AD 49	Paul visits northern Galatia during second missionary trip AD 50	Paul's third missionary trip ends AD 57	Paul imprisoned at Rome AD 60
TIMELINE	**BIBLE EVENTS**	**AD 45**	**AD 50**		**AD 55**	**AD 60**
	WORLD EVENTS	Jews expelled from Rome over controversy about "Chrestus" (probably "Christ") AD 49	Romans learn about soap, from Gauls (France) AD 50	Buddhism of India introduced to China AD 58		Dates are approximate

needing to follow rules, Paul writes, "live by following the Spirit . . . if the Spirit is leading you, you are not under the law" (5:16, 18 NCV).

POINTS OF INTEREST

Anger. "You were foolish; you let someone trick you" (3:1). That's Paul talking. He's more upset in this letter than in any other letter he writes.

He's so angry that he skips the note of appreciation and praise that usually begins each ancient letter, much as modern letters begin with "Dear." Instead, Paul quickly jumps on the Galatians' case: " I am amazed that you are turning away so quickly. . . believing something different than the Good News" (1:6–7 NCV).

DID YOU KNOW?

• Whirling dervishes, Muslim monks who dance into a spinning trance while trying to seek God, got their start in the 1200s in a 4,000-year-old city near Lystra, Galatia, where Paul started a church.

• The Roman province of Galatia got its name from the Gauls of western Europe who began settling there about 200 years before Christ.

Paul's anger reflects the seriousness of the problem more than the frailty of his ego. If the Galatians cling to the revised gospel message they have accepted, Paul knows that as far as they are concerned, Jesus will have died for nothing (2:21).

Makings of the first major split in the church. The first split in the Christian church came over the very issue that erupted in Galatia. The divisive question was this: Do people have to become Jews before they can become Christians? Paul said no. Many other Jewish Christians said yes, everyone must obey the laws of Moses.

If the Jewish Christians had won the debate, Christianity might not have become a major world religion. It could have become just another branch or denomination in Judaism. Added to the Jewish branches of Reform (the least traditional), Conservative, and Orthodox (the more traditional), all of Christianity would be a branch of Jews who accept Jesus as Messiah, but who feel obligated to observe Jewish laws about circumcision, kosher food, and religious holidays.

Paul defending his apostle status. Paul reminds the Galatians of how God chose him to preach especially to the Gentiles, and of how the original disciples of Jesus accepted him as a minister of equal authority. The disciples agreed that Paul and Barnabas "should go to those who are not Jewish" (2:9 NCV).

Paul arguing with Peter. Paul is on such an equal par with the original disciples that he feels free to argue with Peter, leader of the Twelve, when Peter makes a big mistake. This happens when Peter visits the church that Paul and Barnabas are pasturing in Antioch, Syria. Peter, feeling pressured by Jewish Christians who still observe the laws of Moses, stops eating and socializing with Gentile members of the church. According to Jewish law, Gentiles are considered ritually unclean. Jews who come into contact with them have to perform cleansing rituals before they can worship God at the temple.

What Peter's behavior amounts to is religious segregation within the church. At best, both groups would have considered themselves separate but equal. More likely, each group would have considered itself superior.

Other Jews follow Peter's lead, until Paul publicly confronts him, saying: "If the law could make us right with God, then Christ's death would be useless" (2:21 NCV).

Principles of living, instead of rigid laws. Though Christians are free of Old Testament rules, Paul says believers must live godly lives nonetheless. Paul explains that the Holy Spirit leads people away from evil. "The Spirit produces the fruit of love, joy, peace, patience, kindness, goodness, faithfulness, gentleness, self-control" (5:22–23 NCV).

AUTHOR AND DATE

The letter is "from Paul, an apostle" (1:1 NCV) to all the churches in Galatia, a Roman province in western Turkey.

It's unclear exactly when Paul wrote. The letter provides no solid clues about the date, where Paul was when he wrote it, or which churches in Galatia he had in mind. Because the theology in the letter resembles Paul's early letter of 1 Thessalonians more closely than his later letter of Romans, Bible scholars speculate that Paul wrote Galatians sometime around AD 55 or a few years earlier.

ON LOCATION

Paul writes to unnamed churches he started in Galatia, a strip of territory roughly 300 miles long and 100 miles wide, located in western Turkey. It's unknown if Paul intended the letter for churches he founded in southern Galatia on his first missionary trip (churches named in Scripture) or churches he started in northern Galatia on his second trip (churches not named in Scripture). Perhaps he had both in mind.

GALATIANS OUTLINE

Paul argues with Peter (2:11–21).

After Paul leaves Galatia, Jewish-Christian missionaries arrive and contradict his teaching that people are saved only by faith in Jesus. Faith in Christ is not enough, they argue. Anyone who wants to be a Christian must also obey the laws of Moses.

This is an old heresy, Paul explains in his letter of defense to the churches in Galatia. He tells the Galatians that years ago he had to publicly correct Peter for this same mistaken belief. When Paul was pasturing in Antioch, Syria, Peter came for a visit. At first Peter ate with the non-Jewish members and treated them as spiritual brothers and sisters. But later, when other church leaders from Jerusalem arrived, Peter suddenly became afraid of associating with non-Jewish Christians. Apparently these visiting dignitaries believed like other Jews that Gentiles were ritually unclean.

"We know that a person is made right with God not by following the law, but by trusting in Jesus Christ," Paul tells Peter. "If the law could make us right with God, then Christ's death would be useless" (2:16, 21 NCV).

Peter would later side with Paul on this matter in a Jerusalem summit meeting of Christian leaders (Acts 15). And though Jerusalem leaders concur, finding in favor of Peter and Paul, many Jewish-Christian dissenters take their case on the road—to Galatia and beyond.

Equals in the eyes of God (3:26–4:7).

If the teaching of Paul had been eclipsed by that of his opponents who got a foothold in Galatia, Christianity could have turned out much differently. All Christians must have become Jews, bound by the restrictions of Jewish law. Christianity might not have become a major world religion, but only one of several branches or denominations in Judaism. And non-Jews who converted to the Christian branch of Judaism might have been treated as lower-status members, just as Gentile converts to Judaism are in many synagogues today.

Paul wants nothing to do with a status-conscious Christianity that puts some people ahead of others. "In Christ, there is no difference between Jew and Greek, slave and free person, male and female. You are all the same in Christ Jesus. You belong to Christ, so you are Abraham's descendants" (3:28–29 NCV).

Freedom from the restrictive Jewish laws, however, does not mean freedom from accountability. "Do not be fooled," Paul warns, "you cannot cheat God. People harvest only what they plant. If they plant to satisfy their sinful selves, their sinful selves will bring them ruin. But if they plant to please the Spirit, they will receive eternal life from the Spirit" (6:7–8 NCV).

POINTS TO CONSIDER

The traits of a Christian. The traits of a Christian, which Paul identifies in Galatians 5:22–23, are incredibly consistent with traits that Paul mentions in several other letters: 1 Corinthians 13:3–8; Philippians 4:8; and Colossians 3:12–16.

Compare, for example, Galatians and Philippians:

"But the Spirit produces the fruit of love, joy, peace, patience, kindness, goodness, faithfulness, gentleness, self-control" (Galatians 5:22–23 NCV).

"Think about the things that are true and honorable and right and pure and beautiful and respected" (Philippians 4:8 NCV).

Paul, the bitter hypocrite? How could Paul write that God's Spirit makes people "gentle, and self-controlled" (5:23) just a few paragraphs after wishing that Jewish missionary intruders in Galatia "I wish the people who are bothering you would castrate themselves!" (5:12 NCV)?

And why would a gentle, self-controlled apostle ask Galatians who accepted the Jewish version of the gospel this rhetorical question: "How could you be so stupid?" (3:3)?

This is one blistering letter.

Whether Paul let his human emotion get the better of him, only Jesus, who flipped tables of businessmen at the temple can judge (Matthew 21:12). But like Jesus, perhaps Paul knew when a vital issue demanded a stern response.

FOR FURTHER STUDY

- For a report of the Jerusalem summit meeting that debated the same issue the Galatians confronted, read Acts 15.

- To better understand Paul's teaching about salvation through faith, read Romans 3:21–4:25.

Ephesians

Job #1 for the Church

The church has a job. Paul's vision of what that job is may surprise you, for it's one that doesn't show up on agendas of church leadership meetings.

The job is not as material as fundraising, not as mundane as counting warm bodies, not as simple as telling stories of people who lived 2,000 years ago or longer.

Christ's church has a job that's harder, playing a key role in a plan as old as Adam and Eve. God's plan is to save humanity from the destructive effects of sin, and to restore His creation to the holiness and peace it once exhibited. This sounds impossible, but God has been known to do the impossible.

God made human beings to be like him (4:24) and to live with him as his people (1:4). But God's holiness and human sinfulness are as incompatible as matter and antimatter. So God provided a way for humanity to be cleansed of sin: we humans are to do exactly the opposite of Adam and Eve by disobeying God in something we don't fully understand. We are to simply trust that the sacrificial death of Jesus makes us worthy to stand before God: "In Christ we can come before God with freedom and without fear. We can do this through faith in Christ" (3:12 NCV).

Famous Lines

• "Don't go to bed angry" (4:26).

• "Husbands, love your wives" (5:25, KJV).

• "Our fight is not against people on earth but against the rulers and authorities and the powers of this world's darkness, against the spiritual powers of evil in the heavenly world"(6:12 NCV). *Paul explains there are evil spiritual forces that are every bit as real as the physical world. These forces oppose both God and God's people.*

• "Put on the whole armor of God, that you may be able to stand against the wiles of the devil" (6:11 NKJV). *To defend against evil spiritual forces, Paul urges Christians to protect themselves with godly attributes such as truth, justice, and faith.*

The church's job is to be the people of faith—God's people.

How do we measure our success? The measuring is God's job. But the goals before us, Paul says, are unity among believers, following the Spirit within us, maturing in our faith, defeating spiritual forces allied against us, and—perhaps hardest of all—getting along with the people we live with every day.

Can the church ever hope to accomplish all of this? Paul replies confidently, "His goal was to carry out his plan" (1:10 NCV).

BACKGROUND

INFLUENTIAL PEOPLE

Paul, a traveling minister who starts churches throughout the Roman Empire, and who is most successful in non-Jewish cultures (1:1).

THEME

Ephesians reads like a beautiful, poetic sermon written for just about any congregation. It's not a story with a plot, or a letter with a problem-solving agenda. It is, however, a compelling meditation with a deep and lasting message: God has a plan to return unity and peace to his creation, and the church will play a leading role in that plan.

"His goal was to carry out his plan, when the right time came," Paul says, "all things in heaven and on earth would be joined together in Christ as the head" (1:10 NCV).

POINTS OF INTEREST

No problems. After reading 1 and 2 Corinthians and Galatians, this letter comes as a pleasant surprise. Paul isn't scolding anyone, correcting warped theology, or defending his authority as an apostle sent by God.

TIMELINE	BIBLE EVENTS	Paul converts ⌐--AD 35	Paul's missionary journeys begin AD 46 ---┐	Paul writes Ephesians, during Rome imprisonment AD 60 -----------------┐	Dates are approximate
		AD 35	**AD 45**	**AD 55**	**AD 65**
	WORLD EVENTS	Buddhism of India introduced to China AD 58 ------┘		Mayans are building a great civilization in Central America AD 60 --------------┘	

Instead, he's stretching and exercising the faith and mind of his readers, helping Christians improve their understanding of what God is doing in the world and how he is doing it. The short answer to the "what" question is that God is restoring his relationship to human beings, and human relationships to one another. The "how" is through Christ, and the church he started from a motley crew of a dozen common folk, the likes of fishermen and tax men.

The flow of the letter. Paul begins by pulling out a cosmic canvas and painting a picture of God's plan for all of creation—heaven and earth—to be holy and blessed (1:3–23). Next, Paul explains how Christ has made all believers—Jew and non-Jew alike—key players in this plan (2:1–22). Then Paul

> ### DID YOU KNOW?
> • Unlike the Old Testament, the New Testament has no books that are entire poems. Coming closest is Ephesians, which seems to draw heavily from early church hymns and prayers.

explains the role that believers play through the church (3:1–5:20) and through their personal relationship at home and work (5:21–6:9). Finally, with powerful imagery from the battlefield, Paul tells Christians how to tap into God's unlimited power to defeat evil spiritual forces allied against them (6:10–20).

Practical advice for everyday living. The last half of the book throws the spotlight on practical ways for the church to fulfill its role in God's plan.

1. Live in unity. "Always be humble, gentle, and patient, accepting each other in love. You are joined together with peace through the Spirit, so make every effort to continue together in this way" (4:2–3 NCV).

2. Grow spiritually mature and serve others through the church (4:11–13).

3. Seek spiritual renewal. "You were taught to be made new in your hearts, to become a new person" (4:23–24 NCV); "but be filled with the Spirit" (5:18 NCV).

4. Put others first. "Yield to obey each other as you would to Christ" (5:21 NCV). This involves all personal relationships, especially husbands and wives, children and parents, workers and bosses.

5. Resist evil spiritual forces. "Our fight is not against people on earth but against . . . the rulers and authorities and the powers of this world's darkness, against the spiritual powers of evil in the heavenly world. That

is why you need to put on God's full armor. . . And when you have finished the whole fight, you will still be standing" (6:12–13 NCV).

AUTHOR AND DATE

The letter claims Paul as its writer (1:1), and speaks in the voice of a prisoner "in jail" (6:20). For about 1,700 years no one questioned that Paul wrote Ephesians. But in recent centuries, scholars comparing this letter to others that Paul wrote have noticed some substantial differences. For more, see "Who wrote the letter?" in Points to Consider.

If Paul wrote the letter, he may have done so during his two-year imprisonment at Rome, which began about AD 60. If someone else wrote it in Paul's name, applying his theology to later circumstances in the church, the writing may have occurred in the closing decades of the first century.

ON LOCATION

Though the letter claims to be written "to God's holy people living in Ephesus" (1:1 NCV), this introduction is excluded from the oldest manuscripts. Nor does the letter contain any of Paul's characteristic personal greetings to individuals, or references to circumstances in this major port city in western Turkey. Paul may have intended Ephesians as a general letter, for circulation among as many churches as possible. Or perhaps he did address it to Ephesus, fully expecting that believers there would make copies for distribution to other congregations. (See map in Acts, page 362.)

EPHESIANS OUTLINE

Jew and Gentile, united in Christ (2:11–3:13).

From the beginning of time, Paul says, God has wanted human beings "that we would be his holy people—people without blame before him" (1:4 NCV). Yet from Adam's time onward, humanity has chosen sin over obedience. God in his mercy, however, has made provision for people to find forgiveness for sin: first through sacrificial rituals, then through the sacrifice of Jesus, who gave "the blood of his death, and so we have forgiveness of sins" (1:7–8 NCV).

By the time Paul writes this letter, Jews are increasingly rejecting the Christian gospel, and the church is becoming more and more Gentile. So much so, that many non-Jews are developing an us-them attitude, with "them" being the Jews—outsiders to the church.

But the church, Paul reminds his mostly non-Jewish readers, is made up of the forgiven—Jew and Gentiles, and he has united us (2:14).

Unity, Paul says, should be one of the hallmarks of every congregation. For by getting along with each other other, the apostle explains, we fulfill one of the main reasons the church exists. "You are joined together with peace through the Spirit," Paul says. "There is one body and one Spirit" (4:3–4 NCV). That body is the church.

Get rid of malice (4:17–5:20).

Paul says that when people become followers of the Lord, they slowly but certainly begin to resemble their creator. "That new person is made to be like God," Paul says, "made to be truly good and holy" (4:23 NCV).

This doesn't mean Christian never make mistakes and always do the right thing. But it does means they have accepted their role as human beings devoted to God, their holy father. And it means they live in such a way that others can see the resemblance. "Holy," in reference to anything in the physical world, means "set apart" or "dedicated" to God. It doesn't mean "perfect" in behavior.

On the other hand, Paul quickly adds that Christians who are growing spiritually are learning to replace bitterness, anger, and criticism with kindness, mercy, and forgiveness.

"So try to be like him," Paul urges. "You are God's children whom he

Sun
Mon
Tue
Wed
Thu
Frid
Satu
Sun
Mon
Tues
Wed
Thu
Frid
Satu
Sun
Mon
Tues
Wed

loves . . . But there must be no sexual sin among you, or any kind of evil or greed" (5:1–3 NCV).

Put others first (5:21–6:9).

"Honor Christ and put others first," Paul says. Christians who listen to the Spirit of God within them will increasingly learn to do this in all their relationships—especially in relationships closest to home.

Husbands and wives will love and care for one another, each doing as much as possible to meet the needs of the other.

Children, young and old, will treat their parents with respect. This isn't a one-way street. "Fathers, do not make your children angry," Paul instructs. "But raise them with the training and teaching of the Lord" (6:4 NCV).

In ancient times, it was as acceptable for people to have slaves as it is today for corporate managers to have employees. (And many over-worked, underpaid employees today can easily see a parallel.) Paul isn't interested in starting a slave-liberating revolution, at least not from the outside in. What he calls for, however, would eventually accomplish this, by working from the inside out.

"Slaves, obey your masters here on earth with fear and respect and from a sincere heart, just as you obey Christ. You must do this not only while they are watching you, to please them" (6:5–6 NCV).

For slave owners, Paul offers these instructions: "Masters, in the same way, be good to your slaves. Do not threaten them. Remember that the One who is your Master and their Master is in heaven, and he treats everyone alike" (6:9 NCV).

Does this sound like a recipe for Utopia? This is God working his plan through the church. It may sound unrealistic, but Paul assures his readers that "his goal was to carry out his plan, when the right time came" (1:10 NCV).

Dressing for spiritual success (6:10–18).

For the moment, we live in a physical world made up of elements we can see and touch and smell and taste. But Paul says there's an overlapping spiritual world that we can't see, yet it's as real as clouds and rocks and flowers and honey.

Mysteriously, in this spiritual world there are two forces at work.

These are the forces of God and the forces of Satan. Both can influence us—God for the better and Satan for the worse.

In fact, Paul says, the biggest battles we face in this life are not confrontations with other human beings. "Our fight is not against people on earth but against the rulers and authorities and the powers of this world's darkness, against the spiritual powers of evil in the heavenly world. That is why you need to put on God's full armor" (6:12–13 NCV).

Comparing God's arsenal to the uniform of a Roman soldier, Paul tells believers to strap on truth like a belt, God's justice like armor, the good news of peace like shoes, faith like a shield, and God's saving power like a helmet.

Then when evil attacks, through temptation or whatever other means are at his disposal, "you will be able to stand strong. And when you have finished the whole fight, you will still be standing."

POINTS TO CONSIDER

Husbands and wives: Submit to each other. Lots of sermons have touted the verse "Wives, yield to your husbands, as you do to the Lord," (5:22 NCV). Fortunately for the ladies, Paul's thought begins one verse earlier: "Yield to obey each other as you would to Christ" (NCV).

In this letter's original language, Greek, there is just one verb for the entire section that discusses husband and wife relationship. That verb is *submit* in 5:21. Everything that follows is built on this verb, to illustrate how each is to submit to the other.

"As the church yields to Christ, so you wives should yield to your husbands in everything" (5:24 NCV).

"Husbands, love your wives as Christ loved the church and gave himself for it . . . as they love their own bodies" (5:25, 28 NCV).

Who wrote the letter? Most scholars agree that Paul wrote Romans, 1 and 2 Corinthians, Galatians, Philippians, 1 Thessalonians, and Philemon. These books clearly sound like Paul in choice of words, style of writing, and theology. Ephesians, however, uses important words that don't appear in Paul's undisputed letters. And some of the familiar words have been tagged with different meanings entirely. Also, the prose is more flowery and wordy than Paul's other cut-to-the-chase-scene letters.

Sun
Mo
Tue
Wed
Thu
Frid
Satu
Sun
Mo
Tue
Wed
Thu
Frid
Satu
Sun
Mo
Tue
Wed

Some Bible experts suggest that one or more of Paul's associates, such as Timothy, wrote the letter after Paul died. This associate applied Paul's theology to current issues, such as the growing division between Jews and Gentiles, and honored his master teacher by writing in Paul's voice and by signing Paul's name. This was a common practice among Greek and Jewish writers of the time. It was exactly the opposite of plagiarism; it was giving credit instead of taking it, and it was an expression of humility instead of pride.

Other experts argue that Paul was quite capable of growing and adapting, using new terms and vesting old terms with new and rich meaning. The wordy writing, they suggest, may have come from Paul's use of well-known hymns and prayers, which he wove into the letter. And he may have used a writer or secretary, who expressed Paul's ideas in the writer's words, with the apostle's approval.

For Further Study

- Colossians, in both writing style and teachings, is strikingly similar to Ephesians.

Philippians

A JOYFUL LETTER FROM PAUL IN JAIL

Paul does strange things in jail. When he sat in a Philippian jail, the year he founded the church in that city, he sang hymns (Acts 16:25). Now, as he sits in some other jail and writes to his beloved Philippians, he speaks of happiness.

He says he's happy that he has such caring friends. He's even happy that he's suffering for Christ because his suffering is inspiring other Christians to preach more boldly. And he says if need be, he will be happy to die because he will go to be with Christ, which is a much better place than where he is now.

As Paul faces death and ponders his mortality, his thoughts are drawn to the source of immortality. "To me the only important thing about living is Christ, and dying would be profit for me" (1:21 NCV).

Paul wants the Philippians to experience this same peaceful joy when they reflect on their lives. So in the spirit of a gentle father, he advises them "keep on working to complete your salvation with fear and trembling, because God is working in you to help you want to do and be able to do what pleases him. . . . shine like stars in the dark world. You offer the teaching that gives life" (2:12–13, 15–16 NCV).

Paul's words are captivating, coming from the brink of death.

FAMOUS LINES

- "So that every knee will bow to the name of Jesus-everyone in heaven, on earth, and under the earth (2:10 NCV).

- "My God shall supply all your needs according to his riches in glory by Christ Jesus" (4:19 NKJV).

- "For me to live is Christ, and to die is gain" (1:21 KJV). *Paul plans to live for Jesus, then enjoy an afterlife of eternity in heaven.*

BACKGROUND

INFLUENTIAL PEOPLE

Paul, apostle, traveling preacher, frequent prisoner, and founder of the church at Philippi (1:1).

Epaphroditus, a member of the Philippian church who brings gifts from the congregation to jailed Paul (2:25).

THEME

While Paul is in jail, perhaps in Rome during the early AD 60s, a messenger arrives from the church at Philippi, in northern Greece. Some ten years earlier, during Paul's second missionary trip, Paul had arrived in Philippi and established what became the first church in Europe. Throughout his traveling ministry, the Philippians continue to support Paul with money and gifts. As soon as they learn of Paul's imprisonment, they dispatch one of their trusted members—Epaphroditus—who brings the apostle some gifts. These may have included funds to help defray his expenses while enduring two years of house arrest.

Ephaphroditus becomes deathly ill, but manages to recover. Paul then sends him home with a joyful letter of thanks we now know as Philippians. In this letter, the apostle expresses joy for the longstanding support that the Philippians have given him, and for the recent gifts, as well as for the recovery of Ephaphroditus. But Paul also warns the believers that one day they may have to suffer as he is suffering now. "Be brave," Paul says (1:28), for God can use suffering to accomplish good. "What has happened to me," Paul explains, "has helped to spread the good news ... most of the believers have become more bold in Christ and are not afraid to speak the word of God" (1:12–14 NCV).

TIMELINE	BIBLE EVENTS	Paul starts church in Philippi, during second missionary trip ┌-- AD 50		Paul writes Philippians, during Rome imprisonment AD 60 ----┐	Dates are approximate
		AD 50	**AD 55**	**AD 60**	**AD 65**
	WORLD EVENTS		China, Rome conduct trade via 4,000-mile-long └------- Silk Road AD 50	Rome burns; Christians blamed, persecuted AD 64 ------------------	

Points of Interest

No quotes from the Old Testament. Paul is a converted Pharisee, a scholar in the Jewish scripture. So it's unusual for him to write about religious matters without quoting the Old Testament. Yet there's no mention of the Old Testament in this letter. This may be because nearly all the believers in Philippi are non-Jews, unfamiliar with sacred Jewish Scripture. When Paul first first arrived in the town, there apparently was no formal synagogue—just a riverside gathering place outside the city, where a few Jews met for prayer on the Sabbath (Acts 16:13).

Why Paul writes the letter. Paul makes several key points in Philippians, one of his most affectionate letters.

1. Paul thanks the Philippians for their ongoing support, and for their recent gifts (1:3–11; 4:10–20).

2. He warns them that they may have to suffer, as Christ did and as Paul is doing now. But he urges them to stand firm in their faith. And drawing from his own experience, he shows how God can use difficult situations to help spread the good news about Jesus (1:12–29).

3. He urges them to remain united, and to imitate the humility of Jesus, who "gave up his place with God and made himself nothing" and to whom God awarded "the highest place" and "made his name greater than every other name" (2:7, 9 NCV).

4. Paul also warns the Philippians to "watch out for those who do evil, who are like dogs" (3:2 NCV). These are apparently Jews who profess Jesus as Lord, but who insist—against Paul's teaching—that all Christians must observe the Jewish laws recorded in the Old Testament.

Joy. For someone writing from prison and facing the threat of death, Paul speaks a lot about happiness. He uses the word joy in some form or another sixteen times in this short letter.

He remembers the Philippians with joy (1:4). He will be "completely happy" if the believers there will live in harmony with each other (2:2). The Philippians are his "pride and joy" (4:1).

A moving song about Jesus. Paul quotes part of what many Bible experts believe is an early song about Jesus (2:6–11). Paul uses the song merely as an illustration, to urge the Philippians to imitate Christ's humility and his willingness to suffer for others. But the song also shows what the earliest Christians believed about who Jesus is: "truly God," "he became like one of us." He is now "honored . . . above all others," and one day "at the name of Jesus everyone will bow."

AUTHOR AND DATE

Paul, writing from jail in an unnamed city, writes this letter to the Philippians to express thanks for gifts they send him.

If Paul wrote from Rome, as many scholars believe, then Philippians is a product of his two years of house arrest, beginning about AD 60. This would have been during the final years of his ministry, which began with his conversion some twenty-five years earlier.

ON LOCATION

Paul writes from prison to a church in Philippi, a large city on one of the main roads connecting Rome with territories to the east. He visited it twice on his third missionary journey (see map).

Where Paul is during the writing remains a mystery. He speaks of "Roman guards" (1:13) and employees "in the service of the Emperor" (4:22). This leads some to conclude Paul is writing from Rome. But Roman guards and imperial employees are scattered throughout the Roman world. So Paul could be writing from one of many other jails in which he spent time. Paul admits he was imprisoned many times (2 Corinthians 11:23).

Acts names three: Philippi, when he started the church (16:23–40); Caesarea (23:23–26:32), and Rome (28:16–31). Other possible jailings took place in Corinth and Ephesus.

PHILIPPIANS OUTLINE

Paul writes from prison (1:1–29).

When the church at Philippi hears that Paul, their founding minister, is in jail, they send a courier with gifts. In response, Paul writes a joyous letter of appreciation.

"I thank my God every time I remember you," Paul writes. "I thank God for the help you gave me while I preached the Good News—help you gave from the first day you believed until now . . . I have you in my heart" (1:3, 5, 7 NCV).

Paul encourages the people not to feel badly about his imprisonment. He says "what has happened to me has helped to spread the Good News. All the palace guards and everyone else knows that I am in prison because I am a believer in Christ. Because I am in prison, most of the believers have become more bold in Christ and are not afraid to speak the word of God" (1:12–14 NCV).

Paul warns that one day the Philippians may also have to suffer for Christ. If they do, he says, they should be brave and remember that the love of Christ will comfort them.

Jesus, the suffering servant, now glorified (2:1–18).

Not only will the Philippians be comforted, Paul adds, they will be rewarded. To illustrate this, he draws from a beautiful poem about Jesus, perhaps the lyrics of a hymn: "He humbled himself and was fully obedient to God, even when that caused his death—death on a cross. So God raised him to the highest place. God made his name greater than every other name" (2:8–9 NCV).

Paul asks the Philippians to continue being his "pride and joy" (4:1) by living in harmony with each other and by following his example if they have to face suffering. "I keep trying to reach the goal and get the prize for which God called me through Christ to the life above," Paul writes (3:14 NCV).

"Finally," the apostle adds, "think about the things that are good and worthy of praise. Think about the things that are true and honorable and right and pure and beautiful and respected . . . God, who gives peace, will be with you" (4:8–9 NCV).

Sun
Mon
Tue
Wed
Thu
Frid
Satu
Sun
Mo
Tue
Wed
Thu
Frid
Satu
Sun
Mo
Tue
We

=== POINTS TO CONSIDER ===

Citizens of heaven. "But our homeland is in heaven, and we are waiting for our Savior, the Lord Jesus Christ, to come from heaven" (3:20 NCV). When Paul says this, he uses a technical term that appears only here in all of the New Testament. The word is citizen, but it refers to a colony of settlers or retired soldiers who secure a conquered land. This is a term especially pertinent to the residents of Philippi, for this city began as such a frontier town. Residents in cities like this were awarded a legal status equal to that of people born in the imperial capital of Rome.

The Philippians took great pride in their citizenship, because their city enjoyed the highest legal privilege attainable in the empire. Paul wanted Philippian believers to take just as much pride in their church, which he described as a colony of heaven ruled by Jesus.

Three letters in one? Some Bible scholars say Philippians is a collection of three letters. They suggest this because of some abrupt changes in topic and tone, and because Polycarp, a second-century Christian writer, spoke of Paul's "letters" to the Philippians.

Especially obvious, though buried in the middle of the letter, is Paul's sudden and sarcastic attack on Jewish Christians who are trying to convince non-Jewish believers in Philippi to observe Jewish laws. Paul describes these people as evil, as enemies of the cross of Christ, and as behaving like dogs (3:2, 18). This digression seems far astray from a letter otherwise filled with words of happiness. Also, it seems odd to some that Paul waits until the end of the letter to thank the Philippians for the gifts they sent him.

For these reasons, some scholars propose that Paul wrote three letters, and themes all blend together to form a single letter. They add that when Paul urges the Philippians to "face your enemies" (1:28), he is anticipating the harsh comments ahead, with which he condemns Jewish-Christian intruders trying to impose Jewish laws onto Gentiles (3:2–4:3).

=== FOR FURTHER STUDY ===

- To read about how Paul started the church of Philippi, turn to Acts 16:11–40.

- Second Timothy is one of Paul's final letters. It includes a moving passage about his approaching death (4:6–8).

Colossians

FAKE RELIGIONS AHEAD

Just enough truth to be dangerous—that's what Paul sees in a new religious movement catching fire in Colossae. For years Paul has defended Christianity against major religions of the day: Judaism, worship of Roman and Greek gods, along with mysterious cults that promise eternal life.

Now Paul faces a movement led by religious philosophers gifted in the art of accessorizing. These teachers take a little from Christianity, a little from Judaism, a little from the mysterious cults, and suddenly they have a new religion that looks deceptively familiar. This religion teaches that angels exist, it honors religious holidays, and it urges people to seek God. All this looks so familiar, in fact, that it makes the Christians of Colossae begin to wonder if this new teaching is simply a more insightful way of interpreting old truths.

It's not, Paul insists. It's just another set of human teachings that "comes from the ruling spirits of this world, and not from Christ" (2:8 NCV).

For the people of Colossae—and for Christians of all ages who become perplexed by new takes on old-time religion—Paul offers sage advice: "As you received Christ Jesus the Lord, so continue to live in him. Keep your roots deep in him and have your lives built on him" (2:6–7 NCV).

What people need is not "fancy talk" (2:3), not "senseless arguments" (2:8), not "human teachings" (2:8)—just Jesus Christ.

Background

Influential People

Paul, traveling minister who starts churches throughout the Roman Empire and who advises even churches he has not started—such as the one in Colossae (1:1).

Epaphras, founding minister of the church in Colossae, and an associate of Paul (1:7).

Theme

While sitting in prison awaiting trial, Paul gets word that Christians in Colossae are confronting a new teaching that could destroy the church. The threatening movement seems to blend elements of many religions into a convincing belief system.

"Be sure that no one leads you away," Paul warns. "With false and empty teaching that is only human, which comes from the ruling spirits of this world, and not from Christ" (2:8 NCV).

Paul reminds the Colossians that they accepted Jesus Christ, and they should now follow him "just as you were taught" (2:7 NCV).

The apostle closes his letter with a list of everyday traits that true Christians exhibit, as well as traits they shun (chapter 3).

Points of Interest

The problem. When Paul hears that a religious teaching that combines Jewish beliefs and other religions is making inroads into the church at Colossae, he writes a letter to urge the people to trust only in the power of Jesus to save them.

It's unclear what the heresy is, or even if it has a name. Paul's rebuttal, however, gives clues about what the heresy emphasizes.

1. Follow rules about food, religious holidays (2:16–17), and circum-

					Dates are approximate
TIMELINE	**BIBLE EVENTS**	Paul converts AD 35	Paul's missionary journeys begin AD 46	Paul writes Colossians, during Rome imprisonment AD 60	
		AD 35	**AD 45**	**AD 55**	**AD 65**
	WORLD EVENTS		Buddhism of India introduced to China AD 58		Mayans are building a great civilization in Central America AD 60

cision (3:11). These teachings may have come from Judaism.

2. Deprive your body, to show you have control over it (2:21–23). This resembles the ascetic practices of isolationist religious groups such as the Jewish Essenes who produced the Dead Sea scrolls, and of Christian monks in later centuries.

3. Worship angels, who provide visions, more knowledge about God, and more access to him (2:18). This emphasis on having secret knowledge about God and salvation may represent the seed of a heresy that develops into a major movement in the second century: Gnosticism, from a word for "knowledge."

The supreme power of Jesus. Paul refutes this speculative religion by reminding the Colossians that their salvation doesn't depend on such a wide variety of spiritual power sources. Christ is the supreme power on which people depend.

> **DID YOU KNOW?**
>
> • The 1983 film *Tender Mercies*, for which Robert Duvall got the Oscar for best actor, takes its title from the King James Version's translation of "gentleness," a trait that describes God (Psalm 25:6) and God's people (Colossians 3:12).

Christ's sacrifice eliminates the need to observe ancient Jewish rules, which were built around the sacrificial system (1:20). Christ is Lord of the "body," a word that symbolizes both the church and the individuals in it (2:19–23). And Christ had a role in creating all life, including angels (1:16).

A song about Jesus. To refute the heresy, Paul draws from what may have been a well-known song about Jesus. At least part of the hymn appears in 1:15–20. These lyrics, with Paul's additional comments, produce the New Testament's strongest statement about the authority of Jesus.

Instructions for daily living. After teaching about the power of Jesus to save, Paul shows how Christians should respond: adopt attitudes and a lifestyle that reflects a close relationship with Jesus. "Since you were raised from the dead with Christ, aim at what is in heaven . . . clothe yourselves with mercy, kindness, humility, gentleness, and patience. Bear with each other, and forgive each other. If someone does wrong to you, forgive that person because the Lord forgave" (3:1, 12–13 NCV).

AUTHOR AND DATE

The writer is identified as "Paul, an apostle of Christ Jesus. I am an apostle because that is what God wanted" (1:1 NCV). For background on why some scholars doubt this, read "Who wrote the letter?" in Points to Consider.

Because of similarities between this letter and the letter written to the Ephesians, both were likely penned about the same time. If Paul wrote the letter, he may have done so during his two-year imprisonment at Rome, beginning about AD 60. If someone else wrote it as a tribute to Paul, applying the apostle's theology to the heresy confronting Colossae, the writing may have occurred in the closing decades of the first century.

ON LOCATION

Paul writes from jail (4:3), perhaps in Rome, to a church he has never visited. Colossae is 100 miles west of Ephesus, where Paul once lived for two years. The church was apparently started by a student minister Paul sent: Epaphras (1:7). (See map in Acts, page 362.)

COLOSSIANS OUTLINE

Jesus at creation (1:15–20).

A new teaching that urges people to pray to angels arrives in Colossae, a busy city on an important east-west trade route in Turkey. Paul feels compelled to write to the believers there and remind them to hold fast to their traditional faith, which they received from one of his associates.

There's no need to pray to angels, Paul says. "Jesus Christ is exactly like him. . . Through his power all things were made—things in heaven and on earth" (1:15, 16 NCV). Paul explains that faith in Christ is all that anyone needs for salvation.

Jesus, taking our sins to the cross (2:6–23).

The heretical teaching, which Paul calls "senseless arguments," apparently has a long to-do list for people who want God's forgiveness that leads to salvation. In addition to praying to angels, people are expected to observe rules and religious holy days dictated by the teachers.

This is all wrong, Paul argues. God took away our sins when he "nailed it to the cross" (2:14 NCV). We become God's people not by obeying rules, praying to angels, or discovering spiritual secrets in visions. We become his people by trusting him.

Paul illustrates this with the familiar ritual of baptism. "When you were baptized, you were buried with Christ, and you were raised up with him through your faith in God's power that was shown when he raised Christ from the dead. When you were spiritually dead because of your sins and because you were not free from the power of your sinful self, God made you alive with Christ, and he forgave all our sins" (2:12–13 NCV).

Other than believing this, Christians have no required to-do list for salvation.

Like the people of God (3:1–25).

In words resembling Ephesians 4 and 5, and probably written about the same time, Paul says that genuine Christianity shows itself in the way people live.

"You have begun to live the new life, in which you are being made new and are becoming like the One who made you" (3:10 NCV). Paul says this means, for one thing, that we learn to control our bodies—not as ascetics do by depriving themselves of nourishment—but by doing away with harmful thoughts.

In addition, we try to become more kind, patient, and forgiving, all of which are motivated by nothing less than love.

When we're in doubt about what to say or do, Paul offers this suggestion: "Everything you do or say should be done to obey Jesus your Lord" (3:17 NCV).

═══ POINTS TO CONSIDER ═══

Paul's touch. Though some scholars question whether Paul or a later associate such as Timothy wrote this letter, the message reflects what Paul said in many other letters.

For example, one repeated theme is that as far as Christ is concerned, all believers are equal: "In the new life there is no difference between Greeks and Jews, those who are circumcised and those who are not circumcised, or people who are foreigners, or Scythians [people from southern Russia, known for their savagery], there is no difference between slaves and free people" (3:11 NCV). Paul says much the same in other letters: Romans 10:12; 1 Corinthians 12:13; Galatians 3:28; and Ephesians 6:8.

Who wrote the letter? For many of the reasons that some scholars think Ephesians was written after the death of Paul, they think the same of Colossians. The writer's use of words and ideas don't mesh well with those of Paul in other letters.

For example, Paul often confronts opposition by using the style of a well-reasoned argument or debate. In Colossians he uses a more poetic style that joyously celebrates Jesus. Also, Paul writes with uncharacteristically long and complex sentences, which most English translations simplify.

In addition, part of the heresy addressed in the book seems remarkably close to Gnosticism, a movement that became popular only in the second century. And other teachings, such as the portrayal of Christ at the beginning of creation (1:16), appear only in Christian writings believed to have been written near the end of the first century—some thirty years or more after Paul died.

Bible experts who argue that Paul wrote Colossians say the variations show he was able to change with the times, using new terms and giving old terms new meaning. The wordy writing, they suggest, may have come from Paul's use of well-known hymns and prayers, which he wove into the letter. Also, the heresy in Colossae may have been the seed from which Gnosticism grew.

For Further Study

- The letter of Colossians resembles Ephesians in both tone and teachings. Both, for example, have advice for everyday living, and both emphasize the church, which the writer symbolically calls the body of Christ.

Sun
Mo
Tue
We
Thu
Fri
Sat
Sun
Mo
Tue
We
Thu
Fri
Sat
Sun
Mo
Tue
We

1 Thessalonians

WHEN WILL JESUS COME BACK?

The infant church of Thessalonica, in ancient Greece, wants Jesus to come back soon and whisk them off to the eternal delights of heaven. This seemingly is their greatest desire—the one subject they think about most.

It's not hard to understand why. Paul is able to spend only a few weeks with them, before he is run out of town by Jews who believe he is preaching heresy. Left behind, and alone, is this unorganized core of converts, united only by their experience of salvation and the belief that one day the Lord will return to take the faithful to their everlasting reward in heaven.

Though the Thessalonian believers stand united, they stand alone—or so it must have seemed—for they begin cultivating a lifestyle of holiness while living in a sprawling port city that teems with immorality, greed, and deception. In addition, they worship Jesus as God's Son and as ruler of the heavenly kingdom, while Jews insist God has no son and Romans in the city worship the emperor, ruler of the largest earthly kingdom.

For Thessalonians, and all Christians who feel out of sync in their world, Paul encourages them not to focus their energy on the return of Jesus. Instead, we are to work hard, live honorable lives, and earn the respect of others. By doing this, we draw people to Jesus just as a lighthouse draws to safety one list ship after another.

> ### FAMOUS LINES
>
> • "The Lord will come like a thief in the night" (5:2 NCV). *When asked about the timing of Christ's return, Paul replies with this phrase, meaning that no one can predict the Second Coming.*

BACKGROUND

INFLUENTIAL PEOPLE

Paul, leading minister to the Gentile world, and founder of the congregation at Thessalonica and other major cities throughout the Roman Empire (1:1).

Timothy, Paul's associate who visits Thessalonica then reports back to Paul about the progress of the new converts and the questions they have (1:1).

THEME

About 1,000 miles into his second missionary trip, Paul has a captivating vision one night: he sees a man pleading with him to leave Turkey and come to Macedonia, a Roman province in northern Greece. Paul complies, taking the gospel to Europe. He arrives in Philippi, but stays only a short time before he is charged with disturbing the peace and is forced to leave town. He proceeds on to Thessalonica, capital and largest city of Macedonia. Some 200,000 people live in this busy port town on the main east-west trade route to Asia.

Paul preaches in the synagogue for about three weeks before the Jews realize that what he's teaching requires an end to traditional Judaism. They riot, forcing Paul to escape to Athens, 200 miles south. But not before some Jews and many non-Jews convert to Christianity.

Within perhaps a month or two, while Paul is staying in Corinth, he sends his young associate, Timothy, to check on the Thessalonian believers. Timothy returns with a good report. But he also brings word that the people are facing persecution and that they have questions about the Second Coming. By this time Paul is deeply involved in starting the Corinthian ministry; he can't leave. So he comes up with an innovative solution that's not unlike a correspondence school. He decides to encourage and teach the believers of Thessalonica by letter.

TIMELINE	BIBLE EVENTS	Paul's missionary journeys begin AD 46 --------------	Paul starts second missionary trip AD 50 --------------	Paul writes Thessalonians while in Corinth AD 51 ----------------------	Dates are approximate
		AD 40	**AD 45**		**AD 50**
	WORLD EVENTS	China, Rome conduct trade via 4,000-mile-long Silk Road AD 50 --------------	Jews expelled from Rome over controversy about "Chrestus" (probably "Christ" AD 49 ---------		
			Isthmian Games held at Corinth AD 51 -------------		

Paul praises their faith, answers their questions about the Second Coming, then urges them to live in a way that would please the Lord.

POINTS OF INTEREST

The Second Coming. The questions most on the minds of new converts in Thessalonica have to do with the return of Jesus. Questions like these: When is he coming? How can we know he will accept us? What will happen to Christians who die before Jesus arrives?

Paul says no one knows when Jesus will return, but he assures the Thessalonians that as long as they trust in Jesus for their salvation, they won't be disappointed. As for dead Christians, Paul says they will not miss out on eternal life. After they die, they will be "will rise first" (4:16 NCV).

> ### DID YOU KNOW?
> • First Thessalonians is probably the oldest piece of literature in the New Testament, written about twenty years after the death and resurrection of Jesus. The Gospels, describing the life of Jesus, were written a decade or more later, to preserve the stories the disciples had told.

Paul covers several topics in this short letter, but the Second Coming is the main idea. Every chapter ends with a reference to it. And 4:13–5:11 describes what it will be like, beginning with the call of an angel and a trumpet blast, and concluding with Christians rising into the heavens to meet the Lord in the air.

Guidelines for holy living. Thessalonica is anything but a city of saints. It's a thriving port town on a major trade route. So it has all the sinfulness of any large city, along with the emphasis on sex that could be expected in a town that draws traveling merchants and sailors just passing by.

Paul knows that it's hard to live in a town like this without getting swept into the powerful current of passion and greed. So he gently warns the new believers, "He wants each of you to learn to control your own body in a way that is holy and honorable" (4:4 NCV). Instead, Paul says, "Do all you can to live a peaceful life. Take care of your own business, and do your own work as we have already told you . . . then people who are not believers will respect you" (4:11–12 NCV).

No quotes from the Old Testament. Paul was raised a Pharisee, a Jewish scholar. When he talks about religious matters, it's common for him to draw from his expertise and quote the Jewish Scriptures. The fact that he doesn't do this in his letter to the Thessalonians suggests that most of the believers there are non-Jews, unfamiliar with Scripture.

The story of Paul's visit to Thessalonica, reported in Acts, suggests that only a few Jews accepted his message, compared to "many of the Greeks who worshiped God" (Acts 17:4 NCV). God-fearing Greeks are non-Jews who worship in the synagogue, but who stop short of converting to Judaism. Major roadblocks to conversion are the painful rite of circumcision and the restrictive dietary regulations of the Jews.

By the time Paul writes this letter, there may be even fewer Jewish Christians—perhaps none. He describes congregation members as having "stopped worshiping idols and began serving the living and true God" (1:9 NCV).

AUTHOR AND DATE

The letter is written by Paul, who is accompanied by his traveling associates Timothy and Silas (1:1). Bible experts agree that this letter reads like other authenticated letters of Paul. Early Christian writers, beginning with Marcion in AD 140, confirm that Paul was the author.

Paul wrote this letter in about AD 51, during his second missionary trip, while he was starting a church in Corinth. For archaeological evidence supporting this date, read "Gallio was here" in Points to Consider.

ON LOCATION

Thessalonica is a bustling trade town in northern Greece. The city profits from a port in the Thermatic Gulf of the Aegean Sea, and from its location on the Via Egnatia, an east-west Roman road that stretches across northern Greece and into Turkey. Paul writes the letter from Corinth, some 250 miles south. (See map in 1 Corinthians, page 384.)

1 Thessalonians Outline

The Second Coming (4:13–5:11).

During Paul's second missionary journey, which takes him into what is now Greece, the apostle spends only a few weeks in Thessalonica. But this is long enough to convince many people that the Messiah has come, been executed, and raised from the dead. It's also long enough to instill in the new converts an urgent sense of expectation; they believe Jesus will return at any moment.

Some apparently quit their jobs, feeling that they shouldn't waste their time on trivial matters. As the waiting goes on for weeks and perhaps months, the people begin to have doubts about what Paul told them. They want to know when Jesus is coming and what is going to happen to Christians who die before he arrives.

Paul writes that no one knows exactly when Jesus will return: the event will be as unexpected "like a thief that comes in the night" (5:2 NCV). This Thief, however, will be welcome because he will come to take his followers to heaven.

Paul outlines the course of events: "The Lord himself will come down from heaven with a loud command, with the voice of the archangel, and with the trumpet call of God. And those who have died believing in Christ will rise first. After that, we who are still alive will be gathered up with them in the clouds to meet the Lord in the air. And we will be with the Lord forever" (4:16–17 NCV).

In the meantime, Paul says, believers should not be idle, but should work hard, live godly lives, and patiently endure the religious persecution they will most certainly encounter.

POINTS TO CONSIDER

Gallio was here. An ancient Greek inscription adds evidence that Paul was, in fact, at Corinth in about AD 51, when he wrote to the Thessalonians.

Acts 18 says the Corinthian Jews brought Paul up on charges before Gallio, governor of the southern Greek province of Achaia, and that Gallio threw the case out of court.

An inscription found at Delphi, a worship center in the region, confirms that Gallio was governor of Achaia from about AD 51–53. Gallio was also the brother of Seneca, a philosopher and a tutor of Nero. Seneca describes his brother as fair and likable. "No other human being is so charming to just one person as he is to all people," Seneca writes.

Paul misjudged the Second Coming. Paul not only preached that Jesus had come to save human beings from sin, but he also taught that Jesus was coming back. And from what Paul told the Thessalonians, he seemed certain the Second Coming would happen in his lifetime.

This is implied in the answer he gave to people wondering what would happen to Christians who died before Jesus returns: "We who are living when the Lord comes again will not go before those who have already died" (4:15 NCV).

Not only did Paul believe in the imminent return of Jesus, he managed to pass this sense of the approaching Second Coming on to his converts. Some believers apparently had gone so far as to quit working to wait for the Great Return (4:11–12; 2 Thessalonians 3:6–15).

Paul, however, tells the Thessalonians to get back to work and to remember that no one can predict when Jesus will return.

Later in Paul's ministry he realizes he will not live to see the Second Coming. "The time has come for me to leave this life," he writes to Timothy, his close friend (2 Timothy 4:6 NCV). When that moment arrives, Paul believes he will be raised to life and ushered into the presence of God. As he once explained to the Corinthians, to be absent from the body is to be present with the Lord (2 Corinthians 5:8).

FOR FURTHER STUDY

- To learn how the church at Thessalonica began, read Acts 17:1–10.

- For Paul's follow-up letter, read 2 Thessalonians.

- For Paul's most extensive statement about the return of Jesus, read 1 Corinthians 15.

2 Thessalonians

OBSESSED WITH THE SECOND COMING

Once people start thinking about Jesus coming back to earth at any moment and whisking them to heaven, it's hard to think about much else—especially if life is as tough as it was for the persecuted Thessalonians.

Preoccupation with the Second Coming can sidetrack Christians, however, as it did in Thessalonica. Instead of going out to spread good news that Jesus came, Christians hang out and wait for better news that he has come back. Some actually quit their jobs.

This sabotages the mission Jesus gave the church: "Be my witnesses" (Acts 1:8 NCV). Paul knows this, and in the first letter tells the believers to keep busy. In this second letter, he puts it more bluntly: "We hear that some people in your group refuse to work. They do nothing but busy themselves in other people's lives. We command those people and beg them in the Lord Jesus Christ to work quietly and earn their own food" (3:11–12 NCV).

To get their minds off the Second Coming, Paul reminds them of other end-time events that must come first. We don't know how the Thessalonians reacted to this, but in later centuries Christians became preoccupied with "signs of the times." They tried to figure out where they were on God's end-time timetable.

For those of us who know believers doing this, Paul says, "Do not treat them as enemies. Warn them as fellow believers" (3:15 NCV). And what exactly did Paul say kindly? "Work quietly" (3:12 NCV). Perhaps he also reminded them of what the angels told the disciples after Jesus ascended into heaven: "Men of Galilee, why are you standing here looking into the sky?" (Acts 1:11 NCV).

BACKGROUND

INFLUENTIAL PEOPLE

Paul, leading minister to the Gentile world, and founder of the congregation at Thessalonica and other major cities throughout the Roman Empire (1:1).

THEME

Sometime after Paul writes 1 Thessalonians, primarily to answer the church's questions about the Second Coming, Paul writes a second letter that arrives perhaps a few months later.

Excitement about the Lord's return has nearly consumed the believers. Part of the reason, perhaps, is because of Paul's teaching while he was in town, and his follow-up letter urging the Christians to remain alert and ready for Jesus' return. In addition, the believers are facing a lot of persecution—the violent kind that earlier had driven Paul out of town. These believers would have welcomed a quick escape to eternal bliss.

Paul, however, reminds them of events that must happen before the Lord returns. And he tells the believers to get on with their lives, sternly rebuking those who have quit work to await the Great Return.

POINTS OF INTEREST

Second Coming. Like 1 Thessalonians, the main reason Paul writes this letter is to clear up confusion about the Second Coming.

The return of Jesus is apparently all the Christians want to talk about. This excitement is likely fueled by Paul's earlier preaching on the subject, by his letter urging them to stay alert, and by a wave of anti-Christian persecution.

"The Man of Evil." To calm the believers down and get their minds focused on working in this world instead of anticipating the next, Paul

TIMELINE	BIBLE EVENTS	Paul's missionary journeys begin AD 46	Paul starts second missionary trip AD 50	Paul writes Thessalonians while in Corinth AD 51	Dates are approximate
	AD 40		**AD 45**		**AD 50**
	WORLD EVENTS	Jews expelled from Rome over controversy about "Chrestus" (probably "Christ") AD 49	China, Rome conduct trade via 4,000-mile-long Silk Road AD 50	Isthmian Games held at Corinth AD 51	

reminds them of his earlier teaching about events that will precede the Lord's coming.

"That day of the Lord will not come until the turning away from God happens and the Man of Evil, who is on his way to hell, appears. He will be against and put himself above any so-called god or anything that people worship . . . The Man of Evil will come by the power of Satan. He will have great power, and he will do many different false miracles, signs, and wonders. He will use every kind of evil to trick those who are lost" (2:3–4, 9–10 NCV).

The people of Thessalonica know exactly what Paul is talking about: "I told you when I was with you that all this would happen. Do you not remember?" (2:5 NCV). But we don't know what he's referring to. Bible experts have suggested several possibilities.

1. "The Man of Evil" may be an evil religious leader who is an antichrist, opposed to everything Jesus stands for. John refers to many antichrists (1 John 2:18).

2. He could be a wicked spiritual entity.

3. Or perhaps "the wicked one" refers to the Roman Empire, or to an emperor. If so, Paul would have had good reason not to be more specific in this public letter. One of the characteristics of end-time literature, a genre called apocalyptic, is that the writers often use code words that the recipients understand, but that no one else does. This allows writers to criticize powerful leaders without getting caught.

Persecution. The Christians of Thessalonica are suffering because they are Christians. Paul writes that he knows they are "being treated badly and are suffering many troubles" (1:4 NCV). It's probably the same kind of violence mixed with legal wrangling that had earlier forced Paul out of town (Acts 17:5–10).

These harsh conditions would have added fuel to the bonfire of hope for a speedy return of the Lord.

Christians not working. Since Christians were sure that Jesus was coming right away, some apparently saw no reason to plant crops, work in their shops, or repair their houses. In time, these people began to live off the generosity of others. Paul has stern words for these folks, and how to treat them. "We command you to stay away from any believer who refuses to work," he says. "You yourselves know that you should live as we live. We were not lazy when we were with you. And when we ate another person's food, we always paid for it . . . we gave you this rule: "Anyone who refuses to work should not eat" (3:6–10 NCV).

AUTHOR AND DATE

The letter begins by announcing that it comes from Paul and his associates, Timothy and Silas. It ends with Paul's signature: "I, Paul, end this letter now in my own handwriting" (3:17 NCV).

Some Bible scholars, however, suggest that one of Paul's associates may have written the letter on his behalf, perhaps after his death. They base this on the observation that the teaching about the Second Coming is different from that in the first letter. Also, the second letter is written in a more formal style, and it uses some terms that don't appear in any of Paul's other letters—such as the words translated "the Evil One" (2:3 NCV). Other scholars argue that the changes in the second letter reflect the changing situation in Thessalonica. For more on this, see "Second Coming, revised" in Points to Consider.

Because the two letters address the same topics, they were probably written about the same time, perhaps a few months apart. Paul likely wrote them during his two-year stay in Corinth, which began in about AD 50.

ON LOCATION

Thessalonica is a bustling trade town in northern Greece. The city profits from a port in the Thermatic Gulf of the Aegean Sea, and from its location on the Via Egnatia, an east-west Roman road that stretches across northern Greece and into Turkey, Paul writes the letter from Corinth, some 250 miles south. (See map in 1 Corinthians, page 384.)

7:00

8:00

9:00

0:00

1:00

Noon

1:00

2:00

3:00

4:00

5:00

6:00

7:00

8:00

9:00

0:00

POINTS TO CONSIDER

Siding with the prophets. When Paul says a wicked and God-insulting leader will come before Jesus returns, the apostle is confirming end-time prophecy from the Old Testament. Daniel speaks of an evil leader who will "say things against the God of gods" (11:36 NCV) and of "blasphemous things" (9:27 NCV) that will desecrate God's holy temple.

Jesus also spoke of this "blasphemous object" (Matthew 24:15 NCV), which may have been a prediction about the Roman destruction of the temple in AD 70 as well as a horror yet to come. John, writing in Revelation perhaps in the AD 90s, tells of a coming "beast" (13:5–8 NCV) who will claim to be God and who will rule the earth for a time. In the end, John says, the beast will be destroyed. Paul describes the death this way: "The Lord Jesus will kill him with the breath that comes from his mouth" (2:8 NCV).

This is a powerful description that connects Jesus to Creation. God "breathed the breath of life into the man's nose" (Genesis 2:7 NCV), and at some time in the future Jesus will breath the life out of "the wicked one."

Second Coming, revised. Paul's teaching about the Second Coming of Jesus is so different here than it is in 1 Thessalonians that some scholars doubt Paul wrote the second letter.

In 1 Thessalonians, Paul tries to prepare the church for the soon-approaching return of Jesus. He calms their anticipation by urging them to go about their lives, yet he cautions them to stay alert and be ready when Jesus comes (1 Thessalonians 5:4–8).

In 2 Thessalonians, however, Paul backpedals so much that he looks as though he's in full retreat. It's unclear if Paul was refuting that "the Lord has already come" (2:2 NCV) or that the coming was near. The original Greek could be translated either way. But whichever the case, Paul threw cold water on the anxious crowd by reminding them of his earlier teaching about the events that must precede the Second Coming.

We know very little about what these events are, but they involve the arrival of a mysterious entity or organization that Paul describes as "The Man of Evil" through whom "He will do many different false miracles, signs, and wonders" (2:9 NCV).

Paul probably didn't backpedal because he had changed his mind about the Second Coming. He probably saw that Second Coming fervor was getting out of hand in Thessalonica. And he realized he needed to calm the people down so they could get on with the business of living and serving God.

FOR FURTHER STUDY

- Read 1 Thessalonians, the letter Paul wrote the congregation first.

- To learn how the church at Thessalonica began, read Acts 17:1–10.

- For Paul's most extensive statement about the return of Jesus, read 1 Corinthians 15.

Sun
Mo:
Tue
We(
Thu
Frid
Satu
Sun
Moi
Tue
We(
Thu
Frid
Satu
Sun
Moi
Tue
We(

1 Timothy

TIPS ON HOW TO BE A PASTOR

Four years in Bible colleges, three years in seminary. That's the prescribed course of study for many ministers today. But for those interested in Paul's priorities for church leaders, there's a thirty-minute correspondence course: his two letters to Timothy, who is pastoring in Ephesus, and his one letter to Titus, on the island of Crete.

Timothy and Titus had each served several years of rigorous apprenticeship. They had accompanied Paul on some of his missionary trips, and they served as trusted emissaries who delivered his messages to churches and helped answer questions and defuse explosive situations. Timothy, for example, draws the unenviable assignment of delivering 1 Corinthians, Paul's letter to the troublesome congregation that hadn't bothered to discipline a member who was committing incest with his stepmother (1 Corinthians 4:17; 5:1).

> **FAMOUS LINES**
>
> • "The love of money is the root of all evil" (6:10 KJV).

Even after years of experience, both men receive continuing education on the basics of ministry, courtesy of their protective mentor. Because of these letters, we discover not only some of Paul's ministry fundamentals—such as resisting the temptation to get rich—we also learn that Paul believes older, seasoned ministers should gently share their wisdom with younger ones.

Paul supported the ministers in his care. Congregations can do the same.

BACKGROUND

INFLUENTIAL PEOPLE

Paul, traveling minister who covers some 10,000 miles and starts churches throughout the Roman Empire (1:1).

Timothy, one of Paul's most devoted traveling companions, whom Paul appoints to lead the church in Ephesus (1:2).

PLOT

When Paul leaves Ephesus to travel on to Macedonia in northern Greece, he assigns his associate, Timothy, to stay behind and lead the congregation. The Christians there are being confronted and confused by several religious teachings. Paul believes that Timothy can help the Ephesians sort out the truth and the lies.

Sometime later, perhaps while Paul is in Greece, he writes Timothy this letter giving guidance on a wide array of issues that surface in local congregations. These topics include conducting worship services, choosing church leaders, ministering to the poor, and even ministering to the rich.

POINTS OF INTEREST

Lots of advice for ministers. The three letters of 1 and 2 Timothy along with Titus are known as the Pastoral Letters because they contain Paul's advice to these two men who are pasturing churches.

False teachings. Based on what Paul writes, it seems that the Ephesians are grappling with at least three kinds of religious teaching, all of which are at odds with Christianity.

1. References to "stories that are not true and on long lists of names in family histories" (1:4 NCV) and to "teachers of the" (1:7 NCV) point to the Jews, who take great pride in their family tree. The "stories" may refer to Jewish legends, which are popular in Paul's day.

TIMELINE	**BIBLE EVENTS**	Paul arrives at Ephesus, staying more than 2 years AD 53	Paul imprisoned at Rome AD 60	Paul writes 1 Timothy, possibly after release from Rome AD 63	Paul executed, possibly after second imprisonment in Rome AD 67
		AD 50	**AD 60**		**AD 70**
	WORLD EVENTS	Rome burns; Nero blames Christians, launches persecution AD 64		Nero commits suicide AD 68	Dates are approximate

2. "They forbid people to marry and tell them not to eat certain foods" (4:3 NCV). This clue points to monklike ascetics who try to make themselves holy by controlling their bodies. But in the process, they treat important elements of God's good creation—such as sex and food—as though they are sinful. Some later Christian leaders fast so much that they do permanent damage to their digestive systems—among them, Protestant reformer Martin Luther.

> **DID YOU KNOW?**
>
> • Though Paul argues that Jewish laws have become obsolete, including the law of circumcision, he arranges the rite of circumcision for Timothy, whose mother is a Jew. Evidently, this is to help Timothy get along with the Jews. Paul adamantly refuses, however, to have another associate circumcised: Titus, a full-blooded Greek (Galatians 2:3–5).

3. "Stay away from foolish, useless talk" (6:20 NCV) implies that the second-century heresy of Gnosticism (from a word meaning "knowledge") is already getting started. Paul's Greek word for "smart" is *gnosis*. The Gnostics believe they have received from God unique knowledge about their true nature, and this knowledge guarantees them eternal life. Some Gnostics teach that nothing their bodies can do will affect the fate of their souls—so they do as they please. Others go to the opposite extreme, trying to strengthen their true spiritual nature by depriving the body of physical necessities.

Qualifications for church leaders. Among the ranks of church leadership, the highest standards are required of the officiating minister. Ministers must have a solid reputation, strong social skills, and be able to teach (3:2). Paul has nothing but harsh words for profiteering preachers who love money and "think that serving God is a way to get rich" (6:5 NCV).

Church officers who help the minister should be honest, generous, and firm believers in the teachings about Jesus. Before they are appointed to their position, "test them first" (3:10 NCV). This is not a job for new and struggling Christians.

AUTHOR AND DATE

The letter begins: "From Paul" (1:1 NCV). When Christian leaders in the early centuries referred to 1 Timothy, they identified it as the work of Paul. In fact, the reason the letter survives in the New Testament is because early Christians accepted it as Paul's. for arguments suggesting that someone else wrote it, see "Who wrote Timothy and Titus?" in Points to Consider.

Scholars aren't sure when Paul wrote the letter. Paul says that after the two visited Ephesus, he left Timothy behind and continued on to Greece without him (1:3). But this doesn't fit with the travels described in Acts; Timothy accompanied Paul to Greece (Acts 20:4).

Some suggest Paul wrote this letter after the events described in Acts. If so, Paul was released from imprisonment in Rome in about AD 62, then made a fourth missionary trip. During that trip, as the theory goes, Paul assigned Timothy to Ephesus, then was later arrested and sent to Rome again. This time he was executed in about AD 67, during Nero's persecution of Christians.

ON LOCATION

Paul addresses his letter to Timothy in Ephesus, apparently writing from the northern Greece province of Macedonia. (See map in 1 Corinthians, page 384.) Ephesus, a harbor town in western Turkey, is one of the largest cities in the Roman Empire. The town boasts a population of somewhere between 200,000 and 500,000. Ephesus is also a Roman seat of government, home to Rome's governor of Asia. In addition, the city is a famous center of worship to Artemis, a fertility goddess whose temple there is four times larger than the Parthenon in Athens.

1 Timothy Outline

Paul writes to Timothy (1:1–20).

Timothy has learned a lot from Paul during the many years they traveled together, starting churches throughout the eastern Mediterranean, and dealing with questions and problems that arise later. But now Timothy is on his own, pasturing the church in Ephesus. Paul loves this young man like a son; he continues to train and encourage him by offering advice about how to run the church.

"I asked you to stay longer in Ephesus when I went into Macedonia so you could command some people there to stop teaching false things," Paul reminds Timothy. "The purpose of this command is for people to have love, a love that comes from a pure heart and a good conscience and a true faith" (1:3, 5 NCV).

Early church worship service in a private home (2:1–3:16).

Paul gives his coworker, whom he addresses as "my child" (1:18 NCV), advice on more than how to cope with false teachings. Paul tutors him on the wide range of topics that any local church leader would confront: how to conduct worship services, how to choose church leaders, and how to minister to the different kinds of people in the church.

In church services, for example, Paul says, "I want the men everywhere to pray, lifting up their hands in a holy manner, without anger and arguments" (2:8 NCV). Paul also wants the people to dress modestly, remembering that they come together to focus on God, not to show off their wardrobes, jewelry, and makeover hairstyles.

Church leaders, Paul says, "must not give people a reason to criticize him, and he must have only one wife. He must be self-controlled, wise, respected by others, ready to welcome guests, and able to teach." In addition, the apostle says, they should "be gentle and peaceable, not loving money" (3:2, 3 NCV).

In advising young Timothy about ministering to various groups, Paul says, "Do not speak angrily to an older man, but plead with him as if he were your father" (5:1 NCV). In addition, Timothy is to treat older women "like mothers," and younger women as "like sisters" (5:2 NCV).

After packing a wealth of practical counsel into this short letter, Paul closes with a final request and a promise.

"Timothy, guard what God has trusted to you" he says. "Grace be with you" (6:20–21 NCV).

POINTS TO CONSIDER

Timothy, Paul's best friend. Though some scholars question that Paul wrote 1 and 2 Timothy. Paul's young associate was a prime candidate for the assignment in Ephesus and for the fatherly letters that came afterward.

Timothy was Paul's closest friend and a devoted associate who worked by his side among congregations in Turkey, Greece, and Italy. When believers of Thessalonica had questions about the second coming of Jesus, it was Timothy that Paul trusted to deliver his two letters and help resolve the confusion. And when Paul spent two years starting the church in Corinth, Timothy was at his side assisting in the preaching duties.

There's yet another reason Timothy was a logical choice to pastor the Ephesians. He was from the same Greek culture they were. Timothy grew up in Lystra, about 300 miles east of Ephesus. Yet Timothy also understood the Jewish community as well, because his mother and grandmother were Jews (Acts 16:1; 2 Timothy 1:5).

Who wrote Timothy and Titus? Some scholars doubt that Paul wrote the two letters to Timothy and the single letter to Titus. These scholars suggest that someone else penned the words after Paul died, perhaps drawing from his letters and sermons and applying them to later circumstances. This was a common and accepted practice among Jews and non-Jews of the time. (For more on this, see "Who wrote the letter?" in the Points to Consider section for Ephesians, page 413.)

One reason many Bible experts believe this is because some of Paul's pivotal ideas—such as those about faith, Jewish law, and righteousness—are treated differently in this letter. Here, for example, "faith" means Christianity. But in Paul's other letters, it describes a person's trusting relationship with Jesus.

Other scholars argue that Paul wrote the letters, as second-century church leaders testify. These Bible experts say that the differences in word use and the absence of themes important in Paul's other letter (such as the ministry of the Spirit, and freedom from Jewish law) confirm that Paul wrote these near the end of his ministry, perhaps ten to fifteen years after his first letters.

Women in the church. Paul told Timothy that women in church "should be silent and not be allowed to teach or to tell men what to do" (2:12). This is much the same message that Paul gave to the church in Corinth. Yet in congregations where there were no problems among the women, Paul puts no restriction on them. (See "Women, keep quiet in church," in the Points to Consider section of 1 Corinthians, page 384.)

FOR FURTHER STUDY

- To read about the founding of the church in Ephesus, turn to Acts 18:18–19:14.

- For insights into the Ephesus congregation by the turn of the first century, read Revelation 2:1–7.

- Paul gives further ministerial advice in the letters of 2 Timothy and Titus.

2 Timothy

THE LAST WORDS OF PAUL

When we know we're about to die, the last words we speak and the last actions we perform show what is most important to us.

The last we hear of Paul he's chained inside a Roman dungeon, awaiting execution. The imperial trial may still be underway, and if so, it's not going well.

Paul unrolls a strip of parchment, perhaps given to him by Luke, the only colleague in the area who hasn't abandoned him. Then Paul writes a letter to the man who is likely his best friend on earth, Timothy.

A preacher to the end, Paul repeats some of what he has said before: Don't be ashamed of the gospel. Don't be fooled by false teachings. Live like children of a holy and loving God. Timothy, who had traveled with Paul for many years, must have heard this a hundred times. But the words are important enough to Paul that he says them again.

> ### FAMOUS LINES
>
> • "I have fought the good fight, I have finished the race, I have kept the faith" (4:7 NKJV). *Paul's reflection on his life as he sits in prison, expecting to be executed soon.*

Paul's final action—his last known request—is one that any hospice nurse would understand: "Come to see me as soon as you can" (4:9). Paul wants to die in the company of those he loves.

In words and actions, Paul shows what is most important to him: the gospel he has preached, and the people he has loved.

BACKGROUND

INFLUENTIAL PEOPLE

Paul, traveling minister who starts churches throughout the Roman Empire, but who is now in jail awaiting execution (1:1).

Timothy, one of Paul's most devoted traveling companions, whom Paul appoints to lead the church in Ephesus (1:2).

THEME

The end is near for Paul, and he knows it. So he writes this, his last and most moving letter. He addresses it to Timothy, a young friend he thinks of as a son. Paul is not writing from the comfort of the house arrest described at the end of Acts. Though he's in Rome—as he was before—he now languishes in a cold dungeon, chained like a dangerous criminal.

Paul is lonely, having been abandoned by colleagues who apparently realize the hopelessness of his situation. He asks Timothy to come and be with him before his execution. He also warns his devoted friend that sufferings are bound to come his way too. Perhaps Paul is writing in the mid-60s, when Emperor Nero is having Christians killed throughout the empire—many in arenas, as blood-spectacle entertainment. But Paul urges Timothy to be brave and to cling to the hope of spending eternity with Jesus.

POINTS OF INTEREST

The intimate tone of the letter. Notice how personal the letter is—at times even private. Though Paul intends for the entire church of Ephesus to read it, and he refers briefly to false teachings, end times, and the traits of godly people, the aging apostle—perhaps now in his late 50s—is talking especially to Timothy. "You are like a dear child to me," Paul writes (1:2).

TIMELINE	BIBLE EVENTS	Paul imprisoned at Rome AD 60		Paul writes 1 Timothy, possibly after release from Rome AD 63	Paul writes 2 Timothy, possibly after another imprisonment in Rome AD 67
		AD 50	**AD 60**		**AD 70**
	WORLD EVENTS	Rome burns; Nero blames Christians, launches persecution AD 64			Dates are approximate
				Nero commits suicide AD 68	

The approaching death of Paul. This letter may be the last surviving words of Paul, for he is convinced he is about to die. Paul has already endured at least part of a trial—perhaps all of it (4:16). And he's not expecting to be released.

"Bound with chains like a criminal," Paul writes (2:9 NCV). He is further restricted, and humiliated, by having to wear a chain (1:16 NKJV).

But in a poignant and inspired moment, Paul expresses his incredible faith. "My life is being given as an offering to God, and the time has come for me to leave this life. I have fought the good fight, I have finished the race, I have kept the faith. Now, a crown is being held for me—a crown for being right with God" (4:6–8 NCV).

> ### DID YOU KNOW?
>
> • One of the oldest structures in Rome is Mamertine Prison, a dungeon carved out of solid rock 600 years before Christ. Early Christian writers say Paul was kept there before his execution.

Paul's request for Timothy to come. Like the last request of a dying man, Paul asks for his dearest friend to make a 1,000-mile journey across land and sea.

"I want very much to see you," Paul writes (1:4 NCV). "Do your best to come to me as soon as you can" (4:9 NCV). Most of Paul's other associates have deserted him, and he is obviously lonely. He is also cold, and apparently hungry for God's Word, for he kindly asks Timothy to "When I was in Troas, I left my coat there with Carpus. So when you come, bring it to me . . . along with my books, particularly the ones written on parchment" (4:13 NCV).

A call to courage. Timothy is going to face persecution, Paul says he is certain of that. "But you should control yourself at all times, accept troubles, do the work of telling the Good News, and complete all the duties of a servant of God" (4:5 NCV). This certainly would have frightened Timothy. But Paul adds a comforting note of assurance: "You then, Timothy, my child, be strong in the grace we have in Christ Jesus" (2:1 NCV). Everyone who remains faithful to Jesus, Paul says, will rule for an eternity with the Lord (2:11).

AUTHOR AND DATE

The letter is from Paul, in a jail at Rome (1:1, 16–17). He is writing to his young friend Timothy, whom he appointed to lead the church in Ephesus. Some scholars say that this letter, like 1 Timothy and Titus, was written a generation after Paul, perhaps to address Christian persecution going on at that time. (See "Who wrote Timothy and Titus?" in the Points to Consider section of 1 Timothy, page 445.) Others argue that the deeply personal nature of this letter confirms what early church leaders believed—that Paul wrote it.

It's unclear exactly when Paul wrote the letter. One popular theory is that Paul was released from the Roman imprisonment described at the end of Acts. But after continuing his missionary work he was again arrested, taken to Rome, tried during Nero's crackdown on Christians, and executed in about AD 67.

ON LOCATION

Paul writes from a jail in Rome. (See map in Acts, page 362.) He addresses the letter to Timothy, pastor of the church in Ephesus, a major Roman city about 1,000 miles east, along the Mediterranean coast of Turkey.

2 TIMOTHY OUTLINE

Paul writes his last known letter (3:10–4:18).

As death approaches, the elderly and imprisoned Paul sits alone with his memories.

"Timothy," he writes, "a dear child to me" (1:2 NCV). Paul says he remembers a time when Timothy cried, and Paul remembers laying hands on this young friend, blessing him for ministry. "I want very much to see you," Paul pleads, "so I can be filled with joy" (1:4 NCV).

A wave of anti-Christian sentiment and persecution is apparently sweeping across the empire, forcing the more timid believers to keep their faith a secret. But Paul pushes Timothy toward courage and boldness: "So do not be ashamed to tell people about our Lord Jesus, and do not be ashamed of me, in prison for the Lord" (1:8 NCV).

"Everyone who wants to live as God desires, in Christ Jesus, will be persecuted," Paul explains (3:12 NCV). But how people respond to this suffering, Paul says, will determine our destiny: "If we say we don't know him, he will say he doesn't know us." On the other hand, "If we died with him, we will also live with him" (2:11–12 NCV).

"Come to me as soon as you can," Paul asks.

Then, drawing the letter to a close, Paul expresses confidence in the Lord even in the face of death. "The first time I defended myself, no one helped me. . . But the Lord stayed with me and gave me strength so I could fully tell the Good News to all those who are not Jews. . . he will bring me safely to his heavenly kingdom. Glory forever and ever be the Lord's. Amen (4:16–18 NCV).

POINTS TO CONSIDER

Roman persecution was real. The violent persecution that Paul describes in this letter matches what Roman historians said about how the government treated Christians.

Paul speaks of once being spared from "lion's mouth" (4:17 NCV) and "fought wild animals in Ephesus" (1 Corinthians 15:32 NCV). In both cases, Paul may have been speaking figuratively. But for many Christians during Nero's wave of terror in the mid-60s, there was nothing metaphorical about the wild beasts and executioners they faced in Roman arenas.

Historian Tacitus, writing about the fire that consumed two-thirds of Rome in AD 64, expresses his sentiments toward the "detestable superstition" of Christians—whom Nero blamed for starting the fire. Yet even Tacitus felt that Nero's tortures were excessive. The historian reports that some Christians were covered with fresh animal skins, then torn apart by starving dogs. Other believers were nailed to crosses, or were burned alive.

Even Nero's suicide in AD 68 didn't end the persecution. In the decades that followed, the oppression came and went, like a tide rolling in and out. Pliny the Younger, Roman governor of a territory near Timothy's church in Ephesus, revealed as much in a report he sent to Emperor Trojan in AD 112. Pliny said he had tried many people accused of being Christian. "I asked them whether they were Christians, and if they confessed, I ordered them executed."

The last days, 2,000 years ago. Paul wrote about "the last days" as though they were just around the corner. He said that in those final days of human history, before Jesus returns, "people will love themselves, love money, brag, and be proud. They will say evil things against others and will not obey their parents or be thankful or be the kind of people God wants. They will not love others, will refuse to forgive, will gossip, and will not control themselves. They will be cruel, will hate what is good, will turn against their friends, and will do foolish things without thinking" (3:1–3 NCV).

The list goes on.

Then Paul told Timothy, "Stay away from those people" (3:5 NCV), as though Timothy would witness the last days.

Was Paul wrong?

If Paul expected Jesus to return within a few years, then he was wrong about that. But throughout the Old and New Testaments, "the last days" was a phrase that meant more than the months or years just before the Second Coming. It also meant "the age of the Messiah." The birth of Jesus became not only the event around which the human race built its calendar; that birthday also marked the beginning of the end of God's plan to save the world from sin.

When will God finish what he started?

Only the Father knows," Jesus said (Matthew 24:36).

FOR FURTHER STUDY

• Paul gives more advice to ministers in the letters of 1 Timothy and Titus.

MINISTERING TO LIARS AND LAZY GLUTTONS

Some pastors *feel* as if they're ministering to a congregation of two-faced folk. In the case of Titus's church, however, this was widely assumed to be true.

Paul quotes one of Crete's own highly respected writers and teachers as saying, "Cretans are always liars, evil animals, and lazy people who do nothing but eat" (1:12 NCV). Ancient Greek writings confirm this snake's-eye view of Cretans, for in Greek, "cretanize" is a verb that means "to lie."

Paul assigns Titus to organize churches among these people, ironically giving him an order that must have sounded like an oxymoron: appoint as church leaders Cretans who "must not be guilty of doing wrong" (1:6 NCV).

FAMOUS LINES

• "Cretans are always liars, evil beasts, lazy gluttons" (1:12 NKJV). *The words of a Cretan writer and prophet, whom Paul quotes apparently to warn Titus that ministry in Crete will be a challenge.*

The apostle and his associate know the reputation of the Cretans, and that it's deserved (see "Paul slanders the Cretans" in Points to Consider). But the ministers also apparently remember what Jesus said when religious folks scolded him for hobnobbing with liars, crooks, other shady characters: "The Son of Man came to find lost people and save them" (Luke 19:10 NCV).

Paul reminds Titus that Jesus can make a difference for people everywhere, even on Crete, because Jesus made a difference in them: "We also were foolish. We did not obey, we were wrong . . . People hated us, and we hated each other . . . Being made right with God by his grace, we could have the hope of receiving the life that never ends" (3:3, 7 NCV).

BACKGROUND

INFLUENTIAL PEOPLE

Paul, traveling minister who covers some 10,000 miles and starts churches throughout the Roman Empire (1:1).

Titus, one of Paul's non-Jewish traveling companions, whom Paul appoints to organize the churches on the island of Crete (1:4).

THEME

During one of his missionary trips, Paul visits the island of Crete, south of Greece. Paul feels the need to continue his journey, but he leaves behind one of his traveling associates, Titus, "so you could finish doing the things that still needed to be done and so you could appoint elders in every town, as I directed you" (1:5 NCV).

Sometime later, Paul writes this short letter to Titus. Paul may have written about the same time he wrote 1 Timothy, after assigning Timothy to the church in Ephesus. Both letters cover much the same material. Paul instructs Titus in the qualities that he should look for when selecting church leaders. Paul also tells Titus how to advise different groups of people in the church. Older women, for example, "not speaking against others or enslaved to too much wine" (2:3 NCV).

Paul closes the three-chapter letter by urging Titus to insist that the people get along with one another and get away from false teachers.

POINTS OF INTEREST

Advice for a minister. This letter is a seasoned minister's advice to a younger minister. Bible experts call the three letters of 1 and 2 Timothy and Titus the Pastoral Letters, because they contain Paul's counsel to these two men who were once his traveling associates but who are now pasturing churches.

TIMELINE	BIBLE EVENTS	Dates are approximate		Paul writes Titus, possibly after release from Rome AD 63	Paul executed, possibly after second imprisonment in Rome AD 67
		Paul imprisoned at Rome AD 60			
		AD 50	**AD 60**		**AD 70**
	WORLD EVENTS	Rome burns; Nero blames Christians, launches persecution AD 64		Nero commits suicide AD 68	Rome destroys Jerusalem and temple AD 70

Qualifications for church leaders. Part of Titus's assignment in Crete is to choose leaders for each church on the island. Because Paul knows that a bad leader could kill a congregation, he gives Titus a list of qualifications. Church leaders "must not be guilty of doing wrong, must have only one wife, and must have believing children. They must not be known as children who are wild and do not cooperate" (1:6 NCV). In addition, Paul says, church officials "must not be guilty of doing wrong, being selfish, or becoming angry quickly. They must not drink too much wine, like to fight, or try to get rich by cheating others. Overseers must be ready to welcome guests, love what is good, be wise, live right, and be holy and self-controlled" (1:7–8 NCV).

> **DID YOU KNOW?**
>
> • Half a million people live in Crete today, and most consider themselves members of the Orthodox Church of Crete, a branch of the Greek Orthodox Church. There are more than 3,000 Orthodox churches on the island.

False teachings. Titus faced some of the same kinds of religious competition that Timothy does in Ephesus. "Stay away from those who have foolish arguments and talk about useless family histories," Paul says. "And argue and quarrel about the law. Such arguments are useless and senseless" (3:9 NCV; this advice is similar to 1 Timothy 1:4, 7). Paul is apparently talking about Jewish Christians, many of whom take great pride in their family tree and believe that all Christians—even non-Jews—should obey the Jewish laws that God gave to Moses. Paul teaches that the age of the Law came to an end when Jesus was sacrificed for the sins of humanity (Colossians 2:14).

AUTHOR AND DATE

The letter is written "From Paul" (1:1 NCV) to Titus, who is directing the work of several churches in Crete. Some scholars, however, suggest that one of Paul's associates wrote the letter after Paul died, drawing from the apostle's letters and sermons, then applying the messages to problems that developed later in Crete. (For arguments about who wrote the letter, turn to "Who wrote Timothy and Titus?" in the Points to Consider section of 1 Timothy, page 445.)

It's uncertain when the letter was written. There's no mention of Paul visiting Crete, either in the stories of Acts or in any of his letters outside this one. For this reason, some suggest Paul wrote the letter after the events described in Acts. If so, Paul was released from imprisonment in Rome in about AD 62, then made a fourth missionary trip. During that trip Paul likely assigned Titus to Crete, then was later arrested and sent to Rome again. This time Paul was executed in about AD 67, during Nero's persecution of Christians.

ON LOCATION

Paul addresses his letter to Titus, who is organizing churches on the island of Crete, some 100 miles south of Greece. (See map in Galatians, page 404.) The island is about 150 miles east to west, and 35 miles north to south—in square miles it's about the size of Rhode Island. This is a short-term assignment for Titus. Paul says he will send a replacement soon and that he wants Titus to join him in Nicopolis, a city on the western coast of Greece.

TITUS OUTLINE

Titus teaches a congregation in Crete (2:1–2:11).

After Paul arrives on the island of Crete and starts churches in several cities, he decides to move on. But he assigns Titus, one of his associates, to stay behind long enough to appoint church leaders and to clear up confusion about some false teachings that quickly begin to threaten the churches.

Paul keeps in contact with Titus by letter, advising him how to choose good leaders and how to fight teachings that undermine Christianity.

Church leaders, Paul said, should have a solid reputation and a friendly disposition. And these leaders should be in full agreement with the core teachings of Paul, which emphasize that salvation comes through faith in Jesus—not through obeying Jewish laws.

Paul suggests a two-prong attack against false teachings.

First he urges Titus to fight false teachings with true teachings: "You must tell everyone what to do to follow the true teaching" (2:1 NCV). Paul then explains how Titus can measure his effectiveness: faith in Jesus should begin expressing itself in the lives of the people. Elderly men will become more patient, elderly women will give up gossiping, young women will become more kind, and young men will learn self-control.

Second, Paul tells Titus to stay away from false teachers who stir up trouble in the church. "After a first and second warning, avoid someone who causes arguments. You can know that such people are evil and sinful; their own sins prove them wrong" (3:10–11 NCV).

Paul concludes with the same prayer that ends many of his letters: "Grace be with you all."

Sun
Mo
Tue
We
Thu
Fri
Sat
Sun
Mo
Tue
We
Thu
Fri
Sat
Sun
Mo
Tue
We

POINTS TO CONSIDER

Paul's teaching: Obey rulers. The writer's choice of words and teachings suggest to some scholars that Paul didn't write this letter. And the implied well-developed organizational structure of the church suggests that the writing took place decades after Paul, when the church began growing more institutionalized. Yet some of the core material in Titus repeats what Paul said in other letters.

For example, Paul told Titus, "Remind the believers to yield to the authority of rulers and government leaders, to obey them, to be ready to do good" (3:1 NCV). Paul said the same thing to Christians in Rome, in a letter that most scholars agree is genuinely his (Romans 13:1–2).

Paul slanders the Cretans. "Stupid, vulgar, or insensitive person." These are modern definitions of a *cretin*. Paul offered his own similar definition of Cretans by quoting a couplet from the sixth century BC poet and prophet Epimenides: "Cretans are always liars, evil animals, and lazy people who do nothing but eat" (1:12 NCV). To this poetic verse, Paul adds a nod: "The words that prophet said are true" (1:13 NCV).

Why would Paul slander the very people he says he's trying to help?

Perhaps Paul said what he did because the islanders had earned their bad reputation, and Paul didn't want Titus to think that ministry problems in Crete were the fault of the minister.

A thousand years earlier, Crete had been famous for its skilled architects and engineers; Greeks traveled there to study the architecture. But later, business moved elsewhere and Crete became infamous for harboring pirates and mercenaries.

FOR FURTHER STUDY

- For more of Paul's advice to a minister, read 1 and 2 Timothy. The letter to Titus is so much like 1 Timothy that both may have been written about the same time.

Philemon

A RUNAWAY SLAVE TURNS HIMSELF IN

Paul has a gift for being politically incorrect on social issues.

Take slavery, the subject of his letter to a Christian slave owner named Philemon. Paul is as out of sync with our day as he is with his own.

We want him to take a stand against slavery. We want to hear him tell Philemon to free the runaway slave Onesimus—and any other slaves he has.

On the other hand, the people of Paul's day would have been shocked at how freely he associates with slaves. And they would have taken him to task for insisting that everyone deserves equal treatment, slave or free. After all, they would argue, how could any slave owner treat a slave as if he's free? Would a man work your fields all day, every day, for nothing but room and board? And could you snatch a citizen out of his home and sell him for a profit?

The answer seems obvious. You can't treat slaves as though they're free until you free them—which is exactly what Paul wants Christians to discover, and what he wants Philemon to do to Onesimus.

Two thousand years later humanity has made progress. Most of our cultures have gotten rid of slavery. Yet that's just a mile marker along the road that Paul mapped out for us. He's pointing us farther up the hill, to equality.

BACKGROUND

INFLUENTIAL PEOPLE

Paul, traveling minister who starts churches throughout the Roman Empire and who advises even churches he has not started—such as the one in Colossae (1:1).

Philemon, a Christian slave owner, master of Onesimus, and one in whose home the Colossians meet for church services (1:1).

Onesimus, runaway slave converted by Paul and sent back to his master (1:10).

THEME

Onesimus, a runaway slave, meets Paul and converts to Christianity. Paul, consistent with his teaching in several letters, convinces Onesimus to return to his slave owner, Philemon.

Paul wields influence over Philemon, a church leader, and he uses it on behalf of Onesimum. From jail in an unnamed city—perhaps Rome—Paul writes a short but gripping letter for Onesimus to take to Philemon. In this letter Paul asks Philemon to receive the slave in kindness. Paul also hints—from the letter's beginning to its end—that Philemon should free Onesimus so he can help Paul.

POINTS OF INTEREST

A masterpiece of tactful persuasion. Paul doesn't come right out and ask Philemon to free Onesimus. But Philemon would likely have realized that this is what Paul wanted. The pressure Paul applies, though subtle, is certainly not gentle. It's powerful and compelling. Consider these seven pressure points:

1. Paul compliments Philemon on his growing faith in Jesus and his "love you have for all God's holy people" (5 NCV)—slaves included.

TIMELINE	BIBLE EVENTS	Dates are approximate		Paul's missionary journeys begin		Paul writes Philemon, during Rome imprisonment	
			Paul converts				
			⌐----- AD 35	⌐------------ AD 46		⌐---------------- AD 60	
		AD 30	**AD 40**	**AD 50**	**AD 60**	**AD 70**	**AD 80**
	WORLD EVENTS		100-year anniversary of Spartacus's doomed slave revolt AD 28	Buddhism of India introduced to China AD 58 -------		6,000 captured Jewish rebels become Nero's slave labor force AD 67	

2. "I wanted to keep him [Onesimums] here with me so that in your place he might help me," Paul writes. "But I did not want to do anything without asking you first so that any good you do for me will be because you want to do it, not because I forced you" (13–14 NCV). The implication is that Paul, as an apostle, has the authority to order Philemon, a church leader, to free Onesimus and return him to Paul's side.

3. "No longer as a slave, but better than a slave, as a loved brother," Paul adds. "Welcome Onesimus as you would welcome me" (16–17 NCV). Certainly Philemon would not punish a visiting Paul as he would a runaway slave.

4. Paul says he will pay back anything Onesimum may have taken to finance his escape, "charge that to me," Paul says, adding, "you owe me for your own life" (18–19 NCV). Paul apparently converted Philemon. The implication is that Philemon owes Paul, and in gratitude should write off any debt.

> **DID YOU KNOW?**
>
> • The Old Testament says that Jews can sell themselves into slavery to other Jews. But the law requires that all such slaves be freed every seventh year (Exodus 21:2).

5. This is not a private letter. It's to Philemon and "the church that meets in your home" (2 NCV). Others will read it and realize what Paul is asking Philemon to do—peer pressure at its finest.

6. When Paul gets out of jail, he plans to visit Philemon (22). This will be one awkward meeting if Onesimus is not free by then.

7. Paul is not alone in asking for kindness on behalf of the slave. Paul sends greetings from four associates, including Mark and Luke, implying that they support his request.

A lighthearted play on words. To lighten up the deadly serious topic of runaway slaves, Paul makes a play on words. The slave's name, Onesimus, means "useful." Paul acknowledges that Onesimus caused trouble for Philemon, the slave owner. But Paul argues that things are different now: "In the past he was useless to you, but now he has become useful for both you and me" (11 NCV).

AUTHOR AND DATE

"From Paul, a prisoner of Christ Jesus . . . to Philemon . . . and to the church that meets in your home" (1–2 NCV). Philemon lived in Colossae, in western Turkey.

It's uncertain when and where Paul wrote, though some ancient manuscripts add a postscript saying he wrote from Rome during his two-year imprisonment, which started in about AD 60. Some scholars doubt this. They argue that Rome, 1,000 miles from Colossae, is a long way for a runaway slave with limited resources. They suggest Paul wrote from a closer jail, perhaps in nearby Ephesus.

ON LOCATION

Philemon and Onesimus live in Colossae, about a weeklong trip east of Ephesus, Turkey (Colossians 4:9). (See map in Acts, page 362.)

PHILEMON OUTLINE

A runaway slave returns to his master (1–25).

Onesimus, a slave living in western Turkey, gets a chance to run away—and he takes it. During his flight to freedom, however, who does he run into but Paul, the apostle who teaches, "Slaves, obey your masters here on earth" (Ephesians 6:5 NCV). Paul converts Onesimus to Christianity, then convinces him to return to his master, Philemon, a church leader in Colossae.

Fortunately for Onesimus, Paul also teaches that slave owners should reciprocate, treating slaves with respect, and keeping in mind that "the One who is your Master and their Master is in heaven, and he treats everyone alike" (Ephesians 6:9 NCV).

Paul, writing from prison somewhere, sends Onesimus home with a letter to Philemon. "I am sending him back to you, and with him I am sending my own heart," Paul writes. "I wanted to keep him with me" (12–13 NCV). That's a strong hint for Philemon to free Onesimus.

The apostle promises to pay back anything Onesimus may have taken before leaving. Then Paul asks Philemon to welcome Onesimus not as a slave, but "as you would welcome me" (17 NCV).

Without actually using the words, Paul pleads for Philemon to send Onesimus back to him as a free man.

══ POINTS TO CONSIDER ══

Bishop Onesimus. About fifty years after Paul, a church leader named Ignatius wrote a letter to Bishop Onesimus, leader of the church in Ephesus.

It's uncertain if this bishop is the same slave who once lived in nearby Colossae. But it is possible. If Paul wrote the letters of Ephesians, Colossians, and Philemon all during his imprisonment in Rome—as many believe—the Ephesian people may have met Onesimus while he was on his way back to his master. This is quite possible because Onesimus traveled with Tychicus, who delivered the letters of Ephesians and Colossians (Ephesians 6:21; Colossians 4:7–9).

Many scholars who doubt that Paul wrote Philemon from Rome suspect he wrote from jail in Ephesus. If so, the Ephesians

Sun
Mon
Tue
Wed
Thu
Frid
Satu
Sun
Mon
Tue
Wed
Thu
Frid
Satu
Sun
Mon
Tue
Wed

would have become acquainted with Onesimus during his conversion and perhaps after his return to Paul, if Philemon took the hints and freed him.

Paul's stand on slavery. Though Paul never outright said slavery is acceptable, he never condemned it, either. And when a runaway slave showed up, Paul converted him to Christianity and then returned him to his slave owner. Runaway slaves who returned were not usually welcomed with a hug. They were punished, sometimes executed, as an example to others.

The apostle's decision to send Onesimus back not only put the slave at risk; it seemed to condone slavery, and it certainly set back any movement that would have outlawed this flesh-peddling institution. It took nearly 1,000 years for the church to discover that there's nothing Christian about slavery. In the meantime, slaves served church members, ministers, and congregations.

Paul wasn't interested in starting a slave-liberating revolution, at least not from the outside in. What he called for, however, would eventually accomplish this by working from the inside out.

As he told the Ephesians, "Slaves, obey your masters here on earth with fear and respect and from a sincere heart, just as you obey Christ. You must do this not only while they are watching you, to please them. With all your heart you must do what God wants as people who are obeying Christ" (Ephesians 6:5–6 NCV). And for slave owners Paul offered these instructions: "Masters, in the same way, be good to your slaves. Do not threaten them. Remember that the One who is your Master and their Master is in heaven, and he treats everyone alike" (Ephesians 6:9 NCV).

Instead of changing the system that would influence people, Paul changed people who would influence the system.

For Further Study

- For more on Paul's view of slavery, read 1 Corinthians 12:12–31; Galatians 3:23–4:7; Ephesians 6:5–9; Colossians 3:11–4:1; Titus 2:9–10.

Hebrews

ADVICE FOR CHRISTIANS ABOUT TO GIVE UP

Hebrews is a book for potential Christian dropouts.

In a first-pass read, it looks as if the unidentified writer has targeted only Jewish Christians on the verge of returning to their spiritual roots: Judaism. The writer certainly has targeted these people, because in this, the longest sustained argument in the Bible, he presents a staggering array of evidence to convince them that Jesus Christ—and faith in him—fulfills God's promises to Israel. He says that the old covenant, or agreement between God and Israel, has given way to the new agreement that Jeremiah predicted. God's law written on scrolls has been replaced by God's law written on the human heart. And animal sacrifices for sin have become obsolete because of the sacrificial death of God's Son.

> ### FAMOUS LINES
>
> • "Jesus Christ is the same yesterday, today, and forever" (13:8 NCV).
>
> • "Faith means being sure of the things we hope for and knowing that something is real even if we do not see it" (11:1 NCV).

This is a book for Jewish Christians, all right. But it's also a book for any other Christians facing obstacles to their faith: temptations, frustrations, disenchantment. The second thoughts that first-century Jewish Christians experienced were likely generated by Roman and orthodox Jews who were persecuting them.

Whatever the obstacle, the writer to Hebrews encourages Christians to keep their eyes on the finish line. "We should remove from our lives anything that would get in the way," he says. "So let us run the race that is before us and never give up. Let us look only to Jesus, . . . sitting at the right side of God's throne" (12:1–2 NCV).

BACKGROUND

INFLUENTIAL PEOPLE

Jesus, God's Son, who establishes a new agreement between God and humanity—a covenant better than the one instituted by Moses and practiced in the temple (2:9).

THEME

About a generation after Jesus' resurrection, some Jewish Christian are beginning to abandon the early Christian movement and return to the Jewish faith, perhaps because of persecution. To win back their loyalty, an unidentified church leader writes the book of Hebrews, an essay arguing that faith in Christ is better than Judaism.

The writer makes three main points: (1) Jesus is superior to Old Testament heroes, including the prophets, Moses, and even the angels. (2) Jesus is superior to the high priest, who serves and intermediary between God and humanity. (3) Jesus is a better sacrifice than any animal offered on an altar.

Further, the writer adds, Jesus has rendered obsolete the old agreement, which was based on rules preserved on the pages of the first five books in the Bible. In its place is a new agreement, based on laws God has written onto the human heart. For Jewish Christians, the writer explains, there is no turning back—for there is nothing to turn back to.

POINTS OF INTEREST

Old Testament quotes. To convince Jewish Christians that the Christian faith is both God's idea and an outgrowth of Judaism, the writer quotes about forty passages of the Old Testament to support his arguments.

For example, he says animal sacrifice isn't what pleased God. Animal

				Dates are approximate
TIMELINE	**BIBLE EVENTS**		Unidentified author writes Hebrews ----- AD 65	
		AD 60	**AD 70**	**AD 80**	**AD 90**
	WORLD EVENTS		Jews in Israel revolt ----- AD 66 Rome burns; Christians blamed, persecuted AD 64	Rome destroys Jerusalem and temple AD 70	Roman bishop, Clement, quotes Hebrews AD 95 ---------

sacrifice was simply a means to an end—a way to remind people that sin is wrong. To prove his point, he quotes Psalm 40:6 NCV "You do not want sacrifices and offerings." That passage goes on to reveal that what God really wants is for people to trust and obey him.

Jesus, the better way. Notice that the writer compares Jesus to many people and practices revered in Judaism. Notice, too, that Jesus always comes out the winner.

Better than angels, prophets, Moses. Angels worship him (1:6). Prophets are only spokespersons for God; Jesus is God's Son (1:1–2). Moses told God's people what the future would be like; Jesus is in charge of the future (3:5–6).

Better than a high priest. High priests intercede for the people in a temple; Jesus intercedes in heaven (7:23–8:1). High priests have sinned; Jesus has not (4:15).

Better than animal sacrifices. An animal is usually sacrificed for one sin, one person; Jesus was sacrificed for all the sins of all people (9:26).

> ### DID YOU KNOW?
>
> • "Remember to welcome strangers, because some who have done this have welcomed angels without knowing it" (13:2 NCV). Examples from the Bible include Abraham (Genesis 18), Gideon (Judges 6), and Manoah (Judges 13).
>
> • The sacrifice of Jesus ended the need for people to offer sacrifices to God. Forty years later, Rome forcibly terminated the Jewish sacrificial system by destroying the temple, which has never been rebuilt. A 1,300-year-old mosque now sits on the Jerusalem hilltop where Jews once worshiped.

AUTHOR AND DATE

The writer doesn't identify himself. In the mid-century, some Christian leaders attributed the book to Paul. But it is unlikely that Paul wrote it. He identified himself in his other letters, and he wrote in a simpler style. Hebrews was likely written by someone who, unlike Paul, had never seen Jesus but who had heard about the Lord from eyewitnesses (2:3).

Two strong candidates for authorship are Barnabas and Apollos, associates of Paul. As early as AD 200, a theologian named Tertullian quoted from Hebrews, which he identified as "an epistle to the Hebrews under the name of Barnabas." Barnabas was co pastor with Paul at a church in Antioch, Syria. Later, Barnabas served as a missionary who preached throughout the Eastern Mediterranean. Apollos was "a good speaker who knew the Scriptures well" (Acts 18:24 NCV). It would take a well-educated Jew to write Hebrews, which is among the most sophisticated writing in the New Testament and which is so intimately connected to the Jewish Scripture.

The date of the writing is also uncertain. It was likely written sometime in the AD 60s, as the second generation of Christians began to emerge as church leaders. The book's many references to the Jewish temple and sacrificial system suggest the writer completed it before AD 70—when Rome destroyed the temple, bringing the sacrificial era to an abrupt halt. Clement, a church leader in Rome, quoted several sections of the book in a letter he wrote in AD 95.

ON LOCATION

The message seems addressed to Christians all over the Roman Empire, but especially those of Jewish heritage. The writer sends greetings from believers in Italy, suggesting he lived there, perhaps in Rome (13:24). This possibility is strengthened by the fact that in AD 95, Clement, bishop of Rome, quoted from the book. (See map in Acts, page 362.)

HEBREWS OUTLINE

Jesus at the right side of the Father (1:1–14).

To Jewish Christians on the verge of quitting Christianity and returning to Judaism, the writer of Hebrews reminds them of what they will be leaving.

Jesus, the writer explains, is superior to prophets, Moses, and even angels. "When the Son made people clean from their sins, he sat down at the right side of God, the Great One in heaven . . . God never said this to an angel: "Sit by me at my right side" (1:3,13 NCV).

Hebrews also presents Jesus as superior to any high priest who had ever interceded to God for the people. Jesus doesn't need to address God through rituals at a temple; Jesus has direct access to God in heaven.

The sacrifice for sins (10:1–18).

Jews who want forgiveness offer an animal sacrifice. This is not to placate an angry God, but to give the people a means of forgiveness and a graphic reminder of the seriousness of sin. When Jews lay their hands on the head of an innocent sheep—symbolizing the atonement that the animal will make for their sin—and when the people see the blood drain out of the animal, the life-and-death seriousness of sin becomes dramatically real.

"Life of the body is in the blood," God told Moses, "and I have given you rules for pouring that blood on the altar to remove your sins so you will belong to the LORD" (Leviticus 17:11 NCV).

But as promised through the prophets, God establishes a new means of forgiveness. Jesus died as the final sacrifice, replacing the sacrificial system. "With one sacrifice," Hebrews explains, "he [Jesus] made perfect forever those who are being made holy" (10:14 NCV).

Abraham comes to Canaan, proving his faith (11:1–40).

Faith means being sure of the things we hope for and knowing that something is real even if we do not see it," Hebrews says. "Faith is the reason we remember great people who lived in the past" (11:1–2 NCV).

Drawing from a huge cast of Old Testament heroes, the writer proves his point that God is pleased by the trust that people have in him. Faith

Sun
Mon
Tues
Wed
Thu
Frid
Satu
Sun
Mon
Tues
Wed
Thu
Frid
Satu
Sun
Mon
Tues
Wed

is more important to God than the Jewish rituals ever were—even before they became obsolete. Before Israel had a system of laws and religious rituals, the faith of godly men and women gave God immense pleasure—people like Abel, Noah, Abraham, Sarah, Isaac, Jacob, and Moses.

The writer urges his readers to hold firmly to their faith in God's Son: "Those who are right with me will live by faith" (10:38 NCV).

Points to Consider

The promised new covenant. Jews were understandably reluctant to abandon the laws and rituals prescribed in their holy Scriptures—rules that God Himself had given through Moses, their most revered prophet. The Law, as the rules are called, represented Israel's part of an agreement God made with them. If the Jews obeyed these laws, then God would protect and bless their nation.

That's a big "if." Throughout Israel's long history, the people repeatedly broke the Law—sometimes abandoning it entirely, when godless kings reigned.

"I will make a new agreement with the people of Israel and the people of Judah," God said through the prophet Jeremiah. "It will not be like the agreement I made with their ancestors when I took them by the hand to bring them out of Egypt.

I was a husband to them, but they broke that agreement," says the LORD. "This is the agreement I will make with the people of Israel at that time," says the LORD: "I will put my teachings in their minds and write them on their hearts. I will be their God, and they will be my people" (Jeremiah 31:31–33 NCV).

The writer of Hebrews explains that "God called this a new agreement, so he has made the first agreement old. And anything that is old and worn out is ready to disappear" (8:13 NCV). As Moses delivered the first agreement to Israel, Jesus delivered the new one: "Those who are called by God can now receive the blessings he has promised, blessings that will last forever. They can have those things because Christ died so that the people who lived under the first agreement could be set free from sin" (9:15 NCV).

No second chance? To Jewish Christians thinking about returning to Judaism, the writer of Hebrews offers an ominous warning. He says that if Christians turn their backs on Jesus, "It is impossible to bring them back to a changed life again." To do so, he explains is, "nailing the Son of God to a cross again and are shaming him in front of others" (6:6 NCV).

This is a passage that has mystified Bible scholars.

To the casual reader, the words can sound like a minister's last, desperate, exaggerated attempt to keep a group of members from leaving the church: "Walk through that door and you've forever walked out of God's kingdom!"

Some scholars take the passage literally, insisting that Christians who recant faith in Jesus are hopelessly lost. Other scholars suggest that backsliders are people who have merely sampled Christianity but have never experienced a genuine faith in Jesus.

Still others argue that the believer's faith is authentic, yet so is that person's right to accept or reject Jesus—even after conversion. Fallen believers such as this remove themselves from the foot of the cross and relocate themselves among the jeering crowd of sinners that crucified Jesus. And because God refuses to drag people into his kingdom against their wills, there is nothing he can do to save them. If they want back inside, these scholars contend, repentant backsliders have only to follow this advice of Jesus: "Ask, and God will give to you. Search, and you will find. Knock, and the door will open for you" (Matthew 7:7 NCV).

FOR FURTHER STUDY

- The writer of Hebrews compares Jesus to the priesthood and sacrificial system of the Old Testament. To review some of the source material with which the writer worked, turn to Leviticus, especially chapters 1–9.

James

REAL CHRISTIANS DO MORE THAN TALK

James has little patience with do-nothing Christians. When confronting them, sometimes he's diplomatic, and often he's not.

"You foolish person! Must you be shown that faith that does nothing is worth nothing? Abraham, our ancestor, was made right with God by what he did when he offered his son Isaac on the altar. So you see that Abraham's faith and the things he did worked together. His faith was made perfect by what he did" (2:20–22 NCV).

Clearly James is quite tired of hearing Christians talk the talk. He wants to see some proof that the faith they're talking about is real. So James writes a short letter of instructions for Christian living. In it, he tells believers exactly what he expects of them.

For starters, they'll remain faithful even when others attack their beliefs. And when they see someone in need, they'll lend a hand. And when they have an opportunity to slander someone, they'll keep their mouths shut.

> ### FAMOUS LINES
>
> • "Resist the devil and he will flee from you. Draw near to God and he will draw near to you" (4:7–8 KJV).
>
> • "Always be willing to listen and slow to speak" (1:19 NCV).
>
> • "Faith that does nothing is worth nothing" (2:20 NCV). *James teaches that true faith isn't kept inside; it's expressed through acts of kindness.*

The entire book is a series of examples showing how James expects Christian faith to express itself in wise and compassionate ways.

The language is often vivid and picturesque—sometimes even forceful. But James knows that it can take a lot of energy to propel dead weight into motion.

BACKGROUND

INFLUENTIAL PEOPLE

James, possibly the brother of Jesus and leader of the church in Jerusalem (1:1).

THEME

The letter of James is not a story with a plot. It doesn't even seem to address a particular problem. Instead, it's a collection of practical lessons about Christian living.

Among the lessons are these: If you are poor, don't worry about it. If you are rich, worry like crazy—and give some money to the poor. Don't give in to temptation. Be slow to get angry. Don't treat rich people better than poor people. Do kind things for others. Watch your mouth. Run away from the devil and into the arms of God. Pray for people who need God's help.

POINTS OF INTEREST

Practical advice for everyday living. James is brimming with practical advice on how Christians should live. Some scholars call it Wisdom Literature of the New Testament, because it sounds so much like the wise sayings of Proverbs. In fact, much of what James says has been said before in Old Testament writings.

Here are a few excerpts of his advice:

"People who think they are religious but say things they should not say are just fooling themselves. Their "religion" is worth nothing" (1:26 NCV).

"You show special attention to the one wearing nice clothes and say, 'Please, sit here in this good seat.' But you say to the poor person, 'Stand over there,' or, 'Sit on the floor by my feet' " (2:3 NCV).

TIMELINE	BIBLE EVENTS			Dates are approximate
		Paul starts churches on first missionary trip ---- AD 46	James leads church council in Jerusalem -------- AD 49	
	AD 40	**AD 50**	**AD 60**	**AD 70**
	WORLD EVENTS	Jews rebel against Rome AD 66 ---------	Rome destroys Jerusalem and temple AD 70 --------	

"Do not tell evil lies about each other" (4:11 NCV).

"You rich people, listen! Cry and be very sad because of the troubles that are coming to you. . . The pay you did not give the workers who mowed your fields cries out against you" (5:1, 4 NCV).

Jewish perspective. If you read carefully, you'll notice that the letter sounds as though it's written by a Jew, for Jews.

James addresses his letter to the twelve tribes, a common way of referring to Israel. He uses the Greek word for synagogue to describe the meeting place mentioned in 2:2. He uses the Hebrew title for God, *sabaoth*, in "Lord All-Powerful" (5:4). And he often speaks of the Jewish law, always with reverence (2:8–13).

> **DID YOU KNOW?**
>
> • Martin Luther, father of Protestant religions, said this book doesn't belong in the Bible. He said it emphasizes good works too much and faith too little. Luther lived in a day when most Christians believed they were saved through church rituals, not through faith in Jesus.

Paul, on the other hand, does not always show such enduring respect for the Jewish law. When writing to his predominantly non-Jewish constituency, Paul says, "Now the way of faith has come, and we no longer live under a guardian" (Galatians 3:25 NCV). For more on the apparent clash between James and Paul, see "James vs. Paul" in the Points to Consider section.

AUTHOR AND DATE

The writer identifies himself only as "James, a servant of God and of the Lord Jesus Christ" (1:1 NCV). At least four men in the New Testament share this name, including an apostle. But since early Christian times the writer has been identified as the oldest of Jesus' four younger brothers (Mark 6:3). James rose to become leader of the Jerusalem church. He also headed the first church council meeting, which ruled that Gentiles did not have to follow Jewish rules about circumcision and food (Acts 15).

It's uncertain when James wrote the letter. A Jewish historian named Josephus, who lived in the first century, said Jewish leaders stoned James to death before Rome destroyed Jerusalem in AD 70. So if the brother of Jesus wrote is, he must have done so before then. Some scholars say that the Jewishness of the letter suggests it was written when most of the church was still Jewish—before Paul began to enjoy sweeping success among the Gentiles. If so, the letter could have been written in the AD 40s and might be the oldest literature in the New Testament.

ON LOCATION

James writes to "to all of God's people who are scattered everywhere in the world" (1:1 NCV). This may mean Jews who have become Christians. Or it can mean the entire Christian church, which James may be portraying as the New Israel. (See map in Acts, page 362.)

JAMES OUTLINE

Christians are people helping people (2:14–26).

My brothers and sisters," James says in an open letter to Christians throughout the Roman Empire, "if people say they have faith, but do nothing, their faith is worth nothing. Can faith like that save them? A brother or sister in Christ might need clothes or food. If you say to that person, "God be with you! I hope you stay warm and get plenty to eat," but you do not give what that person needs, your words are worth nothing. In the same way, faith by itself—that does nothing—is dead" (2:14–17 NCV).

James anticipates that some Christians will disagree with him. Some, he says, may argue that belief in God is enough. But James replies that even demons believe in God.

"Just as a person's body that does not have a spirit is dead, so faith that does nothing is dead!" (2:26 NCV).

Harnessing the power of the mouth (3:1–12).

Probably the most memorable piece of advice James gives is that people should watch what they say: "If people never said anything wrong, they would be perfect and able to control their entire selves, too" (3:2 NCV).

The tongue is small, James adds, but so is a ship's rudder, and so is the spark that starts a forest fire.

"People can tame every kind of wild animal, bird, reptile, and fish, and they have tamed them," James observes. "But no one can tame the tongue" (3:7–8 NCV).

For people with a tongue that flaps viciously in the heated breath of anger, James says simply, "always be willing to listen and slow to speak . . . because anger will not help you live the right kind of life God wants" (1:19–20 NCV).

═══ POINTS TO CONSIDER ═══

Rich vs. poor. One way to tell that James is an authentically Christian book is to study what he says about the rich and the poor.

The prevailing belief among Jews in Bible times is that the wealthy are rich because God has rewarded them for their goodness. Jesus and His followers, however, side with Old Testament prophets like Amos who say that too often the wealthy get rich by trampling poor into the ground and then robbing them.

"It's easier for a camel to go through the eye of a needle than for a rich person to get into God's kingdom," Jesus said (Matthew 19:24 NCV).

James, like his big brother, has strong words for the rich: "Your life on earth was full of rich living and pleasing yourselves with everything you wanted. You made yourselves fat, like an animal ready to be killed. You have judged guilty and then murdered innocent people, who were not against you" (5:5–6 NCV).

James vs. Paul. Paul says we're saved by faith alone, not by anything we do (Ephesians 2:8–9). But James argues that faith without deeds is worthless: "Can faith like that save them?" he asks (2:14 NCV). That's a rhetorical question; he expects us to answer no.

Critics of the Bible, and even famous Christians like Martin Luther, see a stark clash between James and Paul.

But James doesn't argue that we're saved by doing kind works—that we earn our salvation. Instead, he says that genuine faith in Jesus will naturally express itself in kindness. In a way, James is saying that if sin were a disease, and salvation were the cure, compassion would be a side effect we'd have to live with.

Paul agrees. He tells believers of Ephesus. "You are God's children whom he loves, so try to be like him. Live a life of love . . . But there must be no sexual sin among you, or any kind of evil or greed" (Ephesians 5:1, 2, 3 NCV).

The two men apparently came at the topic of faith from different perspectives. James seems to have ministered among do-nothing believers. And Paul has seen his share of I-can't-do-enough Gentiles who thought they needed to obey all Jewish laws and customs to earn salvation. Both extremes are wrong.

We're saved by faith. And when we're saved, it shows, because authentic faith works.

FOR FURTHER STUDY

- For more wise sayings, read the Old Testament books of Proverbs and Ecclesiastes.

1 Peter

WHEN WE SUFFER
BECAUSE WE'RE CHRISTIAN

It's unnatural for humans to suffer in silence. Somebody has to tell us to do it—especially when we know we're right and that we're suffering unfairly.

For Christians scattered throughout western Turkey, suffering simply for being Christians, Peter is that somebody.

Not only do we have to be told to suffer in silence, we need an explanation—a really good explanation. Peter gives several. For example, Christians who show respect to political authorities and who live a godly life have the power to "stop foolish people from saying stupid things" (2:15 NCV). Also, Christian women married to unbelievers have the potential, through kindness, to "persuaded to believe without anyone's saying a word to them" (3:1 NCV).

Peter doesn't go so far as to say that Christians should seek out opportunities to play the martyr—as Christians in

later centuries will do. But he does say, "When people insult you because you follow Christ, you are blessed" (4:14 NCV). In the anti-Christian climate of the mid-first century, it is inevitable that Christians will face persecution—they don't need to go looking for trouble. It will come. And when it does, Peter asks the believers to think of themselves not as victims, but as teachers with a unique opportunity to show others what Christians are really made of—and to follow in the footsteps of Jesus.

BACKGROUND

INFLUENTIAL PEOPLE

Peter, leader among the twelve original disciples of Jesus (1:1).

THEME

Christians in five Roman provinces throughout western Turkey are facing serious persecution because of their belief in Jesus. Romans no longer consider Christianity as a branch of Judaism, which is an approved faith. So Roman authorities begin pressuring Christians into accepting the Roman culture and gods, and not stirring up the Jews with their disturbing message about a messiah. Refusal to comply with Roman expectations can mean threats, confiscation of property, attack, and even execution.

Peter writes to sustain and inspire the believers. He reminds them of Christ's sacrifice, and what that means for eternity: "You were bought, not with something that ruins like gold or silver, but with the precious blood of Christ" (1:18–19 NCV).

The apostle then urges Christians to live the righteous life to which God has called them. He says they should respectfully submit to those in authority, yet be prepared to gently defend the Christian faith.

POINTS OF INTEREST

Persecution. Notice that the people Peter writes to are clearly facing persecution for their faith. The apostle refers to their condition throughout his short letter. "It is better to suffer for doing good," Peter says, "than for doing wrong" (3:17 NCV).

Submission. To Christians faced with severe persecution, and who are perhaps tempted to fight back, Peter urges submission at all levels of society.

TIMELINE	BIBLE EVENTS		Peter writes the letter called First Peter AD 64 --------------------------		Dates are approximate
		AD 40	AD 50	AD 60	AD 70
	WORLD EVENTS	Jews expelled from Rome over controversy about "Chrestus" (probably "Christ") AD 49 --------------	Rome burns; Christians blamed, persecuted AD 64 ---	Peter possibly executed in Rome AD 67----	Nero commits suicide AD 68

He urges submission of constituents to political rulers, of slaves to masters, of wives to husbands, and of young men to elders. To support his case, Peter appeals to the example of Jesus, who submitted to insults, beating, and death, yet without retaliating in any way.

Quotes from the Old Testament. Peter is a man especially interested in taking the news of Jesus to his own people, the Jews. This shows in his use of quotes from Jewish Scripture, known among people today as the Old Testament or the First Testament. In urging believers to cling to their trust in the promises of God, for example, Peter quotes poetry from the prophet Isaiah:

> "All people are like the grass,
> and all their glory is like
> the flowers of the field.
> The grass dies and the flowers fall,
> but the word of the Lord will live forever" (1:24–25 NCV).

> **DID YOU KNOW?**
>
> • The Roman Catholic Church considers Peter the first in a long line of church leaders first called bishop of Rome and later called pope. They base this on what Jesus tells Peter: "you are Peter. On this rock I will build my church, and the power of death will not be able to defeat it. I will give you the keys of the kingdom of heaven; the things you don't allow on earth will be the things that God does not allow, and the things you allow on earth will be the things that God allows" (Matthew 16:18–19 NCV).

AUTHOR AND DATE

The letter is "from Peter, an apostle of Jesus Christ" (1:1 NCV). The writing style is refined Greek, a surprising literary style for a Jewish fisherman. But Peter admits "I wrote this short letter with the help of Silas" (5:12 NCV). Perhaps Peter's words were polished by Silvanus, also known as Silas—a Christian who traveled with Paul throughout the Greek-speaking world (Acts 15:22).

Peter may have written the letter during unofficial, localized outbreaks of persecution in the early 60s. Or perhaps he wrote later, after Nero blamed Christians for torching Rome in AD 64.

The AD 95 writings of Clement, a church leader in Rome, seem to reflect an awareness of 1 Peter. And Christians writing in the second century, such as Polycarp, quote the book.

ON LOCATION

Peter writes to Christians scattered throughout five Roman provinces in western Turkey. (See map in Acts, page 362.) It's uncertain where Peter is writing from. He sends greetings from "Babylon" (5:13). This could refer to cities of that name in Iraq or Egypt. But it might be a code name for Jerusalem or Rome. Jews start calling Rome "Babylon" as early as AD 70, when Rome destroys Jerusalem. Perhaps they used the nickname even earlier. The Jews associate these two empires because each one is wealthy and evil, and because each one levels Jerusalem and destroys the temple.

1 PETER OUTLINE

Roman soldiers arrest Christians (4:12–19).

Christianity begins as a Jewish movement, led by Jews and embraced primarily by Jews. For this reason, Romans treat Christians with the same tolerance as Jews—for Judaism is an approved religion.

But as the decades pass, and violent clashes persist between Jews and Christians, it becomes obvious to everyone that Christianity is more than just another of the many branches or denominations of Judaism. It's a new religion—and a troublesome one at that. Romans shy away from new religions, and they shut down troublesome ones. That's because Romans want stability in their empire. As far as they are concerned, Christianity is just another mysterious cult with secret meetings and possibly disgusting rituals. Communion services, in which bread and wine represent the body and blood of Jesus, produce rumors of cannibalism. And the custom of greeting spiritual "brothers" and "sisters" with a kiss generates gossip about incest.

"Always be ready to answer everyone who asks you to explain about the hope you have," Peter advises. "but answer in a gentle way and with respect. Keep a clear conscience so that those who speak evil of your good life in Christ will be made ashamed" (3:15–16 NCV).

"My friends," Peter adds, "do not be surprised at the terrible trouble which now comes to test you. Do not think that something strange is happening to you. But be happy that you are sharing in Christ's sufferings so that you will be happy and full of joy when Christ comes again in glory" (4:12–13 NCV).

═══ POINTS TO CONSIDER ═══

Submission limited. Peter spent so much time cautioning people to be submissive—even to tormentors—that he seemed to have no backbone at all.

Nothing could be farther from the truth. When he and John were arrested and appeared before the seventy-man Jewish Council, which served as the national legislature and high court, Peter was anything but submissive. The Jewish elders ordered him to stop teaching about Jesus, and Peter replied,

"We cannot keep quiet. We must speak about what we have seen and heard" (Acts 4:20 NCV).

When Peter and the other apostles were arrested a second time, they all faced a possible death sentence from this same council that conspired to execute Jesus. Furious, the high priest insisted on knowing why they flagrantly disregarded the high court's order.

"We must obey God," Peter replied, respectfully but sternly. "Not human authority!" (Acts 5:29 NCV).

There are times to submit to leaders. But following leaders away from God is not one of those times.

Women, the weaker sex. After urging wives to submit to their husbands, Peter commendably called on husbands to show consideration for their wives. Unfortunately he did so in words that are today politically incorrect. Peter said men should "live with your wives in an understanding way, since they are weaker than you" (3:7 NCV).

In what way did Peter think women are weaker? He didn't explain.

Perhaps he meant physically and mentally. In his day, men provided much of the brawn and brains for the family. Women worked in the home. And as youngsters, they were denied the education that boys received in the synagogue.

Peter also may have been thinking of the social plight of women. In the courts, they were treated as minors who had no legal voice or civil rights. They were the property of their fathers and then of their husbands. When their husbands died or divorced them, they were left with nothing but the dowry they brought to the wedding, and with any compassion that extended family and friends might show them.

FOR FURTHER STUDY

- Second Peter is a sequel, warning against false teachers in the church.

- Some of the themes in 1 Peter seem drawn from Paul's letters to the Ephesians and the Colossians. For example, compare 1:1–3 with Ephesians 1:1–3; 3:1–7 with Ephesians 5:22–31; and 2:18 with Colossians 3:22.

2 Peter

WHY HASN'T JESUS COME BACK YET?

For thirty years or more, apostles and other church leaders have been assuring first-generation Christians that Jesus is coming back soon. As far as many in Generation-Christ are concerned, he's late. And the apostles are wrong.

Perplexed believers start looking for answers. Smooth-talking spiritual guides arrive on the scene, full of answers. Peter, however, says that what they're full of is nonsense. Like the fraudulent Christians that Jude writes about, these smart-sounding teachers say it's okay for Christians to sin, since Christians have already been forgiven of sin. These teachers practice what they preach. Peter says they're immoral, greedy, and headed for trouble.

The apostle's message for all Christians confronted by questionable teachings is this: don't give up the faith.

Peter reminds us that history is filled with examples of how God deals with sin. And as far as the Second Coming is concerned, Peter says, that's in God's hands. The Day will come, he adds, and Christians should never lose hope of that. Yet "since you are waiting for this to happen, do your best to be without sin and without fault" (3:14 NCV).

BACKGROUND

INFLUENTIAL PEOPLE

Peter, leader among the twelve original disciples of Jesus (1:1).

THEME

Fraudulent Christians teaching a new and distorted gospel begin making headway in the churches throughout the Roman Empire. The apostle Peter has mysteriously received word from heaven that he will die soon. So he writes a short, final letter to warn believers not to get taken in by these false teachers. "They promise them freedom," Peter says, likely referring to freedom from moral rules. "But they themselves are not free. They are slaves of things that will be destroyed. For people are slaves of anything that controls them" (2:19 NCV).

Peter assures the church that God will punish people who twist the gospel of Jesus Christ into a counterfeit, do-as-you-please religion: "They are being kept for the Judgment Day and the destruction of all who are against God" (3:7 NCV).

Instead of following these false teachers down the wrong path, Peter says, Christians should follow the example of Jesus and the directions given by the apostles and Paul.

POINTS OF INTEREST

Warnings about false teachers. This is the primary motive behind the book. Peter writes from death's doorstep to send a final, urgent message to the Christian community that has been invaded by heretical teachers.

"You will have some false teachers in your group," Peter says (2:1). They have caused many people to suffer, so they themselves will suffer. That is their pay for what they have done. They take pleasure in openly

TIMELINE

BIBLE EVENTS		Peter writes the letter called Second Peter AD 65		Dates are approximate
	AD 40	AD 50	AD 60	AD 70
WORLD EVENTS	Rome burns; Christians blamed, persecuted AD 64	Peter possibly executed in Rome AD 67	Nero commits suicide AD 68	Romans decimate Jerusalem AD 70

doing evil, so they are like dirty spots and stains among you. They delight in deceiving you while eating meals with you. Every time they look at a woman they want her, and their desire for sin is never satisfied. They lead weak people into the trap of sin, and they have taught their hearts to be greedy. God will punish them (2:3, 13–14 NCV).

Explanation for the delay of Christ's return. After waiting several decades for Jesus to return "soon," as the apostles have long been preaching, some believers are starting to wonder if He's ever coming back. Fraudulent teachers apparently capitalize on this impatience and start convincing people that Jesus is not returning.

Peter explains the delay this way: "To the Lord one day is as a thousand years, and a thousand years is as one day. The Lord is not slow in doing what he promised—the way some people understand slowness. But God is being patient with you. He does not want anyone to be lost, but he wants all people to change their hearts and lives.

But the day of the Lord will come like a thief" (3:8–10 NCV).

> ### Did You Know?
>
> • The Bible doesn't say how Peter died, but early Christian writers say he was crucified upside down in Rome on Vatican Hill, near where the pope now addresses the crowds. Archaeologists have found an ancient shrine to Peter on that site.

AUTHOR AND DATE

The letter is "from Simon Peter, a servant and apostle of Jesus Christ" (1:1 NCV). But Christian scholars from as early as the second century have doubted this, and suspect the letter was written in Peter's name (see "In search of an author" in the Points to Consider section).

If Peter wrote the letter, as many scholars believe, he likely wrote it just before he died. He said in the letter that he has been told by Jesus that he will soon die (1:14). The Bible doesn't say anything about his death, but early Christian writers report that Peter was crucified upside down in Rome during Nero's persecution of Christians (AD 64–68).

Scholars who believe the letter was written by someone other than Peter suggest it was penned anytime from AD 100 to 150.

ON LOCATION

The letter doesn't identify where it was written, or to whom. Peter does say "this is the second letter I have written you to help your honest minds remember" (3:1 NCV). His audience may be the same as in 1 Peter: churches in five Roman provinces throughout western Turkey. (See map in Acts, page 362.)

2 PETER OUTLINE

False teachers in the church (2:1–22).

In an open letter to all Christians, Peter reveals that he expects to die soon. Because of this, his letter serves as a last will and testament. He expresses three deep desires: that Christians will continue growing in the faith (chapter 1), that they will reject false teachers (chapter 2), and that they will live in patient anticipation of the Second Coming (chapter 3).

The false teachers that Peter warns about are apparently infiltrating the church and teaching that, since Jesus has delayed his return for so long, it's obvious he's not coming back (3:4). They also seem to teach that there will be no Judgment Day and that Christians can live any way they please, as long as they profess Jesus as Savior.

Peter describes these teachers with blunt condemnation: "They have caused many people to suffer, so they themselves will suffer. That is their pay for what they have done. They take pleasure in openly doing evil, so they are like dirty spots and stains among you. They delight in deceiving you while eating meals with you. Every time they look at a woman they want her, and their desire for sin is never satisfied. They lead weak people into the trap of sin, and they have taught their hearts to be greedy. God will punish them!" (2:13–14 NCV).

The harvest of trouble they'll reap, Peter explains, is the judgment of God. The apostle illustrates his point by drawing on past judgments: the Flood, Sodom and Gomorrah, and the profiteering prophet Balaam. The Israelites killed Balaam for luring some of their people into sex rituals in worship of Baal, a Canaanite fertility god (Numbers 31:8, 16).

"Dear friends," Peter concludes, "Do not let those evil people lead you away by the wrong they do. Be careful so you will not fall from your strong faith. But grow in the grace and knowledge of our Lord and Savior Jesus Christ" (3:17–18 NCV).

══ POINTS TO CONSIDER ══

How to spot a false teacher. The fraudulent Christian teachers whom Peter writes about sound much like some of the same people Paul encountered. And Peter's advice for dealing with the religious frauds is on target with what Paul said in many of his letters.

Peter says these teachers profess to know Jesus, but they live like the devil—engaging in orgies and profiteering (2:13-14). Paul, writing the heresy-plagued church of Colossae, warns believers to "put all evil things out of your life . . . and greed" (Colossians 3:5 NCV).

Both writers also agree that any and all teachings about Christianity need to be measured against the original teachings of Jesus and the apostles. If new teachings don't measure up, they are false. "Remember the command our Lord and Savior gave us through your apostles," Peter writes (3:2). Teachings contrary to this, Peter says, are nothing but "they brag with words that mean nothing" (2:18 NCV).

Paul puts it this way in a letter to his friend and associate, Timothy: "useless talk . . . falsely called "knowledge" (1 Timothy 6:20 NCV). Paul adds, "Anyone who has a different teaching does not agree with the true teaching of our Lord Jesus Christ and the teaching that shows the true way to serve God. This person is full of pride and understands nothing" (6:3-4 NCV).

In search of an author. The most common criticism of this letter is that the apostle Peter didn't write it, contrary to what 1:1 says. The letter is written in a less refined Greek than 1 Peter. The writer also implies that the letters of Paul have already been collected and are revered as part of Scripture: after speaking of Paul's letters, Peter refers to "other Scriptures too" (3:16). Furthermore, writing in the name of a respected teacher was a common practice among Greeks and Jews. It was the opposite of plagiarism; it was applying the master teacher's theology to current issues and then humbly giving credit to him instead of taking it.

These clues suggest to some scholars that the letter was written long after Paul and Peter died. Both men were likely killed during Nero's persecution of Christians in the mid 60s. Second Peter may not have been written until AD 100 or later, these scholars say, when the church clearly begins treating selected Christian writings as sacred.

Like some modern scholars, early Christian scholars also doubted Peter wrote the letter. These men include Origen (185 –253) and Eusebius (265-340). On the other hand, Bishop Clement of Rome, writing in AD 95, may refer to the teachings of Second Peter, though stopping short of quoting the letter.

Scholars who say Peter wrote the letter argue that he admitted having help writing the first one; this could account for the difference in style (1 Peter 5:12). And by the time Peter wrote this second letter, near the end of his life, some of Paul's letters would have been in circulation for ten years or more, and increasingly regarded as authoritative.

FOR FURTHER STUDY

- In wording and content, Jude has striking parallels to 2 Peter. Compare Jude 4–13, 16–18 with 2 Peter 2:1–17; 3:1–3.

- For other warnings about false teachers, review Colossians, 1 Timothy, Titus

1 John

BATTLING WARPED TEACHINGS ABOUT JESUS

Pilate had a great question for Jesus, but his timing was all wrong.

This Roman governor asked, "What is truth?" (John 18:38 NCV). It was a superb question because in Pilate's day, as today, the world was full of competing religions and philosophies.

Pilate's question showed horrible timing, however, because Jesus had just given the answer: "I was born and came into the world: to tell people the truth" (John 18:37 NCV). His teachings are the truth. In fact, he is the embodiment of Truth (John 14:6). Pilate was looking Truth (John 14:6). Pilate was looking Truth in the face, and he couldn't recognize it.

More than fifty years later, Christians started having trouble recognizing the truth too. They didn't seem sure about who Jesus was and what exactly he taught. A main problem was that some professing Christians started adding to the good news, trying to make it better. They made it worse. For example, by the time the apostle John had become an elderly man, someone came up with the idea that Jesus was just a spirit who only looked human. A religious movement started, and churches split.

For perplexed believers, John wrote a sermon called 1 John. In this essay he points Christians back to the basics—to Jesus' original teachings about what to believe, how to behave, and how to know they are true children of God. John also reminds the Christians that they have the added benefit of the Holy Spirit, who teaches from the inside out. "Christ gave you a special gift that is still in you, so you do not need any other teacher. His gift teaches you about everything, and it is true, not false. So continue to live in Christ, as his gift taught you" (2:27 NCV).

What is truth?

It's in our hands when we hold the Bible, and it's in our hearts when we accept Jesus. And we can know that we belong to the Truth.

BACKGROUND

INFLUENTIAL PEOPLE

Jesus, God's Son, who has come to earth in human form to offer eternal life to everyone who believes in him (1:3).

John, one of the twelve original disciples of Jesus, and probably the author of this letter along with 2 and 3 John, the Gospel of John, and Revelation.

THEME

Churches split after a group of Christians deny that Jesus was truly human. These unorthodox Christians, apparently forefathers of a heresy that explodes into full bloom during the second and third centuries, believe that everything physical is flawed and evil—including the human body. They teach that God, on the other hand, is completely spiritual and good.

Christians who embrace this premise are forced to conclude that Jesus only appeared to be physical—but was really spiritual. Furthermore, they argue that the Crucifixion plays no role in salvation, since the Son of God was not really killed. Salvation, they explain, comes from secret knowledge about how to transcend the body. This secret knowledge, apparently expressed in rituals and words, eventually gives the religious movement its name: Gnosticism, from *gnosis,* the Greek word for knowledge.

"I am writing this letter about those people who are trying to lead you the wrong way," John says. "So we can see who God's children are and

		Jesus crucified	First John	John writes Revelation from exile on Patmos island			Dates are approximate
	BIBLE EVENTS	AD 30	written AD 90	AD 95			
TIMELINE	**AD 30**	**AD 40**	**AD 50**	**AD 60**	**AD 70**	**AD 80**	**AD 90**	**AD 100**
	WORLD EVENTS	Pilate begins 10-year rule as Judean governor AD 26	Mount Vesuvius destroys Pompeii, Italy AD 79		Emperor Domitian, persecutor of Christians, begins 15-year reign AD 81		Paper invented in China AD 103

who the devil's children are: Those who do not do what is right are not God's children, and those who do not love their brothers and sisters are not God's children" (2:26; 3:10 NCV).

When confronted by such false teachers, Christians should "Be sure you continue to follow the teaching you heard from the beginning" (2:24 NCV).

POINTS OF INTEREST

Antichrists. "You have heard that the enemy of Christ is coming," John writes. "And now many enemies of Christ are already here" (2:18 NCV). John describes these individuals as enemies of Christ who "were in our fellowship, but they left us. They never really belonged to us; if they had been a part of us, they would have stayed with us. But they left, and this shows that none of them really belonged to us" (2:19 NCV).

These former church members have seceded from the union of believers, formed their own congregation based on ideas blended from a variety of religions, and are trying to lure new members from the church.

> ## DID YOU KNOW?
>
> • As Jesus hung on the cross, he entrusted his elderly mother to the care of an unnamed disciple he loved deeply. Since at least the second century, Christian writers have identified this disciple as John.
>
> • Jesus nicknamed John and his brother James the "sons of thunder," apparently because of their fiery temperaments. True to his nickname, John boldly calls professing Christians "liars" if they teach anything contrary to the original message about Jesus.

Opposites. Notice the contrasting figures of speech that are identical to those used in John's Gospel: truth vs. lies, love vs. hate, light vs. darkness, life vs. death.

Not all religious issues are black and white. But as far as John is concerned, the heresy that apparently emerges in the Ephesus region is clearly in the wrong. He describes its advocates as liars incapable of teaching the truth. These people are enemies of Christ because, instead of loving the church, they hate it. This hatred proves they remain in spiritual darkness, which will lead to their spiritual death.

A sermon. First John reads more like a sermon or an essay than a letter. Missing are an opening and closing, commonly used in letters. Many scholars suggest John wrote this message to deal with a regional problem, and that these words become a circular letter read aloud in many churches.

AUTHOR AND DATE

Like most New Testament books, the author is not identified. But the themes and the style of writing (simple Greek) are strikingly similar to those of John's Gospel. Early Christian writers from at least the second century have attributed both books to the apostle John, a fisherman, and one of Jesus' closest disciples. John may also have been a first cousin of Jesus.

It's uncertain when the book was written. Christian leaders in the second century said John wrote it in Ephesus late in the first century, roughly AD 90 or perhaps later.

ON LOCATION

John likely wrote during his old age, while living in Ephesus. The first documented use of the letter is in Ephesus. (See map in Acts, page 362.)

1 JOHN OUTLINE

Jesus: God in the flesh (4:1–6).

Within half a century after Jesus died and rose again, Christians are becoming increasingly confused about who he is and why he came. Some are starting to accessorize their faith with teachings from other religions and philosophies. Drawing from the insights of respected Greek philosophers who teach that divinity is a mysterious ideal that is both invisible and eternal—not physical and temporal—some Christians conclude that Jesus could not have been human. He was a spirit, they argue, who only looked human.

The church grows uncertain about what to believe. "So do not believe every spirit, but test the spirits to see if they are from God," John writes. "This is how you can know God's Spirit: Every spirit who confesses that Jesus Christ came to earth as a human is from God. And every spirit who refuses to say this about Jesus is not from God" (4:1–3 NCV).

John adds that there is yet another way to identify if professing Christians are really of God: God's children "do right" and "love each other" (3:10).

"We know we have left death and have come into life because we love each other," John explains. "Whoever does not love is still dead" (3:14 NCV).

POINTS TO CONSIDER

Evidence favoring John as writer. There are plenty of reasons to conclude that the apostle John wrote this letter—reasons beyond the similarities between 1 John and the Gospel of John, Irenaeus, a church leader who lived about AD 140–203, quoted extensively from the book and attributed the work to John. Other church leaders who lived about the same time attributed it to John as well: Clement of Alexandria, Tertullian, and Origen. An even earlier Christian, Polycarp of Smyrna (about AD 69–155), seems to have drawn from 1 John when he insisted that anyone who does not confess that Jesus came in the flesh is an antichrist.

The early church fathers said John wrote in Ephesus, during the final years of his life. This region, in what is now western Turkey, was a virtual stew of varied cultures and religions—an ideal location for mixing new batches of creatively blended religions, like those described in the Gospel and letters bearing John's name.

The end is near. "My dear children, these are the last days," John writes (2:18 NCV). That was about 2,000 years ago, or 17 million hours.

"The last hour" is a phrase, like "the last days," which means more than the months or years just before the Second Coming. It also means "the age of the Messiah," fully inaugurated by the death and resurrection of Jesus. This phrase is similar to one that John uses repeatedly in his Gospel when speaking of the Crucifixion. When Jesus realizes it is nearly time for him to fulfill the reason he came to earth—to die—he says "the time has come" (John 17:1 NCV).

"The last hour" can refer to events immediately preceding the Second Coming, but it also marks the beginning of the end of God's long-term plan to save the world from sin. Here, John likely intends the latter meaning. In Old Testament time, God's plan involved animal sacrifices. In New Testament times, the plan features the ultimate sacrifice: God's Son.

FOR FURTHER STUDY

• For more of John's writings dealing with similar religious issues, read 2 and 3 John, along with John's Gospel.

NO WELCOME MAT FOR HERETICS

Second John reads a bit like a P.S. to 1 John.

The apostle John, presumed the writer, condenses the five-chapter message of his first letter into a mere thirteen verses. In addition to repeating and abbreviating his warning against false teachers who argue that Jesus was not human, John adds that Christians should not show hospitality to these teachers.

In Bible times, Christians aren't the only ones traveling around the land and preaching. So are quasi-Christian evangelists, trying to spread the word that spiritual things are good and physical things are evil, and that because of this, Jesus was only a spirit who looked human. It is customary in early Christian days for believers to invite into their homes any traveling evangelists, and to later send them on their way with provisions for the trip.

> ### FAMOUS LINES
>
> • "Love each other" (1:5 NCV).

John warns church members to be discerning about who they support. He says if people don't preach the genuine story of Jesus, "do not welcome or accept that person into your house. If you welcome such a person, you share in the evil work" (10 NCV).

This doesn't mean we should turn all sinners away from our door. Jesus came to help sinners. He even sought them out (Luke 15:2–7). But John teaches that we shouldn't encourage and support their sin.

BACKGROUND

INFLUENTIAL PEOPLE

The church leader, identified in many translations as "the Elder," probably the apostle John, one of Jesus' twelve original disciples (1:1).

A very special woman and her children, probably a figure of speech for the church and its members (1:1).

THEME

The apostle John seems to have a soft spot in his heart for an unnamed church that he identifies only as "the chosen lady and her children" (1:1 NCV). So he writes a special letter to this congregation, repeating some of what he has said in 1 John. Then he adds a warning against showing hospitality to traveling evangelists who teach false doctrines.

Though 1 John reads like a sermon or essay—without an introductory greeting and a closing that are common in letters—2 John has both of these. Perhaps 1 John is a general message circulated among all the churches in John's region, and 2 John is a personal letter to an individual church—a letter that accompanies their copy of 1 John.

AUTHOR AND DATE

The writer is identified as "the Elder" (1:1 NCV). The writing style, ideas, and testimony of Christian leaders in the second century indicate the writer was the apostle John. This close disciple of Jesus was also probably author of 1 and 3 John, along with the Gospel of John and Revelation. One central theme in 1 John is truth—an important idea in a day when the church was being bombarded with lies about Jesus. This theme is repeated in John's Gospel as well as 1 and 3 John.

Like 1 and 3 John, it's uncertain when 2 John was written. Christian leaders in the second century said John wrote it in Ephesus late in the first century, roughly AD 90 or perhaps later.

3 John

SHOWING HOSPITALITY TO CHRISTIANS

The most personal of John's three letters, 3 John is the only one addressed to an individual: Gaius, a kind believer who is part of a church led by Diotrephes, a minister who runs the congregation like a rebel general runs a junta.

John commends Gaius for obeying the true teachings about Jesus, and especially for showing hospitality to Christian missionary—possibly some John has sent into the area. John knows that Gaius might be punished for this since Diotrephes rejects all outsiders who might undermine his authority. And he boots people out of the church who refuse to do the same.

"My dear friend," John writes to Gaius, "do not follow what is bad; follow what is good. The one who does good belongs to God. But the one who does evil has never known God" (11 NCV).

Even in the beginning years of Christianity, believers face stern and influential enemies within the church—fraudulent Christians who worship values cherished in the kingdom of this world: power and prestige. John's advice to believers is to keep doing what they know God wants them to do: obey the truth, love others, and support those spreading the gospel, regardless of the risk.

BACKGROUND

INFLUENTIAL PEOPLE

The church leader, identified in many translations as "the Elder," probably the apostle John, one of Jesus' twelve original disciples (1:1).

Gaius, a Christian commended for showing kindness and hospitality to Christian travelers (1:1).

Diotrephes, a dictatorial church leader who abuses his authority by excommunicating those who disagree with his policy of refusing to welcome Christian travelers (1:9).

THEME

In the early decades of Christianity, the organization is loose; local churches are guided by letters and representatives sent from leaders scattered around the Roman Empire. In one unnamed church, a minister named Diotrephes "who loves to be their leader" (9 NCV). He refuses to respect the authority of the apostle John and even spreads malicious rumors about him. When John writes to this church, Diotrephes apparently refuses to even read the letters in public. And when John sends representatives, Diotrephes refuses to welcome them. Furthermore, this autocratic church leader excommunicates any members who do welcome them.

The apostle John writes to Gaius, a member in this troubled church. John commends Gaius for showing hospitality to all Christian travelers and urges him to keep doing this no matter what Diotrephes says.

John concludes his letter by saying he hopes to see Gaius soon, so they can talk in person. When John arrives, he says, he will deal with Diotrephes.

AUTHOR AND DATE

As in 2 John, the writer is identified as "the Elder" (1:1 NCV). The writing style, ideas, and testimony of Christian leaders in the second century indicate the writer was the apostle John, who also likely wrote 1 and 2 John, along with the Gospel of John and Revelation.

As with 1 and 2 John, it's uncertain when 3 John was written. Christian leaders in the second century said John wrote it in Ephesus late in the first century, roughly AD 90 or perhaps later.

Jude

IF WE'RE FORGIVEN, WHAT'S WRONG WITH SIN?

Christians in the first century called themselves followers of the Way, meaning the way to eternal life, through Jesus. Some, however, were followers of the Shortcut. They believed they had found an easier way to heaven, through a colossal loophole.

The loophole was this: Jesus had forgiven them of sin. Therefore, they figured, sin didn't matter anymore. They could sin all they wanted; they were forgiven. Besides, they reasoned, God's grace is greater than all our sin.

There's a place for creativity in the kingdom of God, but this is a bit much. Jude knows that professing Christians who are carriers of a light view of sin can infect and destroy an entire congregation. Sin is serious business. In Old Testament times, ani-

> ### FAMOUS LINES
>
> • "God is strong and can help you not to fall. He can bring you before his glory without any wrong in you and can give you great joy. He is the only God, the One who saves us. To him be glory, greatness, power, and authority through Jesus Christ our Lord for all time past, now, and forever. Amen" (24–25 NCV). *The benediction of Jude's letter.*

mals died as a reminder that sin is a matter of life and death. In New Testament times, God's Son died to save us from sin—not so we could sin all we wanted, but to free us from the power that sin has to enslave us. As Jesus once put it, "everyone who lives in sin is a slave to sin" (John 8:34 NCV).

"Fight hard for the faith," Jude writes (3 NCV).

As long as there are followers of the Shortcut, preaching the gospel of the Loophole, Jude says there needs to be knowledgeable Christians who can point to examples in Scripture—such as grumbling Israelites on the Exodus, or sex addicts in Sodom—and say, "Don't forget what happened to those people" (5).

BACKGROUND

INFLUENTIAL PEOPLE

Jude, author of this letter, and possibly a brother of Jesus (1:1).

THEME

Jude writes a forceful letter to an unnamed church, warning the people about Christian impostors who have infiltrated the congregation and who are rising to positions of leadership.

These fraudulent Christians are teaching that it's okay for Christians to sin, since Christians have already been forgiven of sin. "God treats us much better than we deserve," Jude seems to be saying, "so it is all right to be immoral" (4). These people practice what they preach. Jude describes them as filthy minded, shameful, and selfish (12).

"I wanted very much to write you about the salvation we all share," Jude says. "But I felt the need to write you about something else: I want to encourage you to fight hard for the faith" (3 NCV).

Using a wide array of examples from the Old Testament and from revered Jewish literature not included in Scripture, Jude shows that God punishes sin. "Also remember the cities of Sodom and Gomorrah," Jude says, citing one memorable case study. "In the same way they were full of sexual sin and people who desired sexual relations that God does not allow. They suffer the punishment of eternal fire, as an example for all to see" (7 NCV).

Jude asks true believers to take a stand for what they know is right.

AUTHOR AND DATE

The writer is "Jude, a servant of Jesus Christ and a brother of James" (1 NCV). Many scholars believe Jude is also the brother of Jesus. They draw this conclusion partly because "Jude" is a form of the Hebrew name Judah, which is Judas in Greek. Jesus had brothers named Judas and James (Matthew 13:55). James rose to leadership within the Jerusalem church, which may be why Jude identified himself as the brother of James.

Another possibility is that Jude was one of the twelve disciples (Luke 6:16). This seems unlikely, however, because the writer speaks of the apostles as though he is not one of them (17–18).

There is nothing in this letter to identify when it was written. It could have been written during the lifetime of Jesus' brothers. Paul addressed some of the same issues within about thirty years of the Crucifixion. For example, he felt compelled to remind Christians that they should not take advantage of God's grace by continuing to sin (Romans 6:1–2).

Jude could have addressed his letter either to Jewish Christians or Gentile Christians. The many references to Jewish Scriptures and legends, however, suggest that Jewish Christians would have found the arguments especially convincing.

Revelation

THE END IS JUST THE BEGINNING

By some the most avoided book of the Bible, while by others the most closely studied, Revelation can seem bizarre, scary, and thoroughly mystifying. What, for example, is a modern Christian to make of heavenly creatures "with eyes all over them, in front and in back" (4:6 NCV)?

Revelation is also perhaps the most misunderstood book of the Bible. When Iraq, for instance, has taken provocative, threatening action, some interpreters have turned to Revelation 18 to warn that the end is near, and Babylon is about to fall. (The ancient ruins of Babylon are near Baghdad.) Yet the first readers of this book saw the name "Babylon" but read "Rome." Jews had used Babylon as a code name for Rome ever since AD 70, when Rome did to Jerusalem what Babylon had done centuries earlier: burned and leveled it.

This closing book of the Bible is an encrypted message written especially for persecuted Christians near the end of the first century. Those believers have the key to interpret much of what the writer, John, says. We have only part of their ancient insight into the dramatic symbols John uses. But this is more than enough to decode the main message: Evil and its followers don't win; God and his followers do.

In the end—when the age of fallen human beings gives way to the

> ### FAMOUS LINES
>
> - "I am the Alpha and the Omega, the Beginning and the End" (1:8 NKJV). *Alpha and Omega are the first and last letters of the Greek alphabet.*
>
> - "God will wipe away every tear from their eyes" (7:17 NCV). *Figurative language to describe the absence of sorrow in God's heavenly kingdom.*
>
> - "I saw a new heaven and a new earth" (21:1 NCV). *In a vision, John sees God restore creation to the paradise it was before sin entered.*

new age of fully redeemed beings—God will restore the paradise that was lost through the sin of Adam and Eve. He will make a new creation and populate it with happy, resurrected humans who want to live with him forever.

BACKGROUND

INFLUENTIAL PEOPLE

John, author of the book, who describes his captivating visions of the future; possibly one of Jesus' twelve original disciples (1:1).

Jesus, Son of God, who returns to earth to judge all people and to take his followers to heaven (1:1).

THEME

John, exiled to a small and rocky island apparently for refusing to worship the Roman emperor as god, experiences a long series of dramatic visions. Some visions are bizarre—even horrifying. Others are beautiful and deeply comforting. But all of them prove to John that his faith is real, and that no matter what Rome or any other power tries to do to God's church, the Lord and his people will prevail.

The writer describes his visions in stark and often disturbing detail. He speaks of international chaos, God's people martyred, world-shattering catastrophes, and cosmic upheavals. Humanity and the world cease to exist.

But in their place, God restores paradise lost. Human beings become spirit beings, fully capable of enjoying God's new creation for the rest of eternity.

TIMELINE	BIBLE EVENTS		Paul and Peter executed in Rome ┌-- AD 67	John writes Revelation from exile on Patmos island AD 95 ----------------	Dates are approximate
		AD 60	**AD 70**	**AD 80**	**AD 90**
	WORLD EVENTS		Rome burns; Nero blames Christians, launches └-- persecution AD 64	Rome destroys Jerusalem and └--------- temple AD 70	Emperor Domitian assassinated, ending his persecution of Christians AD 96 ----------------

POINTS OF INTEREST

Apocalypse, the genre. The unique style of writing in Revelation is called apocalyptic, from the Greek word apocalypses, which means "reveal." That's where the book gets its name.

This writing paints a graphic picture of the present evil world, followed by a glorious future—and it does so through dramatic visions, strange symbolism, and code words. The point is to comfort persecuted readers by assuring them that their difficult circumstances won't last forever—God will punish the wicked, reward the righteous, and usher in a new and wonderful age.

One reason the writer uses extraordinary symbolism is to prevent government authorities from deciphering the message. The Roman emperor, for example, would not take kindly to someone saying that God is going to destroy both him and his empire. Yet that's what John means when he says "Ruined, ruined is the great city of Babylon!" (14:8 NCV). After Rome decimated Jerusalem in AD 70, just as Babylon did in 586 BC, many Jews began referring to the Roman Empire as Babylon.

> ### DID YOU KNOW?
> • Armageddon, the place where Revelation says the final battle between good and evil will take place, is a huge valley plain in northern Israel (16:16). Over the past 4,000 years there have been no less than 22 invasions into this valley. In John's time, Armageddon (Hebrew for "mountain of Megiddo") was already a name synonymous with war.

Though the key for decoding much of the symbolism is lost, some remains. Revelation itself reveals the code for some of the less dangerous ideas: stars are angels and lampstands are churches (1:20). The heavenly Jerusalem is the church, the bride of Jesus (21:9–10; compare with Ephesians 5:25–32).

Numbers. To secretly communicate his message, John supplements his strange symbolism and fantastic word pictures with a perplexing use of numbers.

Seven. One of John's favorite numbers is seven, which he uses more than fifty times. He talks about seven churches, seven spirits, seven golden lampstands, seven stars, seven seals, seven trumpets—and the list goes on. Throughout Jewish history, seven symbolizes completion; it was on the seventh day that God rested after finishing Creation.

So when John dictates letters to seven churches, praising their good traits and warning them of their weaknesses, he and his readers may have understood that he was addressing the entire Christian church. In fact, the church today still looks to these letters for guidance. Since the number symbolizes something that is complete, it's little wonder John uses it so much in a book about the end of human history and the fulfillment of God's plan of salvation.

144,000. This number, which appears in Revelation 7:4, may be another one that symbolizes completeness. In Revelation it could mean "all God's people." John shows that this number comes from the twelve tribes of Israel: twelve times twelve, with multiplied thousands—suggesting the new Israel, which is the entire assembly of God's people.

666. Known as the Mark of the Beast, 666 is likely a coded reference to Nero—Rome's most vicious persecutor of Christians. John gives this clue: "This takes wisdom. Let the one who has understanding find the meaning of the number, which is the number of a person. Its number is 666" (13:18 NCV).

Hebrew and Greek letters have numeric equivalents. When the numbers that spell the Hebrew name of Nero Caesar are combined, the total is 666.

Connections to the Old Testament. Revelation is full of allusions to the Old Testament. Nearly 300 of the approximately 400 verses have some connection to the Old Testament.

For example, the vision John has of God's throne and the song John hears the heavenly beings sing are much like those described by Ezekiel and Isaiah (compare 4:1–8 with Ezekiel 1 and Isaiah 6:3).

Also, the plague of "hail and fire mixed with blood" (8:7 NCV) is reminiscent of the thunder, hail, and fire of the seventh plague on Egypt (Exodus 9:22–26). And the plague of locusts, coming with smoke that blots out the sun (9:1–3), is based on Joel 1–2.

AUTHOR AND DATE

The writer identifies himself as John. But which John? Christian writer Justin Martyr (about AD 100–165) is the first person on record to identify the author as the apostle John, one of the closest disciples of Jesus, and author of the Gospel of John and the three letters of John. About 100 years later, other Christians began to challenge this. Dionysius, a theologian from Alexandria, Egypt, said the writing style is not at all like the other works of the apostle John. However, the frequent references to the Old Testament and the style of the Greek that the writer used suggest he was a Jew from Israel.

John may have written this masterpiece of mystery during the Christian persecutions late in the reign of Nero, in the mid 60s. But most scholars date the book to the final years of the Emperor Domitian, who was assassinated in AD 96. Late in his reign, Domitian forced his subjects to address him as "Lord and God." Those who refused were harshly punished. Many Christians were exiled to penal colonies or executed.

ON LOCATION

John writes from fifty miles offshore of western Turkey, on the rocky island of Patmos, about ten miles long and five miles wide. He begins the book with letters addresses to churches in seven cities near the coast of western Turkey. The futuristic visions that John writes about involve the entire planet. He says the last battle between good and evil will take place in the Valley of Armageddon, known today as Megiddo, and that God will make a new Jerusalem. Since the genre of the book is apocalyptic, characterized by extreme symbolism, scholars debate whether John had any of these actual sites in mind.

REVELATION OUTLINE

John sees a vision of heaven (4:1–5:14).

Roman authorities exile a Christian leader named John to a small and rocky island fifty miles off the coast of western Turkey. John apparently receives this punishment for refusing to worship the emperor as a god. Actually, this punishment is comparatively light, because many other Christians are executed for such insolence. Perhaps John receives a lighter sentence because of his advanced age.

On this island of Patmos, John begins to experience a long series of dramatic visions. First, he receives divine insight into seven prominent churches in western Turkey, and he dictates letters of commendation and warning to each.

Afterward, he finds his spirit standing in the very throne room of God. What he sees is much like that which the prophet Ezekiel saw hundreds of years earlier (Ezekiel 1). In the background, heavenly beings continually praise God in words and song. One such song is similar to what the prophet Isaiah once heard in a vision: "Holy, holy, holy is the Lord God Almighty. He was, he is, and he is coming" (4:8 NCV; see Isaiah 6:3).

Suddenly John sees God holding a scroll locked with seven seals. Among all the beings in the heavenly court, only Jesus is deemed worthy to break the seals. As Jesus breaks each one, John experiences a new vision—including terrifying scenes of the four horsemen of the Apocalypse, who represent conquest, war, famine, and lethal disease.

Silence falls as Jesus breaks the seventh seal. Suddenly, seven trumpets blast, one after another, each one heralding destruction, persecution, martyrdom, or God's punishment for humanity's evil.

Rider on a white horse (19:11–20:11).

As the visions progress, John sees two hideous monsters born of Satan. Some scholars interpret them as symbolizing the Roman Empire, or perhaps humanity's evil. Others see in them the Antichrist, assisted by a Satanic prophet who performs miracles that convince humanity to worship the Antichrist.

After seeing all this tragedy, John witnesses a glorious sight: a rider on

Sun
Mon
Tue
Wed
Thu
Frid
Satu
Sun
Mon
Tue
Wed
Thu
Frid
Satu
Sun
Mon
Tue
Wed

a white horse, preparing to lead the army of heaven into battle against all the forces of evil—natural and supernatural. The rider wears a robe engraved with his title: KING OF KINGS AND LORD OF LORDS. The rider is Jesus Christ, coming as the warrior king that the Jews expected to see in their messiah.

John witnesses a great battle in which the heavenly forces strike a coalition army belonging to "the beast and all kings of the earth." Jesus wins. The soldiers of the evil army are annihilated, their bodies left as carrion for scavengers. The two beasts and Satan are condemned to everlasting torment in a lake of burning sulfur.

Judgment Day (20:11–15),

John then sees what happens next, at the end of human history. He sees Judgment Day.

"I saw a great white throne and the One who was sitting on it," John writes. "And I saw the dead, great and small, standing before the throne" (20:11–12 NCV).

Heavenly authorities open "the book of life." Then all the people who have ever lived are judged according to what they have done in life. The judge is none other than Jesus, of whom Paul wrote, "God and Christ Jesus, the One who will judge the living and the dead" (2 Timothy 4:1 NCV).

"And anyone whose name was not found written in the book of life was thrown into the lake of fire" (20:15 NCV).

Scholars debate what that means. Some interpret the description literally, arguing that sinners follow their lord and master, Satan, to his eternal fate. Others say this graphic image symbolizes separation from Christ—that people who want Jesus, and people who want nothing to do with Jesus, each are given their heart's desire.

Heaven, eternal reward of the faithful (21:1–22:6).

I saw a new heaven and a new earth," John writes. This is the same new creation that Isaiah had spoken of hundreds of years earlier. Quoting God, Isaiah wrote: "I will make new heavens and a new earth . . . people will be happy forever. . . There will never again be heard in that city the sounds of crying and sadness" (Isaiah 65:17–19 NCV).

Since the dawning of human history, when Adam and Eve contaminated God's good creation with sin, God has been working his plan to remove all traces of defilement. "It is finished" God now says. "I am the Alpha and the Omega, the Beginning and the End. I will give free water from the spring of the water of life to anyone who is thirsty. Those who win the victory will receive this, and I will be their God, and they will be my children" (21:6–7 NCV).

With this, God and his people settle in for an eternity. Evil is gone. Beauty, tenderness, and joy fill the realms of paradise restored.

The Second Coming (22:7–20).

I am coming soon!" Jesus tells John. "I will bring my reward with me, and I will repay each one of you for what you have done" (22:12 NCV).

"Let whoever is thirsty come" Jesus adds, for all to hear, "whoever wishes may have the water of life as a free gift" (22:17 NCV).

To all John has witnessed, both the tragic and the wondrous, he has but one short response: "Come, Lord Jesus!" (22:20 NCV).

POINTS TO CONSIDER

Letters to the seven churches. Though it's unclear if the letters John addressed to seven churches were intended for them alone, or for the entire church, John carefully chose word pictures appropriate for the churches.

To the church in Laodicea, an immensely wealthy city famous for its eye ointments and medical center, John says, "you are really miserable, pitiful, poor, blind . . . Buy from me medicine to put on your eyes so you can truly see" (3:17–18 NCV). Further, he calls them "lukewarm" (3:16 NCV), an ironic description for a people located just a few miles from hot springs, a popular attraction for tourists and the sick.

To the church in Smyrna, home of a large and militant group of Jews, John says he understands how hard it is to live there as a Christian. "I know the bad things some people say about you. They say they are Jews, but they are not true Jews. They are a synagogue that belongs to Satan" (2:9 NCV). Polycarp, bishop of Smyrna, was arrested for his faith and burned to death there in about AD 155.

Hell. Punishment for doing wrong is something most people seem to understand and accept. But eternal torture in a lake of burning sulfur is quite another thing—especially if the torturer is God, whom the Bible describes as the essence of love (1 John 4:8).

Part of the problem in understanding what God's end-time punishment for sinners will be like is that the Bible has to resort to word pictures from the physical world to describe what will take place in an entirely different, spiritual dimension. John says Satan and his followers will be thrown into "the lake of fire that burns with sulfur" (19:20 NCV) where they will suffer "day and night forever and ever" (20:10 NCV, see also 20:15). Jesus confirms that sinners are "in danger of the fire of hell" (Matthew 5:22 NCV), a place outside of the kingdom of God where people "will cry and grind their teeth with pain" (Matthew 8:12 NCV). Surprisingly, Jesus also describes this as a place of darkness (Matthew 8:12). Yet fire displaces darkness.

What exactly is that place of fire and darkness, which the Bible sometimes calls hell? Hell is a word that comes from the Hebrew term *gehenna*, an ever-smoldering garbage dump in a valley outside ancient Jerusalem. Here is where people threw their trash, as well as the corpses of executed criminals. The Jews in Jesus' time used this place as a figure of speech to describe God's punishment of sinners on Judgment Day.

From beginning to end, the Bible is clear that people have to suffer the consequences of their sinful choices. God honors their decision to reject him, his love, and his rescue from sin and judgment. But how those who reject him will suffer remains in the hands of God who "what he does is perfect" and "he is always fair" (Deuteronomy 32:4 NCV).

FOR FURTHER STUDY

- For other apocalyptic writings in the Bible, read Isaiah 24–27; Ezekiel 38–39; Daniel 7–12; Joel 2; Zechariah 9–14; Matthew 24; Mark 13; Luke 12.

THE APOCRYPHA
BOOKS LEFT OUT OF THE OLD TESTAMENT

Jews wrote many revered books during the final centuries before Christ, and even up until Rome destroyed Jerusalem in AD 70—books eventually eliminated from their Bible but kept in some Christian Bibles.

These are books about dramatic Jewish history, romance, wise sayings, prayers, and miracles. Jews respected these books enough to include them in the Septuagint, an ever-expanding Greek translation of sacred Hebrew writings, started in the 200s BC. Yet when Jewish scholars later decided to agree on an authoritative collection of Scripture, they eliminated these books known as the Apocrypha, a Greek word meaning "hidden." The Jews believed the books were not as reliable as those kept.

When Christian scholar Jerome translated the Jewish and Christian Scriptures into a Latin edition of the Bible in about AD 405, he included some of the Apocrypha. But even those he bothered translating he considered less than sacred, criticizing them as "the crazy wanderings of a man whose senses have taken leave of him."

When 16th-century Protestant reformer Martin Luther broke from the Roman Catholic Church, he decided that the Christian Bible should include only the Old Testament books in the Hebrew Bible. As a result, the Protestant Bible is shorter than both the Catholic Bible and the Eastern Orthodox Bibles (Eastern churches had split from the Catholics about the time of the Crusades, in AD 1054).

There's no standard list of Apocrypha books.

The Roman Catholic Church accepts seven: Tobit, Judith, 1 and 2 Maccabees, Wisdom, Sirach, and Baruch—along with additions to Esther and Daniel (in sections called the Prayer of Azariah and the Son of the Three Jews, Susanna, and Bel and the Dragon).

The Eastern Orthodox Church accepts all those in the Catholic Bible, and adds several more. The Greek Orthodox, for example, adds 1 Esdras, the Prayer of Manasseh, 3 Maccabees, and Psalm 151.

The Slavonic Church adds 2 Esdras. (Slavonia is part of southern Europe that suffered in the war of Bosnia and Herzegovina, which ended in 1995.)

Other Eastern churches add 4 Maccabees.

Here's a short introduction to each of these apocryphal books and portions of the books.

Tobit. This is the story of Tobit, a Jewish man who is deported with his family to Nineveh, capital of the Assyrian Empire, after Assyria conquers Israel. Against imperial law, Tobit boldly continues giving a proper burial to executed Jews. One night after doing this, then sleeping outside, he is blinded by sparrow droppings that fall into his eyes. For eight years he prays that God will cure him. This prayer is answered when his son, at the instructions of the archangel Raphael, smears Tobit's eyes with bile from a fish.

Judith. A beautiful Jewish widow, Judith saves her city that is besieged by an Assyrian invasion force. She leaves her city and offers her services as an informant. The general gladly accepts and invites her to a small party with the hope of seducing her. By party's end, the general is drunk and passed out on his bed. Judith stays with him, under the guise of spending the night with him. Instead, she cuts off his head and takes it back to her city. At her urging, the Jews launch an attack at first light. When the Assyrians try to awaken their commander, they discover his headless corpse, panic, and run for their lives.

Esther additions. The Old Testament story of Esther, a Jewish woman and Persian queen, does not mention God at all. But 107 extra verses in the Greek version mention Him more than 50 times. For example, the original story written in Hebrew tell of the Persian king having a sleepless night. But the later Greek version explains why: "The Lord took sleep from the kings."

Wisdom. Traditionally attributed to Solomon, this collection of wise sayings was composed in Greek, perhaps in the first century BC. The writer speaks of righteous people receiving God's gift of immortality, an idea not taught in more ancient Jewish writings. The writer also brags that Jewish wisdom, which comes from God, is greater than the wisdom of the Greeks, who are renowned for their sages.

Sirach. Called by early Christians as Ecclesiasticus, meaning "church book," Sirach is a 51-chapter collection of maxims, sacred songs, and reflections about life—much like the books of Proverbs and Psalms.

Early Christians used this book in worship rituals. The author is a respected sage and teacher named Jesus the son of Sirach, a man who lived about 200 years before Christ, when Israel was dominated by successors of Alexander the Great.

Baruch. This story is set among the Jewish exiles taken to Babylon, after the Babylonian Empire decimates Jerusalem in 586 BC. The writer claims to be Baruch, assistant to the prophet Jeremiah—though the book of Jeremiah says both men escaped to Egypt (43:6–7). The five-chapter book includes a confession of the Jewish nation's sins, along with a prayer for deliverance, and a song of praise about the wisdom God has given Israel through his commandments.

Letter of Jeremiah. Often treated as the sixth chapter of Baruch, this claims to be a letter that the prophet Jeremiah sent to Jewish exiles in Babylon, warning them not to worship idols while they are there.

Prayer of Azariah and the Song of the Three Jews. Added to the Greek edition of Daniel, this work tells of Daniel's three friends who survive in a fiery furnace. The prayer is by Azariah, better known by his Babylonian name of Abednego. The song that follows is what he and his friends—Shadrach and Meshach—sang while in the furnace.

Susanna. Also added to Daniel is this story of Susanna, a beautiful and rich young woman who is said to have launched Daniels career as a prophet. Two respected but lustful Jewish leaders falsely accuse her of having an affair, after she refuses to have sex with them. Young Daniel publicly and separately interrogates the two men, revealing inconsistencies in their stories. Susanna is saved and the two men face the punishment they intended for her: execution.

Bel and the Dragon. In yet another addition to the Greek version of Daniel, the prophet Daniel uncovers hoaxes about two Babylonian gods: Bel and a serpent. (1) Bel: Each evening the Babylonians place food in the temple of their god, Bel. By morning, the food is gone. One evening Daniel scatters ashes on the temple floor, and the next morning points out footprints to show that priests came in through a secret passage and carried the food away. (2) Dragon: Babylonians also worship a serpent, which Daniel feeds a lethal mixture of tar, fat, and hair. The concoction expands inside the "dragon," making it explode.

1 Maccabees. This book tells about the Jewish revolt and war of independence after Syrian occupiers desecrate the Jewish temple and try forcing the Jews to abandon their religion. Leading the resistance is a priest and his five sons, known as the Maccabees. After winning the war they set up what becomes known as the Hasmonean dynasty, which rules Israel for a century—until Rome arrives.

2 Maccabees. This supplements the story of the Jewish war for independence, focusing especially on how God helped the Jews win against incredible odds.

1 Esdras. The books of 1 Esdras through 3 Maccabees are in the Bibles of Greek and Russian Orthodox churches, though not in the Roman Catholic Bible. First Esdras summarizes the fall of Jerusalem and the exile of the Jews to Babylon, then concentrates on the Jews returning to Israel and the rebuilding of the temple and the capital. Much of the material is found also in the book of Ezra. In fact, Esdras is the Greek form of the Hebrew name Ezra.

Prayer of Manasseh. Manasseh was one of the most wicked kings in the history of the Jewish nation. He worshiped idols, and even sacrificed his sons in pagan offerings. The Prayer of Manasseh claims to be his prayer of repentance, perhaps written to justify his long and apparently successful reign. In ancient times, many Jews associated success with God's approval.

Psalm 151. This is a short song that David is said to have sung after defeating Goliath, the Philistine champion. A copy of the song was found among the famous Dead Sea Scrolls. It was written in Hebrew during the first century before Christ.

3 Maccabees. The title of this book is misleading; the story has nothing to do with the Maccabean heroes who fought and won the Jewish war of independence in the mid-100s BC. Instead, the story is set a half-century earlier and deals with the struggles of Egyptian Jews suffering under an oppressive king. He assembles them in an arena and tries to crush them with a herd of elephants. But God makes the animals turn and trample the armed Egyptians behind them. The king repents.

2 Esdras. This book appears in the Slavonic Bible. Most of the book tells about the visions that the prophet Ezra has concerning the last days of human history. These include the signs that the end is near, the suffering that will occur, and God's deliverance of the righteous.

4 Maccabees. This book appears in some other Eastern church Bibles, and is an appendix to the Greek Bible. Set just before the Jewish revolt and war of independence in the mid-100s BC, this book is an emotional plea for Jews to continue obeying the laws of Moses—even though Judaism has been outlawed by Syrian occupiers, and observant Jews are being executed.

INDEX

INDEX